VIOLENCE
AS
COMMUNICATION

D1520865

Alex P Schmid
and
Janny de Graaf

VIOLENCE
AS
COMMUNICATION

Insurgent Terrorism and the Western News Media

 SAGE Publications · London and Beverly Hills

For information address

SAGE Publications Ltd
28 Banner Street
London EC1Y 8QE

SAGE Publications Inc
275 South Beverly Drive
Beverly Hills, California 90212

British Library Cataloguing in Publication Data

Schmid, Alex P.
Violence as communication:
insurgent terrorism and the Western
news media.
1. Terrorism
I. Title II. Graaf, Janny de
322.4'2 HV6431 81–48144

ISBN 0-8039-9789-2 (c)
ISBN 0-8039-9772-8 (p)

SECOND PRINTING, 1983

CONTENTS

TABLES AND DIAGRAMS

FOREWORD
by Denis McQuail

This book is likely to appeal to at least three distinct audiences – those concerned with the study of mass communication, those interested, from whatever perspective, in the phenomenon of terrorism and those who work in, or have responsibility for, the news media. Each of these audiences tends now to be quite well served with literature, but the novelty of this book is to connect terrorism, news and political and public response within a single framework and one which gives rise to questions of the most pressing kind. While the answers given are still very tentative, the directions for thought indicated by this framework are both fascinating and promising.

We are reminded, first of all, of the ambiguity of the concept of terrorism, the multiplicity of types and causes which are concealed by the factual similarity of terroristic acts in their consequences – usually the injury to some innocent third party. We are reminded also of the thin line between the terrorism of those in authority and that of insurgent groups or individuals. The very labelling of an event as terroristic or not has become a sensitive matter and the power to give or withhold that label may itself be an object of competition. One of the themes which is explored in some detail is the complex interplay between the symbolism and the reality of insurgent terrorism, an interplay in which the media are caught up without being able to play a very determinate role. It is hardly surprising that the public, which means almost everyone, for which the media are the only timely source of information, is often uncertain and alarmed when confronted with news of terrorism.

In the public debates of recent years arising from the apparent spread of terroristic activity of all kinds, the role of the news media has been given considerable attention. They are associated with terrorism as the bringers of news and by their frequent involvement as intermediaries between the parties involved. This association has led to speculation about the possible causal influence of the media on the events which they set out to report. This general supposition has been a recurring motif of scientific as well as public discussion for several decades and has led to a good deal of largely futile research, with little result beyond confirmation of the initial starting point – the predilection of the media for portraying violence in all its forms. It is refreshing to see this theme dealt with as an interaction between sequences of historical events and the reporting of them and the authors present circumstantial evidence for linking the two. They leave us with little doubt, at least, that the concept of 'harmful news' has to be taken seriously and that the question of media responsibility at the time of terrorist events is both urgent and hard to deal with.

Most significantly, perhaps, Schmid and de Graaf focus on a conception of terrorism as itself a means of communication, a way of ensuring public attention and even of channelling particular messages to chosen targets. This is not the only meaning of terrorism, but it may be a key to the rise of terrorism in recent years and an important way of expressing the causal connection between the two phenomena. It draws attention away from issues of media responsibility and the pros and cons of censorship, although both are important and dealt with here, and towards the ways in which the media are used by terrorists and by the authorities. The extent and variety of actual or planned manipulation of news in terroristic situations is in itself very striking and the evidence brought together raises considerable doubts about the possibilities for objective news coverage under the typical conditions of such events. In doing so, the book is an addition to a growing body of evidence which brings long-standing journalistic myths of objectivity and freedom of action into question. It is useful to be reminded of the close involvement of media institutions in the relevant structures of power in which terroristic happenings find a place. It is not the general good faith or intentions of the media which are questioned, but their capacity to perform their self-chosen tasks.

This is not a polemical or one-sided book, although, as the authors remind us, it is hard to have a complete view when one set of participants (the terrorists) are rarely inclined to confirm or deny the inferences which are drawn about their motives and behaviour. It is, however, a book with an ultimate purpose — the promotion of conflict resolution without violence. It contributes to this end by detailed recommendations and judgements and also by offering, in a literal sense, a more global perspective on the problem. The authors take a cool look at the established structures and practises of news journalism under conditions of high competition for audiences within a world news system. They make a connection between fundamental aspects of the structure and the actual reporting of terrorist events by way of the immensely strong emphasis which is placed upon violence as a news value. The human basis of audience interest in violence can hardly be changed in the short term, but some of the operating conditions of the whole media system need not be so resistant to alteration. In particular, we are reminded of the severe limitations on access and thus the effective denial of the right to communicate through normal channels. The relevance to the theme of insurgent terrorism lies in the strong incentive to gain access by playing upon the media's own appetite for violence.

The search for guidance in handling the coverage of terrorist incidents in Western countries and the debate over possible changes in the 'world information order' do not seem very directly connected and have not been discussed together in the past. It is a great merit of this book and a mark of its depth and scope that it does make the connection in a thought-provoking and undogmatic way. It may act as a reminder that it is not only in the interests of the Third World to look again at the manner of our international exchanges of news and information. There potentially are negative repercussions for us from information imbalance, just as there are from economic imbalance.

University of Amsterdam
July 1981

INTRODUCTION

This book is — to our knowledge — the first extended study treating the relationship between insurgent terrorism and the Western news media in a comprehensive way. There have been a few studies that deal with individual cases (such as the press reaction to the Moro abduction in Italy) or with particular aspects, but no attempt has so far been made to link the rise of modern insurgent terrorism to the rise of the mass media, as the present work attempts to do. Given the paucity of previous research in the field, our study cannot be anything than exploratory. Nevertheless, we have aimed at developing a framework for analysis that differs significantly from the existing approaches to explain the recent rise in terroristic activity.

SCOPE OF THE STUDY

The title of this book, *Violence as Communication*, hints at this new framework of analysis. Instead of treating acts of terrorism as 'senseless violence', we see them as a kind of violent language. The subtitle of the book needs some elaboration. We have confined ourselves mainly to *insurgent* terrorism (social-revolutionary, separatist and single issue terrorism aiming at the top of society) excluding other forms of political terrorism such as vigilante terrorism or state terrorism. It can be argued — and there are some good reasons for it — that state terrorism is the main terrorist problem in a world where as many as 117 states violate human rights in one way or another. How the mass media treat state terrorism or, in many cases, keep silent about it, is admittedly a burning topic but it is not the one we have chosen. Our concentration on insurgent terrorism evolved gradually in the research process as we came to realize what varied uses it makes of the mass media while state terrorism (with a few exceptions such as show trials) generally shies away from the media. As the interaction between insurgent terrorism and the mass media is so much denser we decided to restrict our attention mainly to this topic.

The second word which needs defining is *terrorism*. The term has become subject to inflation and we use it in a much more narrow sense than is usually done, narrower than political violence, narrower as well than (urban) guerrilla violence. The reason for our restricted use of the word lies in the genesis of modern terrorism as we perceive it and will be explained in detail in chapters one and two. Here it is sufficient to say that we label terroristic only those deeds of violence in which violence is mainly perpetrated for its effects on others than the immediate victims. The third word in our subtitle, *Western*, is not quite synonymous with the geographical notion of the term; Japan, for instance, is also included. It is, however, also not quite synonymous with 'capitalist'. In many cases Western media are state-controlled or publicly-owned and as such removed from profit-based market considerations. While the formal form of control is not private ownership these media often copy or follow the pattern of market-based media. 'Western' therefore refers to a cultural pattern based on capitalism but at the same time broader than it. To some extent our use of the word Western is admittedly pretentious: we read only six of the Western languages and while some additional sources were accessible to us through translations, our survey falls short of covering the entire Western world with all its variety. The fourth word in our subtitle, *news*, needs little explanation. Terrorism is also a favourite topic of Western entertainment media and the word 'news' limits the field of analysis, excluding cinema movies, science fiction, thrillers and other fictional treatment of the subject. The fifth word, *media*, stands for public or mass media — newspapers and magazines on the one hand and the electronic or audiovisual media, radio and television, on the other. The time-span covered by this study is the period 1968–1979, although there are some references to earlier occurrences of terrorism.

ORIGIN OF THE STUDY

The present work is an outgrowth of a 'Pilot Study on Political Terrorism' which we wrote in 1977 for the Dutch Advisory Group on Research into Nonviolent Conflict Resolution. In this pilot study we proposed as one of several desirable studies a study on terrorism and the mass media. Since the Advisory Group redirected its research focus at that time the study was finally sponsored by a different body. The Dutch Ministry for Science Policy gave us a grant for a six month's study and when first results looked promising financed a prolongation of another four months. Ultimately it took us more than twenty months to write this book. The fact that part of the study was financed by a government source does not mean that we were subject to any sort of control, influence or censorship. The responsibility for the content of the study rests with the authors alone.

The second source of inspiration for this study was the 7th General Conference of the International Peace Research Association in Oaxtepec (Mexico) in December 1977. At that conference a Peace and Communication group was established which decided to dedicate one of its research efforts to the topic 'The Misuse of Journalism for Insurgency and Counterinsurgency'. Finally, this study has also a more personal intellectual origin. Our research was inspired by the question of why violence receives so much attention while nonviolence receives so little, why the belief in the power of violence is so strong and that in the power of nonviolent methods to bring about change is so weak.

STRUCTURE OF THE STUDY

One can study terrorism and the mass media for three main reasons: to come to know more about terrorism, to come to know more about the media or to come to know more about their relationship. Originally our main attention was devoted to the first aspect. But the more we learned about the relationship between insurgent terrorism and the mass media the more our attention shifted to the media. Naturally, the question of what can be done to curb insurgent terrorism played a role. This brought us to a discussion of the repression attempts by governments which take the form of media censorship. As peace researchers our inclination is to solve social problems by conflict resolution rather than by conflict repression. Therefore we have also tried to identify those elements in the Western information order which invite the use of violence and we have suggested ways to transform this information order. From these shifts in focus in the research process the present work obtained its structure: the first chapter deals with the insurgent terrorists, the second with the uses the media make of insurgent terrorism, and the third with the various relationships between media and terrorism. Chapter four deals with the question of censorship, and the final chapter discusses and questions the present information order.

DATA BASE AND METHOD

We have used three different kinds of data in this study. On the one hand we have collected and evaluated most of the existing and available literature on terrorism and to a lesser extent on the mass media and the few works dealing with both areas. The bibliography reflects this data base. The second data base — which finds its expression in the notes but not in the bibliography — is the media themselves — mainly newspapers and magazines but also radio and television. The third data base was interviews with journalists and written questionnaires to journalists and editors. Our questionnaire was distributed in the first instance to the participants of an International Press Institute conference in November 1978 in London which dealt with 'European Terrorism and the Media'. Later it was also sent to other journalists. Apart from the interviews and questionnaires (the details about them can be found in the notes) we also gained many data and insights from correspondence with journalists, scholars and friends in both the field of terrorism and the field of the mass media. These contacts, while numerous, do not find an adequate reflection in either bibliography, notes or acknowledgements since in most cases the information was provided in exchange for the promise of anonymity. One data base we could not tap were the insurgent terrorists themselves. We have, however, made use of written and taped sources which they have produced and we have analyzed their actions so that the picture is less one-sided than might be feared.

The careful reader will notice a preponderance of English-speaking and especially American sources. There are three main reasons for this. One is that much of our research was carried out in the Library of Congress in Washington, DC and, to a lesser extent, in the British Library in London. The second reason is that American society is more open than most others: an information request to a US television network is more likely to be honoured than one to a West German one in a delicate area such as the coverage of terrorism. The third reason is that research on terrorism and on the media is most advanced in the United States and the number of sources reflects this. On a deeper level this preponderance is probably also an outflow of the world information order which is discussed in the final chapter. In a way this order has preshaped the data base which was available to us. Due to this our study has much more to say on the relationship between government and media than on the media-induced effects of insurgent terrorism on the people. We regret this but cannot change it. The accessible data bases were to a significant extent prestructured and, with our limited resources, we could not afford to generate data of our own on a scale large enough to provide some balance. The top-directedness of data collection and evaluation in social hierarchies makes it cheaper and simpler to measure the reactions of the relatively few in government than of the many among the people. The news-gathering practices of the media are based on this and so also are studies which take media output as source material. One mitigating factor in the top-bottom imbalance is the issue of secrecy which sur-rounds government actions and reactions in the field of terrorism. With close-lipped government officials and deadlines at hand, reporters have often to take recourse to interviewing the common man in the street so that by default the balance is partly restored. Another data problem, which will be addressed in the text rather than here, stems from the fact that most of our data on insurgent terrorism are ultimately based on media accounts which makes it problematical to discuss the relation-ship between news media and insurgent terrorism objectively, given the fact that we see one through the other.

Here we are in fact discussing methodological problems. Our approach has been comparative. By putting terrorist and media prac-tices from various time and place settings in comparative perspective we have attempted to gain an insight into their common properties. Spreading our attention so wide (nineteenth and twentieth century, Middle East, Western Europe, North and South America), however, also meant that the samples of incidents from which we drew our con-clusions were smaller than we would in many cases have wished. For some of our propositions the empirical data base has been too narrow to allow firm generalizations to be made. Nevertheless, we have aimed at generalizations where these could be responsibly done, for without them it would have been impossible to develop a broad framework for analysis. Our aim was to discover the 'big picture' and given our limited means we felt that too much methodological rigour was not in place. In this regard we have to some extent traded relevance for rigour. Since this work is covering new ground we found it more important to act as pathfinders than as topographers.

SOME REMARKS ON THE TEXT

This study can be read in two ways: either from beginning to end, or, for those with a predilection for theory, by starting with the fifth chapter before looking at the empirical evidence. Those wishing to quote from our quotes are warned that some of them have been translated from a third language back into the original one so that the exact wording of a quote might differ slightly from our translations. A shorter and slightly modified version of the first chapter has been published in the *Proceedings of the 8th IPRA Conference* (New York, Campus, 1981). An audiovisual version of parts of this study has been produced in collaboration with NCRV and was broadcast on 29 October 1979 on Dutch television. The present text is, except for the main title and some editorial changes, identical to the one published in November 1980 in Leiden as an institute publication of the Centre for the Study of Social Conflicts. The original text included, however, as Part II, a Dutch case study which is here summarized only in the Appendix. Together with another case study on South Moluccan terrorism and Dutch public opinion, this case study was published in Dutch language by Intermediair Bibliotheek, Amsterdam, in early 1982.

ACKNOWLEDGEMENTS

This book could not have been written without the assistance of scores of informants, scholars and friends. Since some of the people who helped us most have been promised anonymity it is somehow unfair to list the others. Yet some have to be singled out. No one has been more helpful than Professor A. J. F. Köbben, director of the Centre for the Study of Social Conflicts (COMT) at Leiden University. Without his support this study would never have been financed and without the hospitality he gave us at his institute it could never have grown into a full-size book. His criticism of our work saved us from more than one blunder and many of his suggestions have enriched our study. Thanks are also due to two other members of the COMT, Henk Tromp who read and commented on our text and Jan Brand who was helpful in many ways. Professor H. Daudt and Professor H. W. Tromp who acted as supervisors for this study are also to be thanked for their contributions. Tineke van der Heide deserves thanks for typing the manuscript. Hans van der Dennen aided us at an early stage by granting us access to his incomparable bibliography on political violence. Teri Pung helped to make a research stay in Washington agreeable and went out of her way thereafter to locate some hard-to-find items. Special thanks are due to Dr Michael Sommer from the Department of Journalism of California State University at Northridge for allowing us to use some of the statistical data he and his associates have aggregated. Thanks are also due to Henk Mochel of NCRV television for giving us a chance to visualize part of our material in the series 'Wereld van het Nieuws'. Tapio Varis and Dallas W. Smythe contributed, through their personal example as well as through their work, more to this study than they were aware of. Our final thanks go to our many informants who shared their perceptions and opinions with us in interviews, questionnaires and letters.

While they all helped to make this a richer book, the responsibility for its shortcomings rests with us alone.

Leiden, May 1981

1. TERRORIST USES OF THE NEWS MEDIA

MODERN TERRORISM –
ORIGIN AND DEFINITION

In the late nineteenth century two new phenomena entered social life: the mass press and modern insurgent terrorism. Both owed much of their existence to recent technical developments: dynamite, discovered in 1866, and the rotary press, introduced in 1848 and perfected in 1881. The two inventions soon started to interact. '*Truth* is two cents a copy, dynamite is forty cents a pound. Buy them both, read one, use the other', the anarchist paper *Truth* declared.[1] The link between the invention of dynamite and of the mass media is of course not that direct. *Truth* was but a small San Francisco paper not printed on a rotary press and dynamite was not the only weapon of terrorism. The rotary press was in the hands of an establishment definitely opposed to insurgent terrorism. Modern terrorism itself, first employed on a systematic scale during the Reign of Terror under Robespierre in France, was originally an instrument of those in power rather than of those trying to take state power.

Yet terrorism and mass communication are linked to each other. Without communication there can be no terrorism. Robespierre's Reign of Terror was stopped on the ninth Thermidor (27 July 1794) by denying him and St. Just access to the speaker's forum in the French convention. Deprived of their main medium, their terrorism

9

collapsed.[2] In the hundred years between the state terrorism of the French Revolution and the heyday of anarchist terrorism modern mass communication became a reality. Before technology made possible the amplification and multiplication of speech, the maximum number of people that could be reached simultaneously was determined by the range of the human voice and was around 20,000 people. In the nineteenth century, within one lifetime, the size of an audience was expanded twenty-five to fifty times. In 1839 the New York *Sun* published a record 39,000 copies; in 1896, on the occasion of President McKinley's election, two US papers, belonging to Pulitzer and Hearst, for the first time printed a million copies. William McKinley paid dearly for this publicity.[3] In 1901 he was killed by an anarchist, Leon Czolgosz, who explained his deed with the words: 'For a man should not claim so much attention, while others receive none'.[4] Another anarchist, Luchini, the murderer of the Empress Elizabeth and who was a collector of news clippings, said he had longed to kill 'somebody important so it gets into the papers'.[5] While this can be interpreted as Herostratism,[6] which predates the advent of the mass media, there is, at least in Czolgosz' argument, something that is linked to the rise of the mass media. To understand this link we have to recall what changes the advent of the mass press brought about.

In its fight against absolutism the bourgeoisie had propagated the notions of freedom and equality. In the American Constitution, ratified in 1788, these bourgeois demands became for the first time a legal right. In Europe the fight against the remnants of feudalism and absolutism was only won after 1848. The press, which became a periodic phenomenon in the seventeenth and eighteenth centuries, was one of the most important instruments for bringing about the changes desired by the rising capitalist class. The gradual decline of state censorship led to the creation of a public sphere beyond the courts where people could freely vent their ideas. But the freedom of speech, which in principle (though not in practice) was for anyone, became, with the growth of the press, a right that gave unequal chances of expression to different people. The freedom of the press, derived from the individuals' freedom of speech, superimposed itself on it.[7] Through the concentrations in press ownership and the increase in copies the new press barons were able to throw on the public market in the late nineteenth century, public opinion formation again became in effect the domain of the few. The rise of the mass press had in practice all but destroyed the theoretical equality of freedom of speech. Czolgosz' argument reflected this new situation. The dynamite the anarchists used served, in a sense, to overthunder the noise of the rotary press. Auguste Vaillant, the anarchist who threw a bomb in the French national assembly in 1893, expressed this with the words: 'The more they are deaf, the more your voice must thunder out so that they will understand you'.[8] The unequal chances of expressing oneself, brought about by the rise of the big press, contributed to the rise of terrorism as 'expressive' violence.[9] There was another way, however, in which the same process that had reduced the effective right to communicate opened new avenues of communication. To understand this we have briefly to sketch how the capitalist press evolved.

In its historical development the bourgeois press has gone through three phases, or perhaps more correctly, been of three types. On the one hand there was, around 1800, the commercial newspaper, which, with its news on arriving ships and announcement of goods that were for sale, served to increase the capitalist market. For its revenue it depended on advertisements. The second type of newspaper was less concerned with selling goods than selling ideas. It was the partisan newspaper fighting for political causes such as defending bourgeois freedoms against absolutism. Its chief source of revenue came from the political party who issued it. The commercial and the partisan newspaper often overlapped and the first generally evolved into the second type without losing its original function.

With the spread of literacy, the increase in the buying power of the masses and the advent of the rotary press, a third type of newspaper appeared on the scene around 1850, firstly in the United States, the cheap daily press.[10] Its main function was no longer to sell capitalist goods or ideas but to sell itself. Rather than merely supporting business, it had become a business in itself. It wanted to attract as many people as possible and therefore brought news that the people found attractive. This third type of press, the 'yellow press', as it was first called, concentrated on sensational news like catastrophies, scandals, crime and war. Interested primarily in increasing its readership, this press had in fact detached itself considerably from the economic and political bases of capitalism and parliamentary democracy. Through its size, its commercial power to expose advertisements to mass audiences and its political power to shape public attitudes, this press became an autonomous cultural actor. This press, most clearly in the muckracking period before the First World War in the United States, could defend labour against capital and attack grafting politicians.[11] Although itself a capitalist business, this type of press could, if it was helpful in getting more readers, take positions that were in fact contrary to capitalist interests in general. The rise of this mass press had shifted the balance from news as information to news as commodity. The moral and commercial values of a piece of information on an event could stand in complete opposition to each other. Journalists and newspaper owners could, as persons, abhor violence. Yet as professionals and entrepreneurs violence was for them interesting marketable news. Morally bad news could be commercially good news. The Boer War, for instance, contributed significantly to the doubling of the sales of the London *Daily Mail* in the years 1898–1900.[12] 'Bad news', in the words of a journalist adage, 'is good news, good news is bad news, and no news is bad news'. In most cases the commercial and the cultural functions of news did not directly clash. But there were areas where they did and in these areas of cultural contradictions of capitalism stepped the nineteenth-century terrorists by creating bad news. The capitalist transformation of values was exploited by the anarchist terrorists to regain the freedom of expression which the same process of the rise of the mass media had taken away.

Most of the news of the nineteenth-century establishment press was dedicated to the actions of the powerful in society. Yet by affecting the lives of the powerful the powerless could also enter the pages of the press and thereby shape public opinion. The *attentat* on famous persons became the first form of modern terroristic violence. Unlike in tyrannicide, from which terrorism took its first form, the elimination of the enemy was no longer the primary goal. The goal was to reach public opinion, to send a message that made all the powerful tremble and gave the powerless hope. The victim was instrumental and no longer automatically identical with the enemy. A look at the reasoning of the nineteenth-century anarchist and social-revolutionary terrorists illustrates the evolution of the terrorist doctrine.

The nineteenth-century middle- and upper class revolutionaries who wanted to liberate the masses had been facing the problem that their pamphlets had a limited distribution and could not reach the illiterate. To communicate with the masses words and ideas proved insufficient and had to be complemented by deeds that would speak for themselves. Paule Brousse, an early proponent of the 'Propaganda of the Deed', saw the 'Exemplary Deed' as a method 'to show them (the masses) that which they were unable to read, to teach them socialism in practice, to make it visible, tangible, concrete'.[13] The method had obvious advantages. The dissemination of revolutionary propaganda would no longer have to rely solely on the small-circulation pamphlets often clandestinely printed but would be taken over by the official bourgeois press and to those who could not read, word-of-mouth accounts of the successful killing of a king or minister would provide communication. The national press and the international news agencies, aided by the telegraph, could carry the news of violent deeds to remote regions and countries, thereby providing a free and fast external communication network for the terrorists. Terrorism, or the 'Russian method', as it was also called, found its imitators in such faraway places as India, without a Russian member of the Narodnaya Volya ('People's Will') ever travelling there.

The Russian revolutionaries of the late 1870s, after having tried in vain to talk directly to the people, were the first to develop a theory of terrorism. They had most likely taken their inspiration from the Czars themselves. For many years Russian government had instigated the assassination of Turkish officials in the Balkan parts of the Ottoman empire in order to provoke the Orthodox Christians there to revolt.[14] The use of this method by Narodnaya Volya represented the adoption of a violent practice formerly held to be the exclusive prerogative of the state. 'Public opinion is ultimately gained by great victories', the war-theoretician Karl von Clausewitz had maintained.[15] Narodnaya Volya hoped to achieve the same by a series of small victories, as the movement's programme of 1879 makes clear:

Terroristic activity, consisting in destroying the most harmful persons in the government, in defending the party against espionage, in punishing the perpetrators of the notable cases of violence and arbitrariness on the part of the government and the administration, aims to undermine the prestige of the government's power, to demonstrate steadily the possibility of struggle against the government, to arouse in this manner the revolutionary spirit of the people and their confidence in the success of the cause, and finally, to give shape and direction to the forces fit and trained to carry on the fight.[16]

Although the members of Narodnaya Volya killed a Czar and high government officials, the victim himself was relatively unimportant to them — what counted was the message. The choice of the victim, however, was such that the message was clear.

Five years after the programme of Narodnaya Volya was set up, a German-American theorist of terrorism, Johannes Most, carried their line of thinking further:

Everyone now knows, for example, that the more highly placed the one shot or blown up, and the more perfectly executed the attempt, the greater the propagandistic effect.... Once such an action has been carried out, the important thing is that the world learns from it *from the revolutionaries*, so that everyone knows what the position is.... In order to achieve the desired success in the fullest measure, immediately after the action has been carried out, especially in the town where it took place, posters should be put up setting out the reasons for the action in such a way as to draw from them the best possible benefit.[17]

In practice, however, explaining the deed by posters could be a risky business which would often lead to an explanation before the courts. The courtroom in fact became another forum for captured terrorists and with the press being present, a terroristic act could gain a second wave of publicity. Fascinated by those anarchists who proudly accepted responsibility for their political crimes, the late nineteenth-century press gave ample space to terrorist deeds and thereby probably contributed to the spread of this new style of political confrontation.[18]

Individual terrorism in itself was, as many adherents of the Propaganda of the Deed realized, *as violence*, not very effective. Peter Kropotkin, one of the anarchist theorists, admitted that a few kilos of dynamite could not demolish the historical structures created over thousands of years. Yet, *as propaganda*, terrorism was effective. 'By actions which compel general attention', Kropotkin held, 'the new idea seeps into people's minds and wins converts. One such act may, in a few days, make more propaganda than a thousand pamphlets. Above all, it awakens the spirit of revolt....'[19] Terrorism cannot be understood only in terms of violence. It has to be understood primarily in terms of propaganda. Violence and propaganda, however, have much in common. Violence aims at behaviour modification by coercion. Propaganda aims at the same by persuasion. Terrorism is a combination of the two. Josef Goebbels, Hitler's Minister of Propaganda, once said: 'We do not talk to say something, but to obtain a certain effect.'[20] Equally terrorism does not murder to kill somebody, but to obtain a certain effect upon others than the victim. Terrorism, by using violence against one victim, seeks to persuade others. The immediate victim is merely instrumental, the skin on a drum beaten to achieve a calculated impact on a wider audience. As such, an act of terrorism is in reality an act of communication. For the terrorist the message matters, not the victim. In the nineteenth century the victim was practically always from the enemy camp, often a symbol of oppression, whose destruction signalled a message of terror to other oppressors and one of hope to those who longed for liberation so strongly that the atrocity of the deed vanished before the desirability of the end. While in the nineteenth century the deed had to be so specific that it would, as it were,

speak for itself, developments in communication technology have since
allowed for an ever-increasing distance between victim and message. Yet
in its substance terrorism has not changed fundamentally in the hundred years that separate the beginnings of anarchist terrorism from
contemporary terrorism. In recent years social scientists have made many efforts to come to
a satisfactory definition of terrorism but so far no consensus has
emerged. One scholar, Professor Robert Friedlander, for instance,
defined terrorism as 'abominable means used by political fanatics for
contemptible ends'.[21] Others, exasperated by the careless use of the
word terrorism, deny that terrorism is an authentic social phenomenon
and call it a 'political epithet', holding that the conventional way of
analyzing terrorism was 'a vain artifact of intellectual caution and
"professional" taxologizing'.[22] In our view terrorism can best be understood as a violent communication strategy. There is a sender, the
terrorist, a message generator, the victim, and a receiver, the enemy
and/or the public. The nature of the terrorist act, its atrocity, its
location and the identity of its victim serve as generators for the power
of the message. Violence, to become terroristic, requires witnesses.
'Kill one, frighten ten thousand', a Chinese proverb says. If the killing
of the one is done primarily for the purpose of frightening thousands
then we speak of terrorism. The word 'terror' means chronic fear and
terrorism would then refer to the systematic production of chronic
fear. But fear is only one effect of such violence and the full meaning
of terrorism would be lost if one would fix one's attention exclusively
on this fear effect. We therefore define terrorism as *the deliberate and
systematic use or threat of violence against instrumental (human)
targets (C) in a conflict between two (A, B) or more parties, whereby
the immediate victims C − who might not even be part of the conflicting parties − cannot, through a change of attitude or behaviour,
dissociate themselves from the conflict.* Since the aim of terrorism is
behaviour modification of the enemy and/or a public and not of the
immediate victims, a certain arbitrariness in the selection of the
instrumental targets is characteristic of the terrorist form of violence.
Through his violent act, the terrorist seeks to activate a relationship
between victims and enemy, whereby the latter is made responsible
for the former before a public. The enemy is usually personified; but
it can also be the public's *apathy* to the aspirations or grievances of
the terrorists.[23]
    Without communication, as we have said at the beginning of this
chapter, there can be no terrorism. Since victim and enemy are not

identical, the violence perpetrated against the victim by the terrorist has to be communicated to the enemy. In the case of state terrorism, the disappearance and torture of a victim might be made known to his family and friends only by word-of-mouth or a letter smuggled out of prison. Insurgent terrorism, on the other hand, does not shy from publicity but actively seeks it. The news media play a prominent role in linking up the terrorist with his victim, his enemy and the public at large. In the following pages we will discuss the various uses terrorists make of the media. Our main emphasis will be on the period 1968–1979, when television, linked up internationally by satellite, provided a similar audience increase as did the rotary press in the days of anarchist terrorism.

CONTEMPORARY INSURGENT
TERRORISM

The twentieth-century communication revolution has changed the face of insurgent terrorism. In the nineteenth century nonstate terrorism took one basic expression: selective assassination without warning. J. B. S. Hardman, describing the late nineteenth-century terrorism, wrote that 'The terrorist does not threaten; death or destruction is part of his program of action....'[24] Today's insurgent terrorists use a variety of tactics such as hijacking and kidnapping which do not result in immediate and certain death. The time span between initiating a terrorist act and the execution of the violent deed can be weeks and even months. Rapid private and public transportation has allowed for the movement of the victim and anonymous communication has made the threat itself a major component of terrorism. Present-day terrorism can attach meanings to an act of violence which are not self-evident. This has led to an enlargement of the group of possible targets of terrorism. If the meaning of a violent act no longer depends on the specific identity of the victim but can be constructed separately by the terrorists, almost anybody can serve as a target of terroristic violence. While it is still true that the impact of a terroristic deed is greatest when the victim is central to the conflict at hand, the reverse is paradoxically also possible – at least in democracies where the common man counts. Victims who are manifestly neutrals in a conflict (children for instance) can also serve as strong message generators as long as the terrorists' adversaries can be held responsible for the fate of the victims. The spatial and social distance between victim and target, however, must, for making the terrorist threat effective, be bridged by a public network of communications that links them in time.

The shrinking of time needed to relate events, made possible by the communication revolution, is a major element which has increased the usefulness of the media for terrorists. Until telegraphs became common in the 1840s, messages could generally not travel faster than their human or animal carriers. The invention of the wireless in the 1890s increased the speed at which messages could be transmitted to 186,000 miles per second. Wired and wireless communication, however, became a really powerful instrument for terrorism only when the number of message receivers far outstripped the number of senders. A political assassination such as the one of Abraham Lincoln in 1865 took weeks and months to be known to all those who attached a meaning to the existence of the American president. When John F. Kennedy was shot in Dallas in 1963, more than 70 percent of all Americans learned about the event within half an hour.[25] The power which the mass media in this case bestowed on one individual (if Lee Harvey Oswald was the (only) one responsible) was to produce emotional reactions among some 130 million people almost instantly. The Kennedy murder was not a terroristic act since victim and target were identical but the possibilities offered to the assassin are also available to the terrorist; his real target is not the victim but often the public out there. The transmission of the terrorist message to a mass audience is the main use terrorists make of the media.

What the rotary press did for the nineteenth-century terrorists, television is doing for contemporary terrorists. The mass circulation papers of the late nineteenth-century could each reach around a million people within twelve hours. Satellite-linked television can today reach around a billion people instantly, that is, if the TV-watchers are already tuned in to an event such as a world soccer championship. The possible instant audience for today's terrorists is, in other words, as big as one quarter of mankind. The nearest terrorists got to this maximum feasible instant audience was during the Munich Olympic Games in 1972, which were televised to an estimated 800 million people.[26]

Between the mass press and mass television stand historically two more media, the radio and the movie, which both became mass media in the interwar years. Radio, and to a lesser extent film, were however largely controlled by states and as such became primarily instruments of state terrorism rather than insurgent terrorism, which is the theme of our study. A broader analysis than the present one should, however, not neglect to analyze the media uses made especially by fascist states.

Hitler himself admitted that 'without the motor car, sound films and wireless there would be no victory for the National Socialist Party'.[27] The way the leaders of the Third Reich utilized film as an instrument of intimidation already foreshadowed the uses that insurgent terrorists of the 1970s would make of television. What was still lacking then was the simultaneity which today's electronic world communication provides. But the mechanism was basically the same as the following example illustrates. Shortly before the Nazi invasion of Norway the German government arranged a film demonstration for Norwegian officials. The movie shown to them had been filmed by Nazi propaganda units and depicted how endless columns of German tanks and squadrons of aircraft laid Poland into ashes. The intent of the demonstration was to bring home to the Norwegians how utterly hopeless it would be to resist such a victorious war machine.[28]

While the effect of this quasi-terroristic use of the medium of film is hard to assess in this case (Norway capitulated quickly when the Nazis invaded the country in 1940), another example, involving radio, shows that the effects of media-induced terror can be drastic. Again it is not a pure example of terrorism, but it serves as a demonstration of the potential of the media for terrorist uses. After the British had announced their decision to withdraw from Palestine in the late 1940s, Zionist terrorists of the Stern gang and the Irgun Zwai Loumi (National Military Organization) attacked an Arab village, Deir Yassin, and massacred 250 men, women and children. The Arab Committee in Jerusalem decided, after some hesitation, to make this event public, hoping that it would stir up the Arab governments to take up arms against the Jewish settlers. Instead, the spreading of the news about the massacre caused panic among the Arab population of Palestine and in a short period 540,000 of the 700,000 Arabs on Israeli territory fled from their homeland.[29] The bitter irony of this case was that the terrorizing message was issued not by the terrorists or the media as independent news assemblers but by part of the victimized group itself.

Self-victimization, however, also exists as a conscious terrorist strategy as the Cyprus experience exemplifies. The strategy of the Cypriot patriots under General Grivas in the fight against the occupation of their island by the British in the 1950s was summarized by a Cypriot who told a British diplomat: 'Of a stupid man (the peasants) say, "He thought he could beat his wife, without his neighbors hearing". In this case the neighbors are your own Labour Party (which was then in opposition), U.N.O., and many others. We are provoking you to beat

us so that our cries reach their ears.'[30] The Cypriot terrorists assassinated British soldiers to provoke reprisals against the population in order
to induce the media to report the repressiveness of colonial rule so as to
alienate various foreign publics from the British Conservative government. The military losses of the British in their struggle against the
terrorist EOKA (Ethniki Organosis Kyprion Agoniston – National
Organization of Cypriot Fighters) were too small to force them out of
Cyprus but the political repercussions of the confrontation nevertheless
forced them to leave. The Cypriot terrorists had the good fortune that
their island was within reach of the Western media, without whose
presence this strategy could not have worked.

Most colonial countries were not so fortunate and the national
liberation fighters had to use guerrilla rather than terrorist tactics to
achieve independence. A notable exception was the Algerian FLN
(Front de la Libération National – National Liberation Front) which
made an effective use of the media presence in their struggle against
France. After having fought a little-noticed guerrilla war in the countryside against the French army the Algerian nationalist leaders turned to
terrorist tactics which would finally bring them closer to a political
(not military) success in 1962. The change in tactics was rationalized
by the FLN leader Abane Ramdane with the words: 'Is it better for our
cause to kill ten of the enemy in the countryside of Telergma, where no
one will speak of it, or one in Algiers that will be mentioned the next
day in the American press?'[31] The location of the foreign press's correspondents had become one of the determinants for the location of the
struggle. While wars attract journalists, journalists attract terrorists.
The logic is impeccable: relatively small-scale violence witnessed by
many can have effects greater than large-scale violence witnessed only
by a few.

To understand this logic fully it is necessary to place it against the
evolution of modern warfare. In conventional war two states opposed
their military forces in battles whose outcome decided the war. Only
a limited portion of the population was engaged in the violent confrontation and the majority of people were badly and belatedly informed
about the conflict. In short campaigns at least, their opinion on the
conflict had no significant material influence on the conduct of a war.
As communication technology improved and war correspondents made
their entry on the battlefield, the views and moods of the onlookers to
the conflict became important. The state of popular opinion at home
could become more decisive than the fate of the soldiers in the field
for the continuation of the war and ultimate victory. Governments

consequently introduced censorship on the homefront and used propaganda to weaken the enemy's homefront as well as to strengthen their own. In civil wars the position the noncombattants took became even more decisive for the eventual outcome of a confrontation. The Maoist doctrine of guerrilla warfare maintained that it was crucial for the guerrillero to mobilize those people who would be mere onlookers in a conventional war. Clausewitz, the classic theoretician of war, had held, as we mentioned earlier (p. 13), that public opinion was gained by great victories. Mao turned this notion on its head and maintained that winning public support was the precondition for the great victory. If public opinion could be won the defeat of the enemy would be a foregone conclusion. The aim of the guerrillero was therefore in the early stages of a confrontation to win the people to his cause and not to defeat the enemy. Attacks on the enemy were to be staged not primarily to achieve physical results with the enemy but psychological results with the people. In other words, the effect of a violent act, rather than the violent act itself, mattered.[32] Insurgent terrorism draws heavily on this line of thinking and carries it to extremes. At the same time insurgent terrorism is undercutting the moral basis of this doctrine of guerrilla warfare by abandoning in practice the requirement that the people have to be on one's side. For many contemporary terrorists the winning of the attention of the mass media seems to have replaced the winning of the allegiance of the masses.

In the following pages we will attempt to illustrate the various uses nonstate terrorists make of the mass media. Our focus will be on four regions: Latin America, the Middle East, the United States and Western Europe.

Latin America

Urban guerrilla warfare in the Latin America of the 1960s and 1970s is usually contrasted with the previous rural guerrilla concept based on the Cuban experience. A leading proponent of the Cuban model was Ché Guevara who — except in his last days in Bolivia — saw little in the use of terrorism, arguing that 'terrorism is of negative value, that it by no means produces the desired effects, that it can bring a loss of lives to its agents out of proportion to what it produces'.[33] Yet Castro and his few 'barbudos' had in fact used some quasi-terrorist strategies in the 1950s which were far from lacking in success.

Given Cuba's almost total economic and political dependence on the

United States, Castro's strategy aimed at portraying his movement in the Sierra Maestre as a credible alternative to the country's dictator, Fulgencio Batista. His goal was to alienate American public opinion from Batista and thereby force the US government to cut its support for the unpopular ruler. As part of his movement's strategy to attract attention the world-famous Argentinian motor racing driver Juan Manuel Fangio was abducted from the Lincoln Hotel in Havana. Batista's police was unable to trace the whereabouts of the champion and the media attention focused for weeks on the kidnapping. Not only was the inefficient Batista regime humiliated and foreign attention directed on the injustices committed by the dictator, the kidnappers received also favourable publicity from Fangio himself, who, upon release, praised them for the good treatment he had been given. This propaganda success stimulated Raul Castro, the brother of Fidel Castro, to repeat this performance with US citizens in Cuba. They were treated with equal courtesy by the June 26 Movement (the date of their kidnapping) and promptly, upon release, also issued statements favourable to the guerrilleros and their aspirations.[34] The *New York Times* despatched Herbert Matthews as correspondent to cover the June 26 Movement, other journalists followed, and soon the name Fidel Castro had a familiar ring in the United States. The military strength of Castro's movement remained limited but the stream of reports about it magnified its exploits to such an extent that Batista's forces became demoralized. Batista looked foolish and cruel, lost the support of the Cuban and American public and finally became an easy prey for the rural guerrilleros and their urban supporters.

Decisive as this quasi-terrorism (quasi — because the victims were not threatened with death) had been for preparing the victory of Castro and his followers, the exegetes of the Cuban success tended to play down its role in their victory. Guevara, Castro and Régis Debray formulated two major theses for the liberation of Latin America. One maintained that the rural areas had to be the main scene for insurrection, whereby the guerrilla movement had to draw its support from the campesinos. The second thesis held that it was not necessary to wait until a society was ripe for revolution. It was sufficient that a small resolute minority of trained fighters started the revolution from a small 'foco' (focus). The subsequent failure of all rural Latin American guerrilla movements to repeat the Cuban success led to a rethinking of this doctrine, which was, however, only partial: the rural concept was de-emphasized, but not the foco concept. The result was the emergence of the urban guerrilla.[35]

The most influential theoretician of the urban guerrilla was the
Brazilian ex-communist Carlos Marighela, whose *Minimanual of the
Urban Guerrilla* became a standard work for insurgent terrorist movements not only in Latin America but also in many developed countries.
In his booklet Marighela urged the urban guerrilla to 'read the newspapers carefully and follow other communications media'.[36] He then
details the various uses that can be made of the media:

To kidnap figures known for their artistic, sporting or other activities who have
not expressed any political views may possibly provide a form of propaganda
favourable to the revolutionaries, but should only be done in very special circumstances, and in such a way as to be sure people will accept it sympathetically.
Kidnapping American personalities who live in Brazil, or who have come to visit
here, is a most important form of protest against the penetration of US imperialism
into our country.... Terrorism may also include destroying human lives, and
setting fire to North American business establishments or certain plantations. If
the intention is to loot stocks of food, then it is important to make sure that the
people benefit from it, especially at times or in places where there is great hunger
or life is very expensive. In the work of revolutionary terrorism the guerrilla must
always be adaptable. The work of armed propaganda really means the sum total
of the actions achieved by the urban guerrillas, especially those carried out by
force of arms. *Modern mass media, simply by announcing what the revolutionaries
are doing, are important instruments of propaganda.* However, their existence
does not dispense fighters from setting up their own secret presses and having
their own copying machines.... Comrades with inventive minds can design cata-
pults for distributing such pamphlets and manifestoes; they will also try to get
taped revolutionary messages out on the transmitters of radio stations....
    The war of nerves – or the psychological war – is a fighting technique based
on the direct or indirect use of the mass media.... Its purpose is to demoralize
the government. By it we can spread false, or contradictory, information by
sowing anxiety, doubt and uncertainty among the agents of the régime. In psychological warfare the government is at a disadvantage, and therefore will censor the
means of communication. Censorship of course has a boomerang effect, since it
leads to unpopularity....[37]

Marighela, who headed the Acção Libertadora Nacional (ALN –
National Liberation Action), hereby assigned several tasks to the media,
depending on them not only for publicizing the deeds of the terrorists
but also for winning new recruits for the armed insurrection. He
expected that the exemplary deeds would, when made known by the
media, mobilize all sorts of social discontents. By simply reporting the
news of, say, a successful guerrilla payroll robbery, the media would, in
his view, in fact provide a free advertisement for the revolution. People
would get 'ideas' and follow the example. Spontaneous groups would
emerge that would operate independently, without being controlled by

a hierarchical organization while the media would provide them with a sort of external communication network.[38] The strategy depended on the assumption that the media would play the terrorists' game. As another Brazilian urban guerrilla leader, Ladislas Dobor, explained: 'Armed action, which means living in small, clandestine cells, reduces the possibility of contact with the population. We must rely on the repercussions of our actions'.[39] For these 'repercussions' the Brazilian terrorists had to rely on the media. The bourgeois press — 'ever greedy for news that increases the sale of its papers' — as one member of the Vanguarda Popular Revolucionaria (VPR — Popular Revolutionary Vanguard) held,[40] indeed played their game as long as the dictatorial military government allowed it — which was not very long. When the media could no longer provide free publicity, the terrorist propaganda was spread by force. Radio and TV stations were occupied and the urban guerrillas broadcast their slogans and messages, including a tape with one of Marighela's speeches, to the population.

Another method of reaching the people was to include the broadcasting of a message in the demand package for the release of a kidnapped diplomat. When the American ambassador Charles Burke Elbrick was abducted on 4 September 1969 in Rio de Janeiro by the ALN and the Movimiento Revolucionario-8 (MR-8 — Revolutionary Movement of the Eighth), they demanded and obtained not only the release of fifteen political prisoners but also the publication of a manifesto which exposed the cruelties committed by the military regime and called upon the people to overthrow it.[41] As the official radio station broadcast the manifesto people in many places appeared with their transistor radios on the streets, which turned the event into a demonstration against the regime.[42] Yet the tactic did not work well enough. The repressiveness of the regime was too thorough, the muffling of the media too easy for the generals and the impotence and apathy of the masses was too great. One marxist critic later blamed the terrorist middle class revolutionaries with these words: 'The armed organizations of the revolutionary left have nevertheless overestimated the "mobilizing" value of terrorist attacks.... In fact — and here the *class content* of the overestimation of terrorism shows itself — these militants let themselves be tempted by the free publicity they received in the bourgeois press... and mistook the fuss made about their bombs by the class enemy for the support of the masses.'[43]

While the Brazilian terrorists were active in a vast country with 100 million people under a military dictatorship, their Uruguayan counterparts, the Tupamaros, operated in a small country of less than three million people in which control of the capital, where half of all the people lived, was practically synonymous with control of the country. Montevideo has a well-developed communication system, literacy was above ninety percent and the country was, in the 1960s, a politically stable democracy. The preconditions for a successful campaign of urban terrorism looked in many regards better here than north of the border. The Tupamaros movement, founded in 1962–63 by Raúl Sendic, grew in the period 1965–1970 from less than fifty members to an estimated 3,000 and managed to transform the political situation of the nation so thoroughly that Uruguay became, in the words of US Senator Frank Church, 'the biggest torture chamber of Latin America', with the highest per capita rate of political prisoners in the world and one quarter of all Uruguayans fleeing into exile.[44]

The exploits of the Tupamaros, widely reported by the international press, have offered an example to countless terrorist movements abroad, while the lessons that could be learned from their failure have received little publicity. Here we will discuss their strategy only in so far as it relates to the media. One of their public relations techniques was 'armed propaganda', the staging of attacks against the authorities that were intended to demonstrate to the people the weakness of the government and the military strength of the Tupamaros. On the second anniversary of Ché Guevara's death in 1969 they occupied the town of Pando, which gave them so much publicity that the Argentinian Fuerzas Armadas Revolucionarias (FAR – Armed Revolutionary Forces) copied their exploit in 1970 by occupying the town of Garin.[45] The kidnapping of diplomats and businessmen who were detained in 'people's prisons' also provided them with enormous publicity. The purpose was to impress on public opinion that the government was incapable of stopping them while they were in fact building up a counter-state.[46] Left-wing journalists were invited by the Tupamaros to interview a famous kidnap victim, the British ambassador Geoffrey Jackson.[47] Information obtained from the media not only helped them to prepare kidnappings but also enabled the Tupamaros to adapt their negotiation strategy for the release of the victim to new developments.[48]

In their attempt to create a counter-state the Tupamaros brought kidnapped victims to trial before a 'people's court' and released transcripts of 'confessions' to the media.[49] When they abducted the attorney-general of Uruguay, Guido Berro Oribe, in March 1971, the victim was forced to tape-record a statement to the effect that he had allowed the military to interrogate political prisoners and that some of them were kept in jail even after their original term had been served. By 'liberating' documents from bank vaults they were able to publicize the fraudulent use of public funds which forced the Minister of Agriculture to resign. In another case they produced evidence of tax evasion so that the government had to fine the tobacco magnate Luis Mailhos Queirolo.[50] At least in their early phase of action, the Tupamaros managed to create a romantic and heroic Robin Hood image in the media.[51]

After the Uruguayan president Jorge Pacheco Areco decreed a limited state of siege in June 1969, access to the media became difficult for the Tupamaros and they attempted to produce 'counter-media'. Tactics employed to circumvent the official censorship included the occupation of public meeting places such as factory canteens and cinemas where revolutionary teach-ins were conducted. Since the Tupamaros had many technically trained experts in their ranks they also managed to break into normal media broadcasts with their own messages. This use of the public media was supplemented by the installation of their own pirate radio transmitters.[52] Yet these devices were no adequate substitute for the free ride they had formerly been given by the public media when the newspaper readers in the sidewalk cafés of Montevideo were treated daily to stories of their exploits and the government's incompetence, graft and corruption.[53] Although the Tupamaros were ultimately exterminated by military force (with the help of Brazilian experts), their popularity had already earlier declined as could be witnessed in the election of 1971 in which the Tupamaros-supported Frente Amplio did not do well. The media had been their best allies.

The example of the Tupamaros has been widely followed, perhaps nowhere more slavishly than in neighbouring Argentina where the Trotskyist Ejercito Revolucionario del Pueblo (ERP – People's Revolutionary Army) even adopted the five-pointed red star of the Tupamaros emblem. In terms of media uses the Argentinian terrorists have added little new to the Tupamaros' record, except that they treated the media themselves in a much less friendly fashion. A few examples will suffice to illustrate this. On 9 September 1973 members of the August 22 faction of the ERP kidnapped the executive of the newspaper *Clarin*, and blackmailed the paper to print a frontpage advertisement as well as two inside pages in which they urged Argentinians to support Juan D. Peron in the forthcoming elections. Later a band of terrorists also attacked the offices of *Clarin*, wounding two people and setting the premises on fire.[54] Another terrorist group, the ultra-left Catholic Montoneros, kidnapped in November 1975 a director of the Mercedes-Benz plant in Buenos Aires and forced the company to publish

advertisements in Mexican, North American and European newspapers
wherein the 'economic imperialism' of multinational corporations in
the Third World was denounced.[55] The kidnapping and murder of
journalists and their family members by left-wing as well as right-wing
terrorists (the latter enjoying the tacit support of the government) has
become increasingly common in Argentina. At the end of 1978 no less
than eighty-nine of the 162 Latin American journalists who had been
abducted and often murdered were Argentinians.[56] After the military
coup of 24 March 1975 by General Jorge Videla repression became so
severe (more than 15,000 disappearances of persons and 700,000
people driven into exile)[57] that the left-wing terrorists could not even
exploit the World Soccer Championship in the fall of 1978 for their
purpose, though the temptation to reach a peak audience of one billion
people by satellite-linked television must have been great. The absten-
tion from using terroristic violence on this occasion was not total.
Terrorists had placed a bomb under the soccer press centre in San
Martin but a telephonic warning allowed the evacuation of the 500
persons present in the building so that the explosion cost only the lives
of a few policemen.[58]

As a consequence of the muffling of the press in Latin America by
military governments, urban guerrillas have been forced more and more
to seize media broadcasting stations to get their messages across. An
example is the seizure of the radio station in Managua, the capital of
Nicaragua, by the Sandinian Front in April 1978. In El Salvador the
FARN (Fuerzas Armadas Revolucionarios Nacional — Armed Revolutionary National Forces) guerrilla movement has managed to get
manifestoes published in Central American newspapers, as well as
metropolitan ones, by making publication a condition for the release
of foreign businessmen. In the case of the abducted Philips director
F. Schuitema, the terrorists' message was broadcast to El Salvador by
a Dutch World Broadcasting station from the Caribbean, to comply
with the kidnappers' request.[59]

It is perhaps fitting to conclude this survey of Latin American
terrorist uses of the media with an example of right-wing use, although
it cannot be labelled terroristic in our sense. General Carlos Humberto
Romero, the president of El Salvador (until 1979) who refused to allow
the publication of the FARN manifesto in Salvadorian papers because
it was against the national laws on subversive activities, was himself an
adept media user. On election day in February 1977, Orden, the anti-
communist terror squad controlled by Romero and his National
Coalition Party, seized the radio station of the National Water Authority

and used it to instruct his followers with coded messages. The code word for the opposition votes was 'coffee' and 'sugar' meant votes for Romero. 'Little birds' were election supervisors and 'giving lessons' meant to rough them up. 'Put some *Tamales* in the tank' signified filling ballot boxes with fraudulent votes. Having increased the voting list by 300,000 names (almost as much as the capital's population), Romero had ample room for manoeuvring and naturally won his radio-controlled elections.[60] Compared to Romero, the FARN and most other left-wing Latin American terrorists were indeed inept users of the media.

The Palestinians

There can be little doubt that the most effective recent nonstate terrorist users of the media have been the Palestinian fedayeen. For twenty years the world had hardly taken any notice of the fate of the two and a half million displaced Palestinian Arabs. When less than one percent of them, some 20,000 fedayeen, carried their struggle from Israel's frontiers to the developed countries they were able to command media attention.[61] They not only managed to gain support from Arab nations but also laid links with radicals and terrorists from fourteen other nations.[62] After the Arab defeat in the Six Day War in 1967, the Palestinian leaders set out to conquer human minds rather than lost territories. Their terrorism has served primarily as an instrument of mass communication. A report which a US Senate staff member brought back from a trip to the leaders of the Palestinian Liberation Organization (PLO – El Fatah) brings this out sharply:

Terrorist activities, say top Palestinian leaders, have not been carried out for the sake of their immediate results, or for the purpose of terror in itself, or for personal revenge, or as acts of random criminality. Their purpose, they say, has been broadly political, to draw the attention of the world, and most especially of the United States, to the Palestinian movement and its purposes. Terrorism, they say, has been used by other patriotic movements which lacked other effective means, including the Israelis before 1947, or for that matter, the Americans before 1776.[63]

One of the international terrorists in the service of the Palestinians, the Venezuelan Illich Ramirez Sanchez ('Carlos – The Jackal' in media folklore) has put it more succinctly: '...violence is the one language the Western democracies can understand'.[64] Another terrorist internationalist, a member of the Japanese United Red Army, elaborated on this: 'There is no other way for us. Violent actions, such as those we have used constantly in fighting the enemy, are shocking. We want to shock people, everywhere.... It is our only way of communication with the people.'[65] This communication function of terrorism depends almost entirely on the media's willingness to transport the shock to a world audience. The Palestinians' own communication capabilities alone would never have been sufficient to achieve a worldwide impact. The Palestinian Liberation Organization owned but one newspaper, *Falastin Al-Thawra*, and was dependent on the Egyptian government for the use of a radio station, The Voice of Palestine. The movement was allowed to use other radio stations in Syria, Algeria and Iraq and maintained a number of public relation offices in other countries,[66] yet the effectiveness of the PLO's own direct propaganda effort stayed far behind the one resulting from the coverage they got in Western media. As one Fatah leader put it:

We face a strange stream of journalists coming from all over the world.... As a result, our information offices work incessantly, day and night, and the information which we are meant to hand out objectively has become publicity. On the one hand this has had great success in the world, but on the other it has created an abyss between the faith of the masses and the actual ability and effectiveness of fedayeen activity. The Press in general and the Arab Press in particular have credited us with more potentialities than we have. They have created an aura of legendary power which is a very serious matter, as the masses have begun to expect more from us than we are capable of.[67]

This statement, dating from 1969, precedes the biggest terrorist exploits of the Palestinians and still reflects traces of a pre-terroristic understanding of the use of violence in which act and effect are supposed to stand in some proportional relation to each other.

The great breakthrough into the world of McLuhan came in September 1970 when in a carefully choreographed move three airliners with 276 passengers were hijacked and brought to Dawson's Field in Jordan. A Jumbo jet that had been too big to land on the 'Revolutionary Airstrip' had been blown up in Cairo and this served as prelude to a six-day spectacle in the desert sun. The terrorists of the Popular Front for the Liberation of Palestine (PFLP) made some demands for exchanging hostages against imprisoned Palestinians, but these were almost secondary. The local PFLP responsible, Bassam Abu Sherif, later explained the main rationale: 'It was a direct assault on the consciousness of international opinion. What mattered most to us was that one pays attention to us'.[68] Reporters and television crews from all over the world flocked to the scene and the PFLP organized a press conference in which reporters were allowed to speak to the hostages. Broadcast to millions on television screens, these scenes were also meant to impress the five blackmailed governments to give in to at least some of the terrorists' demands [69] Three of the five governments did give in. The airliners, worth thirty million dollars, went up in flames. The film of the exploding planes, rushed to London by a British journalist in a chartered Caravelle, flashed over the TV-screens of the whole world. The reporter, David Phillips, was commended at the Cannes Television Festival for this world exclusive when he afterwards turned it into a documentary 'Deadline at Dawson's Field'. He had provided the PFLP with publicity worth millions of dollars and it was all free. The link which the media made between the Jordanian desert and the living rooms of countless TV-watchers gave the deed its full meaning.

Without the linking of events which the media provided, some of the Palestinian exploits would have been totally senseless. Take the example of the Lydda Airport massacre of 30 May 1972. Three Japanese, in the service of the Palestinians, arrived in Israel on an Air France plane and opened fire on Roman Catholic pilgrims from Puerto Rico, killing twenty-six of them and wounding many more. Two of the terrorists were also killed. The third, Matsufuji Okamutu, explained the deed with the words: 'The Arab world lacks spiritual fervour, so we felt that through this attempt we could probably stir up the Arab world'.[70] A PFLP spokesman explained that the purpose of the attack had been to 'raise the temperature' in the Middle East and to frighten public opinion in other countries. 'This operation does affect the ordinary Englishman. He will be shocked. What horrible cold-blooded murders. But he will think three times before coming to Israel. Why should I get killed, he will say to himself.'[71] The main sense, if not the only one, such a massacre has is that sense it gains from being reported and explained by the media. The Japanese terrorists had no relation whatsoever with the victims who only served as message generators. The bigger the massacre, the bigger the headlines and the prime time reports on the deed in the electronic media. Had the media reported only that twenty-eight people of Japanese and Puerto Rican origin had been killed in an incident in Israel the news would have been unable to spread fear and apprehension among the hundreds of thousands who visit the holy sites and other places in Israel every year. But this, the terrorists could be sure, was not the way the Western media work. The purpose of news is to be reported. Anybody who can stage a news event gets the price for free in the Western system of free flow of communication.

However, there is also an alternative use of the media wherein the terrorist does not create the main news event but intrudes on somebody else's news event. This happened most successfully at the Munich Olympic Games in 1972. The decision to make top athletes the target of a terrorist operation was dictated by similar considerations that had already led the Cuban guerrillas to kidnap the world motor-racing champion. The victim's news value served as an entree for obtaining news value for the perpetrators. One of the key organizers of the Munich attack, Fuad al-Shamali, formulated the strategy a few months before the Olympic Games: 'We have to hit them at their weakest point. Bombing attacks on El Al offices do not serve our cause. We have to kill their most important and most famous people. Since we cannot come close to their statesmen, we have to kill artists and sportsmen.'[72]

The choice of site, the Olympic Games, had been suggested four years earlier in Mexico by athletes adhering to the Black Panther movement who had used the honour ceremony for political demonstration. Outside the stadium in Mexico City students had equally tried to use the presence of the media to highlight their grievances before world opinion. But their attempt had been crushed by the police at a cost of more than one hundred students' lives. In Munich, however, the Palestinians were successful. On 5 September 1972 eight Black September terrorists captured the attention of an estimated 800 million spectators.[73] They demanded the exchange of 200 detained Palestinians against the eleven Israeli athletes.[74] But it was clear that the main purpose of the operation was not material but psychological. Abu Ijad, co-founder of El Fatah and chief of intelligence of the PLO, named three goals for this action:

1. Strengthening of the existence of the Palestinian people;
2. Echo with the international press assembled there; and
3. Liberation of fedayeen imprisoned in Israel.[75]

By placing the military objective last, Ijad implicitly admitted the propagandistic nature of the action. The first goal could, of course, be achieved only via the second. Another Arab explained it with these words:

We recognize that sport is the modern religion of the Western world. We knew that the people of England and America would switch their television sets from any programme about the plight of the Palestinians if there was a sporting event

on another channel. So we decided to use their Olympics, the most sacred ceremony of this religion, to make the world pay attention to us. We offered up
human sacrifices to your gods of sport and television. And they answered our
prayers. From Munich onwards nobody could ignore the Palestinians or their
cause.[76]

In Munich the Palestinian terrorists had carried their war to where
the cameras were and they got the coverage they had sought. The media
did not hesitate to broadcast live the bloody spectacle unfolding in the
Olympic village and satellites transported the pictures of the ski-hooded
terrorists to all continents. At one point in the transmission of the
events to the United States coverage was dropped for nearly ninety
minutes. This, however, had nothing to do with the media no longer
wanting to play the terrorists' game. The cause was rather a rivalry
between two major US television networks for satellite transmission
rights, during which CBS (Columbia Broadcasting System) forced ABC
(American Broadcasting Company) to stop its coverage. 'You're in this
business to win', a CBS spokesman explained[77] and this was akin to
the terrorists' motives. In the Arab world Black September met widespread understanding and even approval for its action. Thousands of
Palestinians joined the terrorist organizations in the wake of this public
relations success.[78] That the action had been unsuccessful in military
terms (five of the terrorists got killed, three were apprehended, the hostages were all killed and no exchange of 'prisoners' took place) did not
detract from the psychological success. On the contrary, the suicidal
nature of the attack in fact reinforced its impact. Millions of people
who had up till then never taken any notice of the Palestinian cause
were alerted. While part of the world public reacted with unreserved
condemnation, others argued that if Palestinians were so dedicated
that they sacrificed themselves for their cause, there had to be something worthwhile about it. What the Palestinians wanted, a nation-state
of their own, was plausible enough to other patriots in the world. It
was not as highreaching and immaterial as world-revolution and accom-
modation was not impossible.

Two years later, in 1974, when PLO leader Yassir Arafat made a
widely televised speech before the General Assembly of the United
Nations, this notion that the Palestinians had to be accommodated
somehow, had become a widely shared opinion. This break-through
to quasi-diplomatic recognition would probably not have been possible
without the Arab oil-weapon looming in the background. What had
prepared it psychologically, however, was undoubtedly the terrorist

strategy aimed at world opinion. Zehdi Labib Terzi, the PLO's chief observer at the United Nations, admitted this in so many words: 'The first several hijackings aroused the consciousness of the world and awakened the media and world opinion much more — and more effectively — than 20 years of pleading at the United Nations.'[79] Throwing bombs, the Palestinian example demonstrates, can be an effective communication strategy. 'We would throw roses if it would work', one fedayeen has said.[80] Roses, however, have a lower news value. Once world notoriety had been achieved, the PLO began to distance itself from further terroristic acts, blaming them on uncontrollable extremists. Terrorism had brought the movement internationally to the point where other channels of expression became available.[81] With a budget of around $ 350 million (in 1975) the PLO had become rich enough to obtain publicity by paid advertisements in the world press.[82]

The guerrilla fight against Israel from the surrounding countries still used elements of terrorism, but world opinion has generally placed it in the more legitimate context of a national liberation war. However, the media continue to play an important role in these cross-border intrusions. Viewing the Middle East as a powder keg where World War Three is most likely to begin, the media had, by the mid-1970s, stationed about 300 foreign correspondents, 120 of them full-time, in Israel.[83] Every small incident — be it only that ten school girls in Bethlehem burn a car tyre — is picked up by them and reverberates around the world. Relatively small as the physical results of Palestinian cross-border operations have been — sixty-two Israelis were killed in 1974, thirty in 1975 — the intensive coverage given to these incidents has made them look like major events.[84] And that seems to be the major reason why they are undertaken. When on 15 May 1974 members of the Popular Democratic Front for the Liberation of Palestine (PDLF) killed a large number of children in Maalot the operation was designed to call attention to the demands of the Arab guerrillas and to create for them a major role at the planned peace talks in Geneva.[85] The Israeli policy of not censoring all terroristic news has, at times, placed great stress on society. In the case of the Entebbe hijacking in Uganda in June 1976, for instance, part of the Israeli population, alerted by the media, put pressure on the government to negotiate with the terrorists for the release of the Jewish hostages.[86] Yet the alternative, a news blackout, with all the rumours that would go with it, would have been even more difficult to handle. Publicity, on the other hand, can be counter-productive and this is obviously what the Israeli government counted on.

Yet to the terrorists themselves negative publicity has its own value. Carlos, the Venezuelan terrorist in the service of the Palestinians, for instance, held that publicity was a sort of security for him. He believed that the more was written about him the more dangerous he would appear so that policemen would be less inclined to arrest him if they crossed his path.[87] When he led the December 1975 raid against the OPEC (Organization of Petrol Exporting Countries) building in Vienna he clearly capitalized on his media celebrity: 'You will have heard of me already; I am the famous Carlos. You can tell that to the others.'[88] When the Austrian government gave in so easily and speedily to his blackmail, his media-strategy was almost cut short and he insisted that his group should stay in the OPEC headquarters long enough for the television cameras to arrive on the scene.[89] In his demand package he also included the broadcasting of a deliberately confusing anti-zionist statement by Austrian radio.[90] Apart from forcing media to spread terrorist manifestoes, pro-Arab terrorists have also turned to another Latin American tactic, the direct assault on journalists. On 8 February 1978 pro-Palestinian gunmen in Cyprus killed the editor of Egypt's semi-official newspaper *Al Ahram*, Youssef el-Sebai, one of the leading exponents of President Sadat's peace initiative.[91] As in Latin America, the whole circle of terrorist uses of the media from seduction to coercion had thereby been covered by the Palestinians.

The United States

The United States is the most media-saturated nation and in all media developments from the press to radio, movie and television the Americans have pioneered and largely determined the format of these media.[92] Given the absence of censorship and the private ownership of most public media and the fact that 'violence is as American as apple pie', the United States seems to be the country most open to terrorist uses of the media. Due to the relatively low degree of class consciousness, terrorism has, however, in recent times more often taken a criminal than a political expression. In the past, there has, of course, been much terrorism based on racial consciousness. In the following account we will concentrate on the more recent political expressions and use examples of criminal terrorist uses of the media only in those cases where we have encountered no equivalent use by politically motivated terrorists.

The American media distribute a mixture of information,

entertainment and advertisement and the three categories readily overlap. News programmes on radio and television are packaged in a
show-biz format and news anchormen vie with movie stars for top
celebrity status. The technique of using violence to bring over a message
to a mass audience was practised by large corporations long before
political terrorists entered the scene in the 1960s and 1970s. George
Gerbner, a leading communications expert, has categorized eighty
percent of US television content as violent.[93] Advertisers use violent
media content to attract audiences which can then be exposed to commercial messages. The difference with the political terrorists is that the
violence they sponsor is fictional rather than real and that they have to
pay for broadcasting the message. Sometimes, however, real people
imitate the fictional violence and make it real. 'We are what you have
made us', a member of the terrorist gang of Charles Manson explained.
'We were brought up on your TV. We were brought up watching
Gunsmoke, Have Gun, will Travel, FBI, Combat. Combat was my
favorite show. I never missed *Combat*.'[94] For these contagion acts
the sponsors of violent programmes take no credit. They only want
people to imitate the behaviour portrayed in the advertisements, not
in the programmes between them. The latter are meant only to direct
attention to the former. But Denise Susan Atkins motivated the murder
of Sharon Tate and her friends by herself and other members of the
Manson 'family' with the same rationale: 'So that one pays attention
to us....'[95] The motives behind some terrorists and the corporate users
of the media seem to correspond: both want the public to pay attention
to them. Arthur Bremer, the man who crippled the presidential candidate George Wallace in an assassination attempt, was quoted as saying:
'Well, I was on Cronkite's program today'.[96] Self-advertisement appears
to have been his one and only motive.

Other individual terrorist media users in the United States seem to
be motivated by a grievance that, in their view, does not receive sufficient media attention. One case in point is the hijacking staged by a
lone gunman, Ricardo Chavez Ortiz, who forced an aircraft to land
in Los Angeles where he demanded radio and television time to speak
about the needs of the Hispano-Americans. This was granted to him
and after a ninety-minute speech he gave himself up without offering
resistance.[97] Many US skyjackers seem to have been attracted by the
ease with which media-time could be obtained. David Hubbard, a
psychiatrist who has interviewed scores of hijackers, quotes one who
was said to express the opinion of many others: 'Television is a whore.
Any man who wants her full favors can have them in five minutes with

a pistol'.[98] Hubbard held that 'They wouldn't even *think* of bombing
and hijacking, unless you guaranteed them a rostrum. So if the media
cut their coverage down to the importance of other minor news, these
men wouldn't act'.[99]

Hubbard's statement certainly contained much truth in the case of
the five Croatians who on 10 September 1976 hijacked TWA Flight
355. For the price of five one-way tickets from New York to Chicago,
one real bomb and some fake bombs and some pamphlets, worth perhaps $ 500 altogether, they received media exposure worth millions
of dollars if placed as prime-time advertisements. Hijacking a Boeing
727 with sixty-three passengers and the flight crew, these 'Fighters
for Free Croatia' captured tens of millions of people's attention for
some thirty hours. They had placed a primitive bomb, made according
to the instructions of the commercially available *Anarchist Cookbook*,
in a locker of a New York Savings Bank and threatened to explode
another bomb in a crowded place. The Croatians had issued demands
and a 3,500 word manifesto and stipulated that both texts had to
appear in their entirety in the *New York Times*, the *Los Angeles Times*,
the *Chicago Tribune* and the *International Herald Tribune*.[100] Except
for the Paris-based *Herald Tribune*, which had already gone into print,
all other papers complied. Furthermore, the Croatians demanded that
their pamphlets be dropped over Montreal, New York and Chicago.
In their manifesto they advocated the liberation of their homeland
from Yugoslavia and stated their grievances against the Tito regime.
After having released thirty-five of the hostages in Newfoundland, the
terrorists forced the pilot to cross the Atlantic and further pamphlets
were dropped over London and Paris. Those who cared to pick them
up from the streets could read that '...the world will not have peace
until Croatia enjoys all the rights recognized for other peoples and
other nations'.[101] To the passengers they explained that the purpose of
the hijacking was to communicate their grievances to the world. When
they gave themselves up in Paris, one hijacker, dismantling his fake
bomb, declared 'That's show biz!'[102] The whole purpose of the exercise had been publicity and in this they had certainly succeeded.

An interesting example of criminal terrorist uses of the media is
offered by the case of Anthony G. Kiritsis, who on 8 February 1977
took an officer of a mortgage company in Indianapolis hostage.
Kiritsis wired his gun around the head of the victim, Richard Hall,
whom he blamed for his financial difficulties. Barricading himself with
the hostage in his apartment, he was soon visited by local and national
reporters, equipped with minicams. The news coverage was so massive

that the terrorist, fearing that somebody witnessing the abduction might have a heart-attack, included in his demands an indemnity for any damage caused to spectators.[103] Kiritsis used the radio in his apartment to gain intelligence on police movements outside, when an on-the-scene reporter described that the bomb squad was readying some equipment that might be used for breaking into the apartment. The news director of a radio station who had broadcast telephone conversations with the terrorist had to enter as negotiator to calm him down.[104] As a condition for his surrender after the sixty-three hours siege Kiritsis demanded and got a news conference ('Put your cameras on me or I'll shoot'). Two or three stations carried the subsequent obscenity-filled speech live. With the gun still at the head of the victim an intentional or accidental discharge was a real and present danger, while Kiritsis bathed in the media attention, calling himself 'a goddamn national hero'.[105] Kiritsis was just an angry man, declared insane, and the uses he made of the media were unpremeditated and arose from the opportunities offered to him on the scene. Others, however, were more deliberate in their media use.

The rise of the Black Power movement offers some insights into the media uses of a more sophisticated group. In the early 1960s television had become a household article with the majority of black families and the discrepancy between their own reality and what they saw on television — affluent white suburban middle-class life — was a powerful stimulus for revolt. When blacks demonstrated for a bigger share of the American wealth, the television crews accompanying them became their greatest allies. Cameramen, anxious to get gripping action film, occasionally even encouraged the use of violence. In the majority of cases, however, the mere presence of cameras induced demonstrators to 'act'. The police, sensing the electrifying influence of the presence of cameras, in many cases attacked the camera crews (which also served to protect themselves from law suits which might arise if police brutality was recorded).[106] The Black Power movement, which Huey Newton and Bobby Seale launched in October 1966, owed its growth almost entirely to their clever use of the media. Newton sent thirty armed Panthers to the state capitol in Sacramento, California, when legislators debated a bill proposing to outlaw the carrying of loaded guns in the city. The media had been invited by the Panthers to the scene and the show of strength of armed militants on the floor of the capitol, made the headlines and newscasts all over the United States. With this masterly stroke the Oakland Panthers had become national figures and were invited to television appearances and speaking engagements all over the country. The Black Panther paper, founded some two weeks later, first as a monthly and then as a weekly, rose in circulation to 140,000 copies in 1970. In this paper the Panthers advocated guerrilla warfare methods and the indiscriminate murder of 'gestapo policemen'. Although the media publicity had enabled them to issue a paper of their own, they still relied mainly on the big media to spread their message. They admitted this in so many words: 'Millions and millions of oppressed people...will gain through an indirect acquaintance the proper strategy for liberation via the mass media and the physical activities of the party'.[107]

Even more adroit in the use of the media than the black militants were those white middle-class children who discovered the 'happening'. Jerry Rubin, a founder of the Yippie movement (YIP – Youth International Party), outlined some important principles of mass media politics and it is worth while quoting him at length:

TV is raising generations of kids who want to grow up and become demonstrators. Have you ever seen a boring demonstration on TV?...Television creates myths bigger than reality. Demonstrations last hours, and most of that time nothing happens. After the demonstration we rush home for the six o'clock news. The drama review. TV packs all the action into two minutes – a commercial for the revolution. The mere idea of a 'story' is revolutionary because a 'story' implies disruption of normal life. Every reporter is a dramatist, creating a theater out of life....A revolution is news; the status quo ain't. The media does not *report* 'news', it *creates* it. An event happens when it goes on TV and becomes myth. The media is not 'neutral'. The presence of a camera transforms a demonstration, turning us into heroes....Television keeps us escalating our tactics; a tactic becomes ineffective when it stops generating gossip or interest –'news'. Politicians get air time just by issuing statements. But ordinary people must take to the streets to get on television. Our power lies in our ability to strike fear in the enemy's heart so the more the media exaggerates, the better. TV time goes to those with the most guts and imagination....I've never seen 'bad' coverage of demonstration. It makes no difference what they *say* about us. The pictures are the story....The movement is too puritanical about the use of the media. After all, Karl Marx never watched television! You can't be a revolutionary today without a television set – it's as important as a gun! Every guerrilla must know how to use the terrain of the culture that he is trying to destroy![108]

Rubin's philosophy ('History (can) be changed in a day. An hour. A second.')[109] travelled on a road on which terrorism was the almost inevitable outcome. The movement's policy turned from a concentration on winning the masses to one of winning the mass media. In order to capture the media's attention ever stronger impulses were necessary. The rally was better than a press conference. Marches were better than rallies, since the moving crowd looked better on the action-hungry TV-screen. And violence was what the media responded to most.[110] The activists who launched demonstrations could in the evening check on television which scenes were broadcast. Almost invariably those few scenes of violence that occurred in a lengthy and otherwise peaceful demonstration got media exposure. As one editor of a big national television network explained: 'Our job is to cut all dead wood and dull moments'.[111] Instead of presenting a balanced picture of what was happening the media generally preferred to focus on the few peaks of action-packed moments. If the demonstrators wanted to play the media they had to produce peaks. One observer of the American scene described the logical consequences of these media imperatives:

I watched and participated as they (the Movement people) changed their organizations' commitments from community organizing, legal reform processes and other forms of evolutionary change to focus upon television. The goal became less to communicate with individuals, governments or communities than to influence the media. Actions began to be chosen less for their educational value or political content than for their ability to attract television cameras.... A theory evolved: Accelerate the drama of each successive action to maintain the same level of coverage. Television somehow demanded it. As the stakes rose, the pressure mounted to create ever more outrageous actions. The movements of the 1960s had become totally media based by the 1970s. The most radical elements were up to the challenges of the theory of accelerated action. They 'advanced' to kidnappings, hijackings, bombings. The sole purpose of these actions was often no more than media exposure. Sensing that television was now the country's main transmitter of reality, individuals began to take personal action to affect it.[112]

One of the groups that marched along this road to terrorism was the Weathermen, a splinter group from the Students for a Democratic Society (SDS). The Weather Underground bombed highly symbolic targets like the Pentagon and the national Capitol, but placed warning calls before the explosions so that nobody would get hurt.[113] The very fact that they issued warnings was indicative that their aim was not military but psychological. It was a publicity stunt, an act of communication, intended, as one alleged participant admitted, 'to freak out the war mongers' on the one hand and to 'bring a smile and a wink to all the kids in the country' on the other.[114] The Weatherpersons cultivated the media and one of the leaders, Bernardine Rae Dohrn, even managed to place an article in the opposite-editorial page of the *New York Times* while being on the FBI's (Federal Bureau of Investigation) top-ten wanted list. They invited filmmakers to meet them in the underground and shoot footage for presentation above the ground.[115] The film documentary, starring Miss Dohrn, contained an appeal to the young to fight 'American imperialism' from their position 'behind enemy lines'. Proceedings of the movie presumably went to the Weather Underground after the Attorney General had declined to subpoena the producers.[116]

Media people known for their left sympathies were invited by the Weathermen for interviews and allowed themselves to be blindfolded to be driven to their secret hideouts.[117] In their book-long political statement 'Prairie Fire' (1974) they declared that 'Armed actions push forward people's consciousness and commitment; they are a great teacher and example. Yet they must be clearly understandable to the people, identify our enemy precisely, and overcome his massive lies and propaganda.'[118] But this last problem was never overcome by the Weather Underground. They could bomb their names on to the front pages but they could do next to nothing to make sure that the message intended by their bombings was also the message transmitted. Unable to control the way the media portrayed their deeds, they apparently decided to establish their own medium. In 1975 the Weathermen founded the Red Dragon Print Collective which issues a bi-monthly magazine called *Osawatomie*. Writing and printing the clandestine publication, however, seems to have taken so much of their time that bombing has declined sharply.[119] The switch from terrorism to publishing illustrates once more how much terrorism is linked to communication.

Perhaps the most effective use of the media by terrorists in the United States has been made by the Symbionese Liberation Army (SLA). Numbering less than a dozen 'soldiers', this Californian 'army' consisting of some middle-class whites under the leadership of a black ex-convict ('Field-Marshal Cinque'), managed to command media attention for two years by kidnapping Patricia Hearst, the teenage heiress of one of the great fortunes of America. Her father, Randolph Hearst, ruler of a media empire, saw not only his daughter Patty taken hostage by the SLA but also his main paper, the *San Francisco Examiner*. Before Patricia Hearst was kidnapped on 4 February 1974 the only sign the SLA had given of its existence came from the murder of an Oakland school superintendent, Marcus Foster, in November 1973. Once Hearst's daughter was in the hands of the SLA, the *San Francisco Examiner* visibly altered its reporting about the Foster case.[120] In a letter to a San Francisco radio station the SLA demanded that all their communications dealing with Patty Hearst's abduction be published in full in all newspapers and other media, adding that 'Failure to do so will endanger the safety of the prisoner'.[121] The *San Francisco Examiner* complied and the *Oakland Tribune* did so too in the beginning but then refused.[122] The worry of the terrorists that their cause might be treated with silence, was, however, unfounded. The SLA-Patty Hearst story became one of the biggest continuing stories in media history and its aftermath, Patty marrying her body-guard, was reported in the world press even five years after her abduction. In the years 1974–1976 Patty, the hostage turned terrorist, made the cover of *Newsweek* seven times – a record of sorts.[123]

The media treated the public to taped and printed messages from the terrorists and their victim. In a communiqué issued on 12 February 1974 the SLA announced the terms of release for Hearst's daughter: 'quality food' worth $ 70 per package had to be distributed by Hearst to all people in need in California. This demand was quite outrageous; for the 5.9 million poor people in the state the costs of such a pro-gramme would have amounted to some $ 400 million, which might have impoverished even the multimillionaire.[124] The SLA explained this Robin Hood stroke in a taped communiqué: 'Our strategy was to show by example what can be done... this goodwill gesture was intended to give some food to the people while at the same time pointing out our understanding that the people can never expect the enemy to feed them...'.[125] Hearst set up a token two million dollar distribution programme and the sight of thousands of people in Oakland fighting for free food was broadcast by the three major tele-vision networks to sixty million Americans. The Robin Hood image of helping the poor while bleeding the rich made people almost forget the kidnapping which stood at the beginning. One reporter noted that 'the tone of the press (in San Francisco)...is subdued, un-bloodthirsty, even sympathetic toward the SLA'.[126] Hearst, after being blamed by his daughter for not doing his best (it had not been 'quality food'), announced a second food give-away programme worth four million dollars but for reasons that remain unclear the SLA demanded that media coverage of the give-away be suspended.[127] Maybe Patty Hearst had at that time already decided to transform herself into Tania (named after Ché Guevara's companion), joining the SLA. At any rate, on 15 April 1974 she was filmed while robbing a bank. The picture of a millionaire's daughter stealing money appeared for the SLA perhaps even more compelling than pictures of unruly mobs fighting for food. But Patty remained the only convert of the SLA, and the initial skill the terrorists had shown in using the media ultimately remained far behind the use the media made of the SLA.[128] Three movies and eleven books have so far capitalized on the story, not to mention scores of articles.[129]

Another instructive case of terrorist use of the media, though less spectacular than the SLA episode, is the Hanafi incident. On 9 March 1977 twelve members of the obscure Moslem sect Hanafi, led by Hamaas Abdul Khaalis, seized 134 hostages in three buildings in Washington, DC and held them for thirty-nine hours. A radio reporter, Maurice Williams, was shot during the takeover and sixteen others were subsequently injured. Khaalis' main concern was revenge, not publicity. His family had been murdered by a rival sect and he wanted the convicted murderers to be handed over to him so that he could personally bring them to justice. Another of his demands was that a movie released that day, *Mohammad, Messenger of God*, be banned from American screens because he regarded it as blasphemous. While the first demand could not be met, the second was met by United Artists, the company that had produced the movie at a cost of seventeen million dollars.[130] Although the movie was later shown in various cities, the episode represented a temporarily successful terrorist attempt at censoring the media. Had the movie company not voluntarily agreed to withdraw *Mohammad, Messenger of God*, hostages might have died or a court might have ordered the banning of the movie. The prospects opened by the Hanafi incident were in both cases frightening.

The media also played a role in this incident in other ways. Khaalis called up a local television anchorman to discuss his demands and even more often was called up by reporters from places as far away as Australia, Saudi Arabia and Sweden.[131] The media attention alternatively elated and infuriated Khaalis. One Texas station which requested a live radio interview with him was turned down when he found out that it broadcasted with only 20,000 watts: 'You are not worth talking to. I don't talk to radio with less than 50,000 watts.'[132] At one point, the terrorists, noticing cameras opposite the street, threatened to hang two older men with their heads down out of the window, to give the media the spectacle they were looking for.[133] One radio discjockey engaged in a live interview with Khaalis, asked the terrorist whether he had set a deadline. Khaalis did not pay attention to this question (no deadline had so far been set by him), otherwise it might have further endangered the lives of the hostages.[134] Another reporter disclosed that there were still more people in one building who so far had managed to hide. A third newscaster infuriated Khaalis by

calling him a Black Muslim. Khaalis' family had been slaughtered by
Black Muslims and he threatened to kill a hostage in retaliation for the
reporter's remark. An apology which the newscaster made on the
advice of the police saved the situation.[135] But the episode did nothing
to endear the media to the hostages. One of them, himself a reporter,
later summarized his experience in these words:

> As hostages, many of us felt that the Hanafi takeover was a happening, a guerrilla
> theater, a high impact propaganda exercise programmed for the TV screen, and
> secondarily for the front pages of newspapers around the world....Beneath the
> resentment and the anger of my fellow hostages toward the press is a conviction
> gained...that the news media and terrorism feed on each other, that the news
> media and particularly TV, create a thirst for fame and recognition. Reporters
> do not simply report the news. They help create it. They are not objective obser-
> vers, but subjective participants – actors, scriptwriters and idea men.[136]

Following the Hanafi incident, Andrew Young, US ambassador to
the United Nations, suggested that the First Amendment of the US
Constitution, guaranteeing the freedom of the press, should 'be clarified
by the Supreme Court in the light of the power of the mass media'.[137]
Although President Carter felt nothing for this suggestion, the fact
that the issue was raised demonstrated that the terrorist use of the
media and the media use of terrorism had begun to intrude on the
fundamentals of American society.

Western Europe

Until the 1960s postwar Western Europe was, with a few exceptions
such as South Tirol and Northern Ireland (1956–1962), largely free
from insurgent terrorism. Since the late 1960s, however, both (student)
revolutionary and nationalist (ethnic/separatist) terrorism have been on
the increase. In this section we will discuss mainly those aspects of
terrorist uses of the media which have not been treated earlier.

The oldest more or less continuous European insurgent terrorism
has been the one in (Northern) Ireland. Presently some five hundred
terrorists from the Provisional wing of the Irish Republican Army
(IRA), backed by several thousand sympathizers, aim at the reintegra-
tion of Northern Ireland with its half a million Catholics and one
million Protestants into the Irish Republic, which had gained independence from Great Britain in 1921, following a successful terrorist
campaign.[138] Although there are other terrorist groups both on the

Catholic left (Saor Eire — Free Ireland; PLA — People's Liberation Army) and the Protestant right (UVF — Ulster Volunteer Force; UDA — Ulster Defense Association), the Provisional IRA has been the most prominent in the last decade. Their aim is to influence the British to withdraw support from the immigrated Protestant settlers who control the economy and to bring about the withdrawal of Britain's 14,000 troops.

In this propaganda war the IRA Provisionals have been holding clandestine press conferences and they have granted exclusive interviews on television to both the British Broadcasting Corporation (BBC) and the Independent Television (ITV). In one of these interviews David O'Connell, the Provisional Chief of Staff, announced a bombing campaign in Great Britain which materialized a week later when two bars in Birmingham were bombed with the loss of twenty-one lives. Although it cannot be proven, the possibility exists that O'Connell actually used his BBC television appearance to signal the attacks to Irish terrorists stationed in Great Britain.[139] Certainly the impact of the subsequent deeds was heightened by his public announcement. In another attempt to increase the impact of a terroristic act, the Provisional IRA invited an American television documentary group to accompany a terrorist team on a mission. The TV crew filmed how IRA men loaded a car with explosives and drove it to a city street where it was blown up.[140]

The IRA Provisionals have not only used bombs to receive news coverage for themselves but also to prevent other events from receiving prominent coverage. The IRA Chief of Staff admitted that the first car bombs in London were placed there in order to bomb an election in Northern Ireland from the front pages.[141] The strategy worked and taught them another lesson as well. As one IRA source put it: 'Last year taught us that in publicity terms one bomb in Oxford Street is worth ten in Belfast. It is not a lesson we are likely to forget in the future.'[142]

Although the Irish terrorists use the media in their strategy to exhaust the patience of the British public they have not hesitated to attack journalists and their sources directly. Desmond Irvine, the Secretary of the Northern Ireland Prison Officers' Association, was shot dead by the Provisional IRA two weeks after the broadcasting of an interview he gave for the Thames Television *This Week* programme.[143] It seems likely that in this case the medium served as a target identifier for the terrorists. Cases where journalists themselves were punished by the terrorists in Northern Ireland for their news coverage have been frequent and not only the Provisionals but also the Ulster Volunteer

Force have engaged in it. In one case the Provos threatened a journalist because he was not anti-British enough for their taste. Many journalists have, as a consequence, desisted from signing their articles.[144]

Censorship by murder and target identification by the media can also be found in places other than Ireland. An English language daily in Athens, for instance, published a list of seven alleged CIA agents working in Greece, whereupon one of them, Richard S. Welch, was shot outside his home on 23 December 1975.[145] While in this case the connection between the visibility of the prospective victim created by a medium and the consequence seems obvious, in other cases it is not. Yet it seems safe to assume that terrorists, like most other people, get their information mainly from the media and their death lists will reflect this. Cases where journalists themselves became targets are much easier to pinpoint and though they are not yet so frequent in Europe as in Latin America, the list of journalist victims is on the rise. Censorship by murder was for instance practised in the case of José Maria Portell, managing editor of the weekly *Hoja de Lunes*. His paper had published a survey in which the majority of Basque intellectuals interviewed had rejected the idea that the Spanish government should negotiate with the ETA (Euskadi ta Askatasuna — 'Basque country and liberty'). Two days later, on 28 June 1978, Portell was shot dead near Bilbao.[146] In Turkey, one of the countries worst hit by terrorism (in 1978 there were more than 1,400 victims), the owner of the right-wing newspaper *Hursoz*, Ardogan Hancerlioglo, was shot dead in February 1979, the second Turkish journalist killed that month.[147] Another variation, less personal, of terrorist censorship has been attacks on newspaper offices or television transmitters, such as in the case of the Barcelona satirical weekly *Papus* or the Breton Liberation Front (FLB — 'Front de Libération de la Bretagne') attack on the radio and TV installation in Pres-en-Bail.[148] Attempts have also been made to coerce media into publishing information sympathetic to terrorists. One such case involved the occupation of the premises of the left paper *Libération* in Paris by some 150 radicals who demanded the publication of a 'pro-Baader' issue.[149] Such acts have also been committed by individuals who felt that they had to tell the world their message. In 1974 one such individual, Jacques Robert, entered a studio of Radio Luxemburg with a pistol to force a discjockey to yield him the microphone for a political message. Three years later the same individual hijacked a Caravelle with ninety-eight passengers for the sole purpose of having a taped ten-minute message broadcast, an attempt that cost one person's life. In both cases he failed to achieve his purpose.[150]

Rather than reviewing individual cases of terrorist uses of the media in Western Europe we will, in the following, concentrate on two countries, West Germany and Italy, where terrorists have developed the most sophisticated media strategies of all European terrorists. Even less than the left-wing terrorism in Italy, has that in West Germany been able to develop anything that resembles a firm social and ideological basis. The German student terrorists started their actions as a reaction against the Vietnam war. Once the war was over, however, the movement did not decline as in most other countries but retained its momentum in what has been called a 'liberate the guerrilla-guerrilla'.[151] Apart from a few political actions directed against US military installations in West Germany, most of the operations of the Rote Armee Fraktion (RAF — Red Army Fraction) and the June 2nd Movement and their related groups have been actions of self-advertising, revenge, resource provisioning and attempts at liberating imprisoned 'soldiers'. In both the Vietnam and the Prisoner-Liberation phase, but especially in the second, the media have played a crucial role in the strategy of the German terrorists.

In the late 1960s when the Vietnam war stirred the minds of West Germany's youth, the media were generally not very critical of American conduct of the war. When in 1968 some German anti-war protestors set fire to department stores this was meant as an attempt to focus public attention on what was going on in Southeast Asia. 'I am not speaking here about a few burned rubber mattresses (in the department store), I speak about the burned children in Vietnam', one of the arsonists tried to explain to the judge.[152] Such early acts of violence against things were predominantly attempts to communicate their concern about the suffering of the people in Vietnam and to be heard in their protest. 'If they do not listen to us, then we throw a couple of bombs',[153] Hans-Joachim Klein from the June 2nd Movement explained. The strategy to bring home their anti-war message by the sound of bombs was generally unsuccessful; only a few intellectuals understood them. One of the few, however, was a columnist of the left-wing political magazine, *Konkret*, Ulrike Meinhof. In her advocacy for the department store arsonists, Gudrun Ensslin and Andreas Baader, she was, like their lawyer Horst Mahler, identifying more and more with the violent political idealists.[154] In May 1970 she participated in the liberation of Andreas Baader and went underground.

Identification is, in our view, the key process with which the German terrorists worked. Their social consciousness was awoken by their identification with the victims of the Vietnam war and with the poor in the Third World.[155] The public media had helped to foster this identification. As one author put it: 'They got a regular stirring up from "the media" — pity and indignation roused on behalf of story characters, existing or not. Learning about wars, exploitation, oppressions in the same way as they learned about the fate of fictional victims, they felt strongly not because they were a generation of visionaries but because they were a generation of televisionaries.'[156] German postwar youth, which has been called the 'fatherless generation' seems to have had an especially strong urge to identify, which has found its outlets in advocacy for remote causes, since, given their fathers' past, the objects at hand were often ill-suited for adoration. The public media, and perhaps even more the underground press and the alternative left press, had motivated part of them and given them symbols of identification such as Ché Guevara or the Tupamaros.

In a world linked up electronically, reference groups after whom behaviour is modelled need not be personally known to the imitator. Personal knowledge of a subject with which a young person feels a need to identify has an inbuilt corrective, since upon closer knowledge even saints tend to lose part of their halo. Models provided by the media, on the other hand, are not subject to verification and identification can therefore become more intense. 'The longing to belong', Arthur Koestler has written in a different context, 'left without appropriately mature outlets, manifested itself mostly in primitive or perverted forms.'[157] The act of identification which enables us to empathize with others is also capable of leading to vicarious emotions, to anger and aggressiveness towards the apparent source of misery of the person or group we have love and compassion for. Koestler has written: 'The total identification of the individual with the group makes him unselfish in more than one sense....It makes him perform comradely, altruistic, heroic actions — to the point of self-sacrifice — and at the same time behave with ruthless cruelty towards the enemy or victim of the group....In other words, the self-assertive behaviour of the group is based on the self-transcending behaviour of its members, which often entails sacrifice of personal interests and even of life in the interest of the group. To put it simply: the egotism of the group feeds on the altruism of its members.'[158]

In the case of the German terrorists the identification need had brought them to advocacy and partisanship for the oppressed and downtrodden in Vietnam, Palestine, and other parts of the Third World. In the course of expressing their identification they had become victims themselves, of the German prison system. The detained 'idealists' then, in a second phase, became objects of identification themselves. With the help of their lawyers the imprisoned terrorists managed to put this identification mechanism in motion. By portraying the detained terrorists as victims of government torture, these lawyers were able to launch a publicity campaign which made more and more young, idealistic people sympathize with the terrorists. The torture charge — which the RAF's lawyer and co-founder, Horst Mahler, later admitted to be a 'propaganda lie'[159] — was used successfully to attract new terrorists. The detained terrorists 'terrorized' themselves with self-imposed hunger strikes and used the public echo as their recruiting instrument. Since the prison security restrictions were for a long time quite lax, the terrorists could not only communicate with outside sympathizers but also with each other, which enabled them to coordinate their hunger strike actions. Even within the prison walls the hard core of the Baader-Meinhof group managed to intimidate wavering members into participating in this stratagem. One of the members was so afraid of group retaliation that she asked prison officials to put her on the medical 'danger' list though she was not participating in the hunger strike. Another hunger striker, Holger Meins, died after two months, which was a godsend for the RAF.[160] The group needed a martyr and one of the hunger strikers had been given the order to die. When he failed to kill himself, the death of Holger Meins served the group's purpose.[161]

Lawyers and 'Red Help' groups who supported the prison actions from outside made the most of Meins' death and the success of the propaganda campaign can be read from the fact that in West Berlin the president of the High Court, Günther von Drenkman, was shot in his home by a group of young people on the Sunday after Holger Meins' death. In the immediate aftermath of Meins' death, between 9 and 11 November 1974, some fifty demonstrations took place in West Germany, three bombs were exploded before courts in Bochum and Frankfurt and many other public buildings and vehicles were damaged.[162] And, most important, the action, made public by the media, served to win new recruits to the terrorist movement. We have the testimony of one radical turned terrorist that he acquired his first gun when he got the news that Holger Meins had died in prison.[163] Later, when he gained some insight into the propaganda strategy of the movement he admitted that he had 'problems to say that Meins was just a poor victim of the (prison) system'.[164] The weapon of the hunger strike was, in the words of Horst Mahler, used by the detained terrorists 'as a whip against the Left to mobilize them for the interests of the guerrillas'.[165]

But what would have been the effectiveness of hunger strikes if they had not been reported? The public media, fed with medical bulletins about the state of health of the various prisoners, and by interviews with concerned lawyers[166] provided the transmission belt to the left, which for some time was not aware of the game that was being played with them. Attempts at liberating the prisoners, some successful, most not, were undertaken by groups who had in many cases no organizational affiliation but only an ideological one with the terrorists. Since some of the would-be liberators got killed in the exercise and others were imprisoned the pool of terrorists and martyrs with whose lot one could identify grew constantly and so did the number of misled idealists who tried to revenge them or organize their escape. In all this the media played a crucial role. One of the terrorists from the June 2nd movement, 'Bommi' Baumann admitted: 'Without journalistic reporting we would find ourselves facing a certain vacuum. It is through the press that our cause is maintained in the just manner.'[167]...'The RAF has said, this revolution will not be built up by political work, but through headlines, through its appearance in the press, which reports again and again that guerrilleros are fighting here in Germany.'[168]

One of the biggest media successes the German terrorists achieved was with the kidnapping of the mayoral candidate Peter Lorenz in Berlin in February and March 1975. The June 2nd movement abducted the Christian Democratic politician to effect the release of six jailed terrorists and to obtain the suspension of the sentences passed on those Berlin demonstrators who had protested against the death of Holger Meins. As a condition for the exchange they demanded that the national television broadcast the release. Horst Mahler, one of the six prisoners, refused to join his colleagues on their way to South Yemen but obtained the opportunity to make a revolutionary speech on television.[169] The live transmission of the release, watched by millions of Germans, took several hours but in fact the terrorists controlled the medium for much longer. One TV editor has said:

For 72 hours we just lost control of the medium. It was theirs, not ours...We shifted shows in order to meet their time-table. Our cameras had to be in position to record each of the released prisoners as they boarded the plane to freedom, and our news coverage had to include prepared statements at their dictate...It's never ever happened before. There is plenty of underworld crime on our screens but up till now Kojak and Columbo were always in charge...Now it was the real thing, and it was the gangsters who wrote the script and programmed the mass media. We preferred to think that we were being 'flexible', but actually we were just helpless, as helpless as the police and the Bonn government...Surely it must be the first recorded case of how to hijack a national TV network![170]

When the terrorists had arrived safely in South Yemen, pastor Heinrich Albertz, who had accompanied them, returned to the TV-screen with the codeword that was meant to signal to the kidnappers that the operation had succeeded and the victim could be released. The West German government, deeply humiliated, decided after the Lorenz kidnapping not to give in again to the terrorists. So far it has succeeded, though it probably could not have been able to keep that hard-line posture if the June 2nd movement had carried out their plan to kidnap the Roman Pope. As the Palestinians would not back them in this enterprise the plan was finally dropped after Paul VI had been shadowed for a month in April 1976.[171] In terms of news value, the Pope is indeed a target second only to the US president as the attentats of April and May 1981 on President Reagan and Pope John Paul II demonstrated.

In the case of the abduction of the president of the German association of entrepreneurs, Hanns Martin Schleyer, on 5 September 1977, the German government stood firm and applied a news embargo most of the time during the forty-five days until his death. The terrorists had great difficulty in breaking through the government imposed silence although they sent almost 140 communications to more than three dozen media.[172] Most of them were never published and the terrorists therefore tried to send their dispatches to the French leftist paper *Libération*.[173] The abductors even made videotapes of their victim's declarations, one of which indeed reached the public.[174] Without a full wave of publicity, however, the terrorists did not manage to sway public compassion to an extent which would have forced the German government to give in. The victim's hope 'that there are still enough free journalists who are ready to publish these reflections'[175] indicated the purpose which publicity was to serve. When all failed, and even an additional hijacking of a Lufthansa aircraft in Palma, Majorca, on 13 October 1977 did not move the German government to release Andreas Baader, Gudrun Ensslin, Jan-Carl Raspe, Verena Becker and seven other detained terrorists, some of the leading terrorists, those mentioned here by name, carried their propaganda campaign to its logical conclusion. Gudrun Ensslin had coined the formula for hunger strikes and charges of isolation torture as one of using their bodies 'as our ultimate weapon'.[176] Like Ulrike Meinhof before them, Baader, Ensslin and Raspe committed suicide, while Verena Becker tried but failed to kill herself. The manner in which the suicides were committed on 18 October 1977 in the Stammheim prison was apparently intended to suggest that they had been murdered by the German 'fascist' state. Many believed them and the media were full of speculation. Yet in fact they had almost certainly become victims of their own propaganda strategy. With their political suicides they added a new variant to terrorism, pseudo-terrorism. While direct terrorism chooses its victims from the enemy camp and indirect terrorism from people not directly associated with the enemy but dependent on him in one way or another, pseudo-terrorism selects its victims from its own camp with the intention of getting the guilt attributed to the enemy.

Unlike the German terrorists who first fed mainly, though by no means exclusively, on misgivings about a foreign war and later on self-pity about the imprisonment of their comrades, the Italian left-wing terrorists had plenty of social grievances on which to feed. The Italian parliamentary system did not work properly, a Christian Democratic party monopolized the control of the state and corrupted itself in an uninterrupted rule during the whole postwar period. The economic situation of the country has remained precarious and the labour market could not absorb the output of the universities which were dubbed 'unemployment factories'. More than half of Italy's 1.2 million unemployed in 1977 were former university students seeking their first job.[177] Lenin's dictum that terrorism is 'a specific kind of struggle practised by the intelligentsia'[178] seems to be true for much of today's left-wing terrorism in Italy. Although the first terrorist attacks in the late 1960s were launched by fascist groups, left-wing terrorism has since then far eclipsed that coming from the right. Of the 3,251 attentats committed in the fifteen month period 1 January 1978 – 16 March 1979, most were said to be the work of 196 left organizations while only thirteen terrorist movements were operating on the political right. Right-wing extremists accounted for 230 attentats, while about one thousand, almost a third of the total, were accounted for by the Red Brigades (BR – Brigate rosse) alone.[179] Our discussion of terrorist media strategies in Italy will confine itself to this single most important terrorist organization in Italy.

The Red Brigades were founded in 1970 by the sociology student Renato Curcio, and its operations were until 1973 primarily directed against (neo-) fascist sympathizers. After that date the BR switched to targets from the governing party and since the Italian Communist Party (PCI) in its 'historic compromise' of 1978 became a government-supporting pillar, targets have also been selected from the PCI. At first the Red Brigades kidnapped people, mainly plant mangers, without using the victim as a pawn for coercive bargaining. In 1972, for instance, they abducted the director of a Milan plant and took a picture of him with a board around his neck, reading: 'Red Brigades bite and flee.

Strike one to educate one hundred'. The picture was then sent to news-papers which published it.[180] The division of labour between Red Brigades and the media to bring about terror together comes out clearly in this formula. The BR did the striking and the media did the 'educating'. The first act served the second and gained its significance by the fact that it was reported.

In 1974 the BR kidnapped a personnel director of Fiat in Turin. Since Fiat owned *La Stampa*, one of the leading Italian papers, they also caught the attention of this paper. The victim was released after nineteen days. The massive coverage of the incident in *La Stampa* had made the Red Brigades a nationally known organization. Later that year they struck in Genoa, kidnapping the judge Mario Sossi, and pub-lished his 'confession' that the police had been involved in black market arms sales. When the government asked the papers not to print these charges the Red Brigades complained that the government was trying to apply censorship.[181] This reflected their real concern, for without publicity their strategy could not work properly. By reporting the exploits of the Red Brigades, giving the life history of its leaders, stating their grievances, explaining their goals and strategy, the media probably also contributed to the recruiting of new members to the ranks of the BR.[182] Although the media did not sympathize with the terrorists, merely by reporting 'objectively' they provided them with a platform. Those with grievances against the way Italian society was organized were presented with a means of doing something about it. In some a responsive chord was struck and some of those might have followed their exemplary deeds.

How sophisticated the media strategy of the Red Brigades is can be inferred from the fact that they choose Wednesdays and Saturdays as their preferred communication days, knowing that on Thursdays and Sundays papers are thicker and have higher circulation figures. By placing their communiqués just before the evening deadlines for the morning papers, as they frequently do, they give the editors very little time to tailor their messages. In their anonymous telephonic communi-cations they simultaneously call several papers and broadcasting stations in various towns so that the media compete against each other. In this way they have been able to induce papers to bring special editions to the streets and radio and television stations to interrupt their regular programmes. To avoid recognition, the telephonic messages, delivered in a monotonous voice, are short, often only indicating where reporters can find a written message.[183]

In some cases the Red Brigades have also seized private stations in

order to broadcast declarations.[184] Coercion has also been used against
journalists by shooting them in the legs. This happened so frequently
that it did not make the front pages any more. One leading Italian
editor has suggested that they started to aim higher and kill journalists
to get back on the front page.[185] This led to the situation where leading
journalists for a time no longer signed their articles, began to wear
bullet-proof vests, carried guns and drove in bullet-proof cars guarded
by security personnel.[186] The 'crimes' of these journalists were, in the
words of the BR, that they were symbols of the 'lackey press', 'vomit-
ting bad information'.[187] They had, in the eyes of the Red Brigades,
become auxiliary forces to the Minister of the Interior, at the time
Francesco Cossiga, who was charged with fighting terrorism.[188]

The Red Brigades' mastery of communication manipulation has been
most clearly demonstrated in the case of the kidnapping of Aldo Moro,
Italy's top Christian Democratic politician. For fifty-five days, from
16 March to 9 May 1978, when Moro was found dead, they were able
to manipulate the media and through them the public with their communiqués. Feeding the media with false information (claiming that
Moro had been 'executed by suicide' like Ulrike Meinhof), with 'confessions' of Moro before a 'people's trial', disclosing a secret letter of Moro
to Cossiga, suggesting that Moro had divulged state secrets to them —
by these and other means, not the least effective of them being the
strategic use of silence, they held the whole nation in a state of tension
for almost two months.[189] The government tried to stop the media
from publishing certain communiqués but failed.[190] Rivalling factions
within the government leaked additional information in the aftermath
of the affair, including a memorandum wherein Moro distanced himself
from his party, charging it with corruption, cowardice and stupidity.[191]

Since most, if not all communications of the Red Brigades passed via
the media, their role was essential in the strategy of tension the terrorists
applied. As if they were mere marionettes, manipulated from the back-
stage, the media played the role the terrorists had assigned to them.
Although they practically unanimously condemned the kidnapping and
murder of Aldo Moro in their editorials, by merely reporting massively
what news the terrorists chose to release they played their game and
made the tragedy that had struck one family and one political party
the affair of the nation. Pretending to themselves that they were merely
informing the people, the media were in fact inducing identification
among the populace. Most identified with the victim, sharing his sense
of impotence. Others identified with the terrorists, sharing their sense
of revenge. Yet others identified primarily with the governing party

that chose to give a higher priority to the preservation of the process of law than to the life of one individual. The terrorists used the information machines as identification machines that translated the physical violence against one into psychic violence against millions. The nature of modern mass media, their ability to make the experience of one simultaneously the experience of millions, transformed Moro's murder into thirteen million murders on Italy's as many television screens and into fifty-six million murders in the eyes of the Italian people. Of all the terrorist uses of the media, this, the use of amplification and magnification by the media, is the most important one. It gives contemporary insurgent terrorism much of its power and, by implication, its raison d'etre.

Conclusion

In the preceding pages we have attempted to sketch some contemporary insurgent terrorist uses of the news media. Given our limited data base this enterprise could be not much more than a survey of examples. For the reader's convenience we summarize our main findings in the following table. This is not a classification but a simple list, with overlapping elements.

Table 1A
Insurgent Terrorist Uses of the News Media

A. Active Uses

1. Communication of (fear-) messages to mass audience
2. Polarizing public opinion
3. Making converts, attracting new members to terrorist movement
4. Demanding publication of manifesto under threat of harm to victim
5. Using media as conduits for threats, demands and bargaining messages
6. Verifying demand compliance by the enemy
7. Winning favourable publicity via released hostages
8. Linking message to victim
9. Misleading enemy by spreading false information
10. Winning publicity by granting interviews in the underground
11. Intimidating media by killing or wounding journalists
12. Advertising terrorist movement and cause represented
13. Arousing public concern for victim to pressure government to concessions
14. Discrediting victim by making his 'confessions' public
15. Discrediting enemy by making victim's 'confessions' public
16. Deflecting public attention from disliked issue by bombing it from frontpages

Table 1A continued
17. Announcing further actions
18. Using journalists as negotiators in bargaining situation
19. Inciting public against government
20. Occupation of broadcasting stations to issue message
21. Boosting one's own morale; Herostratism
22. Gaining Robin Hood image

B. Passive Uses

23. External communication network between terrorists
24. Learning new coercive techniques from media reports on terrorism
25. Obtaining information about identity and status of hostages
26. Obtaining information on countermeasures by security forces
27. Using media presence at site of siege as insurance against 'dirty tricks' by security forces
28. Creating fear with the enemy by media's exaggeration of own strength, thereby reducing likelihood that individual policemen dare to apprehend terrorist
29. Identifying future targets for terroristic violence
30. Obtaining information about public reaction to terroristic act

What we regard as one of our chief findings, however, is not made explicit in this list. It is, as we have tried to show in our discussion of terrorism in Italy and West Germany, that the terrorists can rely on the media not only as information machines but also as identification machines. This hypothesis seems particularly pertinent to the role of the medium television. While print addresses itself mainly to the intellectual understanding of the reader, television, which is colourful, moving, more picture than sound, seems to be able to bypass consciousness.[192] As such a 'deep' medium television lends itself strongly to identification processes in the watcher. In cases of terroristic news the identification that takes place with each member of the viewing audience can be with various actors: the victim and his family, the terrorist, or the opponent of the terrorist. Which way the identification of the media consumer goes, depends, among other things, on the position he takes in the conflict portrayed, the socialization he has received. The power of terrorism, the disproportion between the actual amount of violence committed and its far-reaching effects, seems to stem mainly from the fact that such an identification takes place in the spectators of violence.

In our initial chapter on the origins and definition of modern terrorism we have tried to interpret terrorism as communication activated and amplified by violence. If this is correct then terrorism should like other communications be open to content analysis.[193] To do this one has to begin by identifying the various elements in the terrorism/communication process. The Lasswellian formula for communication process analysis 'Who says what, through what channel, to whom, with what effect?',[194] which has long served as a basis for analysis, is however not broad enough. To make it fruitful for the analysis of terrorism at least four more elements have to be introduced. The two major ones would be 'with what intention?' and 'by what message generator (victim)?'. The questions 'in what social context?' and 'in what form (how)?' ought also to be added, together with a differentiation of 'to whom?' since there are various important audiences to terrorism — the terrorist himself, his movement, his sympathizers, the enemy, the local, national and foreign public. Only with such a conceptual framework and a reliable data base, both of which are presently lacking, can the various media uses of terrorists be studied in a less cursory way than in this exploratory study.

2. NEWS MEDIA USES OF INSURGENT TERRORISM

From the preceding chapter the reader has already obtained some indirect impressions about the ways the news media use terrorism. Here we will attempt a more systematic treatment of this aspect. Yet there is a methodological difficulty. What we know about terrorism we have learned — with few exceptions — from the news media. In order to judge the media's treatment of terrorism properly we would need two sets of data, one about terroristic events and a second about the news on these events. As it is there are no comprehensive publicly available data of the first kind[1] and there are very few studies of the second kind. One could argue that since insurgent terrorism is so media-conscious, what the news media report is by and large what took place. This, however, is, as we shall see, untrue. Some of the insurgent terroristic events that the media report never took place while others took place but were never reported. Yet others were reported but the guilt attribution was wrong. In fact, we have found that news about terrorism can be highly unreliable. In the following pages we will discuss some of the problems that arise when the media use insurgent terrorist events to make news.

WHAT THE NEWS MEDIA CALL TERRORISM

Terrorism is a word with highly negative connotations, and for good reasons, since innocent people without responsibility for the conflict at hand often become its victims. Yet the term is generally used so loosely that it has almost become a political slogan to denigrate all kinds of violence used by the 'other side'. Take the example of hijacking: when in the early 1960s opponents of Fidel Castro hijacked planes to get out of Cuba they were received almost as heroes in the United States. When US citizens travelled the same way to Cuba they were soon to be labelled terrorists.[2] Depending on who committed it, the same act was labelled differently.

Before we discuss what the Western news media call terrorism we have to clarify our own understanding of it. Taking hijacking as a starting point we also call it alternatively terroristic or non-terroristic but for different reasons. In our definition of terrorism those hijackings which merely serve for escape to another country are not terroristic. Only when passengers and crew are used as pawns between hijackers and a third party, that is when the immediate victims cannot through a change of attitude or behaviour disassociate themselves from the conflict, do we speak of terrorism. In both cases, hijacking for escape and coercive bargaining, the victims may feel intimidated, but in the first case they can save their lives through surrendering to the hijackers while in the second they cannot. Only the latter do we call terrorism. Another act which the media often label terrorism is kidnapping. Again we would differentiate. The classical criminal kidnapping in which the victim is snatched and his relatives or associates are made to pay a ransom to secure his or her liberty we would label terroristic only if the victim cannot affect his own fate.

But an abduction of a person that results in his subsequent death is not always terroristic. Take the case of the abduction of Adolf Eichmann who was snatched in May 1960 by Israeli agents in Argentina, deported secretly to Israel where he was tried and hanged in December 1961. Because the former organizer of the Holocaust was victim and enemy target at the same time, this act does not fall under our definition of terrorism. The successful Israeli operation might have filled other former Nazi leaders still in hiding with chronic fear (terror) but that alone does not make it a terroristic act. Terror might have been a by-product of the action, but it was not its main goal. Two conditions are, in our view, necessary to make an act of violence terroristic: (a) the victim cannot, through his own doing, e.g. by capitulating, save his life, and (b) the victimization is done primarily for its effects on third parties and not because of the victim himself. Since the second condition is hard to assess when an insight into the motives of the perpetrators of violence is lacking, it is sometimes difficult to know whether a particular act of violence can be labelled terroristic. Yet such acts usually do not stand alone. The -ism of terrorism hints at a systematic and deliberate character and in the course of a campaign of violence the motives behind it usually become clearer.

A group that uses tactics of terrorism is often labelled terrorist for all the acts of violence perpetrated by it. Even such acts as an armed bank robbery, when staged by such a group, tend to be labelled as such. Why this is done is easy to understand. It is politically convenient to discredit a political movement by attaching to all its acts a label which stands in high disrepute. A related tactic of discrediting a hostile movement is to call its acts criminal rather than political. In a juridical sense it is true that terroristic acts tend to be criminal because they violate some laws. Yet it is sensible to make distinctions. It seems useful to discriminate between political and criminal terrorism. If the act is committed for personal material gain we call it criminal. If the terroristic act is committed for personal psychic satisfaction we call it pathological. If the act is committed for collective motives without direct personal material or psychic gain intentions we call it political terrorism. These are admittedly ideal-type distinctions and in practice the motives of the perpetrators might overlap or change from one to the other. Yet one of the three motivations, the criminal, the pathological or the political often predominates so that the distinction has heuristic value.

In this study we are preoccupied with insurgent political terrorism but this is not the only kind of political terrorism. Within the field of political terrorism we distinguish among three main types. One is insurgent terrorism, directed against the power holders in a state. A second is state or repressive terrorism, directed against less powerful segments of society. A third we call, for lack of a better name, vigilante terrorism. We use the term for nonstate groups that illegally impose force on other nonstate groups in society by terrorism. Historically, vigilante groups have often served as extra-legal enforcers of establishment supremacy but we would like to use this term in a broader sense for all political actors who use terroristic violence which is not directed at the state power itself nor is exercised on behalf of the state. As far as insurgent terrorism is concerned we also subdivide it into three categories. One aims at taking state power and at revolutionizing the whole society, the second calls for secession of an ethnical or national group from a state and is not concerned with the social order in other parts of the state than the one to which it lays claim. The first we call social-revolutionary terrorism and the second we call separatist, ethnical or, in cases of colonized territories, nationalist terrorism. The third type of insurgent terrorism is less encompassing than the other two. It is ad hoc terrorism by one or a few individuals advocating coercively that the state grant some privilege to a group with which the terrorist sympathizes. We call it single issue terrorism. Table 2A gives an overview of our typology.

Table 2A
A Basic Typology of Terrorism

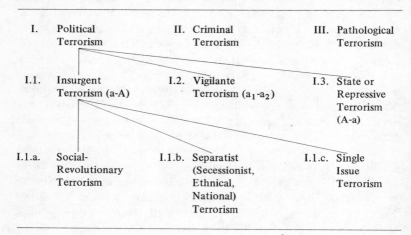

I.	Political Terrorism	II.	Criminal Terrorism	III.	Pathological Terrorism
I.1.	Insurgent Terrorism (a-A)	I.2.	Vigilante Terrorism (a_1-a_2)	I.3.	State or Repressive Terrorism (A-a)
I.1.a.	Social-Revolutionary Terrorism	I.1.b.	Separatist (Secessionist, Ethnical, National) Terrorism	I.1.c.	Single Issue Terrorism

Key: A means State Actor
       a_1, a_2 means Non-state Actors

So far our typology has concerned itself only with domestic or national terrorism. Yet there is also the so-called international terrorism. Its targets are sometimes foreign states and at other times foreign non-state groups. Its perpetrators are often nonstate actors but states also sometimes engage in it. Quite often, however, there is a mix of state and nonstate actors who ally with each other. This allows for a multitude of combinations. If only states are involved as actors and targets we might speak of interstate terrorism. In all other cases one might speak of transnational terrorism. Yet in fact there are so many variations possible that one can better typify them with symbols rather than names. If we use the symbols A and B for states, a and b for nonstate actors in the countries of A and B, the formula A+a-B would for instance stand for a case where the secret service of one state, in collaboration with a multinational corporation or a crime syndicate of the same state, seeks to topple a foreign government with tactics of terrorism.

Table 2B
International (Inter-state and Transnational) Terrorism
An Actor-based Typology with Two, Three and Four Actors

1. A – B	5. A + B – b	11. A + B – a + b
2. A – b	6. A + b – B	12. a + b – A + B
3. a – b	7. A + b – a	13. A + b – a + B
4. a – B	8. A + a – b	14. A + a – B + b
	9. A + a – B	
	10. a + b – A	

Key: A, B means State Actors; a,b means Non-state Actors in Country of A, B

Complicated as this picture of international terrorism might appear to be, it is in fact less complex than the actual international terroristic scene where, for instance (as we have pointed out earlier (p. 27)), Palestinian terrorists are working together with no less than fourteen state and nonstate actors abroad. Taxologizing international terrorism in a world of more than 150 state actors and many more nonstate actors becomes an unrewarding task. In reality most political terrorism is less international than it would seem at first sight. Although the repercussions of it as well as the rhetoric of the terrorist movements might be international, the roots underlying so-called international terrorism are often local.

We have treated definitory and typological questions of terrorism at some length here to reduce the chance of being misunderstood.[3] With such an emotive subject as terrorism it is unlikely that any consensus about its nature will be reached in the near future. Even simpler concepts such as 'soldier' and 'aggression' have kept international bodies such as the League of Nations and the United Nations busy for years with definitory attempts. Those who hold power in the politics of nations often exercise definitory power about political key concepts. Who is labelled terrorist therefore often becomes a question of political opportunism. The terrorists themselves are the first to be aware of the arbitrariness with which the term is used. The 'fighters for Free Croatia' who hijacked a plane in September 1977 expressed it in these words:

We expect all peace-loving forces in the world to describe us as terrorists, criminals, and murderers. From the time of Caesar, through Hitler, Stalin, Franco and Salazar, as well as with numerous other colonial and neocolonial governments, those fighting for national liberation have always been described in such terms. ... One man's terrorist is another man's patriot, depending solely on one's national and political objectives and suitability. The point to be made here, obviously, is not to conclusively define *terrorism*, an impossible and unnecessary task, but rather, to explain the ultimate necessity for our extreme decision and to ask others to judge this decision objectively and unemotionally. We must remember that today's 'terrorists' are often tomorrow's policymakers, having participated in the formation of a new, independent state. ... Thus, the unsuccessful continue to be 'terrorists' but, upon success, are courted by all governments. With this reality reappearing dependably from one day to the next, all ethical and moral revulsion felt for so-called terrorist acts is necessarily irrational.[4]

In their document the Croatian terrorists cited the Nobel prize winner for peace, Sean McBride, who as a former member of the Irish Republican Army (IRA) was a living exemplification of their statement. They might also have quoted another winner of the Nobel Peace Prize, Menachem Begin, prime minister of Israel, formerly leader of the terrorist Irgun movement.

Governments and the media are usually very restrictive with the label terrorist when they speak about violence perpetrated by states. Exceptions to this rule are few and usually reserved for states belonging to a different power bloc. This is not so amazing; in many cases the media belong to the same establishment from which the government is recruited and they share the same value system. In 1974 only thirty out of 138 member countries of the United Nations were judged to have a free press by a symposium on world press freedom.[5] Even in the thirty countries with a politically free press, probably only a few states would tolerate being called terrorist by some local media and those that would allow it are in all likelihood not deserving of this label.

We asked a number of journalists and editors what kinds of (political) violence their medium commonly labels terrorism. In order of decreasing frequency the following acts which we listed to them were mentioned:

1. Hijacking for coercive bargaining
2. Indiscriminate bombing (mentioned as often as 1)
3. Assassination
4. Hostage taking
5. Urban guerrilla warfare
6. Hijacking for escape
7. Torture
8. Kidnapping
9. Sabotage

Since our sample (n=27) was too small and not representative the list has no more than an indicative value.[6] More than three quarters of the respondents said that their medium did not use the term terrorism for violence perpetrated by states. When asked how they would personally define terrorism, twenty-one respondents volunteered a definition (see Table 2C).

Table 2C
Media Definitions of Terrorism

1. Deeds of violence and threats of violence, by which individuals or groups blackmail the legal political establishment. (Editor of Swiss daily)
2. The use of violence for political ends in circumstances in which other means of expression and propaganda exist (In a democratic and not violently repressed society). The use of such violence in any circumstances when it is wholly or mainly directed at causing death, injury or fear to persons not in control of or directly in the service of government (In a severe dictatorship). (Editorial consultant to a number of British dailies and weeklies)
3. Politically motivated violence of a minority group with a high disregard for human values in general and possible innocent victims in particular. (News editor of a Dutch radio station)
4. Acts to achieve political ends by way of illegal means like bombs, guns and others. (Senior staff correspondent of a Japanese daily)
5. An act of violence which involves people who have no apparent relation to those committing the act. (Head of foreign news of a Swedish broadcasting station)
6. A form of violence intended to influence the authorities, which is directed against outsiders or property not necessarily belonging to the state or violence intended to scare people into submission, characterized by its unexpectedness and its unreasonableness. (Chief editor of a Dutch daily)
7. Application of violence for allegedly political aims. (vice-Director of a West German television network)
8. The use of violence for political purposes. (Head of news of a Spanish radio station)
9. Act of despair. (Director of a Dutch broadcasting station)
10. Any activity in which violence – bombing, shooting, killing, etc – is used to attain an objective. This objective would in almost all cases be a political one. (Assistant head of news of an Irish broadcasting station)
11. Violence, physical or psychological, exercised to produce terror for political purposes. (Director of a Spanish broadcasting station)
12. A crime of extreme violence as murder, kidnapping, atrocities, etc committed usually by more or less organized groups usually with political aims. Often a typical feature of terrorism is that it picks its victims at random and that the terrorists fight their 'enemies' through innocent bystanders. (News editor of a Finnish daily)
13. An act (or group of acts) designed to reach a goal by destruction, violence, etc, when other ways of reaching the goal are not possible. Acts must be illegal and wanton in nature. (Public Affairs director of US broadcasting network)

Table 2C continued

14. The use or threat of violence by unconstitutional or illegal organizations or groups against civilian targets, done for political motives. The same definition may apply to an individual hijacker or kidnapper bent on making political propaganda. (Editor of a South African daily)
15. Use of coercion against a person/persons, to reach any goal, with regard to which that person/these persons has no relation, or in relation to which they carry no responsibility. (Head of information of a Dutch broadcasting station)
16. Violent action likely to cause terror to the public including action against the forces of law and order, or against public or private property, such as bombings, arson, armed robberies, etc, or threats of same. (Editor of an Irish daily)
17. Act of violence or threatened violence for illegal purposes, where the violence itself is part of the purpose, as distinct from being an unpleasant necessity to a desirable end. (Correspondent of a British weekly)
18. Forms of excessive violence aimed at the illegal attainment of goals. (Journalist of Dutch daily)
19. A deed of, or a threat with, violence on an organized and planned scale. (Journalist of a Dutch daily)
20. Application of criminal violence against persons and things for the attainment of political objectives. (Editor of a German news agency)
21. Political violence aimed at threatening the general public. (Director of a German broadcasting network)

If we compare these definitions with our own definition (p. 15) we notice that some of them (e.g. nos 5, 12 and 15) come close to our view of terrorism. However, almost all definitions implicitly assume that terrorism is directed against a government, rather than possibly also emanating from the state. Some definitions are so broad that they would also cover macro-violence such as war, at least when war is seen as a continuation of politics by other means. Strong emphasis is generally placed on the illegal and criminal nature of terrorism.

Which definition is the most adequate? If the subject matter is controversial, to attach certain meanings to a word, the power to define, is in fact a political act. A definition allows man to understand his environment in a certain way and structures the order of things for him. Those who have power to define therefore have an interest that their own behaviour is not negatively affected by the definition. In so far as others can be brought to share their view of things they gain power over others. Yet in a democratic society no one's definition should prevail. The same act, perpetrated with the same motives, should be labelled with the same word independently of whether it is committed by those in power or by those less powerful. For this reason we prefer a definition which is detached from the status of the actor.

How do the news media come to their definition or labelling in a concrete situation when violence has to be reported? In many cases, we suspect, they automatically adopt the terminology of the government source that informs them about an act of violence. Horst Herold, until 1981 president of the German Federal Criminal Office (BKA — Bundes-kriminalamt), which is in charge of anti-terrorist operations, hasexpressed his surprise about the ease with which the news media can be brought to accept the information provided by the police if it is preselected and offensively presented. 'The information superiority of the police', he wrote, 'can in this situation not be matched momentarily by the media, which also cannot escape from it due to the pressure for publication arising for reasons of competition; together these two factors effectuate information takeover.'[7]

One would expect that the media are more critical when the news about a terroristic event comes from abroad. Yet a content analysis conducted by Edward Epstein on the coverage of political violence in Latin America in three North American newspapers during a period in 1970–71 also shows a pro-government bias. Epstein analyzed the use of the term terrorism (or a variant thereof such as terror, terrorist) in the *New York Times*, the *Salt Lake Tribune* and the *Los Angeles Times*. He found that 19.7 percent of the 117 articles of the *New York Times* contained the term terrorism. Only in slightly more than one fifth of all cases (21.7 percent) did the word refer to violence emanating from a Latin American government. The other two papers used the term in 18.8 percent (*Salt Lake Tribune*) and 25.3 percent (*Los Angeles Times*) of their ninety-six and 186 articles on Latin America but never referred to government violence with this term. Comparing these newspapers' uses of the term terrorism with the number of times the term could have been used because the situation described was semantically admissible to be labelled as such based on earlier practices of the same paper, Epstein found that the *New York Times* used the term in 48.9 percent of all possible cases, the *Los Angeles Times* in 71.2 percent and the *Salt Lake Tribune* in 66.7 percent of all terroristic situations. The term terrorism was generally used as an expression of 'left-wing extremism', referring to political kidnappings, bombings and assassinations by anti-government organizations.[8] Since many of the repressive activities of Latin American governments, such as the 'disappearances', the torture of political prisoners to deter other political dissenters and the assassinations by government-sponsored death-squads, are undertaken with the same intimidating intentions as those underlying part of the left-wing activities, there is no reason to label them any other than terrorism.

Media news coverage on terrorism sometimes places the occurrence of violence into a criminal context while at other times the context is political. With changing circumstances the labelling can also vary. The different treatment which the United States media gave to Irish and Palestinian terrorism illustrates this. The disturbances in Northern Ireland were reported in the US media from the beginning in political terms. The reason for this presumably lay in the affinity which the Americans felt for a political movement that tries to secede from the British like the United States had done in 1776. Unlike the Irish guerrillas who were generally treated as revolutionaries in the US media, the Palestinians were until 1973 mostly treated as criminals. After the Middle East war and the oil boycott in the same year, the United States government reorientated its policy towards the region and sought a rapprochement with the Arab world. As a consequence the Palestinian terrorists obtained a political status in the US media and were more often termed revolutionaries than merely criminals.[9]

Through their labelling the media can confer different levels of legitimacy on a violent movement. Sometimes the choice of terminology is made quite consciously. The British Broadcasting Corporation (BBC), for instance, holds a weekly meeting of its upper management and senior representatives of the news room which issues directives on nomenclature. Here semantic usage is decided upon and these men determine whether a violent movement will be presented to the audience as consisting of freedom fighters, guerrillas or terrorists.[10] In a BBC memorandum issued on 17 January 1974, the following instructions were given to distinguish between guerrillas and terrorists:

'TERRORIST' is the appropriate description for people who engage in acts of terrorism, and in particular, in acts of violence against civilians, that is operations not directed at military targets or military personnel.
'GUERRILLA' is acceptable for leaders and members of the various Palestine organizations of this kind, but they too become 'terrorists' when they engage in terrorist acts (unless 'raiders', 'hijackers', 'gunmen' is more accurate). ... We should, in a common sense way, treat other guerrilla/terrorist groups in much the same way. We should remember that these people shoot, throw bombs and kill and maim, and often such straightforward and unequivalent phrases as 'the men who killed' may be the best description of all. We should be particularly wary of the word 'commando', which, to our audience, retains its wartime flavour.[11]

This nomenclature seems to leave no room for terroristic violence perpetrated by governments, which saves the BBC from a dilemma. The wars of nations, certainly in the post-World War Two period, tend to produce more casualties among civilians than among the armed forces and where this is deliberately done, the term terrorism might be appropriate if the civilian nature of the target is made the criterion for labelling an act of violence terroristic. The British Army in Northern Ireland has on occasion also deliberately killed unarmed civilians (e.g. on 'Bloody Sunday', 30 January 1972, British paratroopers unprovokedly killed thirteen civil rights demonstrators in Londonderry), yet the BBC would certainly refrain from calling this terrorism. On the other hand, the Irish Provisionals have not confined their attacks to civilian targets but repeatedly hit British military targets in Northern Ireland and abroad. Nevertheless, the BBC pre-eminently uses the term 'terrorist' when covering Northern Ireland.[12]

In our view the mere distinction between military and civilian targets is not sufficient for labelling a violent act either guerrilla or terroristic. A party that engages in political violence, whether it is a state or a non-state actor, usually practises various forms of violence. Some of them might be terroristic in our sense but usually not the majority of them. To label them all terrorist might be good propaganda but makes the task of coping with it no easier. For those who would like to see a higher degree of rule observance in violent conflict it would be sensible to use the term terrorist sparingly and mainly for fighters who do not give their victims a chance to save their lives by capitulating. If the news media would observe a certain economy in the use of the term terrorism, the disapproval which they generally show towards it would be more effective. But we are under no illusion; most of the news media will in all likelihood continue to make the most out of terrorism. Why this is so we will try to indicate in the following section, broadening the discussion to other forms of violence as well.

WHY THE MEDIA COVER (TERRORISTIC) VIOLENCE EXTENSIVELY

The Western news media generally have a certain self-image about their functioning. An important element of this image is that there is a reality out there which the media have to recapture and present to those media users who could not be direct participants in these events.[13] When the media 'mirror' this reality without distortion they are presenting 'objective' news. This view of the functioning of the media, however, has little to do with what actually takes place. For sheer economy of space and time it is not possible to reflect the total reality of what happens between two editions of a newspaper or the main newscasts of a broadcasting station. Eighty and more percent of the news that reaches the media does not reach the public even in abridged form but gets lost in the selection process of the so-called gatekeepers within the media institutions. This filtering out of reality, which is unavoidable, would in itself not be so problematic if the remaining news would give us a 'fair' picture of what is taking place beyond our direct perception. But this is not the case. Half of the world's human reality, for instance, consists of female human beings. Yet when one looks at the news most of the persons appearing in them are male. The 'mirror' of the media is almost blind for half of mankind. That, however, is not necessarily equivalent with distortion. The 'mirror' of the media, it can be argued, is today less blind in regard to women than, say, twenty years ago. The gradual emancipation of women is reflected in greater news coverage of them. The media would then 'mirror' changes in societal importance. But this, too, is a doubtful proposition. Take the example of crime, which is nearer to our topic. If the media would 'mirror' reality changes then one might assume that changes in the actual crime rate would find their expression in the changing amount of news coverage that crime gets in the media. Various studies, however, found that these two magnitudes — amount of crime and amount of crime coverage — fluctuate relatively independently from each other in the written press.[14]

In the following we will offer six possible explanations why violence in general and terrorism in particular do so well with the Western media.

1. One reason for this distortion of reality is that the commercial and the information functions of privately-owned public media are at odds with each other. Crime has always been good news as far as selling newspapers is concerned. The rape and murder of two sisters in Chicago in 1965, for instance, boosted newspaper circulation by 50,000 copies. The following year a rapist running amuck in San Francisco increased sales there by a similar figure.[15] Terrorism sells equally well. In Italy, the circulation figures of *La Stampa* had increased by 35 percent a week after the kidnapping of Aldo Moro.[16] Italy's biggest daily, *Il Corriere*, sold 38.8 percent more copies when Moro was kidnapped, the second day sales were up 40 percent and on the third, eventless, day they were still 19.6 percent higher than usual. When Moro was found dead the figures increased to 56.5 percent, dropping back to 24.7 percent the next day.[17] While it would be simplistic to explain the

media interest in terroristic and other violence by commercial profit motives alone, it is a factor that cannot be dismissed, certainly not in the popular majority press and in the electronic media deriving their income from advertisements based on audience ratings.

2. Behind the media's attention to violence there is also a public interest. It can be argued that the news media (and perhaps also the entertainment media) bring so much violent content because the public demands to be informed about the threatening aspects of life. People might feel a need to know how dangerous the streets have become so that they can take precautions. Yet there is a Catch-22 in this. The more television violence people watch the more they generally tend to be afraid of real violence in the streets.[18] As fewer people dare to go on the streets, mutual social control diminishes which invites more street crimes.[19] The representation of violence in the media may in this way lead to more violence in real life. This in turn would justify even more extensive media preoccupation with violence which would lead to a spiralling, self-fulfilling process. This, however, is only a hypothesis; we know of no research that could substantiate it.

3. A third line of thinking interprets the audience interest in media violence still differently. People in industrialized societies, it is held, lead an alienated life, being caught in the daily routines of sleeping, commuting and working. Deprived of meaningful experiences in their own lives, people turn to the media as a source of substitute experiences. Sex and violence in the media give them the thrill that is largely absent in their own adventureless lives. Chronic boredom, experienced by the majority of the population, stands in this view as the source of the popular demand for arousing media messages.[20] While this applies predominantly to fictional media materials, news can also serve this purpose. Denis McQuail has observed that news can have a 'narcoticising dysfunction', providing melodrama in stories about other people's misfortunes.[21] Frederick J. Hacker, the Austro-American psychiatrist, concludes in the same vein that 'Terrorism had unfortunately become a form of mass entertainment'.[22] A news director of a Boston television station has expressed the view that 'Coverage of terrorists is done to titillate the audience. It's yellow journalism on television. The news departments justify the coverage by saying that "news is news", and the (advertisement) sales department is thrilled to death.'[23] During the Hanafi incident in Washington the news director of another station, noting that his station's news show switched away from the terrorist incident, called up his producer and said in alarm: 'Our audience is leaving us. The minute you change the subject, the audience will leave you!'[24]

4. A fourth line of explanation for the audience interest in media violence takes a different point of departure. Western man, this view holds, has an ambiguous attitude towards violence and authority. As an individual he feels rather powerless in the anonymous hierarchical bureaucratic structures that govern his life. While he looks at the state as his protector and bestows on it the monopoly of societal violence he secretly hates the state at the same time for its all-embracing power. When some individuals dare to challenge the state with outrageous acts he sometimes sides with David against Goliath. The fascination he feels for the insurgent terrorist stems, in this interpretation, from his own submerged urge to rebel. He secretly backs the underdog and experiences 'stealthy joy', as the German student with the cover name 'Mescalero' described it when he analyzed his first reaction to the murder of the German industrial leader (and former Nazi officer) Hanns Martin Schleyer.

There is no doubt that some people admire terrorists and openly show them their support as happened, for instance, in June 1979 in El Salvador when insurgent rebels occupied a number of foreign embassies.[25] Although this is not amazing in countries where the regime in power has a lower moral legitimacy than the terrorists themselves, this same phenomenon can also be observed in more democratic countries. When a US Vietnam veteran of Italian origin, Raffael Minichiello, hijacked a jet-plane in the fall of 1969 and forced it to fly to Italy in the world's longest one-man hijack, he was received by part of the Italian public as a sort of hero.[26] Another US hijacker, operating under the name of D. B. Cooper, who had demanded $ 200,000 and some parachutes, almost became a folk hero and induced a number of others to imitate his feat. In the view of sociologist Otto Larsen, Cooper won his popularity because he had shown that one individual could overcome, temporarily at least, 'the technology, the corporation, the establishment, the system'. 'We all like adventure stories', Larsen suggested. 'That hijacker took the great risk. He showed real heroic features — mystery, drama, romanticism, a high degree of skill and all the necessities for the perfect crime. This man was neither political nor neurotic. His motive was simply $ 200,000 and people can understand that much better.' On the West coast of the United States, where this hijacking had taken place, people bought T-shirts showing a bundle of dollars dangling from a parachute and a song praising Cooper for 'your pleasant smile and your drop-out style' became for a while the discjockies' favourite.[27]

The other side of this ambiguity towards violence and authority is in this view that people at the same time apparently want to see these challengers of authority punished. The fictional crime series on television, where the good guys, the law enforcers, ultimately win over the bad guys, cater for this need. Crime is fascinating but it has to be suppressed. The police capitalizes on this ambivalence by such programmes as 'Aktenzeichen XY ...' in Germany, wherein the public is presented with the reconstruction of real crimes and invited to volunteer information that could lead to the arrest of the wanted criminals. Members of the Red Army Fraction in Germany were sought via this programme.[28] Fascination with media violence, in this view, is an expression of suppressed aggressive impulses of frustrated people, who, unable to admit to themselves that these impulses exist, demand and expect that the crimes they enjoy be punished.[29] Iring Fetscher, referring to the terrorism in West Germany, has written:

In the attitude of the bystanders a dosis of fear for one's own safety mingles with a hidden jealousy towards the perpetrators. In our modern late capitalist 'elbow-society' so many aggressive impulses arise in each individual which he cannot ventilate through the pressure of his societal surrounding, that the 'perpetrators with a clean conscience' are necessarily envied. The suppressed jealousy as well contributes to no small degree to the increase of hate towards the perpetrators. The terrorist as well as the hate-filled square who wishes death to the terrorists and who applauds when hearing about the suicide of RAF-members in prison, experiences psychic liberation. Both are moralists, both are plagued by their conscience. ... Terrorism in industrialized countries is, just as much as the aggressive exaggerated reaction to it, a symptom of the psychic condition of many people.[30]

5. A fifth line of reasoning which owes much to Marshall McLuhan and deals mainly with television argues that the nature of the medium demands or favours violent over nonviolent content. News on television has to be visually attractive. News items on which arresting news reels exist are therefore more likely to be chosen for broadcasting. Edward Epstein has analyzed US television news and found that

Network news stories must therefore be self-contained; there must be a beginning in which the protagonists are identified in a few words and pictures, a climax in which some visual action takes place, and a denouement in which the conflict is resolved. Finally, to retain the interest of a national audience stretching from Maine to Hawaii, network news must be constructed around visual elements that have universal appeal. For example, fires, riots, bloodshed, and armed confrontations, no matter where they occur, can be comprehended at a very basic level by viewers in all parts of the country.[31]

The technical possibilities of the medium television impose news pre-
ferences; a fire at night looks better on the screen than one during
daytime and tends to receive more coverage.[32]

Neil Hickey has noted that many terrorist incidents which are
getting backpage treatment in newspapers receive prominent television
treatment because of their visual attractiveness.[33] David Phillips, a
journalist who has covered many terrorist incidents, has observed that
'A siege makes good television: camera and viewer can squat as patiently
as cats by a birdcage savouring the inaction. Anticipation is the spice of
non-participation'.[34] While it would seem that a hijacked aircraft
standing for hours immobilized in the corner of an airport has only
limited visual appeal, television, by cutting the dull moments out and
condensing the story to ninety seconds or less, can transform it into a
tension-packed event. Insurgent terrorists create visual facts which
favour the event needs of television. The terrorist scenario contains
drama, blood, villains, heroes and innocents in a sensational mix which
corresponds to the characteristics of television stories. The medium
almost cannot help broadcasting a story which seems to be tailored to
fit its standards.[35] However, when such events become routine, media
interest tends to diminish.

Walter Laqueur has called the terrorists the 'superentertainers' of
our time and has said that 'The media are the terrorist's best friend'.[36]
This is a simplification; they are rather unwitting allies. The insurgent
terrorist news promotor and the professional journalistic news assembler
have what has been called in a different context 'parallel event needs'.[37]
They have a common interest in reaching a large audience, both want
attention. It is on this basis that they collaborate instinctively.
Frederick Hacker has written that 'because the terrorists offer very
precious material to the mass media, the mass media generously and
without costs conduct the terrorists' business with real enthusiasm and
with eager professional competence'.[38] With their theatrical acts the
insurgent terrorists serve the audience-attracting needs of the mass
media and where the media are predominantly concerned with holding
the attention of the mass audience (which can be rented to advertisers
or serves as a testimony of public service), this is a symbiosis that is
beneficial for both.[39]

While in the above section television's propensity to use violent
material has been interpreted in terms of the visual value it has to the
medium, there is a broader concept 'news value' to which journalists
refer when they have to explain why they grant certain events more
news coverage than others. Violence obviously has a high news value in

the Western media. In a Canadian study analyzing 12,913 news items on television and in the written press, 24 percent of all items were found to consist of outright violent material and no less than 40 percent of all items were classified as violence-and-conflict-related.[40] This left 60 percent of the news analyzed in this study in the nonviolent category. This 2:3 relation stands in odd contrast to most people's everyday reality in which violence and conflict are exceptional. If the amount of violence in the news were commensurate with the one in reality this would be a world in which life would be almost unbearable.

What determines news value? The term value indicates a reference to the market system. It is no accident that most of the older news agencies were situated close to the stock market. There timely information — news — was closely linked to market requirements. The very concept of news as we know it today is largely a capitalist concept. In traditional societies with very slow change processes there was very little news about distant events for the common people. Leaders, kings, priests were the main recipients of news and for good reasons since sharing knowledge involves sharing power.[41] This situation still prevails in authoritarian societies where people are only given the sort of news which does not endanger the stability of the political system. In the Soviet Union, for instance, the mass media serve as a means of moulding the citizens according to the ideology of the ruling communist party.[42] Since the late 1950s, as a consequence of pressures from foreign radio stations penetrating the Iron Curtain, the Soviet authorities have been gradually forced to adopt some of the news characteristics of the West in order to compete for the favour of the audience. But 'bad' news on crime and accidents is still rarely reported in the Soviet media as it is considered to represent negative developments. This goes as far as that in an aircraft crash not even the families of the victims are routinely informed. Hijackings within Russia receive minimal news treatment and even foreign hijackings get hardly any coverage, presumably because the authorities are afraid of contagion effects. Other acts of violence with political connotations also get only short, backpage treatment.[43] Soviet news, in which information serves agitation (i.e. mass mobilization) behind a party line, is news with a purpose and therefore it is considered to be propaganda in Western eyes.

Western news on the other hand pretends to have no other purpose than to reflect reality.[44] Leaving aside for a moment the profit motive which is a purpose behind privately owned Western media, the question is whose reality Western media reflect. The standard answer is that they reflect public opinion and express it. But some opinions are heard more often and louder than others. The publicized opinion is not the total of public opinion. Those near the top of the social pyramids appear more often in the news and are able to give their opinion on events more often than those at the bottom of society. It seems natural that this should be so: actions and opinions of the powerful affect more people than those of the less powerful. Therefore more people feel a need to know what the powerful are doing and saying.[45] The news assemblers interpret this public interest as news value. What is important to the public has a high news value, what is less important a lower one. But the public media do not only inform, they also entertain. Therefore the interesting, whether it is important or not, can also get news value. Some media place more stress on the things that are interesting (entertaining) to the public than to what is deemed to be important (relevant) to the public. While most media strive to strike a balance between the two poles, there are in Western countries generally two types of newspapers, the quality or minority press concentrating on the important and the popular or majority press stressing the interesting.

The news assemblers have in their professional training been socialized to know which events are fit and profitable to be made public; they have acquired a 'nose for news' as it is called. The criteria for what is news depend on the composition of the medium's audience, its own institutional characteristics and its relationship with various news sources. Although news value is not clearly defined, different media competing for the same audience and with similar institutional structures tend to produce highly uniform news. *Newsweek* and *Time*, two leading US magazines, for instance, quite often have a cover story about the same event. James Lemert, who analyzed the weekday newscasts of two US networks, found that 70 percent of them used identical stories.[46] The selection of news according to news value is done almost intuitively; there are no clearcut rules. In Great Britain there is a rule of thumb for the relative newsworthiness of disasters, called 'McLurg's Law', after a legendary editor, that says for instance that a crash in Europe is more newsworthy than one in Asia. This proximity principle has various expressions, one of which says 'One European is worth twenty-eight Chinese, or perhaps two Welsh miners worth one thousand Pakistanis'.[47] Johan Galtung and Mari Ruge have, in their study on 'The Structure of Foreign News', attempted to make such news values explicit. They found some empirical confirmation for hypotheses such as

— 'The lower the rank of the person, the more negative the event';

— 'The more the event concerns elite people, the more probable that it will become a news item';
— 'The lower the rank of the person, the more unexpected will the news have to be'.[48]

Galtung and Ruge's analysis dealt with foreign news only but these hypotheses would probably also find confirmation in Western domestic news. Insurgent terrorism, consisting of unexpected violent acts by persons with a low rank against elite people, would then have a high news value within the reference system of the Western media, which would account for the fact that it is receiving such attention.

6. An interesting variant of this interpretation has recently been suggested by Giovanni Bechelloni,[49] which we will present here with some additions of our own. The news that is valuable to the media comes from various fields. The oldest field is the government and politics, news from those and about those who control the social order. The second field that the mass media covered was crime, deviance from the social order. Crime reporting became the first journalistic specialization in 1833 and the rise of the mass press owed much to the news interest which crime was able to generate. The advent of mass culture in the 1920s opened a new field, the one of show business with its movie and sport stars. Most news today is about politics, crime and sports. Since the media were and still are in general closely connected with the establishment of society, they tend to share the values of the powerful. The rulers therefore generally tend to be portrayed in a benevolent light by the leading media. The deviants of the established order, especially the criminals, are placed in a bad light. Somewhat outside this value system stand the 'beautiful' people of the world of sports, entertainment, show biz and art. The 'good' (hero), the 'bad' (villain) and the 'spectacular' (star) — those who maintain, disturb or enliven the social order — pre-eminently appear in the news. The 'good' have routine access to news-making due to their power position, the 'bad' gain access to the extent that they endanger the social order and the 'spectacular' gain access insofar as they manage to divert us. This ideal order of things where heroes, villains and stars correspond to the spheres of social order, social deviance and social entertainment is in reality often disrupted. Whenever transgressions between the three spheres take place, news coverage in an uncensored society tends to be expecially intensive. If the 'beautiful' ally with the 'good' (e.g. Grace Kelly marrying the Prince of Monaco) this is big news. If the bad turn out to be good (in the vein of Robin Hood), and even more if the good turn out to be bad (Patty Hearst becoming Tania, Richard Nixon

turning out to be a crook), this is big news. Insurgent terrorism, in this view, receives such extraordinary media attention because it often touches all three fields. Terrorism, it has been observed, is violence for effect, it is theatre.[50] It is also crime and it is politics. This threefold confluence of real life-and-death spectacle, high politics and base crime fits so well into what the Western media are conditioned to cover that they cannot resist giving it full exposure.

In the foregoing pages we have presented some possible explanations why (terroristic) violence has such a high news value. Each of them seems to have some explicatory power but none can, in our view, offer a full answer. It is a subject that deserves more research than it has received so far.

HOW MUCH COVERAGE IS INSURGENT TERRORISM RECEIVING IN THE NEWS MEDIA AND HOW IS IT COVERED?

So far we have only stated that insurgent terrorism receives extraordinary news coverage without substantiating this claim. This we will attempt to do in this section. We would also like to describe how the media cover terrorism. Unfortunately there is very little evidence available on this aspect.

The most important principle governing the amount of exposure a terrorist incident gets by free media is the proximity principle: the closer the terrorists are to a medium and its audience, the more intensive the coverage tends to be. An incident in a national capital where the media are already assembled, receives bigger news treatment than a comparable incident in the provinces. The Hanafi incident in Washington is a good example. The *Washington Star* used the whole front page for reporting the March 1977 incident on the day it began. The *Washington Post* allowed just one more story on the front page, dealing with the ban on saccharin. In the rest of the country the twelve gunmen made banner headlines.[51] An important press conference which President Carter gave at the same time was relegated to the inside pages of the capital's main papers. In this conference a bill to fight youth unemployment was announced as well as a new Middle East peace proposal. The presidential statement also contained a proposal to reduce the US military presence in South Korea and a report on the Salt II negotiations with the Soviet Union. James Reston, a veteran journalist, could hardly recall a single presidential speech with so much news in it.[52] Yet the terrorist news managed to sweep this from the front pages of the capital's leading papers. The electronic media bestowed even more attention on the Hanafi siege. Reporters from all over the country called up the terrorist leader for live interviews. Local television stations interrupted soap opera programmes to treat their audiences to some live drama. Although the situation at the three sites of the siege was stationary most of the time, stations turned back time and again to their reporters on the scene for the latest news.[53]

The Hanafi story was national news and anyone who had something to say on it was courted by the media. In Chicago a telephone caller to the CBS newsroom phoned from the local Hanafi temple and offered an interview. A reporter and an electronic camera crew were speedily dispatched to the site. Nobody knew who the caller was nor what he was going to say but since the six o'clock news was only minutes away there was no time to check his story. At two minutes after six this young Muslim in a rundown house that served as temple was addressing nearly two million people in the competitive Chicago television market. What he had to say did not even directly pertain to the Washington siege.[54] The amount of time and money that the media spent for coverage was impressive. A news director for the Washington WTOP-TV estimated his station's cost for the coverage at between $70,000 and $75,000. The networks spent much more. The National Broadcasting Company (NBC), one of the big three national networks, assigned eighteen camera crews to the Hanafi story, some of whom had to be flown in from places as far away as Chicago and Burbank, California. Altogether about 100 NBC people were covering the incident. For the three days that the Hanafi story was news NBC spent 35 minutes and 50 seconds or 53.22 percent of its total evening network news time on the story. The other two major networks were equally enthralled: ABC spent 65 minutes and 50 seconds or 40 percent of its evening news time on it; CBS 70 minutes or 31.19 percent of its evening news time. All three major networks featured the Hanafi siege as the leading news item on three consecutive evenings.[55] And all this while none of the 134 hostages were killed (although sixteen of them got hurt and a reporter was shot dead).

The hostages were the ones who suffered most from this media attention. When one radio reporter phoned Khaalis and suggested that the police was trying to trick him, the terrorist leader marked ten older hostages for execution should the information be true. To calm Khaalis down the police had to withdraw some sharp-shooters from nearby buildings.[56] One of the terrorist demands had been that the movie

Mohammad, Messenger of God, which the Hanafis regarded as blasphemous, not be shown. The Washington TV station WTTG promptly
showed a brief clip of the film which might have satisfied the curiosity
of the audience but was possibly dangerous to the hostages.[57] In the
eyes of many of the hostages the media reporting showed more understanding for the terrorists than for their victims. Some of them felt
that the media had created the impression that the terrorists had been
kind and merciful.[58] When the ordeal was over and the hostages were
released they fell into the hands of the waiting journalists. Some
hostages, still in a state of shock, tried to hide their faces under their
coats while others who ran away were chased by cameramen.[59] When
one ex-hostage wanted to answer the press others protested. One of
them said: 'They are poison. They don't care about us. They would be
happier if we were dead because that would make a much bigger story'.
After having been exploited by the terrorists, many hostages felt that,
upon release, they were exploited by the media. As one of them said:
'The press is after blood, gore and mayhem. The press revels in sickness
and perversion'.[60]
    The Hanafi incident has not been the only example where the media
squeezed the most out of a relatively minor terrorist incident. The way
the Japanese media treated the 'drama in the mountain forest' on 28 February 1972 is equally instructive. In this case the terrorist actors were
members of the Japanese United Red Army Faction, Rengo Sekigun.
Formed in 1969 the Sekigun had first attracted media attention in March
and April 1970 when nine terrorists with Samurai swords forced an aircraft with ninety-nine passengers to fly to Korea. Before they reached
their North Korean destination they were besieged twice in Fukuoka and
Seoul, lasting five and eight hours respectively, and during which television linked by satellite transmission broadcast their exploit to millions
of people.[61] In February 1972 the Japanese police discovered the headquarters of the Rengo Sekigun in Karuizawa, a resort in the north of
Tokyo. Two terrorists managed to escape while the others barricaded
themselves in a nearby villa, taking the wife of the keeper as their hostage. Negotiations went on for nine days during which the media
gradually built up their coverage to a climax on the tenth day, when
3,000 policemen were ordered to storm the place of siege. Three out of
the seven television stations in Tokyo covered the drama live during ten
hours and forty minutes. Among them was Nippon Hoso Kyokai (NHK),
the Japanese Broadcasting Corporation with its nationwide network.
An estimated seventy million Japanese followed the coverage, among
them, almost certainly, the hostage-takers themselves.[62]

The TV-watchers were treated from 09.40 in the morning onwards
with an almost continuous coverage of the battle between terrorists and
police. After five hours there was a short interruption of the programme to broadcast the return of President Nixon from Shanghai to
the United States. The historic China visit which marked a change in
the power balance in the Pacific basin was of considerable importance
to Japan. Yet it was given only five minutes before the scene switched
back to the drama in the mountain forest.[63] The media shied from no
risk to treat the public with all the details of the battle and bullets hit
not only policemen but also a reporter. The hostage drama had turned
into a spectacle and the media seemed to enjoy it. As one reporter
broadcasting from the scene put it: 'I have never made such a long
newscast in a television transmission. For hours people shoot at each
other. Millions of people all over the country watch it in their homes.
A crime without precedent! And without precedent too is this television
mission!'[64] In the end the single hostage was saved, the five terrorists
were captured. People who had watched the events on television
streamed to the scene and some of them demanded that the terrorists
be killed. One TV-watcher had recognized his son as being one of the
terrorists and committed suicide.[65]

Massive media attention has also been bestowed on the German Red
Army Fraction (RAF) and related movements. West Germany's biggest
press empire, the Springer publishing house, featured headlines such as
'Mao's Embassy in East Berlin supplies bombs against Vice-President
Humphrey', 'Bomb assassination attempt against US Vice-President',
'Free University students prepare bombs with explosive from Peking'
when the young radicals were still throwing paint bags and pudding.[66]
When the student leader Rudi Dutschke was dangerously injured in an
assassination attempt by a right-wing youth in April 1968, students
in Berlin attacked the house of Springer, blaming the publisher for
being an inspirator of the attentat.[67] Years later, the bombs announced
so prematurely became reality when they exploded in Springer's
Hamburg publishing house in May 1972.[68] The Springer press and the
terrorists seemed to feed on each other.

In the case of the kidnapping of the Berlin mayoral candidate Peter
Lorenz in 1975, the two leading Springer papers *Die Welt* (an elite
paper) and *Bild Zeitung* (the country's largest mass paper) devoted
more attention to the affair than to any other single news item in the
period. In the six days from 28 February to 6 March 1975 (from the
day after the kidnapping to the day after the released politician gave
a press conference), *Die Welt* used 42.8 percent of the space of the

political section of the paper for covering the terrorist incident. The *Bild Zeitung* used as much as 72.51 percent of its total political pages for this story. Other major German papers used between 31.7 percent (*Stuttgarter Zeitung*) and 38.68 percent (*Frankfurter Rundschau*).[69]

In one of the few content analyses that have been done on the media's treatment of terroristic news, Gert Ellinghaus and Günther Rager have looked at the communication strategies employed by the Springer media in the case of the Lorenz kidnapping. The authors identified two processes. One of them they termed 'diffusion' by which they characterized suggestive media techniques to portray the deed of a handful of terrorists as the work of a wider group of political opponents. Intellectuals and the political left in general were through this diffusion process indirectly held responsible for the deed of the terrorists so that the terrorist act could be instrumentalized to discredit them as well. The second process which the authors claim to have found in their content analysis they termed 'intimacy building', by which they referred to three techniques. The first they named 'concretism', whereby they described the technique of giving the reader the impression of having total information by treating him to telling details. The net effect of this technique was the creation of tension as in a police thriller. The second technique identified they called 'offers of identification'. The victim, Peter Lorenz, was idealized to invite the reader to identify with him, thereby creating a basis for indignation and blind anger towards the kidnappers. The third intimacy-building strategy the authors found was 'psychologizing' by which they referred to the technique of depoliticizing the terrorist act and reformulating the terrorists' motives in private and psychological terms.[70] While these techniques of news treatment came out most clearly in the Springer press (which controls almost 30 percent of the German dailies market in terms of copies per day), the authors found the same style of reporting, though to a smaller degree, also in other papers.

It goes without saying that the news media can, with such subtle methods of manipulation, to some extent precondition the response of the readers to terroristic news. Where terrorist acts are discriminately aimed at the top power holders of society, the common man might not feel particularly involved. Through an appropriate media treatment of such acts, much can be done to increase the common man's perception that he too is in danger. A leading Italian editor has declared that giving publicity to terrorist acts could serve to help people understand that terrorism was something more than what concerned 'them' — the terrorists and the establishment. Publicity could, in his view, bring people to make up their minds against terrorism. The same editor, however, warned of overdoing it, as this might spread fear and panic among the populace.[71]

Whether the enormous coverage the Moro kidnapping received in the Italian media was the product of a media strategy to involve the common man and rally him behind the forces of social order, or whether it was largely unreflected sensationalism is hard to determine, though we are inclined to see it more in the light of the latter. The coverage of the Moro kidnapping was, in any case, massive and more than commensurate to the uncontestable political significance of the event. During the fifty-seven days of the continuing story, *La Stampa* dedicated on no less than eleven days the entire front page to the affair, while *Il Giornale* and *La Repubblica* did the same on thirteen and twelve days respectively.[72] If the total of information referring to the kidnapping is taken, the picture is even more impressive (see Table 2D).

Table 2D
News Coverage of the Moro Kidnapping in Five Italian Dailies on Three Selected Days
(Percentages refer to proportion of news space on the case to total of political and cultural ('cronaca') news)[73]

Newspaper	19 March	1 April	21 April 1978
La Stampa	37.5	22.85	45
Il Giornale	45.45	27.77	30
La Repubblica	50	22.22	60
L'Unità	62.5	22.72	25
Corriere	33.33	29.41	31.57

Some of these papers occasionally extended the political section to provide space for the big story, while the more common thing was that the news on the Moro case simply killed other news that would ordinarily have received coverage. The cumulative effect of such a one-sided concentration of the news over a period of almost two months cannot have been negligible. If something like a quarter of all topical political information for forty million adult Italians is dedicated to one helpless victim, a helpless police and their clever opponents, a picture of reality is created that cannot be anything else than distorted. In a message the Red Brigades had boasted: 'The hostage is in our hands; we have carried the attack into the heart of the State'.[74] With the help of the media, the Red Brigades, (at that time perhaps three hundred people[75]) indeed came, in one sense, close to conquering the heart of the state, that is, they managed to preoccupy the minds of the majority of people for a considerable length of time.

What contributed to this temporary mental conquest was that much of the Italian press canonized the abducted politician and equated him with the nation. Moro was Italy.[76] At the same time the real Moro, the one who sat in a 'people's prison' and wrote letters to his party asking for an exchange of 'prisoners', was treated by most of the media as if he was already dead. The authenticity of the letters was almost universally denied, they were 'pseudo-letters' from a 'pseudo-Moro'.[77] More than one observer has noted the 'homogeneity which has characterized the newspapers in this period'.[78] This was not the result of a government-imposed directive but, at least in part, of a sort of loosely coordinated self-censorship. It was this practical unanimity of the media, which, in the opinion of an Italian editor, allowed the government to resist pressure to negotiate with the Red Brigades.[79] The terrorists themselves commented on the media's policy by saying that 'the crude exploitation of the emotions of public opinion will have a short life and will turn itself against its own imprudent instigators'.[80] At least one commentator shared this view, holding that 'the press, fearing that the people sympathize with the terrorists, has portrayed them in a manner very much different from how they are, with the result of making them stronger and more well-known'.[81]

Alessandro Silj, the author of a book on the Red Brigades, has made an analysis of the reporting of five Italian dailies during the days of the Moro kidnapping. Since he has done one of the few content analyses on the news treatment of terrorism, it is worth quoting him at length:

In the information/spectacle of the Moro abduction we can, in my opinion, say that the script has been written by the BR (Red Brigades) and that the directing has been in the hands of the press. The director has not even tried to stage a shortened version of the script (the script was too beautiful, the temptation too strong)....It is, at this point, worthwhile to recall the theories of the situationalists, according to whom ours is a society of the spectacle and the terrorist inevitably ends up by assuming the role of the primadonna – in this way terrorism turns into a movie on terrorism....In fact the press did not occupy itself with informing, except as a side activity; above all it has made itself the voice of the points of view of the investigators and one or the other political power....the abduction of Aldo Moro has offered the Italian press the pretext to celebrate an immense intoxicating festival of rhetoric which could not help becoming a grand mystification. (It offered the pretext) as well to battle for or against political positions which have tried, each for its own goals, to instrumentalize the kidnapping. The instrumentalization of a news item is synonymous with disinformation.[82]

So far we have attempted to illustrate how and how much media cover national terrorist incidents, taking examples from the United States, Japan, West Germany and Italy. The manner of media treatment in a domestic context, however, differs from the media treatment of foreign terrorism. In the latter case the ideological hostility or affinity between the medium and the terrorists' goals rather than means seems to be more decisive for colouring the news treatment either positively or negatively. In the case of goal consonance the terrorist acts tend to be treated, as one author puts it, 'as regrettably extreme ways of making a political statement', while in the contrary case they are treated as outrageous crimes.[83] The difference between the treatment of foreign and domestic teroristic news comes out clearly in the case of Northern Ireland, which to the British press was half domestic and half foreign. When the 'troubles' in Northern Ireland started again after 1969, newsmen with different event (interpretation) needs were attracted to the scene. One British observer noted:

Spanish reporters came and saw the afflictions of fellow Catholics. Soviet reporters came and saw the final spasms of British military imperialism. French marxist pressmen saw a liberation movement enacted before their eyes. Maoists came and saw the birth of a European Cuba. But for British broadcasters and journalists the anguish of Ulster lay outside these categories: it lay in the revelation of the existence of inequalities and oppression within these islands of a kind unthinkable in any other part of the country and sanctioned by a kind of helpless feeling of inevitability.[84]

While the foreign media could determine their point of view without much outside pressure, the British media, after having long neglected Northern Ireland, had to find a style of reporting that would at least try to do justice to both sides in what after all was a civil war. The problem which British newsmen faced was basically insolvable. To call a bomb a bomb was no problem, but when the place where it exploded had two names, Londonderry and Derry, the very choice of one name over the other already implied taking sides with either the Protestants or the Catholics.[85] The personal allegiance of journalists in Northern Ireland reporting for the mainland was already a colouring element. The Belfast newsroom of the BBC, for instance, was in 1969 almost totally Protestant. As one newsman put it: 'We take as a fact stuff from Belfast; it's thoroughly checked. The local newsroom is full of violent Protestants. We send over the Englishmen to get unbiased reporting'.[86] Once the British Army moved in, the British media found it even harder not to take sides. The chief leader writer of the

Daily Express held that 'the soldier or the policeman who never knows where the next shot will come from deserves support in a hazardous and desperately difficult task. The snide remark which undermines his morale is almost as bad as the sniper's bullet'.[87] Even the Director General of the BBC felt that he had to take a similar stand: 'But, as between the British Army and the gunmen the BBC is not and cannot be impartial'.[88] Once the Army made its weight felt in Northern Ireland, most of the reporting of the British media became very cautious. The regular recurrence of violent events, in turn, also led to routine standardization of news. A style of reporting has evolved that is largely deprived of contextualization and that tends to record merely the 'who, what, where' of violent incidents.[89] The net result of this has been, as Philip Elliott writes, that it 'makes violence less rather than more explicable'.[90]

This conclusion, as Elliott himself suggests, applies to much conflict reporting in the world.[91] If the local media are unable to give a meaningful picture of a conflict wherein terrorism occurs, foreign media are generally not likely to do much better. Bernard Wember has analyzed the coverage of Northern Ireland on the second German TV network and came to conclusions similar to those of Elliott. Wember found that background, context and political structures were largely lacking while surface phenomena, determined by fleeing topicality, predominated.[92] In discussing the US media portrayal of political violence in Latin America, two other authors have noted, in a similar vein, that the 'urban guerrillas have been presented in the media largely through their actions, with no sense of their history, direction, or social context. Diplomatic kidnappings and occasional assassinations are newsworthy events; but their newsworthiness derives from spectacle and drama and thus obscures the underlying relationship of the urban guerrilla to the revolutionary process'.[93] While the minority press does provide some background in its commentaries and analyses, the electronic media and the popular press frequently discuss (certainly when the reported events are not domestic) no more than the outward features of terroristic events ('Should the government pay ransom or risk the lives of the hostages?', etc).[94]

It is therefore no wonder that to the majority of the public terrorism tends to appear as little else than shocking, senseless violence. To the media-dependent distant observer terrorists often emerge merely as particularly unsavoury troublemakers. What escapes his eye is that insurgent terrorism is generally not the cause of the trouble but a symptom. This lack of understanding in turn is to a significant extent the result of the dominant media's one-sided preoccupation with non-state terrorism. Government repression, which in many cases precedes the arrival of insurgent terrorism, is often excluded in the dominant media's coverage, or, when it is included, it is — in cases of states belonging to the same power bloc as the media — likely to be portrayed as an unfortunate consequence of over-reaction to an insurgent terrorist threat, rather than as one of its main causes. The dominant media's devotion to the coverage of insurgent terrorism rather than state terrorism is partly a result of the close proximity of the media owners to the political power holders. It is also the result of the lower visibility of state terrorism compared to the high visibility of insurgent terrorism. State terrorism is mainly exercised behind closed doors, away from the eye of the camera. While insurgent terrorism seeks the public media to convey its message to a larger audience, state terrorism generally shies from publicity and does not rely on the media circuits to spread its message of intimidation to the groups for whom it is meant. And when state terrorism surfaces the government is usually quick in cen-soring the media. The net effect is an imbalance in the news coverage of terrorism. Informed only by the mass media, the average news con-sumer gets the impression of a unilateral upsurge in mainly left-wing insurgent terrorism. Yet state terrorism is a much more serious problem. In terms of victims the state terrorism in Guatemala, for instance, has cost many more lives in one year than all the international insurgent terrorist incidents of the last ten years together.[95]

THE PROBLEM OF SOURCE DEPENDENCE

In the last but one section we have noted that the use of news on terrorism is partly conditioned by the (perceived) interest of the audience. Yet the journalist, while writing for his audience, gets generally less feedback from it than he gets from his colleagues, his editor and his sources. Compared to the news promotors, the sources the media draw from when they cover terrorism and other events, the news consumers have little direct influence on the journalistic news assemblers. The relationship between medium and source stands at the basis of the news the public gets and the way this relationship is struc-tured largely determines news content. In the following we will analyze the journalist-source relation, the way media and sources interact.

Before we look at news on terrorism in this light some general clarifying remarks are necessary.

Occurrences that are classified as events are either nature-made (earthquakes for instance) or man-made. Among the latter category there are events in which the protagonists are unobserved by the media or are not aware of being observed so that no acting or direct feedback occurs due to the media presence and coverage. In other man-made events the protagonists are aware of the media presence and in increasingly frequent situations the event is taking place mainly or even exclusively because of the presence of the media (e.g. press conferences, demonstrations). In such situations the event creator or event discloser and the medium interact. The interactions between medium and source fall under three major types: there is a gift relation from the source to the medium (the information is provided free), or there is a theft relation (e.g. a journalist 'liberates' documents directly or indirectly as in the case of the Pentagon papers), or — and that is the most common situation — there is an exchange relation, the exchange being either equal or unequal depending on the relative power differential between medium and source. Table 2E provides an overview of some of the more frequent interaction types.

A source that provides information is, if the information affects himself, generally interested that this information is not negative for himself. Usually the source expects some benefit from the information it releases freely so that in fact what at first sight looks like a gift relation is an exchange relation. A journalist is interested in cultivating as many sources as possible. If he wants to use the same source repeatedly he will try not to offend the source by publishing negative news about it. The source, in turn, can create goodwill with the journalist by providing him with exclusive information which can form the basis for a scoop. In this way medium and source develop a relationship that is mutually advantageous. The source gets favourable publicity, the journalist exclusive stories.

Western media, we have said earlier, see it as their purpose to reflect reality while Eastern media have the purpose to provide information that strengthens the position of the Communist party. Yet when we look at the source-medium interaction it is clear that, although the medium might have no other purpose than providing 'objective' information (which is not exactly true), the source on which the medium relies, generally does have a purpose. The purpose of a source can for instance be to discredit a rival through leaking information which throws a bad light on him (e.g. the US Joint Chiefs of Staff leaking information to

Table 2E
A Selection of Medium-Source Interaction Types

1. Medium steals news from source (e.g. the journalist who searched Kissinger's garbage bins in Georgetown)
2. Medium pays source for news (chequebook journalism, e.g. David Frost–Richard Nixon interviews)
3. Medium gets paid by source for news (e.g. Muldergate, South Africa)
4. Medium is blackmailed into publishing news of source (e.g. in the case of Argentinian terrorists kidnapping daughter of editor of *Clarin*)
5. Medium creates news source (e.g. the aborted attempt of CBS in 1967 to finance an invasion force into Haiti in exchange for exclusive rights to the story)
6. Medium is source (e.g. medium announcing that star reporter will join its own news team)
7. Medium observes source (e.g. radio station monitoring police radio and reporting information thus gained)
8. Medium blackmails source (e.g. when medium threatens disclosure if source does not provide certain other information)
9. Medium and source trade information for publicity
10. Source invents event for medium (black propaganda of secret services)
11. Source tricks medium away from event to prevent coverage (e.g. in 1954 the CIA tried to get the *New York Times* correspondent for Middle America away from the scene when the invasion into Guatemala was staged)
12. Source bribes medium with scoops in return for favourable coverage on other occasions

the columnist Jack Anderson about Kissinger siding with Pakistan in the Bangladesh liberation struggle). If a medium is lucky it has several sources which are at cross purposes with each other. In such a situation the medium can get closer to the 'truth' of a story. However, given the pressure of deadlines 'truth' is not often likely to emerge within the twenty-four hours between two newspaper editions and correction of old news is not something the media place great emphasis on. Even when it occurs, the false news has in the meantime already had a true social impact. The source problem is certainly not the only one that stands between news and 'truth'. The interactions of audience-medium, journalist-editor, editor-social system and the one between the different media are all problem areas. Here we confine ourselves to just one, the source-medium interaction which, in our view, is the most important one for the coverage of terrorist news. In cases of insurgent terrorism the sources of the media are, with relatively few exceptions, just two, the terrorists and their opponents, the government and its security forces. In the following two sections we will analyze some of the interactions which we have observed.

The Terrorists as Source

When a journalist uses insurgent terrorists as sources — either directly by interviewing them or indirectly by taking their messages as bases for a story — there is a good chance that he takes over some if not all of the language of his sources. For the same set of things government and insurgent terrorists use different words (see Table 2F), depending on whether they refer to themselves or to the other side. Words carry emotive connotations, imply varying guilt attribution and can serve to neutralize or justify (in-) human acts. If a source can bring a medium to adopt its language it has already won an important psychological victory.

Table 2F
Some In-group and Out-group Labellings for the Same Thing

1. Criminal — Revolutionary	10. Aggression — Preventive Counter-Strike
2. Terrorist — Guerrilla	
3. Murderer — Freedom Fighter	11. Assassin — Avenger
4. Gang — Army	12. Propaganda — Communiqué
5. Subversive element — Liberator	13. Extremist Fanatic — Dedicated Anti-Imperialist
6. Bloodbath — Purge	
7. Lunatic — Martyr	14. Attack — Operation
8. Mercenary — Soldier	15. Hired Killer — Example of Revolutionary Solidarity
9. Threat — Warning	
	16. Murder — Revolutionary Justice

The difficulty the journalist faces is that there are few words that are genuinely neutral since motive and activity are often enclosed in one word. The reporter is therefore compelled to accept one or the other nomenclature, which at the same time implies taking sides. Declining to make a choice, some journalists use alternate terminology, calling a rebel in the same article terrorist, guerrilla or even soldier.[96] What effect media reporting will have depends to a significant extent on the choice of words. Sometimes the insurgent terrorists have very little influence on the way the media report their acts. The terrorists may kill a brutal police torturer only to read in the press that a poor father of ten children was murdered by the lunatic fringe.[97] A simple bombing accompanied by a communiqué mailed to the media, explaining who did it and why it was done, has generally little chance to result in a news item that satisfies the terrorists and informs the public about their rationale. The media often either do not bother to print the message (as has happened with many RAF communiqués in West

Germany[98]) or they interpret it in a way that is diametrically opposed to the self-understanding of the group which perpetrated the deed (as did the British press with messages of the Angry Brigade[99]). In cases of kidnapping and acts of hostage-taking, on the other hand, the media sometimes seem to be prepared not to offend the terrorists needlessly as this might result in harm to the victim. Messages, especially when they come from the victims themselves (even though they might have been dictated by the terrorists), are often reproduced verbatim, as in the case of the Patty Hearst kidnapping.[100]

Sometimes the manner of presentation of the terrorists is so attractive that a medium, out of a quasi-aesthetical feeling, takes over the material. In the case of the Moro kidnapping, for instance, the headline in *La Repubblica* of 17 March 1978 'They have struck the heart of the State' seems to have been directly inspired by a message from the Red Brigades wherein they stated '...we have carried the attack into the heart of the State'.[101] The picture of Aldo Moro before a flag of the Red Brigades, which the terrorists sent to the media, was placed on the front pages of the papers. None of them was apparently content with saying that a photo had been received showing Moro alive but in captivity. None of the major papers thought about taking an archive photo of the Christian Democratic leader.[102] For the Red Brigades this photo, showing Italy's top statesman in shirt sleeves under the star of the terrorists, was undoubtedly a propaganda success, bringing home a message that no written text could have transmitted so powerfully. The source had in this case seduced the media, which with equal lack of caution also reproduced many of the messages that followed this picture. The Italian media's propensity to believe terrorist sources uncritically showed itself most clearly when they gave ample coverage to the improbable story that Moro's body had been dumped in an almost inaccessible frozen mountain lake. The fact that the security forces also fell into this trap was only a small consolation.

A rather blind belief in sources was for a time also shown by Western media in the case of the activities of the Palestinian Liberation Organization. Not only were actual deeds exaggerated by the media, some deeds that were reported had never taken place and were purely imaginary, a joint product of fedayeen boasting and journalist credulity.[103] The ease with which the media sometimes lend credence to doubtful data has been demonstrated as well by Edward Epstein in an analysis on the Black Panthers and the press. After two Black Panther members had died in an encounter with the Chicago police, Charles R. Garry, a spokesman for the Panthers, declared that the two 'were in fact the twenty-seventh and the twenty-eighth Panthers murdered by the police'. The *Washington Post* reported without attribution on 9 December 1969 that 'A total of 28 Panthers have died in clashes with police since January 1, 1968', and the figures were uncritically used almost everywhere, leading to charges of 'a calculated design of genocide in this country' (Ralph Abernathy). When one journalist took the trouble to verify the information by questioning Garry he was told that 'the facts are not necessarily empirical' but was provided with a list naming nineteen dead Panther members. After investigating these cases Epstein found that in only two instances Panthers were killed by policemen whose lives had not been directly threatened by those men.[104] This was considerably less than the number of policemen who had died at the hands of Panthers.[105]

Another source problem poses itself for the journalist when he is interviewing insurgent terrorists, either during an action or in the underground. Where such interviews are carried live by the electronic media the reporter tends to have very little control over his source and in fact becomes a mere show host, providing free publicity for the terrorist. In some cases the reporter can become the accomplice of the terrorists. In an incident in Calgary, Canada, in March 1976, when two robbers, after having shot a policeman, took three hostages, a reporter called them when they were on the point of exchanging their hostages against a number of doses of methadone and said: 'Don't be stupid. If you give up all your hostages you'll have nothing to deal with'. This has not been the only case where reporters, interfering with police-terrorist negotiations, have delayed or prevented surrender.[106] The information value (based on substance) of direct live interviews with terrorists in a siege situation tends to be so low that is does not seem worthwhile to warrant the possible risk to the hostages or the negative public effects.The news value (based on dramatic form), on the other hand, is so high that there will always be reporters who are prepared to take the risk of interviewing terrorists in action. The risk is generally not theirs though there have been cases where talking to terrorists brought discomfort, either by becoming a hostage, as happened to ABC journalist John Johnson[107] or by becoming a terrorist as happened to Ulrike Meinhof who had interviewed (albeit not in a siege situation) Andreas Baader and Gudrun Ensslin.[108]

Quite a different matter to live action interviews are recorded or written interviews with insurgent terrorists and their associates in the underground. The terrorists' statements naturally tend to be self-serving but the journalist himself, chasing the terrorist to get a 'world exclusive', also tends to have self-serving motives. The information value of such interviews for the public, however, tends to be at least as high as the propaganda value for the terrorist. Such interviews are not frequent since journalists are often afraid of being charged with providing a forum to the enemy and giving him a public status. The BBC has in its coverage of Northern Ireland conducted only eighteen interviews with paramilitary spokesmen out of 325 interviews in this context in one year.[109] Direct interviews with terrorists are even rarer. Between 1972 and 1977 the Provisional IRA's Chief of Staff David O'Connell was interviewed only twice by the BBC.[110] The authorities generally strongly discourage media contacts with terrorists. A BBC Current Affairs reporter was jailed for refusing to identify an IRA member on the grounds of professional ethics.[111] In 1979 the British government threatened to take legal action against the BBC because of an interview that had been conducted with a member of the Irish National Liberation Army (INLA) some months after the INLA had murdered the Conservative spokesman for Irish questions, Airey Neave, outside the British parliament.[112] In West Germany, the government has accused seven journalists working for the Westdeutscher Rundfunk (WRD – West German Broadcasting) network of having contacts with anarchist groups. Some of these journalists were subsequently sentenced.[113]

One test of a free press is how willing and able journalists are to resist such government pressures. A study conducted by Vince Blasi in 1972 in the United States throws some interesting light on the question of willingness. Blasi presented a non-random sample of almost 1,000 newsmen with this hypothetical situation:

You have a continuing source relationship with a group of political radicals. They have given you much information in confidence and this has enabled you to write several byline stories describing and assessing in general terms the activities and moods of the group. During the course of this relationship, you are present at a closed meeting with ten of these radicals at which the group vigorously debates whether to bomb a number of targets, including the local police station. The consensus is against such bombing, but two members of the group argue very heatedly in favor of bombing and are deeply upset when the others refuse to go along. These two then threaten to act on their own. The discussion then turns to another topic. Two weeks later the local police is in fact bombed. One officer is killed by the blast and two others are seriously injured.

Blasi asked his sample of newsmen whether they would volunteer the information to the authorities right after the meeting. 26.2 percent answered affirmatively, 55.5 percent answered negatively, while the rest gave no answer. Asked whether they would volunteer the information after the bombing, 37.6 percent answered yes, 36.0 percent no, leaving 26.4 percent with no answer. The willingness to protect their source among this sample was quite high. Even if they were to be subpoenaed by a grand jury to name the members of the group who had advocated the bombing, only 36.9 percent said they were prepared to do so, while 44.1 percent said they would refuse, with 19.0 percent having no answer.[114]

Although these data are partly a reflection of the American media's disenchantment with the Nixon administration, they also reflect the media's endeavour to be an autonomous element. They certainly do not square with the Althusserian view of the capitalist media as simple parts of the ideological apparatus of a ruling class. The journalists' desire to protect their sources is of course also influenced by commercial motives since a good source is good information, which is salable information. In the case of insurgent terrorist sources the public also profits from a journalist's relationship with violent dissenters. It gets a chance to obtain some rare insights into the thinking of the terrorists. Yet such media-terrorist source relations are extremely rare; those insurgent terrorists that have been interviewed were in the majority of cases either imprisoned or had retired. By and large, what we know about insurgent terrorism we do not know because of the media-terrorist relationship, but because of the media-government source relationship, as will be exemplified in the following section.

The Government as Source

If a government is at war with a foreign state it will as a rule censor the dispatches of its war correspondents if these cannot be brought voluntarily to take a 'responsible' and patriotic line. Generals will push their view of reality and if reporters substantially diverge from it they will be either seduced or forced to take the government line. What the journalist writes will be read by the public, the soldiers and the enemy. In so far as it influences the stance of these audiences towards the war, and to some extent it always does, this is affecting the power of the government. The first casualty in war, it has been observed, tends to be truth.[115] Insurgent terrorism is often a part of civil war and the same government desire to influence public perception of the conflict is manifest. As chief and in many cases only source of news about insurgent terroristic events governments are in an excellent position to do so. They are not only able to shape the news on terrorism, they can virtually create it.

In the preceding section we have seen how the Palestinian terrorists could bring the media to report events that never took place. Governments can do this on an even greater scale. Take the case of the Central Intelligence Agency (CIA) of the United States. From parts of the world where there were CIA operatives but no journalists — places like Central Africa or the jungles of South America — these agents have been feeding fictitious stories about in some cases fictitious guerrilla movements to the media. Such stories have been picked up, in one case cited by the Chicago *Daily News* in April 1976, by two hundred newspapers, thirty news services, twenty radio and television outlets and twenty-five publishers. These false stories were spread to manipulate policy decisions of governments but the public is of course fooled as well.[116] Such media manipulations have been done on a grand scale in areas not directly connected with terrorism. In its heyday, the CIA, according to a report of the US Congress, spent 29 percent of its budget on media and propaganda programmes.[117] Part of the news that reaches us on terrorism has no basis in reality. Like terrorism itself it is made for effect. On the other hand there were also terrorist incidents that took place but that were never reported as a CIA source disclosed.[118] If some of the terrorism that takes place is not reported and some that is reported does not take place because governments choose or refuse to be information sources the public gets a distorted view of the reality of terrorism. The remaining information can of course also be distorted when the government has a near total source monopoly.

For this last possibility Northern Ireland offers a good example. One British journalist, Simon Hoggart, has written: 'When the British press prints an account of an incident as if it were an established fact and it is clear that the reporter himself was not on the spot, it is a 99 percent certainty that it is the army's version which is being given'.[119] What is true for the British press is often also true for the foreign press. An American reporter who has visited Northern Ireland several times has noted that in the United States 'news reporting about the North consists largely of wire-service reports based on information from the British Army Information Service in London — a source as reliable as the Pentagon was in telling us about the bombing of Cambodia'.[120]

The British Army in Northern Ireland has been very thorough in its media policy. Army officers have received instruction in how to face a TV camera and in the technique of managing media interviews.[121]

Army press officers are instructed to treat journalists as guests with officer status to whom hospitality is offered. In early 1976 the British Army had over forty press officers in Ulster, backed up by a staff of more than a hundred. Besides these people the British government had another twenty civil servants for media contacts.[122] This information machine that releases news on public disturbances is for journalists a convenient source, which makes it tempting to accept the official version of reality. Very few journalists are therefore diverging from this official line. Those who do have to pay a price. Non-cooperating journalists have been cut off from routine briefings, while journalists that push the Army line might be rewarded with information for an exclusive scoop.[123] To control the activities of the press the Army has also set up personal files on journalists and their contacts.[124] Investigative journalism is in such a situation hazardous for nonofficial sources. Since the British Army is in such a strong position that it can impose its definition of reality on the media, it has, on occasion, not only misled journalists but also fabricated news.[125] The Insight Team of the *Sunday Times* has disclosed that the Army used false information to influence government policy and has set off explosions which were then attributed to IRA terrorists.[126] The Army has also distributed false information implicating a politician in the kidnapping of the West German honorary consul Thomas Niedermayer. A black propaganda section of the Army has been forging IRA documents, posters and even assisted in forging a Sinn Fein newspaper. Furthermore, the Army's special Investigation Branch has equipped plain-clothes soldiers with forged journalists' press cards.[127]

Such examples make it clear that the media are used by both sides, the insurgent terrorists and the government security forces. At times the integrity and independence of the media are directly affected, at others only indirectly. An instance of the latter is offered by the Balcombe Street siege in December 1975. Four IRA men had, after an unsuccessful attack on a restaurant in the West End of London, taken two hostages in a flat in Balcombe Street. The siege lasted six days and the terrorists had access to a radio or television set. In an attempt to induce the terrorists to surrender the police leaked information to the press and the BBC that an assault team from the SAS (Special Air Services — an elite anti-terrorist commando unit) was to arrive on the scene. At the same time a huge screen was erected to block the scene from the eyes of the cameras. The strategy of intimidation through the media worked and the terrorists surrendered.[128]

In another case, the Spaghetti House siege, the use of the media by security forces went considerably further. Three armed West Indians had on 28 September 1975 robbed a Spaghetti restaurant and taken, when trapped by the police, seven hostages. One of the hostages was in the ensuing negotiations traded against a radio. One newspaper, the *Daily Mail*, discovered that the police had placed electronic listening equipment into the restaurant but desisted from printing this upon a request from the police. At the same time the police used radio stations to influence the terrorists. A mock interview in which the police suggested the questions and provided the answers was set up wherein the storming of the place was indicated. This apparently contributed to the surrender of the terrorists.[129] However honourable the purpose of this exercise, the case represented a deception not only of the terrorists but of the public, which was unaware of the uses to which the public media were put. Less problematical than this case was one that took place in Japan, where in 1977 a passenger bus was hijacked in the city of Kochi (Shikoku). The police surrounded the bus and during the negotiations the terrorists demanded that they be provided with the latest edition of the local newspaper. Since the paper could have informed them of the intentions and activities of the police, the paper, *Kochi Shimbun*, made a special edition for the terrorists which excluded all news about the incident.[130] In this case the public was not fooled together with the terrorists and the cooperation between the authorities and the medium was voluntary. American authorities have also taken recourse to having fake newspapers printed and delivered to besieged terrorists. There have as well been cases in the United States where false newscasts were transmitted in order to deceive terrorists. In one case a whole publicity campaign was set up by the US authorities to deter would-be hijackers to Cuba. The tenor of this massive campaign was that Fidel Castro ill-treated hijackers landing in Cuba. This campaign was aimed at potential hijackers who met a psychological profile of persons who respond to reward and punishment. Yet the public and the media who were not aware of what was being played were of course also subjected to this propaganda.[131]

As the last example illustrates, authorities also tend to use the media without the media being aware of it. The German government has on occasion fed the media with distorted information intended to mislead the terrorists.[132] Given the wellnigh information source monopoly governments often have in terrorist incidents such acts are understandable and it is up to the media to remain sceptical. Where lack of caution can lead to, however, has been shown in the Attica prison case in New York (9–13 September 1971). Prison inmates had seized a wing of Attica and barricaded themselves with numerous guards as hostages. Reporters from far and near streamed to the scene and were fed with information by state officials and army officers while troops prepared an assault. The *New York Daily News* featured a headline 'I Saw Seven Throats Cut', while other reports spoke of bestial prisoners castrating guards or throwing them from the walls to die on the pavement below. When the shooting was over forty inmates and guards were dead. Only later did it become known that the hostages had died not at the hands of the rebellious prisoners but had been killed by the bullets of the charging troops. Yet the original false stories had already made their public impact and presumably also served as a justification for the army's action. The media, relying on official sources, had clearly been misled.[133]

Reliance on government sources is strongest when the reported terroristic news is national. But at times a foreign government can also sell its interpretation of reality to distant media. The British *Daily Telegraph* of 16 June 1978 carried a story from Guatemala under the headline '17 police die in terror blast'. The reference was to events that took place on 29 May 1978 in the town of Panzós (Alta Verapaz), where oil had been found. The government had granted land titles to its protégés, taking it away from the local Indian population. This led to a clash between the army and the Quekchi Indians, in which, according to Reuter, 1,000 rebel peasants tried to storm the Panzós garrison, whereby forty-four of them died. This was the official version distributed by the Guatemalan government. Local observers spoke of an unprovoked massacre against Indian peasants who had come to Panzós to present a letter to the mayor of the town in which they protested against the violent attempts of the landlords to deprive them of their remaining land. Landowners together with 150 soldiers fired on them, killing 114 peasant men, women and children while wounding twice that number. The official version of the incident was so untrustworthy and inconsistent that the local Guatemalan press openly mistrusted it. The government version, unsuccessful at home, however, received currency abroad thanks to Reuter.[134]

That government spokesmen on occasion lie to the media is not surprising given the authorities' direct involvement in a conflict with terrorists. At times, such lies can even serve a higher purpose than merely defending the government's vision of reality. One such case where lying appeared morally justified occurred during a siege at the French embassy in The Hague in September 1974. Three members of the Japanese Red Army had taken eleven hostages. One of the hostages had managed to throw a message out of the building, which was noticed by the police as well as the media people. The notice contained information about the state of the hostages, the weapons of the terrorists and the fact that they were listening to British news accounts. The hostage who had written the note asked that none of this information nor the fact that the message had been smuggled out be made known to the press. The official police spokesman, questioned by journalists about this piece of paper, denied that it was a message and spoke of a piece of toilet paper.[135] Clearly the revelation of the message could have endangered the lives of hostages if it had come to the knowledge of the Japanese terrorists.

Government use of the media to protect the lives of hostages and kidnapped persons is perhaps the least problematical area in the government-media source relation. More problematical are attempts of governments to use the media against the terrorists. In Germany, the Bundeskriminalamt issued, immediately after the killing of Hanns Martin Schleyer, nine or ten search movies, which were broadcast over the First and Second TV networks.[136] Such a practice can come dangerously close to a witchhunt, for the persons searched for were after all only suspects and suspects are in Western societies considered to be innocent until they have been found guilty by a court. Until now such methods to appeal for public cooperation have fortunately been the exception rather than the rule. Even more problematical, in our view, are government uses of the media against terrorists where the public and sometimes even the media are unaware of being used. Worst of all are the cases where governments use the source relation with the media against the public in order to impress on it a self-serving interpretation of reality. As we have noted, all of these types of government uses of the media exist, though there is no way of knowing how often they occur and to what extent they manage to fool the public. Governments as sources of news on insurgent terrorism can be just as dangerous as terrorists as sources — but on a much grander scale.

CONCLUSION

The Western media have diverging interpretations of what constitutes terrorism. There is, however, a strong tendency to identify it rather vaguely with predominantly left-wing political violence directed against governments. The high visibility they give to terrorist acts is due to several factors, the most important of them being that the insurgent terroristic act tends to meet the event needs reflected in the news value of the media. The insurgent terrorist news promotor, as source of news, has at times considerable influence on the way the media report his action. Yet his opponents, the government and its security forces, are in fact the main sources for the media in regard to insurgent terrorism. The media do very little investigative reporting of their own in matters of terrorism which makes them dependent on either of these two sources. Since both are direct participants in the conflict, these are self-serving sources that tend to exploit the media mainly for their own advantage. For those media that want to be free and largely autonomous actors in society, the question arises which interest they should serve in a terrorist incident. Naturally the media tend to serve their own interests, selling a big story. But apart from the profit motive which is the necessary basis of the existence of most Western media, the media also serve wider interests, which can bring them into conflict. If they follow the government line they might stand in opposition to the public interest, certainly in cases where the moral legitimacy of the government is as low or even lower than the one of the insurgent terrorists.

In fact the media are in an uncomfortable position. If they censor the terrorist news they are infringing on the public's right to know. If they give extensive coverage they might terrorize the public and become allies of the terrorists. If they follow the government line they might become a propaganda and police tool. Through the way the media present terroristic news, through the selection of some facts out of a multitude of potentially relevant facts, through the associations they lay between the terroristic act and the social context the media can have a profound influence that can create public hysteria, witch-hunts, fatalism and all sorts of other reactions that serve certain political interests — and not only those of the terrorists. Objectivity in media reporting is, in such a situation, difficult. The media might attempt to be as factual in their reporting as some of the British media try to be in regard to terrorism in Northern Ireland but such a seeming detachedness is also not very objective since the lack of contextualization is also a form of distortion.

Although the Western media have now had a full decade to learn to deal with insurgent terrorism, no patent solution about its coverage has emerged. What Steven Rosenfeld wrote in 1975 is still pertinent:

We of the Western Press have yet to come to terms with international terror. If we thought about it more and understood its essence we would probably stop writing about it, or we would write about it with a great deal more restraint.[137]

3. EFFECTS OF MEDIA REPORTING ON INSURGENT TERRORISM

It is a peculiarity of insurgent terrorism that it produces far reaching effects which appear disproportionate when compared to the relatively minor amount of violence actually committed by the terrorists. The amplification and diffusion of the terrorist deed by the mass media is, as we have seen in the previous chapters, the main reason for this. In this chapter we will concentrate on some of these media-induced effects.

In the literature on the effects of mass communication the effects of media portrayal of violence have received an extraordinary amount of attention.[1] Yet this literature has almost exclusively focused on the effects of fictional media violence rather than on violence shown in newscasts.[2] Although the observed effects of fictional and real violence portrayed in the media are said to differ little from each other,[3] the results of research on the effects of violence in the media in general contribute relatively little that might be helpful to us in analyzing the effects of media reporting on terrorism. We will, however, discuss some findings of the relevant mass communication research in the last section of this chapter. In the following sections we will try to analyze, on the basis of often very limited empirical material, some of the effects of media reporting on insurgent terrorism on various groups, namely: (1) the victims of terrorism, in particular the hostages; (2) the government and its security forces; (3) the public; (4) the media themselves; and (5) other (potential) terrorists. It is on this last aspect that most of our attention will focus. The question we will raise in this last section is whether the media portrayal of insurgent terrorism leads to imitation and contagion.

EFFECTS ON HOSTAGES

Before the electronic communication revolution entered the field of news gathering, news assembly and dissemination, the time lapse between the occurrence of an event and reporting about it was in most cases sufficiently large for the event to have come to an end. With technological advances more and more news reporting occurs in 'real' time while the event observed is still running its course. In nuclear physics there is a principle of indeterminacy called after its discoverer the 'Heisenberg effect'. It says that the very method used to find the position of a moving electron (hitting it with a high-intensity beam of light) causes the electron to change its velocity. Applied to journalism this principle has been reformulated as 'the act of reporting changes the character of the events reported'.[4] For journalism this Heisenberg effect has become an issue of increasing concern although many journalists still act as if it were not so, arguing, as one Dutch editor did, 'that — except in extreme circumstances — one should not ask oneself what the social effect of one's reporting is'.[5]

In the reporting of terrorist incidents the Heisenberg effect plays an important role. When committing acts of hostage-taking insurgent terrorists are often equipped with television sets or radio receivers which, in some cases, can also pick up television sound. These form their eyes and ears for following the events beyond their direct perception. The information they obtain in this manner in a siege situation often forms the basis which determines their further actions. Live reporting by journalists can in such cases have a vital or rather lethal influence on hostages. In our own small survey we asked journalists and editors whether their news treatment was influenced by the fact that the terrorists might 'listen-in' and use this information. About one third answered 'always', another third 'sometimes', while one sixth of all answered 'rarely' and an equal number 'never'. Since our sample was too small (n = 26) and not representative, little weight can be given to this outcome. Michael Sommer has, in a larger survey, asked a similar question to US media representatives (Table 3A)[6].

Table 3A
Answers to the Question: 'To what extent do you consider
live/immediate coverage of terrorist acts a threat to hostage safety?'

	Minimal Threat %	Moderate Threat %	Great Threat %	Other %	Don't Know %
TV News Directors	32	32	3	27	6
Radio News Directors	47	19	14	17	3
Newspaper Editors	76	19	0	5	0

In contrast to media representatives, police chiefs in Sommer's survey took a gloomier view, as is revealed in Table 3B which refers only to television.

Table 3B
Answers to the Question: 'To what extent do you consider
live television coverage of terrorist acts a threat to hostage safety?'

	Minimal Threat %	Moderate Threat %	Great Threat %	Other %	Don't Know %
Police Chiefs	7	33	46	7	7
TV News Directors	32	32	3	27	6
Newspaper Editors	67	29	0	4	0

An even stronger position than the one taken by police chiefs was taken by the public in a third survey. In a poll conducted in the wake of the Hanafi incident among listeners of a radio station, 70 percent of the respondents held that media coverage might have threatened the lives of the hostages.[7]

Perhaps more to the point than such surveys are actual examples where media intrusion in an ongoing terroristic act endangered lives. In the Hanafi incident in Washington DC, one reporter said at one point that he believed that the police were preparing to move in with force because he saw ammunition boxes carried into the B'nai B'rith building by police officers. The boxes which the reporter mentioned in his broadcast contained only food, but the comment, in the words of a police source, 'nearly got a hostage killed in retaliation for what the hostage taker thought was a breach of faith by our negotiators'.[8] Yet on the other hand it is only fair to point out that in the Hanafi case the media were not only a danger to the hostages but also an element that helped them. One of the hostages, commenting on the phone calls reporters made to the Hanafi terrorists, held: 'Sure, there are dangers in calling in. But it's also a way to allow the hostage-taker to let off steam. I remember Khaalis coming in and telling us "The whole world is watching me; the whole world is calling me!" It was his moment of glory. Instead of killing us, that became his high point.'[9] While the police negotiators were frequently interrupted by reporters in their attempts to talk to the terrorists, the police did not ask the phone company to pull out the public phone lines as they could have done. It later turned out that it was part of the police strategy to allow these phone calls as they were thought to sap the energy and the anger of the terrorists.[10]

A clear example of how the media can reduce the safety of the hostages was provided by another incident that also took place in the US capital. In 1974 terrorists took over part of the courthouse in the District of Columbia. The hostage-takers kept their victims in a room separated by a two-way mirror from another room, which allowed the police to watch them constantly. In case the hostages' lives were immediately threatened the police could have killed the terrorists by shooting through the mirror. This element of relative safety for the hostages was removed when the media disclosed the fact, whereupon the terrorists ordered the hostages to tape the mirror with newspapers.[11]

There have been cases where the media reporting in all likelihood caused the death of hostages. One such case took place on 22 November 1974, when four hijackers had taken over a VC 10 from British Airways on its way from Dubai to Libya. They demanded the release of thirteen imprisoned terrorists in Egypt and two in the Netherlands in exchange for the hostages. An aircraft which was supposed to carry the freed terrorists from Cairo arrived on the airfield. At this point a local reporter revealed in a live account that there were no freed prisoners on board the Egyptian aircraft and that the terrorists were being hoodwinked. One of the hostages, a German banker, was killed by the terrorists — probably as a direct consequence of this broadcast. Later Egypt released five prisoners and the Netherlands two, whereupon the hijackers surrendered to Tunisian officials upon assurance of protection.[12] Although the terroristic murder was in fact a reaction to the initial Egyptian refusal to deal with them, it was the monitored report that in all likelihood triggered off this execution.

Since false and premature disclosure of information by the news media can be dangerous to the hostages, governments feel, in such

situations, that they have to keep some control on the media. In democratic states the most comprehensive measures in this direction were
taken by the government of the Federal Republic of Germany during
the forty-five days of the Schleyer kidnapping. Although we will
discuss this news embargo in the following chapter (pp. 154—158) we
would like to mention here the consequence of some breaches of this
news blackout. The German magazine *Der Stern* published in its 19
September 1977 edition an account of conversations held by the
government crisis team. It was revealed that the authorities were
unanimous in their decision not to exchange eleven prisoners for
Schleyer. At the same time the government was said to enter into mock
negotiations to win time. This account, which sounded very credible
and which was in all likelihood correct, could have endangered the life
of Hanns Martin Schleyer. When the kidnappers saw that the government was not prepared to enter into a deal they negotiated directly
with the son of the abducted president of the German employers'
association, who was ready to pay the $15,000,000 which the terrorists
demanded for the release of his father. The German news agency DPA
(Deutsche Presse Agentur) revealed this and also mentioned time and
place where the money would be handed over. As a consequence
hundreds of journalists, including two television teams, flooded the
Hotel International in Frankfurt. The terrorists did not contact the son
of the victim. Whether a deal could have been struck is, of course, an
open question, but a chance was lost.[13] Four days later Schleyer was
dead. In the meantime another group of terrorists hijacked the
Lufthansa jet 'Landshut' and forced it to fly to the Middle East. The
news media followed this with maximum attention and reported that
the captain, Jürgen Schumann, was passing information about the
hijackers to the authorities. Via radio the hijackers had learned about
this and the pilot was executed. Thomas M. Ashwood, the chairman
of the Airlines Pilot Association, International (ALPA), was convinced,
after reviewing the evidence, that the media were to a large degree
responsible for the death of the captain.[14] In the same series of events
an Israeli radio amateur had intercepted messages between the German
rescue plane and its home base and he passed it on to the French news
agency. The Israeli television brought the news of the flight of the
German anti-terrorist team GSG-9 (Grenzschutzgruppe-9 — Federal
Border Guard Group-9) to Mogadishu, and two London newspapers
also published the story. It was good luck that the hijackers did not inter-
cept these news stories in the five hours before the successful rescue
operation, otherwise the eighty-six hostages might have lost their lives.[15]

These instances should be sufficient to illustrate the effects media reporting can have on ongoing terrorist situations. To be sure, not all of these effects are negative — terrorists might be calmed down by media contacts, relatives of hostages can be informed that their dear ones are still alive, journalists might serve as successful negotiators, police forces might be deterred from ending the situation at the expense of the hostages through the presence of the media — yet many of them are negative. The media can delay surrender by strengthening the terrorists' sense of power, they can increase their bargaining power by revealing unknown facts about the identity of hostages, they can bring the terrorists to panicky reactions by revealing tactical information about security forces' movements and they can cause distress among the families of hostages by announcing victims where there are none. Many of these negative effects could be avoided if information was held a little longer until the situation was under control. Yet under the competitive conditions with which the Western news media operate this seems extremely difficult. The search for scoops and the rewards that go with them are likely to continue to drive journalists into danger zones. Some effects of media reporting are unavoidable without censorship. In Northern Ireland, for instance, several assassinations took place in the wake of television broadcasts which contained allegations of torture in British prisons. Had the news media censored the information on torture these lives might have been saved. But torture might also cause the death of prisoners and reporting torture might reduce it. Whatever the news media do in such a situation they are damned if they do and damned if they don't.[16]

EFFECTS ON GOVERNMENTS AND THEIR SECURITY FORCES

Effects on Security Forces

The Heisenberg effect affects not only hostages but also the work of the security forces. On numerous occasions the police has had to bear the effects of live reporting on ongoing acts of terrorism. Some examples should suffice to bring this out. In one hijacking in the United States the news media revealed that among the hostages were the children of the State Governor. This caused the hijackers, who listened in, to double the amount of money they were demanding.[17] In another incident where the terrorists barricaded themselves with their hostages in an airport building, the police decided, after negotiations had broken down, to land a SWAT (Special Weapons and Tactics) assault team on the roof. A radio reporter watched them as they were rappelling down on the side of the building and his live report alerted the terrorists. They opened fire and the SWAT team was shot at.[18] In yet another incident a hijacker had seized a Braniff Airlines plane in Texas in January 1972 and demanded a ransom of one million dollars and ten parachutes as well as a gun. The gun which was given to him was fixed so that the firing pin would not strike. A Dallas radio station disclosed this fact and the captain of the aircraft had to keep switching his board radio from the newscasts to leave the terrorist in the dark. After his arrest, the hijacker said, when told about the trick, that he would have shot a stewardess in retaliation.[19] Extortion attempts by criminal terrorists who demanded parachutes for escape were quite frequent at that time. The security forces tried to halt the wave of such attempts by placing transmitters in the parachutes so that they could track the terrorists down when they landed. Within two days after this policy was implemented, the news media revealed this scheme, making the strategy almost worthless.[20]

The search for scoops sometimes makes media people very inventive in getting at information. When the SLA-Patty Hearst story was hot news in California some news media were monitoring the radio frequencies of the Federal Bureau of Investigation (FBI) with mobile scanners. As the FBI was on the point of arresting three members of the Symbionese Liberation Army, a radio station broadcast the news about the impending arrests and the terrorists, hearing the news, were able to evade apprehension.[21] One of our sources has reported a similar case in Turkey where premature media disclosure also allowed the terrorists to escape arrest.

A sore point for the police forces are media interviews with besieged terrorists. During the Hanafi incident, when the police negotiators tried to build up confidence with the terrorists, one talk show journalist warned the terrorists by saying 'How can you believe the police?'[22] Media intrusion can in such cases, as we have noted earlier, break the thought pattern of the terrorists, strengthen them in their perseverance and even give them new ideas which they can use in the war of nerves. The manner of media reporting might infuriate the terrorists, making it more difficult for the police to calm them down. This is not always the case. There have been instances where the police infuriated the terrorists and journalists had a calming effect. Another area of concern is that terrorists might draw wrong conclusions from correct or incorrect media reports or that they might draw the right conclusions, which can be just as dangerous. While the police tries to de-escalate the situation, the news media, trying to make the best of a good story, often work in the contrary direction.

Police strategies to incapacitate terrorists with surprise tactics, when revealed by the news media in detail, make these strategies constantly more risky for future occasions. Rescue operations like the Mogadishu raid have received such detailed coverage that future hijackers are not likely to be taken in by the same techniques.[23] Yet the possibilities of evacuating hostages from an aircraft in the hands of terrorists are quite limited and each new technique revealed reduces the chances of success for the hostages and the security forces.[24] There are various other ways in which the media make the tasks of the security forces more difficult. Television cameras and lights might reveal the position of policemen which endangers them and is likely to make the terrorists more nervous. Reporting the site of an incident draws crowds to the scene which blocks roads. Ambulances can in such cases not pass through, which again might endanger lives. Additional policemen are needed to keep crowds attracted by the media accounts out of the firing zones. Journalists who want information tie down police forces required for other tasks. For the security forces facing terrorists the media are often part of the problem. While it is unfair or even unwise to make the media part of the solution in situations of ongoing terrorism, a neutral stance, which would reduce the obtrusiveness of the media and thereby also reduce the chances of Heisenberg effects might serve all parties concerned — except the terrorists.

Effects on Governments

Given the publicity acts of insurgent terrorism receive in the mass media, such acts cannot fail to have a social impact which is often strong enough to change the political climate in a country. In the German Federal Republic, for instance, about 90 percent of the population believed, according to an opinion poll conducted in the spring of 1978, that the state itself was threatened by terrorism. Most of the respondents put this fear higher than their concern for such fundamental needs as jobs and income in a time of economic recession.[25] Although the level of terroristic violence of the German Red Army Fraction (RAF) and related groups was low compared to Italy or Spain, and although this terrorism was quite discriminate, focusing on public

power holders, the common German man in the street also felt increasingly threatened, as other polls revealed.[26] Since very few people have
had a direct experience with terrorism, this fear must be largely a result
of the media portrayal of terrorism. However, it would be unfair to
attribute it solely to the media's power to magnify and exaggerate
violent phenomena with a high news value. The German conservative
opposition has used the terrorism issue systematically to pressure the
social-democratic government away from its original reform course
into a law-and-order direction. The issue of terrorism has, in the fight
between governing and opposition party, received additional media
coverage above the one directly attributable to the terroristic incidents.

Similar processes to those that led to extensive anti-terroristic legis-
lation in the German Federal Republic have taken place in other
countries. In the last decade no less than fifty-three states have enacted
anti-terrorist measures.[27] Unable to deal a decisive blow at the insurgent terrorists themselves, governments have often limited or completely
prohibited media coverage of such incidents (see pp. 148–150). During
incidents of terrorism, especially when hostages were involved, governments have had to bargain under a glare of publicity with insurgent
terrorists as if they were equal partners. Public opinion in such cases
takes a strong interest in the fate of the hostages and it takes a tough
government to dare to go against public pressure to save the hostages
at almost any price, including giving in to the terrorists. Richard
Clutterbuck has written that 'The strongest single factor which leads
governments to give way to terrorists, internationally and internally, is
television....Governments can only stand firm in so far as they are able
to carry public opinion with them'.[28] There seems to be some truth in
this as far as the few remaining democratic governments are concerned,
although we know of no empirical study which would back up this
claim.

Since public opinion is largely formed by the mass media, governments try to win the media over to their view, either by force or
persuasion. As the strategy of the insurgent terrorists is also based on
having the media on their side, a struggle about media control develops.
For the terrorists it is sufficient that the media emphasize their auto-
nomy from the state, that they report fully the news which *they* are
making. Television with its concentration on emotions rather than
intellect, on action rather than thought, on happenings rather than
issues, on shock rather than explanation, on persons rather than
ideas,[29] is, in this regard, of special value to the terrorists. With some
exaggeration, Brian Crozier has said: 'Media publicity tends, very often,

to favor the terrorist side because of the drama that they represent.... This is not a reflection on the people who are involved in television. It is the character of the medium itself.'[30] Governments therefore often complain that the media enhance terrorists. Such has been the case, for instance, in the Report of the Gardiner Committee (1975) on measures to deal with terrorism in Northern Ireland. This British government committee held that the media had given credence to ill-founded allegations against the security forces, encouraged terrorist activity by giving publicity to its leaders and given, by sensationalized reporting of violent incidents, a false glamour to these events.[31] Such government charges, however, are usually unsubstantiated and so far there is no empirical research that could unequivocally provide a direct statistical correlation between media coverage and terrorism.[32] That does not, however, mean that a functional relationship is not likely, as we shall see in a later section of this study (pp. 125–137).

The influence of the media, especially television, on the outbreak of social unrest, including insurgent terrorism, probably goes deeper than this alone. In Northern Ireland, for instance, television started to make a social impact in the late 1960s when the monopoly of the BBC was challenged by commercial television and when enough television sets had been sold to create a mass audience. This discrepancy between the audience's own reality and the affluence portrayed as typical on television probably helped to kindle discontent with the status quo among many of the deprived. While a majority of the audience might have been narcoticized into a passive consuming attitude by the visual material offered, a minority reacted differently. The British journalist Robin Day has noticed that 'Television brought (promises of change) with increasing impact into the lonely cottages and the shabby backstreets of Northern Ireland. It opened windows onto a broader view of the world; it helped stir a challenge to blinkered bigotry and traditional intolerance....'[33] It is perhaps more than a coincidence that racial violence broke out massively in South Africa in 1976, the year television began to operate.[34] The unrest in Iran that led to a successful revolution was, among other things, triggered off by the television pictures of the demonstrations against the Shah when he visited Washington in mid-November 1977.[35] The outbreak of guerrilla warfare in the highlands of Peru in the early 1960s has also been attributed to the widespread appearance of the transistor radio in the region.[36]

In part, government concern about the media's role in terrorism is but a reflection of a general uneasiness with the media as an alternative power system in modern societies that cannot be fully controlled.

Outside Western democracies government control of the media is still or again near total and even in Western societies the influence of government is often great. Charles de Gaulle said many times that whoever controlled television in France would control the country.[37] It is only logical that this works both ways. It is probably more than coincidental that in Spain the former director of state television, Adolfo Suárez, ultimately became the successor to General Franco as head of state. As the authority of the mass media has grown, political authority in democratic countries has, it would seem, declined.[38] Increasingly politics is made in the media, rather than in parliaments. The media promise immediate redress for public causes, while bureaucratic governments work more slowly. Extra-parliamentary civil actions aimed at the media, which have become increasingly frequent since the early 1960s, seem to testify to that. In this regard many terroristic acts are only a culmination of this trend. Writing about the premises of civil actions in the 'Supermedia Age', one author has noted that those premises involve:

1. the commission of a violent and/or illegal act to
2. attract (especially TV) notice, thereby
3. making a direct appeal to public opinion, shortcircuiting the normal government authorities to negotiate grievances in full view.[39]

Such actions can galvanize public attention to a controversial issue much more effectively than could a parliamentary commission of inquiry. The media's ability to produce significant public opinion changes[40] is, for governments not in full control of the media, an increasing source of concern. In times of crises media control is something few governments seem to be able to do without. In any coup d'etat the broadcasting stations are among the most fought for places. In countries with high incidences of insurgent terrorism the media tend to become a battleground; they lose their status of social mirror to become fortresses to be taken, weapons to be utilized, allies to be won or enemies to be divided, as Yves de la Haye has put it.[41]

EFFECTS ON THE PUBLIC

Insurgent terrorist violence is mainly of two kinds. The first kind is discriminate, focused on the power holders in society. Depending on the degree to which the power holders have alienated themselves from the public, acts of terrorism against them will be more or less welcomed or at least excused by segments of the public. On other occasions insurgent terrorists choose a strategy of indiscriminate random violence where the masses' support is not sought by punishing their (alleged) oppressors but by making the masses more afraid of the terrorists than of the power holders, thereby converting them to the terrorist side not by inspiring them with hope but with fear. In practice, however, the distinction between focused (discriminate) and random (indiscriminate) insurgent terrorist violence is more vague. The public's reaction to violence against itself and violence against its rulers probably differs, although leaders will of course try to portray violence directed against them as violence directed against the whole of society. In both cases the public will feel the impact of the government's reaction to insurgent terrorism in terms of sharper controls, frequent arrests, breaches of the private sphere, possible extra-legal governmental activities, and so on. At least those insurgent terrorists who practise discriminate violence hope that the masses will attribute these inconveniences to the other side.

Since few people have direct contact and experience with terrorists, the large majority will get its understanding of the terrorist violence from the mass media. In order to ascertain the effects of the media portrayal of insurgent terrorism on the public, these effects should be weighed against the intentions of the terrorists. The difference between intended and actual effects would then be a measure of the effectiveness of a campaign of terrorism. We know of no research that has been conducted along these lines either in regard to discriminate or to indiscriminate terrorist violence. Such research could of course best be carried out by terrorists themselves. It should be vital for them to know whether their campaigns serve the purposes intended. Given the disastrous consequences of some terrorist campaigns for the terrorists themselves and the people they wanted to liberate, such knowledge might have a cooling effect on many dangerous 'dreamers of the absolute', as Marx called the terrorists.[42] There is reason to believe that insurgent terrorism has many unwanted effects for the terrorists themselves as well as for others. Partly this is a consequence of the fact that terrorism is an extremely crude instrument to persuade people either by fear or hope. The insurgent terrorist messages are transported to the public mainly by the media and the message is thereby almost invariably abbreviated, distorted or even transformed. The victim of terrorism as main message generator may mean one thing to the terrorists (e.g. capitalist exploiter), another to the media (well-respected

businessman and philanthropist) and various things to different segments of the public (family father, church-goer, self-made man, etc.).
The recipients of the message might misinterpret it or competing events
might throw a different light on it.[43] In short, the message sent is
almost never the message received. Furthermore, the public has a
learning capacity. One terrorist act might have one set of effects,
further such acts, however, might have different effects since the public
attitude might in the meantime have changed as a reaction to the prior
act.

The news retention rate of the public also plays a role. Research has
shown that most people can recount little of the news they have just
consumed. The average newspaper reader, it has been found, retains
only about 10 percent of the political news he reads. It is likely that
television, appealing to two senses simultaneously, is more penetrating.
Its sleeper effects, due partly to the subconscious absorbtion of television images, are still insufficiently understood but might be substantial.[44] However, it does not seem unreasonable to assume that
terroristic news, because of the human interest it generates, is retained
at a higher rate than 'normal' news. The net effect would be that
terrorism achieves an even higher prominence in the public's mind
than it already achieves in the public media.[45]

It is highly likely that the public identifies primarily with the victim
of terroristic violence, at any rate when the moral status of the victim
is not lower than the one of the terrorists. Otherwise the fear acts of
terrorism are able to generate among the public would be difficult to
explain. This identification with the victims of terrorism is also strongly
fostered by the media themselves since it tends to increase the
audience.[46] The televised funerals of the armed guards killed during
the kidnapping of Schleyer and Moro in Germany and Italy were said
to alienate not only the general public but also student radicals from
the RAF and the BR.[47] Such publicity, one is tempted to argue, is
counterproductive for the terrorists. Yet whether in fact this is so is
debatable. What might matter for the terrorists is not whether publicity
is positive or negative, but the amount of publicity alone. For them
much publicity – positive or negative – might be good, and little
publicity – positive or negative – bad. This corresponds to the two-
faced nature of social power. Power can be exercised either as power to
attract or as power to deter. Someone can have power because others
admire him and follow him as he does or represents something for
them, real or imaginary. Power can also be exercised negatively by fear,
in which case people refrain from doing something that might displease

the power holder. The terrorist's power is largely of the second kind. The arbitrariness of his violence, which is never absent even in discriminate terrorism, creates a widespread fear of victimization. In Western countries the public fear of becoming a victim of violence might already have been sharpened by the fact that so much of fictional media material is violent. The fictional world of television programmes contains, as George Gerbner has noted, more victims than perpetrators of violence.[48] This material might form a carrier-wave, creating a latent public anxiety on which the terrorists, with their real violence, cash in. 'If terror were not conveyed by the media', Gerbner holds, 'this fear of victimization would not be so pervasive.'[49]

Yet on the other hand it can also be argued that the public's familiarization with television violence has reduced its general respect for violence. Media-transmitted terrorist violence, at times, also seems to serve the same entertainment function that much of fictional violence apparently has for large segments of the public. Sites connected with acts of terrorism can become tourist sightseeing points. When Patty Hearst was kidnapped, tourist buses rolled daily to the mansion of the Hearst family in Hillsborough.[50] Acts of hostage-taking sometimes draw huge crowds when made known by the media.[51] This sort of curiosity might be a testimony to the desensitization of part of the public. How many members of the public reading, listening or watching terroristic news are using the real-life drama as entertainment is difficult to estimate, but it might be a substantial number. The borderline between the public's need to know and need for titillation might be fluid and largely unconscious. The public itself seems to be divided about the issue of media coverage of acts of terrorism. A Gallup poll, conducted in March 1977 in the United States, revealed that 50 percent thought such coverage of acts of terrorism was necessary while almost as many, 47 percent, thought that the coverage of such incidents was overemphasized.[52]

It is often asserted that terrorists want to produce chaos in society with their acts. This is a somewhat doubtful assumption in many cases, probably stemming from an equation of terrorists with anarchists and anarchy with chaos. Yet it is highly likely that insurgent terrorism, like state terrorism, weakens the bonds that hold society together and makes people distrustful of each other. While we possess no data that would confirm this empirically, analogies might be drawn from the social effects of political assassinations of highly-placed persons. Leonard Berkowitz and Jacqueline MacAulay have done a study on some effects of the assassination of President Kennedy. Their statistical analysis of data from forty US cities indicates that Kennedy's assassination was followed by unusual increases in the number of violent crimes.[53] A similar weakening of inhibitions to act socially has also been observed in another study by researchers from Columbia University. They conducted an experiment which involved the dropping of wallets on the street in order to see how honest people were. While the average return rate of the wallets was about 45 percent, the researchers noticed that none of the wallets dropped on 6 June 1968 were returned. This was the day after the assassination of Robert F. Kennedy had been made known by the media. The authors concluded that the bad news damaged whatever social bonds had caused people to return those lost wallets, that it demoralized people and made them act socially irresponsibly.[54] Whether terroristic violence also works this way is an open question. It is conceivable that it works in some cases in the opposite direction, strengthening public cohesiveness rather than weakening it.

In general, we cannot, with our present knowledge, answer the question about the effects on the general public of the media-reporting on terrorism. The public is heterogeneous with no unitary reaction. The media-reporting also varies considerably from medium to medium and from case to case. And terrorism is not a simple phenomenon, there are many varieties of it. The nature of the terrorists' adversary and the social context also co-determine the effects on the public. Yet so much is safe to say: the media can act as instruments of public terror in the service of insurgent terrorists by merely reporting the bad news which the terrorists create.

EFFECTS ON THE MEDIA

Terrorism is 'bad' news and messengers of bad news have been blamed for conveying it even before the mass media came into existence. One consequence of media reporting on insurgent terrorism has been that governments have often tried to suppress this type of news. In many countries the freedom of the press has, as we shall see in chapter 4, been further curbed due to reporting on acts of terrorism. The media have also been object of attack from the side of the terrorists themselves when they were displeased with the nature of the coverage of their acts. Journalists have been kidnapped, wounded and killed, publishing houses have been bombed and transmitters have been blown up. Many times the public media have had to comply with coercive requests to publish manifestoes of terrorists or they have had to comply with government requests to pass information on to terrorists. We have given illustrative examples of this in the preceding chapters. Here we will concentrate on two aspects not covered so far.

The high news value insurgent acts of terrorism enjoy with the Western mass media has not only led to a situation where other less violent news was dropped from the major news casts due to time restrictions. It has also had an effect on non-news programmes. The way the West German television chains switched programmes in response to the terroristic news in the Schleyer kidnapping case exemplifies this. In the period 6 September–20 October 1977 the Second German Television programme (ZDF – Zweites Deutsches Fernsehen) changed its programme fifteen times. The purpose of these changes was, as the ZDF pointed out, to prevent the originally scheduled programmes receiving an inadequate reception with the audience. But what is an inadequate reception? After the eighty-six hostages were liberated in Mogadishu, a soccer game was scheduled for the next day. 117 telephone callers to the ZDF found that a soccer programme lacked dignity in these circumstances, while seventy-one callers asked why there had been some delay in broadcasting the soccer game. In the whole period about 8,000 phone calls from the public were received by the ZDF, 1,300 of which dealt with aspects relating to terrorism. About one thousand calls were complaints about programme changes while some 300 complained that programmes had not been changed under the impact of terrorism.[55] When shortly after the Mogadishu hostage liberation the killing of Schleyer became news, the ZDF followed it up with a short piece of classical music before changing back to the scheduled sports programme. On the other hand it had dropped the scheduled documentary 'The Death of Camilo Torres', which dealt critically with the participation of the Columbian priest in rural guerrilla warfare. Another television chain, ARD (Arbeitsgemeinschaft der öffentlichrechtlichen Rundfunkanstalten der Bundesrepublik Deutschland – Working Community of the Public Law Broadcasting Corporations of the German Federal Republic, responsible for the First German Television programme), also cancelled this documentary. After the Mogadishu hostage liberation ARD dropped a documentary on the problem of alcoholism and 'celebrated' the event with an old movie.[56] A third television chain, the WDR (Westdeutscher Rundfunk – West German Broadcasting) had during the forty-five days of tension replaced light entertainment programmes with serious music and serious movies. Special news programmes in this period covered declarations of the German parliament on the issue of terrorism and depicted the funeral ceremonies of the assassinated guards of Schleyer.

While the programme makers rationalized these changes as following the mood of the public, it is arguable that they also helped to create this mood or at any rate reinforce it. To a considerable extent the news media, already handicapped by the governmental news embargo, lost their information function and became instruments for creating and rhythmicizing collective emotions. Given the volatile state of public opinion it would have been wiser if the German mass media had tried to act as a counterpole, bringing sober and up-to-date information, thereby lessening the degree of threat to the nation. The newscasts were far from doing this. News that was twenty-four or even forty-eight hours old and already overtaken by events was broadcast as if it was still relevant.[57] In opinion programmes the German media, like the Italian ones in the case of the Moro kidnapping,[58] did not dare to discuss calmly whether it was really unavoidable to sacrifice the chief hostage for reasons of state. What remains amazing is that the celebrated press freedom in Western democracies can, in times of even minor crises (minor to civil or interstate war), shrink to something that is not far removed from the state of affairs in countries where the government controls the media. How this process works is far from being understood. Our knowledge of the media is largely based, as Yves de la Haye has pointed out, on their study in times of relative tranquility.[59]

In discussing terrorism's effects on the media themselves, we have so far concentrated on the negative side. But bad news has, as the journalistic adage 'Bad News is Good News' indicates, also positive aspects for the media. The drama of terrorism increases public interest in media reporting which leads to higher circulation figures or greater audience ratings, as we have noted earlier. And when the drama is over, the media often try to give the terrorist story a second running by turning it into a documentary, movie or instant book. That is, if the terroristic incident has been bloody enough to warrant the commercial risk. In the case of the Hanafi incident this was obviously not the case. Said one prominent publisher of instant books: 'Had the Hanafis chopped off a single head there would have been a market for a quick journalistic book.'[60] The exercise was well worth while in the case of the Patty Hearst kidnapping. A whole series of books (eleven so far) and three movies saw the light on this topic and there have been rumours that Patty Hearst's father also hopes to make some money with the story in order to recoup at least part of the two million dollars he spent in vain with the food-giveaway programme that was meant to buy her freedom from captivity.[61]

Almost as much post-event publicity as was given to the Patty Hearst story was given to the doings of the Charles Manson 'family'. This strange sect from the US West coast, consisting mainly of a number of homeless girls devoted to a charismatic leader, made its entry into the media with a series of bizarre acts of violence. One of Manson's followers, Lynette Fromme, was reported to have sought publicity for a Manson manifesto with the San Francisco office of the news agency UPI. She was turned down and told to return when she had some 'hard news'. Her subsequent assassination attempt on President Gerald Ford in September 1975 was 'hard news' and she made all the front pages. *Time* magazine secured her memoirs and announced this in the New York papers under the title 'Exclusive Photos and Passages from Squeaky Fromme's Unpublished Memoirs... the World of the Social Misfit and Psychological Cripple...Fascinating, Penetrating Reading in this week's *Time*'.[62] CBS, one of the three major US television networks, cashed in on the Manson story with *Helter Skelter*, a dramatization of the 'family''s killings, which was broadcast in prime time. One critic wrote about it: '*Helter Skelter* was well produced, and therefore even more dangerous. One of the girls, in a breathy whisper, describes to a cellmate the killing of Sharon Tate, complete with the stabbings, the blood, and the possibility of ripping her nearly full-term baby from her body; the scene is overall as sexy – and as horrifying – as any ever on the screen.....'[63]

The movie industry, like the book industry, has taken terroristic events for fictionalized replay. One movie favourable to the kidnappers has been the Costa Gavras film *State of Siege* in which the abduction and killing of the US police advisor in Uruguay, Dan Mitrione, by the Tupamaros was given a sympathetic treatment.[64] More common have been movies that celebrate the successful counteractions against insurgent terrorists. The Israeli Entebbe raid has, apart from forming the basis for several books, also served as a theme for three movies. When one of them ('Unternehmen Entebbe') was shown in the theatres in Germany in 1977, it triggered off three attempts of (fire-) bombing cinemas in Aachen, Düsseldorf and Hannover.[65] This sequence of events, terrorism – movie about terrorism – more terrorism, warrants the question of whether the media are not directly or indirectly (co-) responsible for the present wave of insurgent terrorism. To this question we will address ourselves in the last section of this chapter.

MEDIA-INDUCED CONTAGION OF
TERRORIST VIOLENCE

'Violence breeds violence', an old adage says. Does the media portrayal of terrorist violence also produce more of the same? Before we discuss this question some general remarks about the state of research on violence and the media are in place.

In the study of media effects, no single aspect has received an attention comparable to the one bestowed on the possible nexus between media portrayal of violence and the occurrence of aggression in real life. In general, the study of media effects has, in the more than fifty years of its being a topic for social scientists, gone through three phases. The study of violent effects has followed this general trend except in the first phase when it was not yet a topic. In the first phase the social effects of the mass media were, in the light of the war propaganda of the First World War, judged to be substantial and capable of shaping beliefs, attitudes and behaviour even against personal resistance. The second phase of media research, spanning from about 1940 to the early 1960s, concentrated initially mainly on voting behaviour studies following election campaigns. Findings held that the mass media — radio, press and movies — were relatively impotent and ineffective agents of influence.[66] As far as crime and violence were concerned the media were found to be no direct causal agents but at best reinforcers of the existing individual tendencies of the members of the audience.[67] It was even postulated that the portrayal of violence in the media had a positive 'cathartic effect' in the sense that people could get rid of their own aggressive urges by living them out in fantasy with the help of fictional violence. This hypothesis, for a time strongly pushed by experts from the interested media themselves, has received minimal empirical support and is no longer seriously accepted among researchers[68] In the third phase of research, which is now about fifteen years old and heavily influenced by the emergence of television as a social force, the importance of media effects is judged to be much higher again. At the same time the range of questions asked by researchers has passed beyond merely focusing on attitudinal and behavioural changes induced by the mass media. The impact of the media on knowledge formation, on setting the agenda for public discussion as well as the uses of the media by various segments of the public have become major areas of investigation.[69] In regard to the question of what the impact of media portrayal of violence is, research of the third phase partly moved away from asking the direct question whether violence portrayal produces aggression. Attention is also given to the production of exaggerated fears of victimization which heavy doses of exposure to violent television material can cause. George Gerbner, one of the leading communication researchers, holds that 'The most pervasive effect of broadcast violence is not the imitation of violence, but the spreading of intimidation, of the fear of victimization'.[70] There seems to be also some medical evidence that points in this direction. A survey among the members of the American Medical Association reported that 41 percent of the physicians 'suspected' that some of their patients' behavioural or physical problems might be related to television violence. Another 14 percent of them was even more certain and believed this to be the case.[71]

Recent research on the old question of media violence as cause of aggression has been carried out along three main lines. One school works with the 'arousal hypothesis' which holds that exciting media content (erotic, violent, humorous, etc.) can increase aggression if it is an appropriate response. The implication of this is that the exciting element in the portrayal of violence rather than the violence per se can effect aggression among the audience. The behaviour outcome does not have to be violent but other classes of behaviour may be chosen after viewing violence. The corollary of this is that exciting nonviolent material may also produce a violent behaviour (e.g. a father excited by a televised soccer game hurting his child that disturbs his viewing pleasure by crying). The second major school works with the 'disinhibition hypothesis'. It holds that television violence, especially if it is rewarded, weakens the inhibition of the viewer to engage in similar behaviour and by implication increases his readiness to engage in interpersonal aggression. The third school, which is the most mature of the three, bases its thinking on a 'social learning' theory. It holds that ways of behaving are learned by observation not only of real performance but also of media-ted performance. In this way television violence can lead to the acquisition of aggressive responses which are imitated in appropriate situations in real life.[72] These three schools are complementary rather than exclusive. In our following discussion we will draw mainly from the 'disinhibition' and the 'social learning' schools of thought, trying to relate them to the field of terrorism and the media. We shall do this by dividing the question into three, based on the reasoning that three things are necessary for somebody to engage in violence: (1) the unlearning of possible inhibitions against the use of violence acquired during socialization; (2) the acquisition of 'know-how' about the use of violence (e.g. by learning from models); and

(3) a motivation to act violently. These will be discussed in this order.

Unlearning Inhibitions Against the Use of Violence — The Possible Contribution of Fictional Media Violence to Terrorism

In wars violence is used as a means to enforce compliance to the demands of the opposing parties. To soften up the resistance of the enemy certain promises are usually made to the effect that the life of the adversary will be spared if he complies. In this way soldiers of the enemy are offered the opportunity to capitulate, whereupon they will be treated humanely under conditions laid down in the Geneva Convention. Although the practice is often less humane than the theory, these rules exist. In terrorism the victim cannot capitulate and save his life through demand compliance since the demands are made not to him but to a third party. Such disrespect for the individual which we find in terrorism can, as we shall see, also be found in fictional media violence. Is it possible that the treatment of victims in media violence has influenced terrorists? While we cannot answer this question here, we would like to present some material that sketches the problem.

An act of violence consists of two things: the act of aggression and the act of suffering from the consequences of aggression. In violence portrayals in the media emphasis is placed on the first aspect while the second is largely neglected. This is done for two reasons. One is that the aftermath of violence is long and the act of violence short. Given the time constraints which govern media programming it is logical that the long sufferings of the victim, the weeks in hospital, cannot be covered adequately while a shooting or stabbing takes only seconds to depict. The second reason for this imbalance between aggression and suffering is that showing the agony of the victim is unaesthetic and upsetting to the audience. Some years ago a British commercial television station tried to broadcast a realistic crime series ('Big Bread-winner Hog') in which pain and wounds were portrayed in true detail. This produced such a public outcry that the series had to be discontinued after one sequence.[73] The net effect of this imbalance seems to be that the television watcher cannot develop much sympathy with the victim.[74] This is reinforced by the fact that in fictional crime series the people who have to suffer most are usually 'bad guys' who 'deserve' injury or death.

In order to understand the impact of this distortion arising from the storytelling needs of the media one has to recall how massively the Western media and especially television use violence. Given the trend-setting role of the United States we will confine ourselves to this country. The average American child spends some 15,000 hours in front of the television set before he graduates at age eighteen after 11,000 hours of schooling. In this period he is not only exposed to several hundred thousand television commercials but also to some 18,000 killings and countless other acts of violence which the commercial sponsors finance.[75] This amount was still growing in 1977, the last year for which we have seen data.[76] Such exposure to violence does not end with the formative years. By the time an American reaches the age of sixty-five he will have spent 3,000 entire days, or more than eight years of his life, in front of a tube that feeds him with violence as main diet.[77] Given the fact that viewing habits and programme content in other countries are approximating those of the United States and that US crime series find a large market abroad,[78] the overall picture is likely to be only gradually but not substantially different elsewhere in the Western world.

Television programme makers often argue that violence is a real problem in society and that television has a duty to reflect what goes on in society. This recourse to the mirror function of the media is dishonest. Take the following example: it has been calculated that the average American policeman draws his gun three times in his entire career. This ratio finds absolutely no reflection among police officers in crime series who might draw their guns as many times within ten minutes.[79] The high viewing ratios of television violence programmes do indeed suggest that the viewers like what they get. But they do not suggest that they get what they really like. Being brought up with this kind of television diet, they do not know real alternatives.[80] A drug addict after all also likes what he gets, without it being in his own best interests, and television watching is in some ways comparable to the psychology (though not the physiology) of addiction. When in early 1979 the French television personnel of all three channels went on strike for several weeks, social scientists noticed that the majority of the public, deprived of normal television programmes, reacted like drug addicts with irritation and nervousness and other withdrawal symptoms.[81] Finally, to say that much of television violence is fictional does not excuse it. The public's ability to distinguish between real and fictional television material is limited. There was, for instance, a fictional series, 'Marcus Welby, M.D.', in which the leading character played a physician. The actor received, during the first five years of the programme, no less than 250,000 letters from the public, mostly with requests for medical advice.[82]

Fictional violence is just as likely to be imitated, as we shall see in the following section. A strange kind of schizophrenia seems to affect television producers. On the one hand, they suggest to the sponsors of advertisements that television has massive effects, that the public copies consuming behaviour suggested in alluring commercials. On the other hand, they tend to discard the possibility that the public learns the lessons of television violence which they use to attract a large audience. It seems more sensible to assume, as Nicholas Johnson does, that 'all television is educational television'.[83] If this is so, then what is the lesson? The ethical codes and traditional socializing agencies of Western democracies (school, church, family) teach citizens nonviolence. Yet what has become the most influential unofficial socializer, television, is constantly producing violent programmes. In this clash of norms between traditional humanistic Western values and market-oriented capitalist values, the first have lost ground. Social inhibitions against the use of violence are being eroded and the tolerance of aggression tends to increase.[84] Since this erosion process is gradual it does not easily lend itself to short-term measurement and longitudinal studies in research on media effects are rare.[85]

But such effects of habituation to violence and desensitization towards it are likely to be substantial.[86] Already from an early age children get accustomed to violence without simultaneously learning what its consequences are. Television comic series, for instance, may depict how a 'good guy' smashes a person with a rock, whereupon the victim reinflates like a balloon in the next scene to regain his original form. The humorous connotations of such scenes may ultimately not have the effect of harmlessness but facilitate the acceptance of violence as normal, inconsequential and legitimate.[87] Various studies have pointed out that children who watch violent programmes tend to believe in the legitimacy of violence as a problem-solver and are more willing to resort to it when confronted with a difficult situation.[88] And that also seems to be the lesson which violent television programmes teach to adults. The staff of the American National Commission on the Causes and Prevention of Violence concluded in 1968 that from television 'the overall impression is that violence, employed as a means of conflict resolution or acquisition of personal goals, is a predominant characteristic of life'.[89]

Most of what has been said so far refers to fictional violence portrayals. Not enough study has, to our knowledge, been done about the effects of real violence portrayed in the media. But what little evidence there is in the field of real violence suggests that the portrayal of realistic and even legitimate forms of violence (like self-defence) might have detrimental effects as well.[90] Like fictional violence portrayals real ones also tend to shy away from depicting the full misery of the victim, which can favour the aggressor. Potential aggressors among the audience might in this way acquire a particularly low regard for their own victims. It is, however, important to point out that this is mere speculation. We know of no research that has looked into the media experience of terrorists. The learning of aggression against people the terrorist does not even know beforehand, the unlearning of inhibitions against such behaviour, are probably not only, and in the case of organized terrorists, not even primarily taught by the mass (and underground) media. The terrorist movement and the lessons it may learn from its political opponent are probably more powerful socializers. But criminal quasi-terrorists, who do not systematically engage in terroristic violence, might well have learned their main lesson from the media. Even for some professional terrorists this might hold true. They too may have been heavily exposed to the violent media material which might have undermined their general regard for human lives. We have in this section only been able to raise this question, but it seems to us that research in this area is warranted.

Learning Terrorism from the Media

Nobody is born a terrorist; the tactics of terrorism have to be learned. In this section we intend to demonstrate that the public media play an important role in giving the potential terrorist the know-how he needs. In contrast to the preceding section, there is some empirical material that supports this thesis. The theoretical foundation for this section is provided by the observational learning theory. Its central thesis is that a person observing another person, with whom he identifies to some degree, is likely to imitate the behaviour of the other if this behaviour is rewarding to the model.[91] Much of the power of media programmes stems from the easy identification possibilities with heroes and heroines which are presented to the audience. Movie stars can start fashion trends and even suicide waves. When Marilyn Monroe committed suicide there was a 12 percent increase in suicides the following month in the United States, and even in England and Wales the increase was 10 percent. The rise of suicides is in such cases closely linked to the amount of publicity.[92] Before we look into the question of whether the same is true with regard to particular acts of terrorism, some general remarks about television violence and aggression subsequent to watching it are in order.

Among the public there has never been much doubt about a direct link between media portrayal of violence and crime. A British National Opinion Poll from 1971 showed, for instance, that 70 percent of the respondents thought that press coverage of crime increased criminal tendencies.[93] In the United States a Gallup Poll, conducted in 1977, found that 70 percent of the public believed that there is a relationship between televised violence and actual crime.[94] What seems evident to the public is less certain to social scientists. A British study which analyzed the media consumption patterns of juvenile delinquents concluded that 'the mass media, except just possibly in the case of a very small number of pathological individuals, are never the sole cause of delinquent behaviour. At most, they may play a contributory role, and that a minor one.'[95] On the other hand, one American study, investigating one hundred young delinquents in prison, found that sixty-three of them reported that they have imitated characters seen on television. Twenty-two said that they had tried criminal techniques seen on television. Another twenty-two said that they had contemplated committing crimes seen on television. Seven of the hundred said they had stolen things seen on television.[96]

Scientific studies on the nexus between media violence and aggression have been prolific and the results have often been contradictory. Depending on the definitions used and the methodologies applied such studies have 'proven' just about any proposition in which the researchers or, perhaps more important, their financial sponsors, were interested. Yet it is unmistakable that the weight of the evidence leans towards the conclusion that there is such a nexus. In the late 1960s and early 1970s the US Surgeon General sponsored twenty-three research projects. Although the media industry had a strong influence on the choice of researchers (of twenty-nine names proposed by a group of communication researchers only one was accepted),[97] the result was not very positive for the concerned television networks. Cater and Strickland have summarized the central finding of the Report to the Surgeon General:

What was impressive to the (Surgeon General's) Advisory Committee was that when researchers measured relationships between dozens of variables in many settings by several methodologies, the presence of one variable (the child's viewing of violent television sequences) was associated most consistently with a second variable (the child's subsequent tendency to act more aggressively). The Committee members were not overly impressed with the statistical significance or the accounting for variance of any single study. They were impressed with the central finding of so many studies.[98]

Another author, surveying a larger sample of studies in 1975, wrote:

One hundred and forty-six articles in behavioral science journals, representing 50 studies involving 10,000 children and adolescents from every conceivable background, all showed that violence viewing produces increased aggressive behavior in the young....[99]

Three years later two British authors, discussing a further sample of studies, concluded:

The evidence is fairly unanimous that aggressive acts new to the subject's repertoire of responses, as well as acts already well established, can be evoked by the viewing of violent scenes portrayed on film, TV or in the theatre. There is ample evidence that media violence increases viewer aggression...It is particularly convincing, in our view, that different methods of investigation all point to an association between viewing violence and subsequent aggression. Admittedly many studies have major or minor methodological faults, but these tend to cancel out in view of the fact that different studies have different strengths and different weaknesses.[100]

The fact that in the majority of studies children and adolescents served as test material might raise objections. Children are after all imitators almost by definition. It is also true that we do not know enough about the different effects of violent media material on different personality types.[101] It is often held that only the lunatic fringe might be induced by the media to imitate anti-social behaviour portrayed in the media. Even if this were so, the size of the lunatic fringe is sufficiently large to warrant attention. In Great Britain, for instance, it has been calculated that 1 in 9 women and 1 in 14 men at one time or other in their lives have to be treated in a mental hospital. In the United States it has been estimated in 1971 that 'at least ten million of our young people under twenty-five are thought to suffer from mental and emotional disturbances'.[102] More recently the World Health Organization (WHO) has estimated that about 10 percent of the world population has to be judged to be mentally ill. That amounts to more than 400 million people. Television programmes in major countries are today often watched simultaneously by twenty or more million people.

A lunatic fringe of 10 percent is in such a context an awful lot of people. Many of them might already have lost the inhibition against acting violently, others might also have a personal motive to do so, some have both and all that is needed is a model which they can copy. The media can provide it.

An act of violence, real or fictional, can, when portrayed in the media, lead to an imitative act. The imitative act, in turn, can, when reported by the media, lead to more imitations. In this way reporting can lead to a media-fostered contagion.[103] Almost a century ago the French sociologist Gabriel Tarde, discussing the after-effects of the Jack the Ripper murders, in which lurid news stories about his crimes inspired a series of such crimes, spoke of 'suggesto-imitative assaults'. Tarde postulated that epidemics of crime 'follow the line of the telegraph'.[104] In more recent times such contagion has also been observed with urban riots in the United States in the 1960s, where television rather than the telegraph played the linking role. One US Senate Committee noted that other riots were sparked and ignited in cities within television range of the large city where the pictures originated. The Detroit riots were rapidly followed by riots in smaller surrounding towns and the same was true with the Newark riots.[105] In a study on the Detroit riots one author suggested that television played a role in spreading the *idea of rioting* along with *instruction on how to riot.*[106] A third study showed that 95 percent of the people who watched rioting scenes on television did not go out to participate in them. Only 5 percent went into the streets of Chicago as a consequence of the newscasts. Five percent, however, is a large number of people in a city the size of Chicago.[107]

What applies to rioting might also be true for terrorism. A sizeable segment of public opinion, at any rate, is quite convinced that there is a nexus. A Gallup opinion poll conducted in late March 1977 (after the Hanafi incident) in the United States, reported that almost two-thirds of the public (64 percent) thought that detailed media coverage of acts of terror does encourage similar acts. Less than a third (27 percent) held the opposite point of view.[108] One researcher surveying the opinions of police and correction (prison) officers found an even larger support for this view among a sample of which more than two-thirds had experience of handling a hostage situation. In answer to the question whether media coverage of hostage situations encouraged further hostage situations, 76 percent of the police officers and 70 percent of the correction officers answered affirmatively.[109] The degree of encouragement probably also depends on the success the model action has had. It seems plausible to assume that successful actions are more frequently imitated. On the other hand, would-be terrorists are also likely to learn from the mistakes of others.

In our own survey fourteen out of twenty-six respondents believed that live television coverage of acts of terrorism encourages terrorism. In the case of radio coverage only twelve answered with yes and in the case of newspaper coverage only six believed that there was a nexus between coverage and further such acts. Seven of our respondents said that they had (personal) knowledge of situations where media-reported acts of terrorism led to imitative acts. Our first three questions were in fact an attempt to replicate a larger survey conducted by Michael Sommer. Tables 3C–E summarize Sommer's findings.[110]

The notion that terrorism is contagious is, as the above opinions illustrate, quite widespread, even among parties interested in the contrary. Politicians share this concern. Walter Scheel, the former president of the German Federal Republic, expressed it with the words that 'unless this flame (of terrorism) is stamped out in time, it will spread like a bush fire over the world'.[111] Scheel, however, did not refer to the media's role and this link is indeed not the only one possible. One study analyzing the diffusion of international terrorism found that 'In 78 of the 88 cases of new countries experiencing transnational terrorism after 1968, the country shared a border with a State which had previously experienced incidents'. The author found a contagious process at work within the regions he examined.[112] But that, in itself, does not prove that the mass media act as diffusers. The underground press also plays a role. It might also be possible that groups diffuse insurgent terrorism to other countries either by moving themselves around the world spreading terrorism, or by personally persuading local groups to engage in such acts.[113] For these types of diffusion the cooperation of the mass media is not necessary. It seems to be unquestionable that part of the spread of contemporary insurgent terrorism has to be attributed to such extra-media processes. But not all, and perhaps not even a majority of all acts of insurgent terrorism can be explained in this way.

The media play, in our view, an important role in the diffusion of terrorism. However, it is difficult to support this notion empirically. Quite correctly it has been pointed out that we lack hard data which would allow us to correlate mass media coverage and terrorism.[114] What we are going to offer in the following pages amounts – except for the last of the ten cases cited – to little more than what is called 'anecdotal evidence'. That this evidence is not stronger, however, is in

Table 3C
Answers to the Question:
'Do you believe live television coverage of terrorist acts encourages terrorism?'

	Police Chiefs	TV News Directors	Newspaper Editors
	%	%	%
Yes	93	35	43
No	0	35	33
Other	7	24	24
Don't Know/ No Answer	0	6	0

Table 3D
Answers to the Question:
'Do you believe live radio coverage of terrorist acts encourages terrorism?'

	Radio News Directors
	%
Yes	36
No	42
Other	21
Don't Know	1

Table 3E
Answers to the Question:
'Do you believe newspaper coverage of terrorist acts encourages terrorism?'

	Newspaper Editors
	%
Yes	29
No	57
Other	14

our view not the fault of the assumption but a reflection of the under-developed state of research. Some of the ten cases which we are going to present are not terroristic in the sense of our definition, and of those which are, some do not refer to insurgent terrorism, yet all are, in our view, examples of media-fostered contagion.

Case No. 1

On 4 April 1968 Martin Luther King was killed in Memphis, Tennessee. A week later, on 11 April 1968, the twenty-four-year-old house-painter Erwin Bachmann attempted to assassinate the German student leader Rudi Dutschke. Bachmann, who was strongly anti-communist, had acted alone, belonging to no political group. Upon interrogation he said that he had been inspired to his deed by the assassination of Rev. Martin Luther King, Jr. Dutschke suffered brain injury but survived the attempt. Bachmann, who had a criminal record, was found to be mentally subnormal. He had attempted suicide twice before this deed and succeeded in killing himself in 1970.[115]
Discussion: Bachmann learned about the King assassination from the media. Had the event in Memphis taken place some hundred years earlier the time span between the events in Memphis and Berlin would have been greater due to the slow speed of ships. The second assassination would probably not have taken place at all, since the cue quality of a newspaper report might have been too low to trigger off an imitative assault. The gripping television images of the King assassination, which Bachmann is likely to have seen, might have had this cue quality.

Case No. 2

In the early 1970s the Argentine Montoneros 'kidnapped' the corpse of General Pedro Aramburu from his grave and demanded in exchange for the body that the body of Eva Peron be returned from Spain. Within weeks Burmese terrorists removed the body of former UN Secretary-General U Thant from its crypt and used it for coercive bargaining with the Burmese government. On 2 March 1978 criminals abducted the body of Charlie Chaplin in Switzerland in order to obtain a ransom from his family.[116]
Discussion: The peculiar nature of the act and the geographical distance between these events suggest that the media were the agent that provided the bodysnatchers with a model, at least in the second incident.

Case No. 3

On 5 September 1975 Lynette Alice Fromme attempted to assassinate

President Gerald Ford in Sacramento, California. 'Squeaky' Fromme's deed received enormous publicity. On 22 September 1975 another woman, Sara Jane Moore, attempted to assassinate President Ford in San Francisco. The publicity given to both attempts produced a flood of threats to assassinate Ford, according to the Secret Service.[117]

Discussion: The proximity of the two attempts in time and location, as well as the fact that both would-be assassins were women, suggests contagion. Psychiatrists have suggested that the presence of television cameras might serve as a stimulus for such Herostratic deeds.[118]

Case No. 4

In July 1974 a Committee of the US House of Representatives debated the impeachment of President Nixon before live television. A bomb threat was received which necessitated the interruption of the hearing and a search for possible explosives. This threat was reported to a television audience numbering millions of people. In the following period, seven more bomb threats were registered, 'all apparently generated by the instant, nationwide exposure given the initial threat', as FBI-director Clarence Kelley suggested.[119]

Discussion: The linkage by the media seems fairly obvious. Terrorism can be as cheap as ten cents if the phone call is local. The debate interruption, which can be seen on television, is an instant gratification. Hoax calls following a real crime are a major problem. For obvious reasons, they are, however, rarely reported in the media, or, rather, to the media.

Case No. 5

The movie *A Clockwork Orange*, portraying a youth gang which attacked citizens randomly, has led to the formation of street gangs dressed in the same fashion as in the movie. Several crimes appear to have been modelled after this movie. In July 1973, for instance, a young British schoolboy was tried for murder after he had viciously battered to death an old tramp, acting out in considerable detail scenes from the movie. A Scottish advocate, Herbert S. Kerrigan, recalled three murders in 1975 where the crimes were also triggered off by seeing *A Clockwork Orange*. In the United States, Arthur Bremer, the man who made an assassination attempt on Governor George Wallace, decided to commit a crime after seeing the same movie, as his diary revealed. His first target was Richard Nixon; later he switched to George Wallace, whom he crippled.[120]

Discussion: Cinema movies usually reach a smaller audience than television movies. The size of the screen and the greater explicity of movie violence, however, might stimulate as many from a smaller audience as television does among a bigger audience.

Case No. 6

On 22 August 1972 two gunmen took several hostages among the employees of the Chase Manhattan Bank in Brooklyn. One of the hostage-takers demanded the release of his lover from hospital and a plane to bring them with her out of the country. The FBI killed one of them and managed to overpower the second. This incident formed the basis of the movie *Dog Day Afternoon*. In October 1975 one Ray Olsen took ten hostages in a storefront bank in Greenwich Village, after he had seen this movie. He demanded the release of Patty Hearst and three other SLA members as well as ten million dollars. Finally he gave himself up after a police negotiator had suggested to him that he would be covered live on the eleven o'clock news. On 15 February 1975 two hundred prison inmates in the Concord Reformatory in Massachusetts were shown *Dog Day Afternoon*. After the showing between sixty and eighty inmates began to riot, causing damage of at least one million dollars.[121]

Discussion: From the multitude of real-life events the media pick out some for re-enactment before an audience many times bigger than the one directly witnessing the original event. By making certain experiences known to millions of people, these experiences are more likely to be reproduced again in real life than those which received no media blow-up.

Case No. 7

On 11 July 1974 two convicts in a basement cellblock of the US Courthouse in Washington, DC took hostages. On 13 July inmates from the city jail in nearby Baltimore, Maryland seized three hostages. On 14 July 1974 juvenile inmates seized four hostages in the same jail, after the first incident of the previous day had been solved peacefully. The same day a riot broke out in the Queen's House of Detention in New York City, whereby two guards were beaten and one guard was thrown from a fourth floor tier. Officials believed that the inmates who started the riot had heard news reports about the events in Baltimore and Washington.[122]

Discussion: The coincidence in settings (prisons) and the proximity in time suggest that these riots were triggered off by media reports.

Case No. 8

On 4 February 1974 Patricia Hearst, the daughter of the newspaper publisher William Randolph Hearst, was kidnapped in Berkeley, California, by members of the Symbionese Liberation Army. The case received enormous publicity and was followed by a series of kidnappings in the United States. On 20 February 1974 the editor of the *Atlanta Constitution* was abducted by the 'American Revolutionary Army'. It was demanded that all federal officers resign from office so that free elections could be held. But the kidnappers said that they were in the meantime prepared to release Reginald Murphy, the editor, for $ 700,000. After the money was handed over, the kidnappers, a husband-and-wife team, were arrested. They admitted to having taken their inspiration from the Hearst case. On 6 March 1974 an eight-year-old boy, John Calzadilla, was kidnapped on Long Island. His father, a tyre-company executive, paid $ 50,000 for his release. The next day the police arrested two Cubans who were charged with the crime. On 15 March 1974 the wife of a bank president, Mrs Gunnar Kronholm, was kidnapped in Minneapolis. Her husband had to pay $ 200,000 for her release. On 20 March 1974 a kidnapping attempt was made in London on Princess Anne and her husband. The single kidnapper carried a note in which he demanded $ 4.6 million 'in reparation' for victims of inflation and the Irish conflict, as well as for blacks and workers.[123]

Discussion: Acts of political terrorism that receive prominence in the media are often followed by imitative acts in which the political motive is weak or absent.

Case No. 9

In November 1966 the US television network NBC aired a suspense

drama *Doomsday Flight*. The movie's theme was an extortionist attempt
on an airline. A pressure-sensitive bomb had been placed on an aircraft
which would explode if the plane descended below a certain altitude.
The terrorist offered to disclose the exact location of the bomb on the
aircraft in exchange for money. Even before this television movie was
broadcast completely, one airline received an extortionist phone call
clearly modelled on this fictional scenario. Within a week twelve more
such calls were received. When the movie was shown in Canada in 1970
a similar phone call with an extortionist threat forced a British aircraft
to make an unscheduled landing on a high-altitude airfield. In 1971 the
movie was shown in Australia where it led to a successful extortion
which cost Quantas Airlines some $500,000. When the movie was
shown in Europe similar incidents occurred. In France a man who
claimed to have placed two bombs on a Paris-New York TWA flight
was arrested when he tried to pick up the ransom. *Doomsday Flight*
had been shown two weeks earlier on French television.[124]
Discussion: The peculiar extortionist device, the pressure-sensitive
bomb (real or alleged), used in these attempts links them to each other
and to the movie as diffusor. In this case it is fairly certain that the
media provided the know-how.

Case No. 10

Hijacking is one of the most spectacular phenomena and as such
especially attractive for imitators. Since the first recorded case of
hijacking in 1930 almost 600 attempts have been made whereby some
20,000 passengers have become hostages or captives. Most of the more
than 500 million passengers that use aircraft every year are searched
before they board an aircraft. The search is for weapons. Very little
research has been done about how hijackers got the idea to engage in
such an act. In our view the media play a prominent role in this. The
detailed style of media reporting can directly contribute to waves of
hijacking, as we shall demonstrate below in the case of parachute
hijackings.

In the history of hijacking three major waves can be discerned, each
bigger than the previous one. The first involved aircraft from Eastern
Europe in the early 1950s. These were all attempts to escape from
behind the Iron Curtain and they do not fall under our definition of
terrorism since the passengers were merely captives, not pawns. The
second wave was also an escape wave and involved mainly the United

States and Cuba in the late 1950s and early 1960s. A new wave started in 1968. The seizure of an El Al airliner in the summer of 1968 by Arab guerrillas marked the adoption of the hijacking technique for purposes of terrorism.[125] Soon other political groups as well as criminals took over hijacking for terrorism.[126] Albert Bandura has compared hijackings of US airliners with foreign airliners for the period 1947–1970. Except for the first wave, he found that the two curves paralleled quite closely.[127] This coincidence strongly suggests that contagion is at work. The year 1969 saw no less than seventy-one skyjacking attempts and the news about them produced contagion even in Eastern Europe. While no hijackings had been reported from behind the Iron Curtain for the period 1958–1968, the year following October 1969 saw no less than twelve attempts in Eastern Europe, seven of them successful.[128] These incidents occurred despite a very restrictive reporting style in the communist press. It is, however, likely that these hijackers were listening to foreign broadcasts. The Western media, at any rate, provided ample coverage to all attempts. The Minichiello case, for instance, in which a twenty-year-old Vietnam veteran singlehandedly hijacked a TWA flight from Los Angeles to Rome in November 1969, was treated like an Odyssey by some of the media. Ten days after the Minichiello exploit, a fourteen-year-old boy, David L. Booth, attempted to hijack a plane from Cincinatti to Sweden, armed only with a butcher knife. 'He had been reading and watching television about the (Minichiello) hijacking with interest all last week', his mother was quoted as saying.[129] David Hubbard, the psychiatrist who interviewed scores of hijackers, noted that they often kept scrapbooks of news clippings about other hijackings in order to learn how to do it.[130] In the following, we will discuss a sequence of twenty-seven hijackings where the role of the media appears to have been significant.

The parachute hijackings
1. On 12 November 1971 a twenty-six-year old Scotsman living in Canada, named Paul Joseph Cini, seized an Air Canada DC-8 en route from Calgari to Toronto. He had brought his own parachute and threatened to blow up the aircraft if he was not given money. He received $50,000. The crew managed to overpower the confused hijacker who at one stage mistook a life-saving ring for the parachute. This incident received considerable publicity in US newspapers.[131]
2. On 24 November 1971 a man with the alias D. B. Cooper hijacked a B-727 at Portland, Oregon, close to the Canadian border. He successfully extorted $200,000 and four parachutes, leaving the

aircraft en route to Reno, never to be heard of again. This hijacking received enormous publicity and Cooper became a sort of folk hero. If Cooper had got his idea from Cini, or rather, from what the media reported on Cini, many should get the idea from Cooper or from those who imitated him. A whole series of parachute hijackings followed.[132]

3. On 24 December 1971 E. L. Holt made a hijack attempt from Minneapolis on a B-707. The extortionist wanted $300,000 and two parachutes. He was arrested and committed to a mental institution.[133]

4. On 12 January 1972 a hijacking took place in Houston, Texas. The hijacker, R. Ch. La Point, extorted $1 million and ten parachutes. He was seized in Dallas.[134]

5. On 20 January 1972 a hijacker in Las Vegas extorted $50,000 and two parachutes. After his jump he was arrested in the vicinity of Denver.[135]

6. On 26 January 1972 a hijacker, Merlyn St. George, tried to extort $200,000 and four parachutes at Albany. He was killed by an FBI agent.[136]

7. On 5 April 1972 H. Harjanto hijacked a Vickers Viscount of the Merpati Nasuntara airline on flight from Surabaya to Jakarta. He demanded twenty million rupias and a parachute. He was killed by the pilot.[137]

8. On 7 April 1972 a hijacker, R. F. McCoy, Jr., seized a B-727 at Denver and demanded $500,000 and six parachutes. Following a parachute jump he was arrested.[138]

9. On 9 April 1972 a B-727 was hijacked in Oakland by S. H. Speck. The extortionist demanded four parachutes and $500,000.[139]

10. On 5 May 1972 F. W. Hahneman hijacked an Eastern Airline B-727 from Allentown, Pennsylvania to Washington, DC. He extorted $303,000 and forced an aircraft to fly to Honduras where he parachuted out. He later surrendered.[140]

11. On 23 May 1972 J. V. Baguero Cornejo seized an Ecuadorian aircraft on flight from Quito to Guayaquil. He demanded $39,000 and two parachutes. At Quito he was killed.[141]

12. On 30 May 1972 G. D. J. Silva hijacked an aircraft from Sao Paulo to Porto Alegre, Brazil. He demanded $250,000 plus three parachutes. When troops stormed the aeroplane he killed himself with a pistol.[142]

13. On 2 June 1972 R. D. Heady seized a B-727 on flight from Reno to San Francisco. He was captured with the extorted $200,000 after a parachute jump.[143]

14. On 2 June 1972 William Holder and Katherine Kerhow successfully

hijacked a B-727 from Los Angeles to Algeria, demanding $500,000 and five parachutes.[144]

15. On 23 June 1972 J. M. McNally hijacked a B-727 from St. Louis to Peru, Indiana. He extorted $502,000 and five parachutes. He and a colleague who assisted him from the ground were arrested.[145]

16. On 30 June 1972 B. Carre attempted to hijack a DC-9 from Seattle. He demanded $50,000 and one parachute. Carre was committed to a mental hospital.[146]

17. On 5 July 1972 three men tried to hijack a B-737 from Sacramento to Russia. They demanded two parachutes and $800,000. The hijackers were killed except for the one who was not on board.[147]

18. On 6 July 1972 Francis M. Goodell tried to hijack a B-727 from Oakland. He extorted $455,000 and one parachute, but he was arrested.[148]

19. On 10 July 1972 N. Bachali hijacked a B-737 from Lufthansa in Cologne, Germany, demanding $400,000 and a parachute. He was overpowered in Munich.[149]

20. On 12 July 1972 M. Fisher hijacked a B-727 at Oklahoma City. He demanded one parachute and $550,000. He surrendered at Norman, Oklahoma.[150]

21. On 12 July 1972 two men hijacked a B-727 at Philadelphia, extorting $600,000 and three parachutes. They surrendered in Lake Jackson, Texas.[151]

22. On 10 November 1972 three men hijacked a DC-9 from Birmingham, Alabama, to Cuba with $10 million and ten parachutes. They had threatened to crash the plane into the Oak Ridge nuclear installation. They were sentenced in Cuba.[152]

23. On 15 November 1972 Miloslav Hrabinec seized an F-27 from the Australian Anset Airlines en route from Adelaide to Darwin. He demanded a light aircraft and a parachute at Alice Springs Airport. Finally he killed himself.[153]

24. On 12 March 1974 Katsuhito Owaki seized a B-727 from Japanese Airlines on flight from Tokyo to Naha Okinawa. He demanded $55 million and five parachutes, plus mountain climbing gear. He was captured by the police.[154]

25. On 7 January 1975 Saed Madjid seized a BAC 111 from British Airways flying from Manchester to London. He demanded $100,000 and a parachute and a flight to Paris. He was captured.[155]

26. On 22 February 1975 Joel Siqueira, Jr. hijacked a B-737 from Goiania to Brasilia. He demanded ten million cruzeiros, guns, parachutes and the release of two prisoners. He was captured.[156]

27. On 20 October 1977 Thomas Hannan hijacked a B-737 en route from Gran Islan to Lincoln, Nebraska. He demanded the release of an imprisoned friend, $3,000,000 and two parachutes. The attempt ended in suicide.[157]

In our view, the media must have played a decisive role in fostering the twenty-six parachute hijackings that followed the Cini example. Had the media not reported the detail about the parachutes, most of these imitations would in all likelihood not have taken place. In two cases the hijackers demanded four parachutes as in the successful Cooper case and in two cases the sum of money demanded was also identical to the $200,000 Cooper received. Further evidence that indicates contagion by media reporting is that twenty of the twenty-seven cases took place in North America. In one of these cases the hijacking ended in Central America, which promptly produced two imitations in Latin America within twenty-five days. The wave character of the parachute hijackings also indicates contagion. The Cini attempt was followed by five parachute hijackings within seventy-five days. Then there was a lull of sixty-six days. A further parachute hijacking produced a second wave of fifteen attempts within one hundred days. After another lull of 121 days two such hijackings took place within five days. The last four hijackings stand rather isolated, separated by 482, 301, 46 and 982 days from each other. Yet another indication for media-fostered contagion is that thirteen of the twenty-seven cases were separated by eight days or less from each other. If these acts had been generated independently from each other in the 2,178 days that separated the last from the first attempt, the average interval would have been 80.6 days. Yet twenty-two of the twenty-seven parachute hijackings took place at shorter intervals. The evidence for media-induced contagion is rather strong in the case of the parachute hijackings. The public's right to know would not have been seriously infringed if the detail about the parachutes had been suppressed by the media. On the other hand the passenger who was killed in the seventeenth hijacking might still be alive and the same applies to many of the hijackers.

In the foregoing pages we have tried to muster some evidence of media-fostered contagion of violence in general and terrorism in particular. If the data basis on terrorism in general were as complete as it is in the case of hijackings, the overall evidence would in our opinion be quite impressive. That terrorists do copy each other is quite certain although it is difficult to determine to what degree the mass media were involved. It is, for instance, quite certain that the Tupamaros (MLN — Movimiento de Liberación Nacional — National Liberation Movement) in Uruguay inspired Argentinian terrorists. In this case the direct link was probably as strong as the one the media provided. The Tupamaros were also copied by the German Rote Armee Fraktion (RAF). In this case the role of the mass media was probably stronger although books about the Tupamaros also played a role. The Spanish left-wing terrorists from GRAPO (First of October Anti-Fascist Resistance Groups) adopted the technique of shooting victims in their legs from the Italians and again the media were probably the link.[158]

On a more general level it is probably more than a coincidence that the electronic communications revolution, which was heralded with the institutionalized commercial television-satellite link-up (COMSAT — Communication Satellite) in 1968, fell together with the worldwide student upheavals and the beginning of a new wave of insurgent terrorism. Of course, student leaders as well as terrorists travelled and met to communicate their ideas and coordinate their strategies. But the role of the written and audiovisual media in linking up the different scenes of protest seems to have been more important. Mexican student demonstrators in 1968 used protest techniques which were developed only a few weeks earlier in Paris and television almost certainly formed the medium of their learning. A Nigerian student explained his protest with the words, 'The students at Berkeley are demanding their rights. Why shouldn't we?'[159] The media, in our view, spread the idea of protest as well as the techniques, the know-how of it.

The Media as Motivating Factors for Terrorists

In the two preceding sections we have attempted to show that the media might be capable of fostering violence by reducing inhibitions as well as by providing potential terrorists with the mental resources, the know-how, necessary for committing a violent act. In this last section we attempt to demonstrate that the media can also provide the motivation. There are, in our view, six ways in which the media can motivate potential terrorists.

1. The mass media extend experience, present models, stimulate aspirations and indicate goals. In so doing they can also motivate some people to rebellion. We have pointed to this aspect in connection with the rise of the black civil rights movement in the United States and the awakening of Northern Ireland. The media experience was also a crucial

element for the German student terrorists. Horst Mahler, one of the founders of the RAF, recalled: 'Daily the television newscast reported how many people died (in Vietnam). And we sat in our comfortable armchairs in front of the television set, while they fought. We found ourselves disgusting....Only a shock, something that happens all of a sudden, could lead to self-liberation. All that together formed the basis for the RAF-ideology: a mixture of emotions, perceptions, theory-fragments. And above all the need to do something at last.'[160]

Television offers observation without participation. The viewer is stimulated by the images, identifies sometimes with them, but can do nothing with them. Children who watch television are often found to be hyperactive afterwards. The arousal which television can provide needs an outlet which often does not exist.[161] To see, without being able to interfere with the situation, can create frustration. A feeling of impotence overcomes us when we see starving children two yards in front of us on the television set and we cannot feed them. Some of us will send money to an aid organization but that does not save the child we just saw dying from hunger. Some might feel so enraged that they place a bomb at the door of a foreign embassy if the dictator of the country is held responsible for the children's misery. When some German students in Berlin in 1968 tried to burn down a department store it was meant as a protest against the napalm burning of children in Vietnam. Gudrun Ensslin, one of the arsonists, explained to the judge: 'You can notice that impotence was the basis of this deed. But often justice stands on the side of the powerless.'[162] Can one blame the media for motivating terrorists in this way? In our view it can be done only in a way that is much more fundamental than holding the media responsible for certain programmes which portray violence. The mass media can be made accountable in so far as they are not real communication media. They do not provide communication by the masses and between masses but direct a one-way flow of messages and images to the masses without giving them a chance to participate in the communication process. That some of the media consumers want to talk back and do this by using expressive violence, to which the media respond so well, is, in this light, not so amazing.

2. A second way by which the media can motivate terrorists is the following. The cult of individualism which has taken hold of the Western world since the Renaissance has been enlarged by the mass media into a star cult. Until the arrival of the electronic media the star was something confined to the theatre. Since Hollywood took over the star, he or she has become an object of commercial interests that embodies the

popular fantasies of millions of people all over the world. Stars have become so powerful that many politicians could not resist embellishing themselves with the accoutrements of stardom. A style has developed in public life which places more emphasis on appearance than on substance. The hero of the old days was appreciated for what he did. The star is appreciated for what he projects.[163] Success, in a world increasingly shaped by the mass media, is less the result of real performance than of successful image manipulation. Due to the star system, politics has, in the age of television, become a variant of a beauty contest. The Kennedy-Nixon television debates on the eve of the 1960 presidential elections in the United States marked the beginning; Henry Kissinger's performance in the early 1970s marked the height of political stardom. For the media the adoption of the star system in politics was a welcome development. Events could be explained to the masses as the result of the activities of political stars, conflicts as the clash of personalities. This was much easier to portray than explaining politics as the product of structural arrangements in society and the clash of social forces. This media-fostered overestimation of great personalities as shapers of history might have contributed to the rise of insurgent terrorism (although the notion that history is made by big people is much older). Both the terrorists and the mass media seem to share this assumption which implies that history can be changed by the elimination of big people. Is it too farfetched to assume that some of the terrorists have learned this lesson from the star cult of the mass media?

3. There is another side to this and that brings us to a third way by which the media can motivate terrorists. Above anything else the mass media can provide visibility. Through the media a new category of people has come into existence, the celebrities — people who are known to be known. To be named in the media, to be known, is something that is appreciated highly. The news media, and especially television, create, as Charles Fenyvesi has noted, a thirst for fame and recognition.[164] It is known that some terrorists, like Carlos, enjoyed the publicity that was given to them. While individual publicity is probably a minor motive for members of a terrorist movement, it can be the main one for the 'lone wolf' terrorists such as some of the hijackers. David Hubbard, the psychiatrist who did a seven year study of a large group of airplane hijackers, found that the hijackers he studied 'gave clear evidence from the beginning they intended to capture the attention of the world through the news media and to use it for personal publicity as well as political demonstration'. For herostratic terrorists visibility might be a sufficient motive to act.

4. A fourth way by which the media can motivate terrorists is by inciting them, wittingly or unwittingly, to a terroristic deed. Hubbard found that television reports often crystallized the hijacker's decision to act. Some of the psychotic hijackers he studied interpreted live newscasts about hijackings as 'instructions from God to go and do likewise'.[165] While the media motivate the terrorists unconsciously in such cases, there are also cases where this is done explicitly. When Leon Czolgosz assassinated President McKinley at the beginning of this century a copy of a newspaper was found in his pocket wherein the newspaper magnate William R. Hearst attacked the president. The article concluded that 'if bad institutions and bad men can be got rid of only by killing them the killing must be done'.[166] When Shiran Shiran murdered the US senator and presidential candidate Robert F. Kennedy in mid-1968, a newspaper which contained a violent attack on the victim was also found in his pocket.[167] While in this case the media cannot be rightfully blamed, there are cases which are more questionable. Take the case of Margaret McKearney. On the basis of spurious evidence provided by Scotland Yard this Irish girl was in 1975 decribed in the British Press as 'Britain's Most Wanted Woman Terrorist' (*Daily Mail*), the 'Terror Girl' (*Mirror, Telegraph*), or 'The Most Evil Girl in Britain' (*Express*). The *Sun* called her 'Death Courier' and published photographs which were not those of Margaret McKearney but of someone else who lived in the Republic of Ireland. Styled 'public enemy number one', the terrorist Ulster Volunteer Force threatened her that they would 'get your family — each and every one of you'. On 23 October 1975 two relatives of Margaret McKearney were found shot dead.[168] It is highly doubtful that these murders would have occurred without the witchhunt of the British press.

Another case where a person was assassinated because of planted publicity is the one of the Egyptian Jew Henri Curiel. As an orthodox communist pleading for reconciliation between the Arab world and Israel, Curiel was opposed to political violence ('I hate terrorism', he said). Possibly on instigation of the French secret service (DST), the right-wing weekly *Le Point* published a cover story on 6 June 1976, suggesting that Curiel was the mastermind behind a Soviet-guided terrorist network. This story was picked up by the German magazine *Der Spiegel* (24 October 1977), where it was claimed that he and his organization 'Solidarité' stood at the centre of seventeen terrorist organizations. In 1978 Curiel was murdered in Paris by two right-wing extremists. *Der Spiegel* belatedly sent its excuses to Curiel's widow, admitting that the accusation was unfounded. Although it cannot be conclusively proven, it is not unlikely that the assassins had got their target's name from the media, which in turn were quite likely misled by planted information from the secret services.[169]

5. A fifth way by which the news media can motivate terrorists has to do with the laws that govern news values. News has to be new. When an event that first was news happens again and again it loses some if not all of its news value. The normal is not news anymore. An act of violence which an aggressor wants to see reported in the news has to be more outrageous than previous and rivalling acts. There is a built-in escalation imperative which the laws of news value impose on the terrorist. In this way the media motivate the terrorists to invent more and more bizarre or cruel acts. The penalty of not complying with this news demand is silence. The net result of this 'the worse the better' doctrine is an escalation of violence.[170] This escalation imperative also applies to manifestations below the level of terrorism. During the anti-war demonstrations in the United States a dramatic act was staged at Kent State University by the protesters, because, according to one of its leaders, the protest was beginning to lose network news coverage.[171]

6. This brings us to the sixth and most important way by which the news media can motivate terrorists. In our first chapter (p. 19) we quoted an Algerian rebel leader as saying that it was better for them to kill people in the capital where the American media were than in the countryside where there was no publicity. Here we would like to quote an American journalist referring to the same circumstances. Robert Kleiman, who was CBS bureau chief in Paris during the final phase of the Algerian war, described the situation from the point of view of the media:

The television cameraman or still photographer had quite a problem. How did he manage to get there to take the pictures of the people being blown up? That's what his editors wanted in New York....If the photographer wanted to be sure to get a picture, it was very useful for him to find out when an assassination was going to take place. Many of the most startling pictures of assassinations in Algeria were obtained in that fashion. If the photographer knows there are going to be so many assassinations in a month and he is trying to find out when the next one will occur, so he can photograph it, is he responsible for arranging an assassination, even if he hasn't actually arranged it?....There is a very fine line here between reporting and instigating murder. I can remember the CBS News desk in New York asking why we were beaten on a picture of this kind. There are competitive pressures on reporters and cameramen in the field.[172]

If the media sought contacts with terrorists to get startling pictures and the terrorists killed people to gain publicity, it is quite logical to conclude that the media provided the motive for these acts of terrorism. The collaboration between competitive journalists and insurgent terrorists might not always be so close as in the case just cited. But even if the violent men and those who report on them work at arm's length, the same relationship is latently existing. The high news value which violence has in the Western media is, for some people, motivation enough to engage in types of violence to which the media respond well. Journalists, on the other hand, driven by competitive pressures, have to report such news. There is something paradoxical and perverse in this relationship. Among editors and journalists, but also among governments, discussions increasingly focus on guidelines on the news treatment of terrorism. It is to this discussion that we will turn in our fourth chapter.

CONCLUSION

The effects of media reporting in matters of terrorism are diverse and hard to pinpoint in some areas. They are most concrete in hostage situations where, as a consequence of the journalistic equivalent of the Heisenberg effect, hostages have actually died because of media intrusion. Although media effects in hostage situations can also be positive, it is too simple to conclude that positive and negative effects probably balance each other. The types of media interference that endanger hostages are not necessarily the same as those that can help to preserve hostage lives. Many of the problems the news media create in regard to hostages also apply to their interference with the work of the government security forces. Media reporting on insurgent terrorism affects public opinion and can change the political climate in a country. By presenting their cause through the mass media directly to the public, insurgent terrorists are sometimes also capable of undermining the authority of the established government. The news media themselves therefore often experience, as a consequence of this, censorship by the authorities.

The most serious effect of media reporting on insurgent terrorism, however, is the likely increase of terroristic activities. The media can provide the potential terrorist with all the ingredients that are necessary to engage in this type of violence. They can reduce inhibitions against the use of violence, they can offer models and know-how to potential terrorists and they can motivate them in various ways. While extra-media factors are probably at least equally important elements for many insurgent terrorists, the intra-media elements are in our view sufficient to lead to acts of imitative terrorism by criminal and pathological personality types. The evidence presented in this chapter points to a rather strong relationship between media coverage and the occurrence of certain acts of terrorism, especially in the case of hijackings.

The exculpating view of one of the leading experts on terrorism, Brian Jenkins, that 'the news media are responsible for terrorism to about the same extent that commercial aviation is responsible for airline hijackings' is, in our opinion, a grave underestimation of the role of the media. To state, as Jenkins does, that 'The vast communications network that makes up the news media is simply another vulnerability in a technologically advanced and free society',[173] is, in our view, missing the point completely. By placing a heavier burden on the media, we are, however, not alone. A group of experts that met in 1976 in Washington, DC following an invitation from the US Department of State, distinguished between direct causes of terrorism (such as neocolonialism, ethnic dependence, grievances and frustrations) and permissive causes (factors that make terrorism possible and recommend it as a tactic for extremists). These experts held that 'the availability of publicity through news media was seen as permissive cause in most cases, but it was also recognized that publicity leads to a contagion or imitation effect, which in turn becomes a direct cause of subsequent acts of terrorism.'[174] This is a view which in our opinion is much more to the point although it does not capture the whole web of relationships that link insurgent terrorism and the media. While we have, in this chapter, not been able to present sufficient evidence on all the relationships that there are between media and insurgent terrorism, enough has, in our view, been unearthed to warrant further and more detailed research.

4. INSURGENT TERRORISM AND CENSORSHIP

Media coverage of insurgent terrorism produces, as we have seen in the previous chapter, all sorts of effects. Many of these social effects are negative and the question arises as to whether or not some form of censorship should be considered. The question is not academic. Many governments have imposed censorship on terroristic news. In other countries governments and media have come to some working arrangement on the coverage of terrorism. In yet other cases the media have imposed some restrictions with regard to the coverage of such news on themselves. In this chapter, we will, after a brief introduction, survey (1) government censorship; (2) government-media arrangements, using the examples of Great Britain and the Federal Republic of Germany; and (3) internal media regulations, which we will exemplify with illustrations from the United States. In the last section of this chapter we will enumerate the pros and cons of media censorship in matters of insurgent terrorism.

INTRODUCTION

The freedom of the press has historically developed from the individual's freedom of speech and opinion vis-à-vis the government. The original rationale for the individual's freedom of speech was that it would permit public discussion which would allow truth to win over error

(Thomas Jefferson). But with the rise of monopoly capitalism it became increasingly doubtful whether 'the best test of truth is the power of thought to get itself accepted in the competition of the market', as Oliver Wendell Holmes held.[1] The press barons who became the self-appointed spokesmen of public opinion soon tended to use the freedom of the press doctrine as a smokescreen for their profit-making activities rather than as a vehicle to search for truth. The libertarian theory of the press has found its most pointed expression in a statement of William Peter Hamilton of the *Wall Street Journal*: 'A newspaper is a private enterprise owing nothing whatsoever to the public, which grants it no franchise. It is therefore affected with no public interest. It is emphatically the property of the owner, who is selling a manu-factured product at his own risk...'[2] This kind of business ideology refused to accept any social responsibility for its doing and expressions of it can be found in notions such as:
— What God in His wisdom has permitted to happen, I'm not too proud to print.
— We don't make the news, we just print it.
— Give the people the facts, and they'll make the right decisions.[3]
Such notions denying journalistic responsibility are still strong among Western media spokesmen and even among scholars. For instance, Bernard Johnpoll, Professor of Political Science at the State University of New York at Albany, has written:

It is useless to discuss what the media can do about terror. The media are not judicial institutions; their sole role in modern society is to transmit information. How to erase terror is a juridical and ethical question, not a question of the media.[4]

In the post World War Two period the doctrine of the freedom of the press has been supplemented with one that stresses the 'responsibility of the press' but the rise of the second has not corresponded in any way with the massive changes brought about by the electronic com-munication revolution. As one author has put it, 'Space age technology is saddled with Pony Express notions of journalistic responsibility'.[5]

In today's world communication has become a key to power and information has become so powerful that the control of it can literally be a matter of life and death. The media as main disseminators and gatekeepers of information play a crucial role. If, for instance, the media provide terrorists with information that allows them to construct a hydrogen bomb which enables them to destroy a city with ten million people, the press will no longer be able to decline responsibility. The case is not hypothetical. An American publication, *The Progressive*, wanted to publish an article in which the functioning of a hydrogen bomb was explained. A federal judge, Robert Warren, prohibited the publication, arguing that the duty of the government to protect national security had precedence over the First Amendment of the US Constitution which guarantees the freedom of the press.[6] The explosive material, however, was nevertheless published six months later in an eight-page special edition of the *Madison Press Connection*. The editors of the article declared that they printed it as an answer to government censorship.[7] The people responsible for this publication probably felt that they had done something in defence of the celebrated freedom of the press. In reality, they have reduced our chance to live free from fear of a nuclear holocaust. As long as nations control atomic devices, a fragile but so far successful 'balance of terror' has prevented a repetition or worse of Hiroshima (90,000 dead) and Nagasaki (36,000 dead).[8] Nuclear proliferation to terrorists without a country has been brought one step closer by this irresponsible exercise of the freedom of the press. The legitimate social function of news is, in our view, knowledge increase or uncertainty reduction; this type of news, however, has a contrary effect. If a person shouts 'fire' in a cinema when there is none and people are trampled to death as a consequence, the person who started it all will have difficulty in claiming that he only exercised his constitutionally guaranteed freedom of speech. The press should, in our view, be held responsible for media-made disasters just as individuals are held responsible for man-made disasters.

But what is a media-made disaster? If a radio station broadcasts the daily stock-market quotations and a listener, learning that he has just lost his fortune, commits suicide, the medium cannot in all justice be held responsible.[9] On the other hand, to take a positive example, the introduction of radio night programming in Denmark, which helped people to make it through the night, led to a decrease in the number of suicides. In this case one is tempted to hold the media to a slightly higher degree responsible for it than in the previous example. In a way the media can only be made responsible for effects which are likely or predictable judging by common sense or past experience. There is a category of irrational effects for which it is difficult to blame the media, unless there is a logical pattern underlying them which again makes them to some extent foreseeable. This is, for instance, the case with reporting suicides. It has been established that media reports on suicides — especially in romantic contexts — lead to an increase in suicides among the audience.[10] Partly for this reason suicides usually go unreported in the media.[11] Terrorism can be, as we have seen, as contagious as suicides. If the media can show responsibility and restrictiveness in reporting about suicides, can and should they not do the same in regard to certain types of terrorism?

Over the past decade, acts of insurgent terrorism have reached epidemic proportions. Epidemic diseases like malaria have been successfully fought by killing the disease-carrying mosquito. Epidemics of nonstate terrorism are spread mainly by the modern mass media. The implication seems obvious. By stopping the mass media from carrying news on terrorism the epidemic can be contained and ultimately eliminated. This simplistic line of reasoning has been followed most consequently by a number of governments, as we shall see in the following section.

GOVERNMENT CENSORSHIP ON MEDIA COVERAGE OF INSURGENT TERRORISM

The concept of a free press is presently not held in high esteem by the governments of the world. A symposium on world press freedom, held in 1974, noted that only thirty of the then 138 member countries of the United Nations had a free press.[12] Freedom of the press usually goes along with other freedoms. A Freedom House survey from 1975 noted that about half of the states in the world, comprising half of the world's population, were 'not free', while about 30 percent of the nations received the classification 'partly free'. Since the last category included such cases as Nicaragua under Somoza and South Africa under apartheid, this is a doubtful category.[13] In its 1976 report, the Freedom House survey noted that only 19.6 percent of the world's population live in free countries.[14] A more recent survey of the International Press Institute noted that only twenty-five countries, about a sixth of the total, enjoy freedom of the press.[15]

While in many of these countries media censorship and insurgent terrorism are not directly linked, there are countries where the issue of insurgent terrorism has led to censorship. The government of Uruguay, for instance, began its role as censor in 1967, when it closed the newspaper *Epoca* for printing a communiqué of the Tupamaros.[16] In 1969 the decree of a limited state of siege further eroded press freedom. In 1973 the government passed a law which prohibited 'the publication, by means of oral, written or televised media (of) all information, commentaries or impressions which directly or indirectly mention or refer to those persons who conspire against the nation or against antisubversive operations, excluding official communication'. The press were also forbidden to criticize government measures taken against 'terrorists'.[17]

In Argentina the situation is similar. The government prohibited the media from publishing the names of the terrorist organizations Montoneros and Ejercito Revolucionario del Pueblo (ERP) just as the Uruguayan government had declared the use of the name Tupamaros illegal.[18] By a decree issued in April 1976 the Argentinian media were prohibited from reporting, mentioning or commenting on political violence.[19] Journalists have been arrested for publishing unauthorized information.[20] Views 'attributed to illicit groups' cannot be printed without being first submitted to the censors, according to a new law introduced in 1977.[21] In no Western country has journalism experienced such severe repression as in Argentina since the military coup of March 1976; dozens of journalists have been arrested, kidnapped, and murdered by right-wing death squads who operate in the service of the regime.[22]

What happened in Uruguay and Argentina has also to some degree been true for other countries experiencing insurgent terrorism, such as Brazil (until the recent liberalization), Sri Lanka (where the government in June 1978 prohibited any reporting of terrorist activities)[23] or Lebanon (where reports of violence within the country are censored).[24] In Israel the media have to submit news material on ongoing incidents of terrorism to the Military Censor, who decides whether or not the information is hindering the work of the Police or Defence Forces or is helping the terrorists.[25] In South Africa acts of terrorism receive practically no coverage in the media, except indirectly, since steps taken to combat insurgent terrorism are given comprehensive coverage.[26] In Zimbabwe-Rhodesia media censorship was maintained in the 1960s and 1970s to 'help fight terrorism and subversion' and this applied to foreign media material as well.[27] In the Republic of Ireland, the Irish state broadcasting authority Radio Telefís Eireann (RTE) censors interviews and reports of interviews with spokesmen of the IRA, the Provisional Sinn Fein and the Ulster Defence Association.[28] Even countries on the road to democracy, like Spain, show repressive features. A Dutch newspaper correspondent casting doubt on the Spanish police's version of a terroristic incident was expelled from the country.[29] Foreign television teams wanting to cover terrorism in the Basque province are no longer allowed to work without a special government permit. This news regulation, introduced in April 1979, is based on a law which prohibits public approval of terrorist move-ments.[30] The freedom of the press has also suffered in other areas than news. Not only in Latin America but also in several countries in Western Europe Marighela's *Minimanual of the Urban Guerrilla* has been outlawed.[31]

Government control of media reporting on insurgent terrorism seems to be a double-edged weapon. While censorship might reduce the value of a strategy of terrorism for insurgents it cannot prevent them from engaging in other forms of political violence. Their grievances and aspirations remain, whether they are treated with silence or not. In many countries it is likely that the level of terrorism will increase rather than decrease after the introduction of censorship. The increase is due to the fact that the government or pro-government groups will feel freer to engage in terrorist acts against political dissidents since they can count on not being exposed and criticized by the local media. The mass terrorism of Hitler and Stalin was only possible because the people were not fully aware of what was going on. Government imposed censorship on news of insurgent terrorism can, in our view, be a cure that is worse than the disease.

MIXED (GOVERNMENT-MEDIA) GUIDELINES ON THE COVERAGE OF INSURGENT TERRORISM

In countries with a solid democratic tradition governments facing insurgent terrorists are usually hesitant about imposing censorship on the news coverage of acts of terrorism. In so far as such governments act as a source of news on terrorist incidents they naturally attempt to shape and channel the information in such a way as to best serve themselves. It is usually only a small step from releasing self-serving news to releas-ing false news. The deliberate dispensing of misinformation by the authorities is sometimes known and sometimes unknown to the media. In the first case the media can at least decide whether they want to publish or broadcast the information which is known to be false. When the lives of hostages are at stake a pious lie might be defensible. In the second case the media are spared the decision whether or not they want to propagate falsehoods. But if and when they learn afterwards that they have been misused by the authorities, the loss of credibility of a government source might weigh more heavily in the long run than the short-term tactical advantage gained during a terroristic incident.[32]

To solve such and other dilemmas in a mutually satisfactory manner, government and media representatives, usually after a major incident, meet to discuss codes of conduct to be followed in future incidents. The initiative practically always comes from the side of the government law enforcement agencies. The authorities usually make an appeal to the 'responsibility of the press', hoping to achieve a degree of self-censorship which makes government censorship superfluous. Yet responsibility from the side of the media can only be expected if the government, in turn, also acts responsibly. In Italy, for instance, during the Moro abduction, the government sought to prevent publication by the media of a communiqué of the Red Brigades. When the editor of *Il Messaggero* refused to comply, he was sentenced to three months in jail or a monetary fine.[33] On the other hand, however, rivalling government officials have leaked forbidden information texts to the public if it served their political manoeuvres.[34]

Information about government-media arrangements is very difficult to come by. In the following we will discuss some attempts by US government agencies to come to agreements, followed by two short case histories from Germany and Great Britain.

After the Hanafi incident in early 1977 proposals for media guidelines came both from the media themselves and from law enforcement agencies. A typical proposal of the second type was one made by the former police officer Dr Horstman, which he presented during a panel session on 'Police Relations with Press' in September 1977:

1. Establish a policy of not naming the individuals involved as hostage-takers, the methods they used in doing it, and any of the things they say, including their demands, and specifically why they say they did it.
2. If the media coverage is a part of the demands negotiated, then it should be done in as limited a manner as possible with all other media not participating.
3. The act itself when reported should be shown to be a despicable act committed by losers.
4. The point should be made strongly that no hostage situation has ever been successful for the hostage-takers.
5. No direct calls should ever be made to the hostage-takers. The contact may stir them up and add to their feelings of power which could lengthen the situation or put the hostages in jeopardy.
6. Continuing on-site coverage should be eliminated due to the fact that the media can and has played the part of supplying tactical information to the hostage-takers on what the police may be planning to do.[35]

Such guidelines, containing demonstrable falsehoods (points 3 and 4) and depriving news of almost any meaning for the public (point 1; news without who, how, what and why) serve at best the government but not the media. This is the general weakness of most proposals coming from the side of the authorities. A further, though less extreme example of this tendency can be found in the 'mutual agreement' which the former police chief of Washington DC, Maurice J. Cullinane, offered. His suggestions included the following points:

– Agreement by the media not to telephone a hostage-taker; immediate notification of the police by reporters of any calls from hostage-takers; no publication of such conversations without first conferring with the police negotiators for advice.
– Limited use of live telecasting with no close-ups of the actual windows where police officers may be stationed.
– No identification by media of groups claiming responsibility for bombings; no speculation of what might be happening, with reports confined only to facts released by the police.
– Limitation of details of terrorist acts so there is no provision of a how-to guide for terrorists or portrayal of the hostage-takers as heroes.[36]

The 'mutuality' of the proposal consisted in the promise that a police press secretary would give periodic briefings and that a police hotline would be installed during an incident. In some cases, Cullinane suggested, a media pool representative would be allowed to follow the police-terrorist negotiations, so that he might brief others.[37] Cullinane's proposal fell on deaf ears with the media. His successor, Burtell M. Jefferson, therefore asked for guidelines to be drawn up by the media alone rather than in a concerted effort of media and police.[38]

A more balanced set of guidelines was proposed by the US task force on Disorders and Terrorism in late 1976. In the vein of good advertising it presented what the government wanted to say in a manner the media presumably wanted to hear. The task force acknowledged that 'So long as extraordinary violence is a fact of social life, the media cannot and should not avoid portraying and discussing it'.[39] The authors of the report held that 'Whatever principles are adopted must be generated by the media themselves, out of a recognition of special public responsibility'.[40] The report recommends a 'principle of minimum intrusiveness in their gathering of news relating to incidents of extraordinary violence' and listed five points which should be considered:

a. Use of pool reporters to cover activities at incident scenes or within police lines.

b. Self-imposed limitations on the use of high-intensity television lighting, obtrusive camera equipment, and other special newsgathering technologies at incident scenes;

c. Limitations of media solicitation of interviews with barricaded or hostage-holding suspects and other incident participants;

d. Primary reliance on officially designated spokesmen as sources of information concerning law enforcement operations and plans, and

e. Avoidance of inquiries designed to yield tactical information that would prejudice law enforcement operations if subsequently disclosed.

In a second 'principle of complete, noninflammatory coverage in contemporaneous reporting of incidents of extraordinary violence' the report lists six more items:

a. Delayed disclosure of information relating to incident location, when that information is not likely to become public knowledge otherwise and when the potential for incident growth or spread is obviously high;

b. Delayed disclosure of information concerning official tactical planning that, if known to incident participants, would seriously compromise law enforcement efforts;

c. Balancing of reports incorporating self-serving statements by incident participants with contrasting information from official sources and with data reflecting the risks that the incident has created to noninvolved persons;

d. Systematic predisclosure verification of all information concerning incident-related injuries, deaths, and property destruction; and

e. Avoidance to the extent possible, of coverage that tends to emphasize the spectacular qualities of an incident or the presence of spectators at an incident scene.[41]

The underlying assumption of such recommendations is that the police serves public security and the media serve public information; that both, in their own but sometimes conflicting ways, serve the public interest. Such a harmonious model is seldom in consonance with reality. The government and its security forces have an institutional self-interest and so have the media. The public interest might at times be best served by a democratic government. At other times the media are the truer spokesman of public interests. And there are times and places where the terrorists themselves have a higher claim to represent the public than either government or media. The Sandinistas in Nicaragua can serve as a reminder of this. Media cooperation with government security forces in situations of insurgent terrorism carries the danger that the role of the media as a public watchdog, as a check on government, might be impaired. In talking about guidelines on the coverage of acts of insurgent terrorism one has to ask in whose interest the guidelines should primarily be: in the interest of the hostages, the public, the media or the government. Any government-media guidelines contain the risk that the two most vulnerable parties, the hostages and the public, are served less well by them than the contracting parties. There can, in our view, be little objection to forms of cooperation that serve to limit the risk to hostages. But at times the government appeal to the media to be restrictive in their coverage, an appeal made in the name of hostages, seems to serve quite different and contrary purposes. The example of the news blackout in Germany during the Schleyer kidnapping points in this direction.

**The German News Embargo
During the Schleyer Kidnapping**

In the period before the Schleyer kidnapping the German media had already demonstrated some restraint in reporting on acts of terrorism. Communiqués of the Red Army Fraction which explained the rationale behind their bombings had not been made public by the media to whom they were sent.[42] Whether this restraint was self-imposed or the result of an agreement with the federal government is not clear. Yet what happened in the Schleyer case goes beyond anything so far practised in peacetime in Western democracies in recent times. A degree of cooperation on the part of the media was achieved which resulted in such acts as one popular paper regularly deliberating with the government what the next day's headline in matters of terrorism should be.[43] It amounted more to news management than to news embargo (Nachrichtensperre) which was the term most often used to designate the state of affairs. The background to how this worked in detail is still unclear and the following account probably only shows the tip of the iceberg.

After the kidnapping of Hanns Martin Schleyer on 5 September 1977, the terrorists asked that a communication of theirs, wherein they demanded the exchange of Schleyer for eleven imprisoned terrorists, should be read out in full on television.[44] The German government, however, managed, three days after the kidnapping, to put a lid on the terrorists' use of the media. Klaus Bölling, the chief of the federal press and information office, had reached an agreement with the president of the ARD (the overreaching organization of the German electronic media), Hess, the director of the Second German Television Channel (ZDF), Von Hase, and the editors-in-chief of the news agencies

Deutsche Presse Agentur (DPA) and Deutscher Presse Dienst (DPD) to the effect that they promised to use great caution in reporting on the kidnapping. Communications from the terrorists and their helpers, it was agreed, should be used in newscasts only after prior consultation with the federal government. Having achieved this agreement with the top management of the German media, and having received the approval of the German Press Council, the editors of the remaining German media were requested to observe equal self-restraint.[45]

The appeal was effective and followed with only minor exceptions. Of the 121 dailies, for instance, less than a dozen did not fully respect the government's invitation to observe prudence.[46] While the embargo or news rationing, as it was also called, went on, competitive pressures coming from the few breaks in the common front made the maintenance more difficult but by and large the situation was held under control for almost six weeks.[47] The press office of the German government constantly monitored the communications of the news agencies DPA, DPD, AFP, AP and Reuter (which have bureaux in the German Federal Republic) as well as the news flow of twenty other foreign news agencies. In addition, seventy radio programmes, seven television programmes, fifty-two German dailies, seventeen foreign dailies and fifty magazines were kept under watch. When a piece of information which the German government deemed harmful came from the ticker of a news agency, the government either asked the agency to block the item or issued a denial or an official statement on it. In this way information could be intercepted, negated or placed in a different light even before it reached the public.[48] Government requests to kill a news item also went to foreign media and news agencies.[49] The BBC, for instance, honoured a request to keep the news about the flight of the anti-terrorist team GSG-9 to Mogadishu out of its broadcasts at a critical moment.[50] Since this was merely a de-actualization of news, it is less problematical than some of the practices cited above.

The news embargo in the Schleyer case was never total. There were certain types of news which the government even requested be communicated by the media, such as coded messages from the government to the kidnappers.[51] Later, when the Swiss mediator Payot took over this go-between role from the media, it was made known in the media when messages from the kidnappers or transmissions to them took place, but the content of these communications was not made known. Silence was also maintained in the public media on all decisions of the government emergency commission and the operative centre as well as about the state of the investigative efforts.[52] On the other hand the media were allowed if not encouraged to report on movements of German ministers to places like Algeria, Libya, Iraq, South Yemen and Vietnam. This presumably served the purpose of making the terrorists believe that the German government was looking for a safe-haven for the eleven terrorists that the RAF wanted to have released in exchange for Schleyer. In all likelihood these were mock manoeuvres of the government, intended to win time by creating the impression that the terrorist demands might be met.[53] The strategy of the German government was to use the media while denying, as far as possible, the use of the media to the terrorists. This worked reasonably well — most of their 139 communications to thirty-seven media did not reach the public. In order to get through to the public they tried, with some limited success, to address the media in the neighbouring countries, especially in France and in the Netherlands.[54] Some of these communications surfacing abroad were indeed picked up by the German media.

German reporters carried out investigations of their own but very little found its way to the German public.[55] While these unpublished investigations of reporters allowed the media to some extent to maintain their watchdog function on government acts, the public itself had no way of assessing whether the government policy was correct and in the interest of the German people. According to opinion polls 70 or 80 percent of the German public consented to the imposition of the news embargo.[56] One television director commented: 'A tacit state, ruling over citizens who do not want to ask questions, and journalists, who praise this. Do we live in such a state?'[57] It is true that the government promised the media and the public a post-event disclosure of all important aspects in a special documentation. As it turned out this report was less complete than one would have wished, especially in regard to the investigation of the Schleyer case. Had the Mogadishu raid resulted in the deaths of all eighty-six hostages, as it almost did, such a post-event report would have raised many more doubts.

The original rationale given for the news embargo by the government had been that the terrorists had threatened to kill Schleyer if the authorities did not refrain from public investigative operations. The government was afraid that these operations could not be kept secret and that media disclosure of them would result in the death of the abducted. Furthermore, the government held that it was undesirable for the kidnappers to learn from the media what the strategy and tactics of the emergency commission and the operative centre were. Finally, the government wanted to prevent the mass media allowing themselves to become a platform for terrorist propaganda.[58] In a letter to the editors of the German media the government spokesman Klaus Bölling wrote: 'We all know how much publicity matters to the terrorists and that they try to use press, radio and television as instruments for their purposes. Please help us in thwarting these intentions of the kidnappers.'[59] Bölling justified this appeal to the media by saying that terrorism was not just a threat to the government but to the whole of society, including the press and the licensed electronic media. The purpose of the appeal for self-restraint was, in his view, to help realize the target projections of the federal government, which were to save the life of Schleyer, not to release the prisoners whose exchange had been demanded, and to arrest the kidnappers.

Bölling saw it as a victory for the government that the terrorists were not able to reach the public via communiqués and videotapes. But while the terrorists themselves could not use the media directly as a theatre for action, the frequent programme changes and the transmission of the funerals of Schleyer's guards ultimately had an effect which was perhaps not too different from what might have been without a news embargo. The advantage for the government was that it did not have to admit in public that it was prepared to sacrifice Schleyer and the lives of the passengers and crew of the hijacked aircraft.[60] The government gambled with high stakes and, as it turned out, the gamble was largely successful, the eighty-six hostages in Mogadishu being liberated. Schleyer, it is true, was killed but the suicides of three leading terrorists in the Stammheim prison somehow seemed to compensate for this. But if the Mogadishu raid had not succeeded, the government would have had to pay a high price in terms of losing public confidence. This risk would not have been so high if the public had been continuously informed during the six weeks of the news embargo. All in all, the German experiment with the news embargo can hardly be called a success that is worth emulation by other democratic governments. Certainly not in democracies where people place more emphasis on knowing what is decided on their behalf than seems to be the case in West Germany.

Media control in matters of terrorism did not begin or end with the news embargo during the Schleyer kidnapping. A special clause (Paragraph 88a) has been introduced into the Penal Law Code which prohibits the printing and distribution of publications advocating, threatening, glorifying or training for violence.[61] On the basis of this paragraph people have been jailed for printing documentary material of the Red Army Fraction and the June 2nd Movement, leftish bookshops have been raided for subversive literature and booksellers have been incarcerated.[62] A book on anti-terrorist policies of the German government (*After Schleyer: Special Commandos in the FRG – Rapid Establishment of a New Gestapo*) has been banned because it 'places the state in a bad light'.[63] West German border police have been controlling the reading material of young people against a list of 287 newspapers and magazines which were judged to be extremist or suspicious by the internal secret service.[64] Most of these publications were perfectly legal and did not advocate any violence. Yet their readers' names end up in a computer of the Federal Criminal Office. It conjures up all sorts of Orwellian fantasies.

The British Media and Northern Ireland

In an earlier chapter (p. 94) we have already made some references as to how the British government as a news source on the troubles in Northern Ireland attempts to influence the tenor of press accounts. In this section we will concentrate mainly on the arrangements that exist between the electronic media and government agencies in regard to the coverage of terrorism. For outsiders, these arrangements are hard to follow; within the British establishment the 'old boys' network' is still operative and many arrangements are quite informal and personal so that they do not result in any kind of written agreements.

There is, for instance, a system of D-notices (D for Defence). In order to prevent media coverage on any aspects which the government deems relevant for national security, D-notices are issued to editors, suggesting that an item should not receive publicity. Although this system is meant for external defence matters, it is likely that it has also been used for matters relating to domestic terrorism.[65] At any rate, in the early 1970s a similar news blackout was for a time upheld in connection with the bombing campaign of the anarcho-marxist 'Angry Brigade'. Their bombings of the homes of members of the 'ruling class' were intended as symbolic attacks in order to show to the apathetic working class a way from alienation to revolutionary rank-and-file action.[66] When in 1970 the homes of the Attorney General, Sir Peter Rawlinson, and of the Metropolitan Commissioner, Sir John Waldron, were attacked, Scotland Yard issued memoranda to news editors asking them not to publicize the bombings until inquiries were complete. The news blackout also covered other Angry Brigade bombings but it was broken when the underground press gradually became aware of what was going on. When in January 1971 the home of Robert Carr, the

Secretary of State for Employment, was bombed, Scotland Yard first tried to cover it up by saying that an exploding gas main had caused it, but the journalists arriving at the scene soon found out what the real cause was.[67] Scotland Yard justified its blackout strategy by saying that they were afraid that otherwise imitators bombing for publicity for other reasons might cloud their current lines of inquiry.[68] Scotland Yard has also managed to obtain news blackouts in a case of criminal terrorism. During the kidnapping of a Greek-Cypriot girl in London in November 1975 they were able to persuade the British media to observe a voluntary moratorium for ten days until the case was successfully solved.[69] Criminal kidnapping cases, however, are different from other types of terrorism in that the criminals, unlike the Angry Brigade, do not seek publicity.[70]

The arrangements which the British electronic media have with the government in regard to the coverage of the troubles in Northern Ireland are more in the nature of a truce. As a consequence of statute differences, the government-media relations of the BBC differ from those of the Independent Television Companies (ITV). The latter are licensed by the Independent Broadcasting Authority (IBA). ITV makes programmes and IBA supervises them in accordance with the stipulations of the Broadcasting Act. The IBA has to see to it that 'due impartiality is preserved in matters of political controversy or matters relating to current public policy' (Section I (f) of the 1973 Broadcasting Act). Programmes can also be banned by the IBA if they are likely to 'incite crime and disorder', or if they are offensive to 'good taste and decency' or to 'public feeling'. These are rather flexible categories, and the chairman of the IBA who applies them is constantly exposed to pressures from political parties and the government. He meets with the Secretary of State or the Chief Constable of the Royal Ulster Constabulary (RUC) and it seems that he is less than successful in maintaining the independence of the 'Independent' Authority. In the wake of such confidential meetings the ITV receives suggestions such as that a different reporter should cover a particular aspect of Northern Ireland or that a regular programme like 'This Week' should 'lay off' Northern Ireland for a while.[71] If such suggestions do not produce the desired results, the IBA can ban, postpone and cut ITV programmes. This has happened in numerous instances over the last decade. Among the items that have been censored in one form or another were an item on IRA fund-raising, an assessment of the strength of the IRA Provisionals, an analysis of allegations of police brutality, an account of the Queen's visit to Belfast, a report on Republicanism, to name but a few.[72]

Such instances of direct censorship are less visible with the BBC. Unlike the federally structured ITV, the BBC is an organic whole whose authority rests within the organization with the Board of Governors and the Board of Management. Programme-makers concerned with delicate subjects like Northern Ireland are expected to 'refer up' the hierarchy any difficult decisions.[73] The BBC's News Guide rules on the coverage of Northern Ireland from 1972 illuminate this 'refer up' system:

1. News staff sent to Northern Ireland work through Controller Northern Ireland and News Editor Northern Ireland; they must be consulted.
2. No news agency report from Northern Ireland should be used without checking with Belfast newsroom first.
3. The IRA must not be interviewed without prior authority from ENCA (Editor, News and Current Affairs). There can be no question of doing the interview first and seeking permission for broadcast afterwards.
4. Recordings of broadcasts by illegal radios must not be used without reference to ENCA. (This applies to any illegal radio, not just those in Northern Ireland.)
5. We should not report bomb scares concerning BBC buildings for the obvious reasons that such reports would encourage hoaxers or people who wish to disrupt BBC output. (This too does not apply only to Northern Ireland).[74]

The effect of this system is that it produces a great deal of caution and self-censorship which, however, is interpreted as editorial responsibility.

Political pressure on the BBC is strong. When in 1976 Roy Mason became Secretary of State for Northern Ireland he met with the Chairman of the BBC, Sir Michael Swann, in Belfast and accused the BBC of purveying enemy propaganda, support of rebels and disloyalty. Mason was said to have remarked that if the Northern Ireland Office had been in control of the BBC policy, the IRA would have been defeated. The Conservative opposition party spokesman on Northern Ireland, Airey Neave (since killed by Irish terrorists), also accused the BBC of assisting terrorist recruitment and undermining the police.[75] In such a hostile political environment from both major parties, the BBC has to be very careful. Occasionally a controversial current affairs programme suggested by a producer survives the 'refer up' system. In such cases the BBC's whole institutional weight is put behind the programme and the BBC broadcasts it even against political pressure. These occasional exercises in courageous reporting strengthen the BBC's self-image and its public image as an independent voice, but they can also be interpreted as occasional victories amidst a whole series of silent defeats.[76] Like ITV, the BBC has its share of known defeats. Programmes on Northern Ireland have been banned ('24 hours', February

1971), sanitized ('The Scottish Connection', October 1976), cut ('The City on the Border', May 1978) or changed ('A Bridge of Sorts', May 1978).[77]

The cautious style of reporting on Northern Ireland by the British media has had the net effect that the dominant public view of the situation is that the Irish troubles are largely incomprehensible and irrational.[78] Since much of the reporting on Northern Ireland is a repetitious and rather meaningless bomb and body count this is not surprising. Spectacular acts of terrorism, like the assassination of Lord Mountbatten, which the IRA explained as serving to remind British public opinion of the continued occupation of Northern Ireland,[79] do receive ample coverage. On the other hand, the fact that unemployment in Northern Ireland is twelve percent and two to three times as much in certain Catholic districts and that one quarter of all families in Northern Ireland live below the poverty line receives far less coverage.[80] While this is no excuse for terrorism and, in part, even a consequence of it, the terrorism in Northern Ireland would appear far less senseless to the public if it were aware of such structural factors. From the media, however, the public mainly gets the impression that the terrorists are sectarian fanatics and criminal hooligans. However, in a 'liberated' secret Army intelligence document, *Northern Ireland – Future Terrorist Trends*, written by Brigadier J.M. Glover in December 1978, it is stated about the IRA membership: 'Our evidence of the calibre...does not support the view that they are mindless hooligans....It is essentially a working-class organization based on the ghetto areas of the cities and poorer rural areas'.[81] This gap between the prevalent British public perception of the terrorists and the more realistic but secret Army perception is something for which the British media have to be held co-responsible.

When a nation is engaged in armed conflict, the national media are pressured by the government to show loyalty to the patriotic side. Most governments expect the media to go even further and to beef up public morale to see the conflict through to victory. While the British media in the Irish conflict have not made themselves too guilty of propaganda in the second sense, they certainly have been loyal to the government. A statement of a BBC TV sub-editor seems to be characteristic of the majority of journalists: 'I've always assumed the official line is we put the army's version first and then any other'.[82] But loyalty to the security forces or the state is not what the media in democracies are for. Since they are paid, directly or indirectly, by the public they should be primarily responsible not to the state but to the public. If the government is wrong in its policy, the public has, if the media are independent, at least the chance to criticize the government's policy that is made in its name and with its money and blood. But if the media are first responsible to the state, the public is left without a watchdog. The two major parties in Great Britain have no alternative policies to offer in regard to Northern Ireland.

In the 1960s Vietnam was also not a real party issue in the United States. It was the media, more than any political group, that finally managed to expose the national web of self-deception that had been built up over Vietnam. It is doubtful whether the British media will manage to do the same with regard to Northern Ireland. In an address the former BBC Director-General, Sir Charles Curran, has said: 'We have the responsibility...to provide a rationally based and balanced service of news which will enable adult people to make basic judgements about public policy in their capacity as voting citizens of a democracy....We have to add to this basic supply of news a service of contextual comment which will give understanding as well as information....'[83] This valid pledge, made in 1971, has, in our view, not been made true by the BBC or by the other major British media. The reason for this failure is, in our opinion, to be found in the fact that the media have been too responsible and responsive to the government and not enough to the Irish reality and the British public.

Beyond the case of the British media and Ireland this is the main danger that lies in agreements between government and media regarding the coverage of terrorism. The main victims, the public and the direct victims of terrorism, have no part in such agreements. The price which the government pays for its part in such agreements is that it is deprived of a useful critic. The price the media pay is a loss of credibility with the public.[84]

MEDIA SELF-CENSORSHIP

In countries without state censorship or permanent nation-wide media-government agreements on the coverage of terrorism, the media have in some cases developed internal guidelines of their own, partly in response to the fear that government-imposed regulations might otherwise be forced on them. Many of these guidelines are confidential or even secret and we found it hard to get information about them. An official of the German ZDF, for instance, wrote us that knowledge of their guidelines might be useful to terrorists so they could not be made public.[85]

Guidelines invariably involve some manipulation of the news and if terrorist news is manipulated and censored in a way the public does not know this poses some serious problems in democracies. Media without guidelines of course also follow some unwritten editorial rules which might be even more restrictive than written guidelines. In a way it is more desirable that the media follow some clear and publicly known codes than that they manage the news in some uncheckable way. The written guidelines which we will present and discuss in this section are all of American origin, for the simple reason that the media in the United States are more open in these matters than those of most other Western countries.

In principle, guidelines on media treatment of controversial subjects are nothing new. The Code of the Comic Magazine Association of America, for instance, prohibits the presentation of crime 'in such a way as...to...inspire a desire to imitate criminals'. The Motion Picture Association and the National Association of Broadcasters know similar codes.[86] Such codes, however, are rarely invoked and enforced by professional media councils. They have, to our knowledge, never been applied to the news media's treatment of terrorism. In general, the US news media object strongly to any set of narrow guidelines that would limit their freedom to utilize the often exciting news material which insurgent terrorists provide. Few newspapers or stations feel anything for a news blackout of terrorist incidents. There are, of course, exceptions. When the twenty-two years old millionaire's daughter Alice Amanda Dealy was kidnapped in Dallas, Texas, the media maintained a news blackout on the case and the hostage was safely returned after payment of $250,000. As it was, her father happened to be the owner of local newspapers and radio and television stations which made it easy for him to arrange a blackout.[87]

While self-interest of the media was pretty obvious in this case, there are other reasons why media have begun to have second thoughts about the wisdom of giving insurgent and criminal terrorism such a prominent place. Electronic newsgathering with advanced portable minicams linked via microwaves to the studio has made much of today's reporting such a direct affair that the role of the journalist and editor as middle-man between newsmaker and public threatens to lose its significance. Naturally editors do not want to lose control over programming and this makes them receptive to some types of guidelines. A news director of a television station in Cleveland has said: 'Competition has replaced judgement in covering these stories and we are starting to lose control to the terrorists....We used to cover terrorists with live cameras, but we've since changed our policy'.[88] Dan Rather from CBS expressed a similar notion when he said: '...when violent people are playing to the camera, there's no question that the medium itself can become a kind of hostage, and the reporter has to dodge and struggle to keep from being captured and used.'[89] Another journalist, Stephen S. Rosenfeld, has argued that if it is the purpose of the terrorist to send a message, the media should consider not to send it.[90]

Nobody in the media has so far taken the unilateral initiative not to cover any terrorist story. Where the media are commercial enterprises there is strong competition for market shares and since terroristic acts provide excitement they draw large audiences. Given this situation, not to provide the audience with terrorists and terrorists with an audience means losing money to competitors. Responsible media and journalists withholding information are in such circumstances punished and irresponsible ones are rewarded. One journalist told us that he withheld some information during a terrorist incident since he thought that it might cause damage. He shared this information, however, with foreign journalists who showed no hesitation in using it. Our informant's editor, upon reading the foreign press accounts, blamed the original provider of the news item for not having come up with it himself. Restraints, in other words, are not rewarded in the news business, while scoops are. In search of scoops journalists have gone very far, even offering themselves as substitutes for hostages.[91] In such a competitive environment, guidelines, in order to be workable, ought to be a joint effort of all the news media in a news market. To our knowledge this has, however, so far not occurred. An attempt to develop common guidelines for the New York market has come to nothing.[92]

There have, however, been a number of national and international seminars and conferences where media representatives, either among themselves or in conjunction with people from academia or law enforcement, have discussed the question of media guidelines on the coverage of terrorism.[93] No hard and fast rules have been developed anywhere but a certain consensus about the danger zones in reporting terrorist incidents is being built up. The number of media who have guidelines seems to be on the rise. In our own little survey eight out of twenty-five respondents answered that their medium had written guidelines and fourteen said that they had a certain unwritten policy for handling news on terrorism. In three cases, however, the written guidelines were either those of the government or the police or a joint effort between state and media. In a larger survey conducted in 1977 by the magazine *Television/Radio Age* in the United States, some thirty percent of the responding broadcasting stations announced that they had drawn up written directives for cases of terrorism.[94] Another American survey, also dating from 1977, addressed to broadcasting news directors, found that slightly more than one quarter of the stations responding had adopted written codes for handling terrorist-hostage situations, while almost as many said they were considering guidelines.[95]

The first major station enacting a set of guidelines was the Columbia Broadcasting System (CBS). The president of CBS News, Richard Salant, explained: 'What we're groping for is a way to report these things so as to minimize the dangers to the hostages, minimize the dangers of contagion, but at the same time do our job of reporting the facts'.[96] In the preface to the seven CBS Production Standards it is held that 'the story should not be sensationalized beyond the actual fact of its being sensational' — which is a somewhat enigmatic statement. Coverage, the preface says, should be provided with 'thoughtful, conscientious care and restraint'. More specifically, the seven CBS rules on terrorist coverage say:

1. An essential component of the story is the demands of the terrorist/kidnapper and we must report those demands. But we should avoid providing an excessive platform for the terrorist/kidnapper. Thus, unless such demands are succinctly stated and free of rhetoric and propaganda, it may be better to paraphrase the demands instead of presenting them through the voice or picture of the terrorist/kidnapper.

2. Except in the most compelling circumstances, and then only with the approval of the President of CBS News, or in his absence, the Senior Vice President of News, there should be no live coverage of the terrorist/kidnapper since we may fall into the trap of providing an unedited platform for him. (This does *not* limit live on-the-spot reporting by CBS News reporters, but care should be exercised to assure restraint and context.)

3. News personnel should be mindful of the probable need by the authorities who are dealing with the terrorist for communication by telephone and hence should endeavour to ascertain, wherever feasible, whether our own use of such lines would be likely to interfere with the authorities' communications.

4. Responsible CBS representatives should endeavour to contact experts dealing with the hostage situation to determine whether they have any guidance on such questions as phraseology to be avoided, what kinds of questions or reports might tend to exacerbate the situation, etc. Any such recommendations by established authorities on the scene should be carefully considered for guidance (but not as instruction) by CBS News personnel.

5. Local authorities should also be given the name or names of CBS personnel whom they can contact should they need further guidance or wish to deal with such delicate questions as a newsman's call to the terrorists or other matters which might interfere with authorities dealing with the terrorists.

6. Guidelines affecting our coverage of civil disturbances are also applicable here, especially those which relate to avoiding the use of inflammatory catchwords

or phrases, the reporting of rumors, etc. As in the case of policy dealing with civil disturbances, in dealing with a hostage story reporters should obey all police instructions but report immediately to their superiors any such instructions that seem to be intended to manage or suppress the news.

7. Coverage of this kind of story should be in such overall balance as to length, that it does not unduly crowd out other news of the hour/day.[97]

Another set of guidelines which has been influential is that of the news agency United Press International (UPI). In addition to some points similar to those in the CBS rules, the UPI rules include the following points:

— We will judge each story on its own and if a story is newsworthy we will cover it despite the dangers of contagion....
— We will do nothing to jeopardize lives.
— We will not become part of the story.
— If we do talk to a kidnapper or terrorist we will not become part of the negotiations.
— If there has been no mention of a deadline we will not ask the kidnapper or terrorist if there is one.[98]

NBC, one of the three big US networks, came up with some points like:

— Don't let competitive pressures override professional journalistic judgment on how much to carry and whether to give live outside news programs.
— Assume the terrorists know everything that's being broadcast on radio and TV.
— Qualify all information carried; hold back rumors until you can check them out.[99]

Looking at other guidelines one soon approaches the point of diminishing returns. In addition to points already mentioned, the guidelines of the Chicago *Sun-Times* and *Daily News* contain a point which specifies that 'The senior supervisory editor should determine what — if any — information should be withheld or deferred after consultation with reporters and appropriate authorities'.[100] The guidelines of the *Courier-Journal* and the *Louisville Times* also address themselves to the question of forced rather than free publicity: 'If terrorists demand that we publish specific information, we will agree to do so only if we are convinced that not to publish it would further endanger the life of a hostage'. Furthermore, the two papers agreed to assign experienced staff members to the story.[101] In a few cases guidelines are specific. KGO-TV in San Francisco, for instance, in the words of its director Peter Jacobus 'no longer broadcasts either verbally or visually the names of terrorist organizations. Rather than identifying them specifically, we now refer to them only as "terrorists groups" or "terrorist group". We have also tightened our policy of not reporting bomb threats. No organization's threat or messages are broadcast unless first cleared by myself, by the assistant news director, or by the executive producer.'[102] Some guidelines also recommend avoidance of reports of police movements or stress that a minimum of details on how a terroristic act was committed should be made known to prevent other terrorists from acquiring free know-how.[103]

Many of these guidelines have been introduced in the wake of a particular terrorist incident such as the Hanafi episode in early 1977. They are therefore often no more than a formalization of the lessons learned in one or a few instances. Generally these instances have been acts of hostage-taking in siege situations. For this particular situation they might be useful but they do not address themselves to wider media-induced effects, such as the ones we have discussed in the previous chapter. In fact these guidelines can hardly be called an improvement on conventional news judgment as expressed in the communications we have received from media without written guidelines but with a certain editorial policy in matters of terrorism.

Respondents to our questionnaire who said that their medium had a certain policy for handling news on terrorism mentioned many of the same points contained in written guidelines. In addition they, and some other sources of ours, mentioned aspects such as:

— Inform public without providing propaganda opportunity to terrorists.
— Bring no news that could warn terrorists about police operations.
— Do not help the terrorists unless the authorities demand otherwise.
— Do not publish terrorist communiqués if such communications adversely affect the solution of the case in the judgment of the authorities.
— Hand over incoming terrorist documents to the police.
— Do not make prosecution by law enforcing agencies more difficult.
— Anti-terrorist editorial policy.
— No publicity to hoax calls.
— No spread of fear to the masses.
— No glamorization of terrorists.
— Avoid unnecessary repetitions.
— Avoid bloody scenes.[104]

Some of the respondents to our questionnaire thought that written guidelines were useless in practice, while others held that they assured consistency in reporting and allowed quicker and more effective operation. Most of our respondents regarded restrictions to the public's right to know as justified if the information would aid the terrorists, would affect an impending police action or was likely to cause public panic. Thirteen out of twenty-two respondents said that they would usually voluntarily comply if the government asked for a (temporary) news embargo during a terroristic incident, while six more said that they would listen to the arguments of the authorities and then use their own judgment. Thirteen out of twenty-three respondents said that they had on occasion voluntarily and unilaterally withheld information on aspects of a terroristic incident. But a large majority, twenty-one out of twenty-seven respondents, agreed to the proposition that news market pressures between local media and the presence of the foreign press corps make voluntary restraints very difficult.

The question of censorship, self-censorship and guidelines is to an important extent a question of news-timing. In some terroristic incidents instant coverage is no problem. Timely information in bombing incidents can be a vital public service. Richard Francis, the BBC Controller Northern Ireland, has pointed out how essential such information can be:

> If you are sitting in Belfast in the middle of the afternoon and you hear a loud explosion, your immediate thoughts are of concern for the family – are the children home from school?...has your wife got home from the shops? – and you want to know as soon as possible where the bomb was, whether anyone was injured, and so on. There is a real need for that information, and it is (sic) nothing to do with sensationalism on our part that we broadcast it the moment the facts can be established....In a town like Belfast, which is like a village, rumour can travel faster even than radio....The danger is that without accurate information, people may get it wrong....The possibilities are endless if no details are given.[105]

In such situations media competitiveness can be a blessing rather than a curse since media self-interest and the public interest coincide. In hostage situations, however, the public's right to know or the media's desire to be first with the news and the hostages' right to live might be at odds with each other. In theory it is conceivable that sensitive news could be provided to the public in such situations only via the printed media, while the electronic media which are accessible to the terrorists would subject themselves to temporary restraints. There has indeed been one case in Japan where this division of labour has been applied. In a hijacking incident newspapers were free to report while it was agreed that no news on the incident should be transmitted via airwaves.[106] But if this were to become standard practice the electronic media would feel discriminated against and refuse cooperation. The competitiveness of the media is after all to a considerable extent based on being first with the news. In this respect delayed coverage of terroristic incidents is contrary to the very notion of news.

The government security forces strongly advocate delayed coverage since their own operations can also be hampered by feedbacks of instant coverage. But, on the other hand, the operations of the security forces which might be endangered by media disclosures are at times equally as risky to the hostages as media interference. In our survey respondents to the question of what are the problematical aspects of suppressing news on terrorism, mentioned uncontrolled government actions second only to wild rumours (twenty versus fifteen mentions). A Los Angeles news director held: 'If the media doesn't play an adversary role, the police might take justice further than they should. When we're covering a hostage story, police violence is not our first concern at the height of it, but it is one of the other elements. When the police say, "We don't want you guys around", my first thought is "What are they going to be doing in there?".'[107] The assumption that hostage safety is highest with the police and lower with the media is one that is not always warranted in practice. Media presence at hostage sites can prevent strong-arm solutions at the expense of the hostages.

What is curious about the guidelines on terrorism discussion is that no set of guidelines which we have seen refers to the fact that the media are not only misused by the terrorists, but also quite frequently by the authorities. In response to our questionnaire eight respondents named deliberate misinformation as a problem reporters face when dealing with law enforcement agents during terroristic incidents.[108] Governments have often an active interest in altering the public perception about terrorists and they sometimes falsely report terrorist actions to the press or release 'black propaganda', stories allegedly coming from the terrorists themselves, but in fact issued by the government.[109] If journalists care about misuse of the media in situations of terrorism, these aspects should also receive attention in their guidelines.

While the question of news timing stands central in the guidelines and censorship discussion, there are other areas which are less crucial and where some progress might be made. It should not cause too much pain to the media not to report certain specific details that might serve as instructions for other terrorists. At first sight, it also appears attractive not to mention the names of terrorist groups claiming credit for particular acts. With bombings this might work in the first instance but the terrorist bombers are likely to find ways to be heard. In cases of kidnappings and hostage-taking, the terrorists will, however, find it easy to get their identity across to the public by including self-advertising in their demand package. The Who-did-it is central to any news story and without it news becomes meaningless. A large part of the public wants to know about the insurgent terrorists. In an American opinion survey, mentioned earlier, half of the public thought that coverage of terrorism was necessary. As many as one third of those 64 percent of the public who were convinced that terrorism coverage produces contagion still felt that coverage was necessary to keep the people informed.[110] If the public feels a need to know, the media will find it hard not to respond to this need.

One area where the media in our view are rather too cautious in providing the public with information is the area of interviews with terrorists. While all free media report about the terrorists' bloody acts, very few of them give the terrorists a voice if they do not murder. The broadcasting media in the Republic of Ireland, as we have seen, do not allow interviews with terrorists but they allow their violence to be made known. For reasons best known to themselves many stations and governments are afraid to let the terrorists speak. When the BBC, for instance, planned an in-depth programme about the IRA in 1971, the question of an interview with a terrorist was discussed. The Managing Director of External Broadcasting maintained: 'Even if such an interview was carried out by someone capable of correcting incorrect statements, he was doubtful about the extent to which the views represented by the interviewer could be expected to be as emotionally as well as intellectually penetrating as those of the interviewee.'[111] This sort of hesitation appears to us completely misplaced. The terrorists are not intellectual supermen, their statements are often rather confused and there is a definite need to bring them into contact with common sense. If terrorists want to send a message, they should be offered the opportunity to do so without them having to bomb and kill. Words are cheaper than lives. The public will not be instilled with terror if they see a terrorist speak; they are afraid if they see his victims and not himself. While interviews with terrorists might feed on the voyeurism of the public, they at least do not feed on its sadism as the extensive live reporting on ongoing acts of hostage-taking very well might. If the terrorists believe they have a case, they will be eager to present it to the public. Democratic societies should not be afraid of this. In our view it should even be considered whether terrorists should not be offered a temporary safe conduct to talk to representatives of the public in front of the media.

This proposal is admittedly heretical. But the whole discussion of censorship and guidelines is in a way trying to find a solution in the wrong direction. Many insurgent and pathological terrorists (not the criminal ones) in our view resorted to terrorism as a violent communication strategy because they perceived no other way of getting themselves heard. To advocate censorship of their expressions of violence is in a way advocating double censorship. Their terrorism was, in many cases, born out of a kind of censorship, a censorship not labelled as such but flowing from the restrictive laws of news value of the Western media. To introduce additional laws and guidelines to keep these terrorists from presenting their grievances and frustrations with violence may even increase their level of violence. This is not to say that guidelines are useless and possibly counterproductive. Terrorism is not a simple, uniform phenomenon. Guidelines should reflect this. What might be an appropriate media response in cases of political insurgent terrorism might be a counterproductive response in cases of criminal or pathological terrorism, and vice versa. There should, therefore, be at least three different sets of guidelines. All guidelines should be based on measured effects of impact of terroristic acts. So far there has been no serious research in this field. Guidelines are introduced on the mere basis of unchecked assumptions. The least the media could do before they accept guidelines is to make sure that the guidelines serve the purpose for which they are meant. Guidelines are a form of censorship and it has to be demonstrated that their effects are positive not only for the media themselves but also for the public and, above all, for the hostages. If restrictions are imposed on the news the people get, the least the public should demand is that the nature of these restrictions is known. The present guidelines are often secret and if manipulation of news for higher purposes such as saving hostages has to be introduced, the public should have a right to know this.

CONCLUSION

In the preceding pages we have, often implicitly, enumerated arguments in favour and against some form of censorship on terrorist news. Here we would like to place them side by side (see Table 4A).

The list offers no more than more or less plausible hypotheses whose validity is unproven, and even if the validity of some of them could be established they would not be automatically valid in all places at all times.

If censorship is considered one should ask in whose interest it is. It

Table 4A
Arguments for a Censorship Debate

Arguments for Censorship	Arguments against Censorship
1. Insurgent terrorists use the media as a platform for political propaganda which also helps them to recruit new members to their movement	1. If the media would keep quiet on terrorist atrocities, the violent men might be judged less negatively by sections of the public
2. Since publicity is a major, and in some cases the unique reward sought by terrorists, censorship would make terrorism a less desirable strategy	2. With psychotic terrorists publicity can be a substitute for violence. Without media attention their threats might be translated into acts
3. Detailed coverage of incidents by the media provides potential terrorists with a model that increases their success chance in their own acts	3. Political terrorists boycotted by the media might step up their level of violence until the media have to cover their deeds
4. Information broadcast during incidents can be useful to terrorists	4. If the media did not report on terrorism, rumours would spread, which might be worse than the worst media reporting
5. Media presence during acts of hostage-taking can endanger hostages	5. During siege situations, media presence can prevent the police from engaging in indefensible tactics, causing unnecessary loss of lives among hostages and terrorists
6. Reporting on acts of terrorism can produce imitative acts	6. If terrorism would be treated with silence, governments could label all sort of quasi- or non-terroristic activities by political dissenters terroristic; uncontrolled government actions might be the result
7. In cases of kidnappings, media reports can cause panic with the kidnapper so that he kills the victim	7. If the media would censor terrorism the public would suspect that other things are censored as well; credibility in the media will decline
8. People who have so little respect for other people's lives as terrorists do, should not be enabled to command public attention only because they use violence	8. Suppression of news on terrorism might leave the public with a false sense of security. People would be unprepared to deal with terrorism when directly faced with it
9. Sadism in the public might be activated by reporting terrorist acts	9. The lack of public awareness of certain terroristic activities would keep the public from fully understanding the political situation
10. Media reports on terrorist outrages might lead to vigilantism and uncontrolled revenge acts against the group the terrorists claim to speak for	10. The feeling of being deprived of vital information might create a public distrust in the political authorities
11. Negative news demoralizes the public while 'good news makes us good'	11. The assertion of insurgent terrorists that democratic states are not really free would gain added credibility if the freedom of the press were suspended

might be in the interest of the insurgent terrorists who want to close down an open society. It can be in the interest of the government who jumps at the issue of terrorism to squash all other non-terroristic resistance as well. It might be in the interest of hostages who are spared the agony that inflammatory statements of self-serving media personalities towards excitable terrorists could lead to retaliation against them. It could be in the interest of the media who are besieged by publicity-thirsty herostrats. It might be in the interest of the public whose collective reaction to a terrorist threat might cause more damage than the execution of the threat itself. In practice censorship will in a particular circumstance serve some of these five groups and harm others. Difficult questions will arise. Is the value of a fully informed public higher than the value of a hundred hostages' lives?

The Western media usually defend their freedom to report by pointing to the public's right to know. This notion probably goes back to Thomas Paine who wrote: 'In the representative system the reason for everything must publicly appear. Every man is a proprietor in government, and considers it a necessary part of his business to understand....There can be no mystery.'[112] But the 'public right to know' is, at least in the United States, not a right at all. It is not part of the US Bill of Rights. It appears that it found its way into the media's armour of self-justification in 1945 when the general manager of the Associated Press, Kent Cooper, introduced it. It has no legal standing with courts.[113] The media have, in many countries, a right to report but not a right to gather any news there is. If there was a public right to know anything the editors of the public media could no longer select the news according to their own principles but would have to print it all, which with today's amount of news is impossible. As it is, an average medium makes less than 10 percent of the information it receives public and what is made public about any particular event is only a small part of what is known about it. The details of a story which do not fit into the framework of an editor, because they are boring, commercially uninteresting, contrary to the philosophy of a medium and so on, are left out although some segments of the public might wish to know them. Nobody speaks about censorship in such cases. But if the government interferes with this sometimes very arbitrary 'free flow of information' the cry of censorship is raised. There is much truth in an accusation of Professor Meikeljohn who said that 'freedom of the press had become an excuse for the controllers of mass communication to duck responsibility and to exercise by default the same censorship role which had been denied the government'.[114] The Western news media print, if they can, what they want, which is frequently also what the public wants. They print and broadcast, if they are market-oriented enterprises, what is generally profitable for them to make public. But what is profitable for the media is not always good for the public or sections thereof. Some information can cause damage, to hostages for instance. To suppress details or delay parts of such information is not, in our view, a serious infringement of the public's right to know. There are many more important public issues where the media keep silent because they have, in their view, no news value. It is somewhat dishonest if the public's right to know is selectively invoked by the media to justify the publication of profitable but damaging information.

Some forms of guidelines on media coverage of terrorism seem desirable and defensible. The question is who should formulate such guidelines. If the media do it themselves, they might be too self-serving, steering in the direction that they still want to use the exciting news terrorists provide without allowing themselves to be used by the terrorists. If the government establish such guidelines they will tend to serve the government first and this might be even more harmful. Joint government-media guidelines might best serve the two contracting parties but might neglect the interests of the hostages and the public. The proper body to formulate guidelines in matters of media coverage of terrorism should therefore, in our view, be a public body. The public, after all, pays for the news, the public is influenced by the news and it should have a say in how it wants to be informed on such serious public matters. We are accustomed to elect parliaments that make laws by which we govern ourselves. Should we not, in this Age of Communication, also elect a media council that decides what news is good for us to learn, with due respect for minorities such as hostages? If some news on terrorism has to be censored it should be done by such a publicly elected body.

We have, in this chapter, discussed censorship and terrorism within the framework of the Western information order. But we advocate that a solution should also be sought by questioning this information order itself. This we shall attempt to do in our last chapter.

5. INSURGENT TERRORISM AND THE WESTERN INFORMATION ORDER

In this last chapter we would like to return to some of the issues raised in the first and we will try to broaden the discussion. Our basic premise is that insurgent terrorism can be better understood if it is viewed in the first instance as communication rather than as mere violence. If this assumption is correct, it follows that this type of terrorism has to be explained in relation to the prevailing information order and the news values that are paramount within this order. In the preceding chapters we have tried, as often as possible, to marshal empirical evidence to support our argumentation. In this chapter we can do little more than offer some illustrative material and make some references to authorities in the field of communication research. This study has been an exploratory one and in this concluding chapter we will carry the exploration into even more uncertain and unproven territory.

TERRORISM AS COMMUNICATION

Our point of departure has been to distinguish terroristic violence from ordinary violence between two conflicting parties by introducing a third party. Since normally only two of the three concerned parties are present at the scene of terroristic violence, communication is required to involve the third party. This communication can take place via the mass media but that is not a necessary prerequisite. There was terrorism

before the advent of the mass media and the most widespread type of
terrorism, state terrorism, still largely works without the media. In the
triangle Terrorist-Victim-Target, the victim, who is usually but not
always in some ways associated with the target, serves as instrument to
communicate a message to the target which is meant to traumatize,
demoralize or otherwise influence him (see Diagram 5A).

Diagram 5A
The Triangle of Insurgent Terrorism

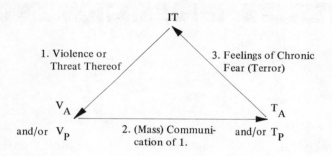

(IT = Insurgent Terrorist; V_A = Victim Belonging to the Camp of the State
Authorities; V_P = Victim Being Part of the Public; T_A = The Authorities as
Target; T_P = The Public as Target)

For the Russian social-revolutionary terrorists of the late nineteenth
century bombing was a form of language. Their bombs were means of
expressing their dissent with the inhuman social order in which they
found themselves, an autocratic order that granted no freedom of
assembly and no freedom of the press. When in the 1880s terrorist
violence occurred in the United States, some of the Russian terrorists
expressed their disapproval, arguing that since the American democracy
granted other channels of expression, terrorism was not justifiable. In
the eyes of Western terrorists, however, the accessibility of the ordinary
channels of communication was largely illusionary. A drastic change
had taken place since the end of the eighteenth century when the
notions of freedom of speech and opinion and freedom of the press
evolved. At that time a typical newspaper was a single sheet, written
often by a single man, with a circulation of a few hundred or at best a
few thousand copies. The size of the media message and the audience of
a medium were not above the one a single man with a single speech to
an audience in the open air could command. Within a century this had

all changed. At the end of the nineteenth century a few press organs such as those of William Randolph Hearst could reach a million people every day, spread over a wide geographic area. And it did not stop there. Today the United Press International (UPI), founded by Hearst, can reach hundreds of millions of people globally with its messages which are translated into forty-eight languages.[1] The freedom of speech, which was intended for everyone, had in effect become very unequal since the chance to be heard had changed so drastically with the rise of the mass media. There was no way in which an irregular handprinted anarchist underground paper could compete with the big bourgeois press. Less and less was it readership alone which accounted for the prosperity and wide distribution of a newspaper but the power to attract advertisements which often paid more than half of the production costs of a paper. And anarchists who did not support the capitalist order in their papers could not expect to get advertisements from the business class. Their papers were therefore condemned to stay small and their influence in shaping public opinion through their own media was almost negligible.

The democratic promise of the American Revolution had been understood by many as an egalitarian promise. People would no longer be ruled by unaccountable rulers from above but would govern themselves by electing law-makers and officials. To do this they required a continuous public discussion in which every voice was heard so that the best course of action could be chosen. That was the democratic theory. The practice turned out to be different. The *public discussion* took place in *private media* and the owners of them made sure that some voices to whom they were sympathetic received a wider audience than others. In the words of A. J. Liebing: 'Freedom of the press is limited to those who own one'.[2] The historical importance of this change has escaped the attention of most observers. When it is expressed in words it is often done in a tentative way, as for instance in the question of Earl L. Vance: 'Is freedom of the press to be conceived as a personal right appertaining to all citizens, as undoubtedly the (US) Founding Fathers conceived it; or as a property right appertaining to the ownership of newspapers and other publications, as we have come to think of it largely today?'[3] This transformation of the freedom of the press from a public freedom to a private property, a subcategory of the freedom of private enterprise, has had a decisive influence on the evolution of democracy. The people were still allowed to cast a ballot every four years or so, but the media owners could influence the public discussion every day. By granting access to the mass media to some but not to others they could direct the course of public discussion, they could choose the subject matter to be discussed and they could, in their editorial columns, pass judgment on the issues and participants of the public discussion. Although taking sides with the underdog, as practised by some journalists in the muckraking period in the United States before the First World War, did counteract this to some extent, muckraking never became the mainstream of Western journalism. The media owners had a power much greater than that of each voter. The news press barons with their unrivalled power to communicate ideas had an instrument to steer or divert the masses that in many ways surpassed the pre-democratic power of feudal barons. With their power to inform, they could effectively form the audience that was theirs. Amitai Etzioni has observed that 'to some degree power and communication may be substituted for each other'.[4] The power of mass communication has been well described by George Gerbner with the words: 'The truly revolutionary significance of modern mass communication is...the ability to form historically new bases for collective thought and action, quickly, continuously and pervasively across the previous boundaries of time, space and status'.[5]

In the eyes of most nineteenth-century terrorists, the power of the bourgeois press was a counter-revolutionary power. By giving visibility to some social phenomena but not to others, the mass media could shape people's perception of the world. Ralph Waldo Emerson's optimistic statement, made in 1870, 'We have the newspaper, which does its best to make every square acre of land and sea give an account of itself at your breakfast table'[6] implied an equality of access to newsmaking which practice did not bear out. The black people of America, for instance, could find little about themselves in the bourgeois press. One analysis, surveying the portrayal of blacks in Californian media for the period 1892-1954, found, for instance, that, except in periods of rioting, less than 1 percent of the total news space was normally devoted to blacks. Even after the major growth of black communities during and after the Second World War, this picture did not change substantially. For the media the black man remained an invisible man, except when he used violence.[7]

Except when he used violence − it was this responsiveness of the bourgeois press to violence from below which the nineteenth-century terrorists discovered and developed into the 'Propaganda of the Deed', or terrorism. The bourgeois press had made crime reporting one of its first specializations in reporting. This recording of social transgressions fulfilled two functions. On the one hand it served to register the threats to the dominant order so that counter-measures could be taken. On the other hand crime reporting had a certain curiosity-satisfying and entertainment function for those segments of the public leading law-abiding lives. The common criminals had little use for this publicity; they preferred to remain anonymous, to avoid visibility. Unlike them the terrorists, using the violent and publicity-bestowing methods of crime, sought publicity deliberately as a means to obtain access to the mass media and through them to a mass audience.

In the nineteenth century the terrorists' targets were mainly authoritarian rulers and their higher servants. This has led some analysts of terrorism such as Walter Laqueur to believe that terrorism owes its intellectual origins to tyrannicide.[8] This hypothesis would be more tenable if terrorism had remained discriminate in the choice of its targets as it largely was in the nineteenth century. It is known that Russian social-revolutionary terrorists refrained from throwing their bombs when the chosen target was in the presence of children. But on the other hand there were already bombing attacks against parliaments and cafés in the France of the 1890s where the degree of discrimination was much lower. And today's insurgent terrorism is often quite deliberately indiscriminate in the choice of targets. In Algeria, for instance, the main victims of terrorism in the period 1954-1962 were natives and not French colonists. In the last decade terrorists have victimized nuns (Argentina), children (the Netherlands, Israel), pilgrims (Israel, Saudi Arabia) and tourists (Spain) — categories of people that have nothing at all to do with tyrants. Partly, this choice of soft targets is a result of the fact that today's rulers are often so well protected that other victims have to be chosen. In a military sense, this type of terrorism is an indirect strategy. But that, in our view, is not the main reason why often innocent people are victimized. The reason is rather that the voice of innocent people is sometimes capable of producing a stronger echo among the population. If Somoza had been kidnapped, how many people in Nicaragua would have wanted him back? But to kidnap the Roman Pope, an innocent man compared to Somoza, as the German June 2nd movement planned in 1976, would have created a directly concerned audience of 543 million Catholics and countless others. The point we wish to make is that the choice of victims made by insurgent terrorists is in the first instance a function of their publicity value, of their communication potential.

Killing a single Jew and getting publicity, George Habash has argued, was more important that killing scores of Jews in battle. The flames in the Marks & Spencer department store in London in August 1969 (the result of a Palestinian incendiary attack), Habash said, were worth as much as the burning of two Kibbutzim, 'because we force people to ask what is going on'.[9] Terrorism, in this sense, is, in our view, best understood as a form of communication. It can be explained in terms of a felt lack of access to communication by ordinary means. Some individuals and groups who are not granted normal access to news-making in the present information order use terroristic violence to gain such access. When President Johnson decided in 1968 not to run for re-election he could command television time to announce this personal decision to a domestic audience of seventy-seven million Americans.[10] On the other hand a young man took some bank employees hostage in Sacramento so that it would be reported in the television news programme that neither he nor his father could get a job.[11] To make a public announcement about their job or lack thereof, the president of the United States had habitual access to news-making while the unemployed man in California had to obtain access by means of a violent disruption, terrorism. When Lynette Fromme tried to make a public statement and went to the UPI office in San Francisco she was told, as we said earlier (p. 116), to come back when she had some 'hard' news She subsequently made an assassination attempt on President Ford to get over her message, which was, according to her own saying, that the media should warn big business to cease destroying the planet.[12] Her previous attempt to deliver such a message without the use of violence had failed; terrorism provided her with a channel to convey her statement. As it was this message was overshadowed by the way it was delivered. The media placed so much attention on the deed itself and the personal psychology of the disturbed girl, that her intended message got practically lost to the public. For the unemployed man and for the disturbed girl, terrorism was a means of getting access to news-making, to deliver a message.

To seek the root for this type of terrorism in tyrannicide seems unwarranted. More to the point are the words of Friedrich Hacker, who wrote:

The terrorist act is an appeal to the environment for help, a drastic challenge to a disinterested, blind and deaf world, which ignores the justified desires and requirements of the unjustly treated, disregarded terrorists. . . .The signal points to a hitherto insufficiently realized emergency and announces that the terrorists are no longer willing to tolerate any longer the past neglect.[13]

The degree of injustice and disregard which the insurgent terrorists feel, however, is a subjective and relative degree and in many cases their evaluation of the situation is not widely shared and sometimes for good reasons. A case illustrating Hacker's point seems to be the Hanafi incident, staged by Khaalis and his friends. Eric Sevareid, the CBS commentator, noted that it was the absence of publicity that drove Khaalis to the act of hostage taking. The fact that the media had paid so little attention to the slaughtering of his wife and children by a rival Muslim group appeared to have maddened Khaalis so much that he decided to stage his triple act of terrorism in Washington, DC.[14] In a more general vein another American observer has remarked:

I think the media, all of us, should be aware of another problem, the growing sense of impotence on behalf of the people. They cannot get into the media. They cannot get their view printed or heard or seen. And this sense of impotence, this sense of frustration on behalf of the people, is what causes them to terrorize the media.... We should be concerned about access to the media. It's much better to let them rant a little bit beforehand than after, with the terror.[15]

What applies to individual terrorists often also applies to terrorist movements. Richard Francis, Director of News and Current Affairs of the BBC, has observed with regard to the political violence in Northern Ireland:

The history of broadcasting in Ireland, and in Northern Ireland in particular, will suggest, I believe, that it was the omission from our air during the sixties of the voices of extremism and the proper examination of the legitimate aims of Republicanism which did...unfortunately, lead to the troubles that have been going on for the best part of ten years.... What the broadcaster has to understand is that people who have been frustrated in achieving those legitimate aims within the democratic framework, have to some extent been forced outside it.... There must be a danger that if you don't heed, listen to, challenge, engage the voices of extremism, then those voices will turn to violent methods and will step outside the democratic process in order to make themselves felt. And I would make a strong plea, certainly in terms of our experience in Ireland, for the broadcaster to take on these responsibilities at the earliest stage, at the lowest level, in order to diffuse that which can be very much worse later on.[16]

Another journalist, David Anable, of the *Christian Science Monitor*, has expressed a similar thought in regard to the Middle East: 'I wonder what agonies we might have saved had the press displayed the Palestinian case *before* violence reached a peak.'[17]

Where individuals or ethnic and revolutionary minorities cannot get their grievances redressed via the channels of politics and where they cannot get their views across effectively via the channels of mass communication, the chance that some of them will resort to terrorism is high. Even for terrorists who seek nothing less than total revolution of society, a problem of communication often stands at the basis of their movements' origin. Take the example of the German student terrorists. In the 1960s the German universities became accessible for a much wider group of people than the sons of the traditional upper class. Young people, often with a great deal of idealism, met in and around universities and engaged in critical political discussions that challenged the prevailing materialism, the sterile cold war rhetoric, the growing militarization and the exploitation of the Third World. The role of Germany's political big brother, the United States, in Southeast Asia, Germany's own relations with the repressive regime of the Shah of Iran were matters of active concern for them. The political convictions that ripened in these discussions, however, were essentially a product of the rather incestuous debate among themselves, with only a few professors and intellectuals participating. The centre of these discussions, further-more, was Berlin, a cold war stronghold away from the political centre of the German Federal Republic and away also from the bulk of the German population. With the debates being so isolated, the young radicals completely lost touch with the views that prevailed in society, while the constant interaction of those opposed to the existing social system led to an intolerant dogmatism.[18]

When in 1967 the Shah of Iran and the US vice-president Hubert Humphrey came to Berlin, these students went to the streets to protest against the inhuman policies for which these men stood. In the German media the Shah had always had a very good press, the majority press occupying itself with the court and family life of the Shah-in-Shah while the minority press generally treated Reza Pahlewi's much pub-licized 'White Revolution' seriously, although it was a sham.[19] The widespread repression in Iran, costing the lives of many ten thousands of people and the activities of the Shah's secret service SAVAK abroad, on the other hand were treated in the media with benign silence. When the student demonstrators wanted to correct this false picture of the Shah and demonstrated in the streets of Berlin, they were attacked and one of them, Benno Ohnesorg, was killed by the police without any provocation on his part. The date of this unpunished killing, June 2nd (1967), was the name which one of the two most important German terrorist movements adopted. The other major German terrorist move-ment, the Rote Armee Fraktion (RAF) can be traced back in its origin to the Humphrey visit and the protests against the Vietnam war. More than a decade later it is clear that the perceptions of these students about Iran and Vietnam were closer to the reality than those that prevailed at the time in the German media. Yet in the late 1960s some of the Berlin students turned to terroristic methods because of a failure to get those perceptions across by conventional means. At the basis of their misdirected course stood, in our view, problems of communication, lack of access to the masses via the mass media.

Once they used violence they got all the attention there was to get but it was not attention to their ends but to their means, which completely transformed the situation. Most political capital to be gained from a continuation of acts of terrorism was harvested by the conservative right-wing forces in German society. With a perverted sort of logic some of the German terrorists still seem to think that this development is helpful for their cause in the same way as some German communists in the early 1930s saw no objection to the Nazis coming to power, arguing that after the Nazis it would be their turn. The activities of the second and third generation of German terrorists can, although some of them are clearly publicity-seeking, no longer be interpreted in terms of lacking access to the media. They have to be seen more as revenge acts and attempts to liberate imprisoned colleagues by people who have almost completely isolated themselves and are mainly concerned with selling their skins as dearly as possible to a security apparatus that shows little compassion and that seems to have an institutional self-interest in exaggerating the danger of the terrorist threat. In 1977, for instance, Germany experienced less than twenty terrorist incidents, yet the police and media-fostered hysteria about them seemed to surpass the reaction in Italy which in the same year had over 2,000 terrorist incidents.[20] While the original terrorists used violence in an attempt to communicate with the apathetic masses, the ongoing terrorist violence is today instrumentalized by their professional enemies to convince the population of the necessity of an all-encompassing internal security system, which in the hands of a different government party than the present one may pose a great threat to democracy in Germany. For the sake of fairness it has to be added that the German government has in the meantime somewhat recovered from the hysterical overreaction of 1977. In late 1979 some conciliatory gestures were initiated which made it easier for terrorists in the underground to return to society.

To avoid misunderstanding, we would like to stress that we do not regard all insurgent terrorism as an attempt to get access to the mass media where other channels are unavailable or thought to be unavailable. While all acts of terrorism are, in our definition, acts of communication, not all of them are aimed at the mass media. In a war of national liberation in a country where the majority is often illiterate and without radios, access to the local media is often not a prime objective, though the winning of foreign publicity might be. In many cases acts of terrorism might simply serve as bargaining instruments to get prisoners released, or to demoralize the enemy without the media being utilized. Acts of terrorism by insurgents can also serve to obtain money by kidnapping as in criminal terrorism. In such cases publicity is incidental for the terrorists and not the primary objective. In the course of a terrorist campaign the number of acts serving such tactical rather than mass communicational objectives might be higher, as it is for instance in Northern Ireland. Yet this should not blind us to the fact that at the beginning of such a campaign by members of down-trodden minorities or groups that feel themselves misunderstood, terrorism is used to communicate grievances and aspirations. There is, however, a strong element of imitation in insurgent terrorism. With the aid of the mass media it has become a fashionable technique of protest. This fashionableness has led to an ubiquity of terrorist acts which tends to deflect the observer's attention from the historical and communica-tional roots of modern insurgent terrorism. In its original form insurgent terrorism is a symptom that something is wrong with the communication system of a society.

In the following pages we will attempt to offer an analysis of some elements of the Western information order which in our view are related to the occurrence of insurgent terrorism.

THE POWER OF THE MEDIA

Power, defined as the possibility to influence the behaviour of others to one's own advantage, is something that is likely to be exercised by and through the mass media since so many people spend so much time with the media. Table 5B gives an impression on how central the mass media have become in the lives of individuals in developed countries.

If we assume that the Dutch figures for sleeping, working and eating are equal to the American ones, amounting to 101.6 hours per week, it is evident that of the remaining 66.4 hours the average Dutch person spends 74.05 percent of his time with the media, while the average American spends 80.53 percent of his time with them. Although these percentages are in practice lower since some activities like eating and listening are done simultaneously, the chance the media have to influence people is second to no other influence in terms of quantity of

Table 5B
Media Consumption in the United States and in the Netherlands.
National averages during one week (168 hours), in hours.[21]

Activity	The Netherlands	The United States
Sleeping	–	53.2 hours
Working	–	40.0 hours
Eating	–	8.4 hours
Watching Television	15.75 hours	26.4 hours
Listening to the Radio	22.75 hours	21.2 hours
Reading Newspapers	3.66 hours	4.2 hours
Reading Magazines	1.90 hours	3.3 hours
Reading Books	1.50 hours	0.06 hours
Attending a Movie (cinema)	0.18 hours	0.2 hours
Listening to Records	3.43 hours	1.3 hours
Total average media consumption time	49.17 hours	56.66 hours

exposure. The situation seems to differ little in the developed socialist countries; Soviet citizens are known to spend up to thirty-five hours per week in front of their television sets.[22] Many of us have passed the point where direct first-hand experience has been replaced by mediated second-hand experience as our main sensory input. While in former times only a few scholars and monks filled their brains with second-hand impressions, this condition has now become fairly widespread due to the pervasiveness of the mass media. This offers the media a chance for remote control without the media consumer being fully aware of it. Ben Bagdikian has put it in these words:

News is the peripheral nervous system of the body politic, sensing the total environment and selecting which sights and sounds shall be transmitted to the public.... Where once priests and kings decided what the populace would hear, the proprietors of the mass media now decide.... For most of the people of the world, for most of the events in the world, what the news system does not transmit did not happen. To that extent the world and its inhabitants are what the news media say they are.[23]

While only a small part of the media output is in the form of news, our minds are formed by news as well as non-news media material. Certain images are put in our heads, social situations are problematized in certain ways, things are depicted as typical or abnormal — in short, norms and values as well as information are transmitted to us overtly and covertly by the media. The image of the world provided by the media tends to find its reflection in the perception of the media users. George Gerbner, who has done much research on the content of violent US television series, has measured some of the distortions that can be attributed to American television. In his field of study, he found that:

Heavy viewers of television were more likely to overestimate the percentage of the world population that lives in America; they seriously overestimated the percentage of the population who have professional jobs; and they drastically overestimated the number of police in the US and the amount of violence. In all these cases, the overestimate matched a distortion that exists in television programming. The more television people watched, the more their view of the world matched television reality.[24]

If media-users are saddled with a view of the world that is not in conformity with reality, their ability to function optimally in reality is obviously impaired. To impose on people certain views on the nature of the world and society, something of which the media are obviously capable to a considerable extent, is to wield a power instrument that is the more efficient the less it is noticed as such.

The mass media have a potential for social control but there is a fierce dispute about the extent of this control. Basically there are two main models. On the one hand there is the Commercial Laissez-Faire Model which seems to be quite popular among the people in the media themselves. It argues that the variety and diversity of information which the mass media direct towards the public leaves the public with a relatively high degree of freedom of choice. By selectively using the media, and by using different media side by side, the public has, in this view, a good chance of being served well by the media in general. The effects of the media are in the Commercial Laissez-Faire Model seen as less pervasive and formative than other exposures of individuals such as personal experience and face-to-face contacts.

On the other hand there is the Manipulative Model, of which there are centrist as well as right- and left-wing versions. All three versions see the media as very powerful shapers of people's minds. According to the right-wing version the media are seen as destroying our cultural heritage by propagating permissiveness and lowering civilized standards. The centrist version of the Manipulative Model sees the media as an integrative force for unity and cohesion in an otherwise divided world. Niklas Luhmann, a German proponent of this version, for instance holds that world society can only be integrated communicatively via the mass media, whose primary social function lies in the 'sharing of all in a common reality, or, to be more precise, in the creation of such a supposition, which then as operative fiction forces itself (on us) and becomes reality'.[25]

The left-wing version, finally, sees the public as an atomized mass, helplessly and unconsciously exposed to messages from a powerful and monolithic source, which diverts the public from the real issues and manipulates them on others.[26] One of the leading proponents of a left-wing version, Dallas W. Smythe, wrote:

To summarize: the mass media institutions in monopoly capitalism developed the equipment, workers and organization to produce audiences for the purposes of the system between about 1875 and 1950. The prime purpose of the mass media complex is to produce people in audiences who work at learning the theory and practice of civilian goods and who support (with taxes and votes) the military demand management system. The second principal purpose is to produce audiences whose theory and practice confirms the ideology of monopoly capitalism (possessive individualism in an authoritarian political system). The third principal purpose is to produce public opinion supportive of the strategic and tactical policies of the state.... Necessarily in the monopoly capitalist system, the fourth purpose of the mass media complex is to operate itself so profitably as to insure unrivalled respect for its economic importance in the system. It has been successful in achieving all four purposes.[27]

So far, none of the contending models and versions thereof has been able to marshal enough empirical evidence to establish its claim to higher explication power. But the Laissez-Faire Model is clearly the weaker model. In practice, most people do not consult different media. According to polls taken in the mid-1970s, three-quarters of all Americans get most of their news from television, while half of them get all their news from that source.[28] And since 'seeing is believing' — a rudiment from the times when people still got most of their experience from participatory observation — television, which is, at least in the United States as far as news is concerned, arguably the worst source, is trusted more than other media.[29] Even if people would consult different media to get a less one-sided view of the reality beyond their perception they would encounter difficulties since the various media are often controlled by the same handful of owners. In the United States, for instance, five giant publishers account for the great bulk of magazines read and five companies produce almost all movies which Americans see. The three major television networks and the major newspaper chains are all controlled by a few banking groups.[30] Comparable situations exist — though in less drastic form — in other countries. Often different products (quality newspapers and mass papers) are in fact produced by the same owner. The influence potential of the mass media is also greater than the Commercial Laissez-Faire Model assumes. The very amount of time people spend with the media makes personal experience and face-to-face contacts for the great bulk of people an unlikely effective alternative source of acquainting themselves with the world beyond their own direct surrounding at a time when major changes take place at frequent intervals. Steve Chibnall has not put it too strongly when he wrote:

The news media are our central repositories and disseminators of knowledge and, as such, exert a considerable influence over our perceptions of group and life styles of which we have little first-hand experience. They have the power to create issues and define the boundaries of debates and, while they may not manipulate our opinions in any direct sense — creating attitudes by changing old ones — they can organize opinion and develop world views by providing structures of understanding into which isolated and unarticulated attitudes and beliefs may be fitted. They provide interpretation, symbols of identification, collective values and myths which are able to transcend cultural boundaries within a society like Britain. Simultaneously, the news media are able to address factory workers in Wigan and solicitors in Surbiton and can realistically expect to be understood and, in situations which are experienced as unfamiliar and where no contradictory preconceptions exist, they can expect to be accepted by both.[31]

There can be little doubt in our view that the mass media can mould mass perception. The media and their habitual sources can direct public attention to some issues in which they have an interest and they can divert it from others which are potentially harmful to their interests. By reporting on certain events and persons the media can confer enhanced status on them and make them look legitimate. They are also able to persuade the masses and mobilize their consent or tolerance as psychological or real weapons (e.g. as votes) in the struggle with rivals.[32]

In order to understand the full power of the media and their news one has to look at some characteristics of power. Social power in societies is relational power. Basically there are two ways in which a power-holder can determine our actions: he can influence our behaviour by credible threats or he can influence it by promising rewards. A ruler gets his followers either because they fear him or because they place their hopes in him. In the second case an identification of the ruled with the ruler takes place that makes the exercise of power an almost effortless affair. This identification with the ruler can be based on the ruler's real representation of the interests of the people, but it can also be based on the mere image of such a representation. To rule by attraction based on the projection of a true or false image is cheap compared to the rule by threat with all the repressive systems which have to be kept in working order. In its crudest form rule by threat is rule by violence and rule by attraction is rule by material rewards. In its more refined form rule by threat is rule by law, whereby the sanctioning power behind it is carefully regulated. Rule by attraction can, in its evolved form, be exercised without material rewards but with the aid of psychic, spiritual and intellectual gratifications, e.g. by providing people with satisfying visions of the world and their place in it. Such cosmological visions can be provided to people by the media and one form of it can be the news. In practice societies are held together by a combination of threats and attractions although the mix between the two varies from society to society. Political theorists interested in finding out what glues people together have usually based their constructions on the latent or overt threat systems. Rousseau, for instance, invented in the eighteenth century the notion of a Social Contract by which people delegated their natural rights in part to the state which in exchange for the monopoly of violence was charged with protecting them. Other theorists have developed different concepts but nearly all of them also take the threat system as point of departure. Recently a new sociological school, ethnomethodology, has placed the emphasis elsewhere. Jonathan Turner has summarized the new perspective in these words:

In fact, the cement that holds society together may not be the values, norms, common definitions, exchange payoffs, role bargains, interest coalitions, and the like of current social theory, but people's explicit and implicit 'methods' for creating the presumption of a social order.... What is 'really real', then, are the methods people employ in constructing, maintaining, and altering for each other a sense of order — regardless of the content and substance of their formulations. While not all ethnomethodologists would go this far, it is a reasonable conclusion that 'order' is not maintained by some society 'out there', but by *people's capacity to convince each other* that society is out there. Furthermore, the substance and content of their visions of society are perhaps not as important in maintaining order as the continually ongoing *processes* of constructing, maintaining, and altering some kind of vision, whatever it may be.

The relevance of this observation for the activities of the media is evident. If the capacity to convince each other is so central, the mass media with their mass audiences are naturally the prime agents in this process. The media in general and the news media in particular are then the main constructors of what ethnomethodologists call an 'occasioned corpus', a *perception* by interacting humans that the current setting has an orderly and understandable structure.[33] We have noted above that one way of regulating behaviour in society is to impose laws. News, in this view, is a second regulatory code system, analogous to law, which conditions our behaviour. One of the proponents of this view describes news as the end product of a continuous processing of raw information which permits organizing social experience in general categories. He defines news as an autonomous regulatory mechanism in social processes with a consequent social integrative function. The genesis of news is in this view analogous to the creation of laws, with the difference that news exists within a much more flexible, almost daily modified system of norms.[34]

The ethnomethodological perspective works on such a level of abstraction that empirical verification is difficult. But the new perspective is refreshing as can for instance be judged from the way two ethnomethodologists look at the media:

We see media as reflecting not a world out there, but the practices of those having the power to determine the experience of others.... In the West as in the East, parallels exist between the event needs of assemblers and promotors (of news). These parallels do not necessarily result from plots, conspiracies, 'selling out' or even ideological communalities.... Though perhaps unaware of the implications of one another's work, they somehow manage to produce a product which favors the event needs of certain social groups and disfavors those of others.... We advocate examining the media for the event needs and the methods through which those with access come to determine the experience of publics. We can look for the methods by examining the records which are produced. Seen in this way, one approach to mass media is to look not for reality, but for the purposes which underlie the strategies of creating one reality instead of another.... Only in the accident, and secondly, in the scandal, is the routine political work transcended to some significant degree, thereby allowing access to information which is directly hostile to those groups who typically manage public event making.[35]

The analogy of law and news sketched above opens the way for some interesting speculations about the role of the mass media in maintaining the established social order. One could, for instance, argue that in some 'democracies' the media have become an alternative system of social control substituting for the political control which universal suffrage has taken from the power-holders. At any rate, there seems to be little doubt that the central battles of politics in democracies are increasingly fought out in the media and through the media rather than in the halls of parliament. The capacity of the mass media to cast a single version of reality at a mass audience with an accompanying chance of shaping simultaneously the experience of millions and rallying their support for a cause, have made them singularly attractive instruments of politics. 'The richness and irony of political life', Molotch and Lester have written, 'is made up of a free-wheeling, skilled competition among people having access to the media, trying to mobilize occurrences as resources for their experience-building work.'[36]

Who has access to the Western mass media? Regular, habitual, massive access is reserved for a few, the powerful, the rich and the media themselves. Independently of who owns the media — listener, reader and viewer collectives, the media workers themselves, sectorial interests such as parties, unions, churches, or economic groups or the government or any combination of the above — the number of people who are allowed to express themselves through the mass media is always inferior to the number of people at the receiving end. The very structure of the mass media determines this, independently of ownership and control arrangements. The most widespread form of media control in the West is private ownership, often, in the case of the electronic media, accompanied by some form of government supervision. Since the mass media are dependent on the powerful in society, they usually grant habitual access to those who might otherwise threaten their continuing functioning, for instance by withdrawing their broadcasting licence. Governments can, in many countries, suggest or even dictate what message the media should carry. Alternatively, they can regulate access to the media by invoking some form of censorship on news and other media material harmful to their interests.

Those who cannot get access to the mass media on the basis of their political power can get it on the basis of their economic power. They can buy a mass medium if they are rich enough, they can stage or sponsor public relation events with news value or they can buy advertising space or time in the media. To catch the regular attention of a mass audience in this way, however, is possible only for the very rich. In 1977 an advertising page in *Time* cost $54,000 and one minute for a television commercial in prime time in the United States cost as much as $120,000. In the latter case the audience is something like thirty million people.[37] Yet the price of winning the attention of the American public is obviously well worth paying, since it can redirect consumer behaviour (more than $500,000,000,000 in annual consumer spending) into a direction desired by those who can afford costly advertisement campaigns, the giant (transnational) corporations. In the United States, where almost as much money is spent on advertising as on education (more than twenty-five billion dollars in 1977, of which more than six billions went on television commercials)[38] the struggle for mass attention is a fierce one. The American Association of Advertising Agencies has calculated that 1,600 advertisements are daily aimed at each individual of which eighty are noticed and twelve provoke some

specific reaction.[39] Among the major weapons used by the advertisers
to penetrate the defence shields of the public are sex and violence. As
primary human notions dealing with life and death they help to establish
a mass audience for those having access to the mass media.

The messages which the powerful and the rich (the two are often
synonymous) broadcast at audiences by way of the mass media are
rarely explicit. Take the following example. The president of Zaire,
General Mobuto, paid Muhammad Ali and George Foreman five million
dollars each for a boxing match in his country. Boxing, a real but
ritualized form of violence, draws mass audiences. But in Zaire there is
no mass television audience since television-sets are available only to the
top layer of society. The millions of people watching the match via
satellite transmission were all abroad. They were obviously interested in
boxing but the interest of Mobuto lay elsewhere. The contest between
the two champions allowed Mobuto to put his name and the name of
Zaire on the map.[40] Millions of people who had never heard of the
country since it became independent from Belgium in 1960 were in this
way influenced to accept the existence of Zaire and its dictator in their
general picture of the world. Muhammad Ali expressed this by saying:
'I never heard of Zaire before I fought there. *Nobody* ever heard of
Zaire before I fought there. Now everybody's heard of Zaire.' Such was
Mobuto's public relation success that the racist white rulers of South
Africa offered forty million dollars to the black champion for a boxing
event in South Africa, presumably to counter anti-apartheid propaganda
abroad. While in this case the black boxer refused to be instrumentalized
for white racism, he somewhat half-heartedly allowed the use of his
person to the American president when Jimmy Carter in early 1980
sought African support for an anti-Soviet boycott of the Olympic
games in Moscow. Muhammad Ali visited several African countries
pleading for a boycott on Carter's behalf.[41]

This capability of conquering part of the minds of people which the
mass media offer to those who manage to get access to them is a form
of power that most people do not realize as such. We think of conquest
in the traditional terms of conquering land. This, however, is a relic of
the bygone days when land was the main source of wealth and power.
It no longer is, but our thinking has not kept up with this change.
J. Tunstall has written: 'When a government allows news importation,
it is in effect importing a piece of another country's politics — which is
true of no other import'.[42] And politics is about power. What is true on
the international level is also true on the national level: just as weaker
nations are penetrated by foreign information, individuals are penetrated

by the mass media to whom they expose themselves. It is to this aspect that we will turn in the following section.

THE INFORMATION ORDER

A fruitful way of looking at society is to see it as a communication system. The size of a society is then given by the communication facilities of the period. Aristotle once said that the size of a political unit was determined by the range of a single man's voice. He was speaking at the time of the Greek City State. Until the nineteenth century distant communication was, with few exceptions (fire signals, message-carrying pigeons), closely linked to transportation by slow-motion earth- and waterbound human and animal carriers of messages. Then a series of inventions (electric single wire telegraph, 1835; rotary press, 1848; dry-plate photography, 1873; telephone, 1876; radio, 1891; movie, 1894; television, 1927; electronic computer, 1946; transistor, 1948; satellite, 1957) made instant global communication increasingly possible and opened the way to a world society.

Yet the result of this development has not been the 'global village' of which Marshall McLuhan spoke. In the Greek Polis the people of the community (insofar as they were not slaves, foreigners or women) met face-to-face on the Agora to discuss political issues. Communication was dialogue, speaking and listening, with an immediate right to respond, to express approval or disapproval. Everyone could, by raising his voice, make himself heard and compel attention according to the strength of his voice, the style of his talking and the weight of his message. The chances of those present to do so were socially not altogether equal but they were technically infinitely more equal than they are today in the electronic global village. Although we have many more channels of communication than the Greeks, who only had speech and the written word, our relative communication ability has, for the great majority, declined, compared to that available to the leaders of the world society. Communication takes place from a sender, via a channel by a message to a receiver. While at the time of the Greek City State every sender was also a receiver and vice versa on at least one of the two channels available (speech and written word), this is no longer so on the main channels of information, the newspapers, radio and television. But communication where not every receiver is also a sender is no longer real communication; for this reason we speak about the information order and not about the communication order in this section. The metaphor of the 'global village' with its undertone of intimacy is, in our view, not an apt one to describe the information order.

What is the present information order? We will try to give a concise answer in two steps. First, we will make some abstract statements of rather apodictical character which, in our view, characterize in varying degrees of accuracy the information order primarily on the national level. In a second step we will offer some data relating to the international information order, which, however, also serve to substantiate some of the claims made in the first step since we view what is euphemistically called the international 'free flow of information' order as an outgrowth of the national 'freedom of the press' doctrine.

The present information order, constituted by the mass media radio, television and newspapers as main sender channels, can be described briefly by looking at some characteristics of senders, receivers and the sender-receiver relationship:

Sender characteristics: Although there are usually a variety of senders in Western nations, ownership concentration has led to a situation where there are only a few strong senders which can command mass audiences on a regular basis. While these few still compete with each other for audience shares, competition occurs mainly on the level of style of presentation rather than substance of message content. Control of the senders is usually in the hands of a few economic groups or the government. Control by the media workers themselves or by receiver collectives is exceptional. In general, the audiences, although they pay directly (taxes, subscriptions, listening and viewing fees) or indirectly (advertising costs contained in consumer product prices) for the senders, have little say in the selection of messages disseminated by the senders. Information is centrally assembled by the senders and distributed on the basis of the ill-defined principles of news values to the audiences. Only a small portion of the incoming information is transmitted to the audiences.

Receiver characteristics: Out of the variety of senders, most receivers choose less than a handful for gaining information about the world beyond their own perception. The possibilities for message verification are for most receivers very limited. Most of the receivers are not themselves information suppliers and have no access to newsmaking. The right to respond to media messages is generally weak. The receiver knows less about the sender and the way he can be influenced than vice versa. Although exposure to the sender is seemingly voluntary, the amount of exposure (1,200 hours per year for television alone by the average American) suggests that some mechanism of psychic compulsion is at work. While information production in a sender is a collective act, the receivers are usually separated from each other. Messages generated by one receiver group are not transmitted horizontally to other receiver groups but processed by the sender who taps the information source and produces a standardized message available to all receivers. Although the amount of information made available to receivers is enormous, the manner of presentation and the inability of the receivers to fully understand and order it, often prevent the receivers being able to use this information constructively.

Sender-receiver relationship characteristics: Information flows vertically from the top of the social hierarchy to the bottom. The message flow is from one to many, rather than from many to one or from many to many. There is practically no feedback, the information flow is a one-way flow, lacking reciprocity. Although the number of information receivers greatly surpasses the number of information suppliers, this majority can not make the senders effectively accountable for the messages sent. The receivers have not been directly asked about the nature of messages they want; they have only been judged on the basis of their message consumption patterns. Since these consumption patterns have been prespecified by the socialization process of the senders themselves, the observed choices of the receivers do not necessarily reflect their real needs. The senders' information represents only an artificially constructed sampling of reality. The receiver is not acquainted with other sampling methods or other samples of reality and cannot choose them. In an information order where messages flow from institutions to individuals, from high to low, from centre to periphery the receivers are atomized, cut off from each other, yet receive identical messages on which to build their experiences. The chances that the conduct of the receivers corresponds with the needs of the senders therefore tend to be higher than that the conduct of the senders corresponds to the real needs of the receivers. While some receiver needs, such as those for entertainment, are only too well served, others, such as those relating to acquiring an ability to transform one's own situation and influence one's own surrounding, are not well catered for. If the basic needs of the receivers are identified as security (in place of violence), welfare (in place of misery), freedom of choice (in place of repression) and identity (in place of alienation), these needs are in our view not so well served by the mass media.

The picture we have just sketched is admittedly simplistic and incomplete; it cannot be otherwise, collapsing, as it does, all senders and receivers into one. However, it will gain some concreteness and plausibility when we look at it on the international level. In the following pages we present a model in which the United States is depicted as sender and most of the rest of the world's nations as receivers.

After the Second World War the United States insisted, largely successfully as far as the First and Third World were concerned, that there should be a 'free flow of information' with no borders hindering the exchange of ideas. The codification of this position occurred in 1948 in the United Nations' declaration of Human Rights. Article 19 of this UN declaration stated that:

Everyone has the right to freedom of opinion and expressions; this right includes the freedom to hold opinions without interference and to seek, receive and import information and ideas through any media and regardless of frontiers.[43]

This fair-sounding declaration stressing receiver rights was in fact utilized to justify sender freedom and the most powerful sender nation was the United States. With this dominant position in mind the US Secretary of State, John Foster Dulles, could say: 'If I were to be granted one point of foreign policy and no other I would make it the free flow of information'.[44] With only 5 percent of the world population, the United States generated almost two-thirds of all communications in the world, as Zbigniew Brzezinski, President Carter's National Security Council adviser at the time of this writing, explained a decade ago:

At this moment, the American society is the one that exercises the greatest influence on all other societies and the one which pushes them to change in a profound and growing manner their appearance and their way of life.... This is in all likelihood the result of the fact that the American society 'communicates' more than any other with the entire world. In total, 65 percent of all of the world's communications originate in the United States.[45]

In his book, *The Media are American*, Jeremy Tunstall has elaborated how the United States became such a sender nation:

In most of the world's countries the media are only there at all, on the present scale, as a result of imports in which the American media (with some British support) predominate. One major influence of American imported media lies in the styles and patterns which most other countries in the world have adopted or copied. This influence includes the very definition of what a *newspaper*, or a *feature film*, or a *television set* is.... And the world, by adopting American media formats, has in practice become hooked on American style media whether these are home-made or imported.... Without the century-long dominance of Anglo-American media products and styles, many aspects of life in most of the world's countries would be different — consumption patterns, leisure, entertainment, music, the arts and literature.[46]

Whatever media channel one looks at, the American dominance is impressive. In cinema movies, Hollywood provided in the 1920s about 80 percent of all films screened in the world.[47] By the late 1940s the share of Hollywood was still almost 75 percent of all movies shown in the world.[48] In the early 1960s Hollywood's cinema movie share dropped but its movies were still seen by some 150 million foreigners every week.[49] Around that time Hollywood's television exports began to eclipse cinema products. A series like 'Bonanza' was in the mid-1960s reaching an estimated 350 million people every week worldwide.[50] Being first with a new medium offered advantages on the world market. In 1950 the United States had over ten million television sets, more than ten times as many as the rest of the world combined.[51] Due to this early lead the United States managed to assume a position of dominance which allowed it to sell twice as many television programmes as the other producer nations combined.[52] By the early 1970s the United States exported between 100,000 and 200,000 television programme hours per year, much more than the nearest contenders Great Britain (ca. 30,000 hours), France (15,000 hours), or the German Federal Republic (5-6,000 hours).[53]

As far as television newsreel is concerned the world market is also dominated by a few 'senders' such as VISNEWS (Great Britain), UPITN (Great Britain-United States), CBS News (United States) followed by DPA-Etes (German Federal Republic) and ABC (United States). Together these provide half of all foreign European television news material and practically all for most Third World countries.[54] While exporting so much to foreign nations, the United States themselves expose their own audiences to very little foreign television material. In this regard it is probably the most isolated country outside the socialist bloc.[55]

The socialist countries themselves are also unequal participants in the exchange of television programmes. While the Eastern European countries associated in Intervision accept about 65 percent of the TV material offered by its West European counterpart Eurovision, only 10 percent of the Intervision material is accepted by Eurovision.[56] The Soviet Union itself is, as far as television programmes are concerned, also a greater importer than exporter. Ten percent of the programmes of the first Soviet TV programme (there are four altogether, at least in the big cities) come from abroad, while the Soviet

Union sells much less to foreign countries.[57]

The Soviet Union, however, plays a leading role in direct radio broadcasting to foreign audiences with Soviet stations transmitting almost 2,000 weekly programme hours in eighty-four languages. But it is doubtful whether the USSR herewith also reaches a comparable share of the audience of 100 million people who listen daily to foreign broadcasts. Altogether some eighty different countries broadcast to foreign audiences, but the bulk of it is provided by those seventeen nations which transmit more than 300 programme hours per week. The United States with its Voice of America, Radio Free Europe and Radio Liberty broadcasts a total of 1,808 hours weekly, but is followed closely by the German Federal Republic, the Republic of China, Great Britain, North Korea and Albania.[58] The Russian and American hegemony in radio broadcasting is also reflected in the international distribution of radio frequencies. Although there are 154 nations in the International Telecommunication Union, in 1979 the Soviet Union and the United States held 50 percent of the electromagnetic spectrum for themselves, while having only 15 percent of the world population. A spokesman for the Third World, the Sudanese minister Ali Shumma, was only slightly exaggerating when he said to the developed nations: 'You have 90 percent of the frequency spectrum and 10 percent of the population. We have 90 percent of the population and 10 percent of the spectrum'.[59] Although not all of these frequencies are used for public voice and picture broadcasting, the overall unequal distribution in communication channels also affects those 10 percent of the cross-border data flow which is attributed to the public media, especially the news agencies. If, for instance, the exchange of electronic media material between the Third World and the United States is compared, the imbalance is such that for every thousand broadcast minutes that flow from the USA to the Third World, only one broadcast minute of Third World material is used by the media in the United States.[60] The chances to influence each other are in this 'free flow of information' system so unequal that the net result is likely to be unilateral cultural domination.

An important element which determines the flow of information is to be found in the economics of advertising. Since most of the Western mass media depend for more than half of their income and sometimes for all of it on advertisements, advertisers or the agencies who do advertising for corporations have the power, through selectively granting or withholding advertisements, to make or break a medium. In Latin America, for instance, more than half of the 107 major advertising agencies operating in the region are controlled by US firms.[61] It has been estimated that almost two-thirds of the advertising income of the Latin American press comes from approximately thirty multinational corporations, most of them of North American origin.[62] In the United States themselves a mere ten corporations bought in the late 1960s 78 percent of all advertising on network television.[63] Since advertising in its present form is also largely an American invention, the lead of the United States has been great. In 1970, for instance, 59 percent of the world's advertising money was spent in the United States.[64] This pre-eminence has led to a situation in which twenty-one out of the twenty-five largest international advertising agencies are American. If the sample is doubled, there are still thirty-four American firms among the fifty biggest in the world.[65]

The oligopolization which characterizes international advertising can also be observed in the international information market. About 75 percent of the total international information market (books, movies, magazines, TV programmes, etc.) is controlled by some eighty transnational corporations, many of them American.[66] A particular role is played by the four big international Western news agencies, United Press International (USA), Associated Press (USA), Reuters (Great Britain) and Agence France Presse (France), which dominate the transnational news flow in the West. UPI serves 600 newspapers and 2,300 broadcasting stations in the United States and has 6,000 customers worldwide. AP serves 1,750 newspapers and 3,100 other US clients and has a total of 8,500 customers worldwide.[67] In the United States some 75 percent of the national and international news read, heard and seen by people came in the late 1960s from AP and UPI.[68] A study of the Latin American press in the late 1960s revealed that AP was responsible for almost half and UPI for more than a quarter of the information carried on foreign issues.[69] AP alone claims to reach more than one billion people every day worldwide via newspapers, radio and television.[70] With bureaux in more than 100 countries and daily cross-border word flows of between 1.5 and 17 million words the four big Western news agencies send many times more information from New York, London and Paris to the Third World than they accept from there.[71] Since newspapers, radio stations and television stations rely on them to a far greater extent than on their own correspondents (which are also very unevenly distributed over the globe), most of the information that millions of media consumers receive from abroad is preshaped and selected by the gatekeepers of AP, UPI, Reuters and AFP. They have the power to plant images and concepts in our heads and to deny us access to other images and concepts which in their view have no news value. Compared to their freedom of expression our individual freedom of expression is completely dwarfed.

While few people realize this information imbalance on the domestic level, more and more leaders of information-dominated nations raise their voices in protest. The president of Costa Rica, Rodrigo Carazo, for instance, has said: 'The poor people of the world want to prevent by all means that the free flow of communication of people by satellites or other transmission techniques stays in the hands of a few'.[72] As far as access to and control over the mass communication media is concerned, all but two or three percent of all people are poor people for whom there is no room at the top of the present information order. The very structure of this order − its verticality, its concentration, its one-way direction − does not allow otherwise.

WESTERN NEWS VALUES AND BAD NEWS

If one looks at communication research one is struck by the fact that comparatively little work has been done on news and news value. There is no commonly accepted definition of news and consequently the question of what constitutes news value is also not settled. Definitions of 'news' vary greatly depending on the interest of the definers. A practitioner of journalism, Arthur MacEwen, William Randolph Hearst's first editor of the *San Francisco Examiner*, for instance, described it by saying: 'News is anything that makes a reader say, "Gee whiz"'.[73] Jeremy Tunstall, a communication researcher, on the other hand has said that '"News" is an Anglo-American market-based concept'.[74] Although something can be 'news' to us without it having to be transmitted by the mass media, news is generally understood to be something that is disseminated by the public media. The media in the West distribute three kinds of ware: information, entertainment and advertisement. News obviously belongs to the first category. Quantitatively it is not the most important of the three categories. RAND field studies on newspapers found that 'In most of the papers studied this ("straight news") constituted about 27 percent of the total paper. Advertisements took 54 to 67 percent of the total paper. Of the nonadvertising space, news took from 62 to 86 percent of space, the remainder being sports, financial and nonnews features.... On almost all papers the advertising department determines total pages to be printed and only after this does news receive its allocation.'[75] Some people buy a paper for the advertisements, others for the entertainment (sports results, crossword-puzzle), yet others, probably the majority, for the news. Since the space for news is limited by the time available for the average media consumer to absorb news as well as by the space or time the media are prepared to allocate to news, a process of selection takes place which makes some events public while giving others no publicity. Those pieces of timely information which survive this process of the media are 'news'. The selection process itself operates chiefly on the basis of the news value of any incoming piece of timely information. Items with a high news value are placed on the first page of a paper or form the leader in a newscast on radio or television. They are also covered at greater length and might even qualify for editorial comment. If an item's news value is exceptionally high, a special newspaper edition might even be printed, other programmes might be interrupted and the aftermath of such an event will be prominent news on subsequent days.

The criteria which editors use to establish the news value of an event differ from medium to medium but the uniformity is in the end more striking than the variations between media. Where media aim at mass audiences they tend to give visibility to the same set of public events, as can be witnessed by comparing the stories on the frontpages of papers serving the same market. Anthony Smith has written:

...when we study the evolving values of news in a given society we are examining a phenomenon which reveals the successive terms on which social order has been established, contested and resolved. It is no accident that we speak of news *values*; the value of something is decided in a market place among buyers and sellers, some of whom are richer than others. The 'values' of the journalist are established under constant pressures within the society he serves.... His so-called 'values' are the interim contracts he makes with his audience as readers and his audience as society.[76]

Journalists often defend their allocation of news value by referring to what Smith terms the 'audience as readers' and what journalists call 'We give the public what it wants'. There can be little doubt that news values reflect to a considerable extent public values. On the other hand, and in our view, much more than public and journalists realize in general, the news values are shaped in accordance with the 'audience as society', by which we understand the power structure of a society within which the production of news takes place. Richard Hoggart, discussing the various filters by which, in his words, 'the news selects itself', refers to 'the cultural air we breath, the whole ideological atmosphere of our society which tells us that some things can be said and others had best not be said. It is that whole and almost unconscious pressure towards implicitly affirming the status quo....'[77]

The news assemblers in the media operate in a field of tension at the one pole of which stands the public and at the other the habitual sources of newsworthy events. In the practice of journalism, newsmen do not aimlessly walk through the streets until they come across some occurrence that strikes them as having news value. Only a small part of the news we get is the result of investigative reporting by journalists who observe unstructured occurrences and transform them into reportable events. The practice is rather that journalists are flooded with invitations to attend events organized by people desirous that these be reported. In most cases the people who produce reportable events are not acting as individuals but are representatives of institutions such as government ministries. Regular news sources gain the status of habitual news makers, and while journalists use them for the convenience they offer in getting access to significant events, these institutions and persons who promote their news in turn also use the news assemblers. Leon V. Sigal has written: 'What the news is depends very much on who its sources are.... While the camera might belong to the newsman, the lights are in the hands of their sources, who tend to aim them in directions which they find advantageous, leaving many things in shadow and still more in total darkness'.[78]

If a habitual news source is not getting the kind of news coverage it desires from a journalist or medium it will stop the flow of news to it. If, on the other hand, a medium does not get the kind of news it wants from a source it will look for another source. Since both alternatives produce some inconveniences for both news promotor and news assembler they will usually try to maintain some working relationship. Only in exceptional cases will one side attempt to break out of this source-media relationship. A recent case in point is the Organization of Petrol Exporting Countries (OPEC). Dissatisfied with the negative news coverage they got from Western news agencies, the OPEC members decided to create a news agency of their own to get their story across to the public.[79] However, only few sources have the economic and political power for such a drastic step. In many cases the power relationship between source and media is such that the first depends more on the second than vice versa. This certainly applies to all the non-habitual sources of the media. Among them are often fierce struggles to get into the news. Once they have managed to do so their concern is to stay in the news and to advance to the status of habitual sources to whom special places and pages in the media are allocated. To be constantly in the news is for most people and institutions a desirable state of affairs. The visibility that goes with it can be translated into economic power as can be witnessed from movie stars or it can be translated into political power as happened to the Nazi party in interwar Germany. (In order to boost their membership the Nazi movement had their public meetings deliberately disrupted by 'communist provocateurs' so that some violence occurred which the bourgeois press would then report on its front pages, thereby giving the movement publicity with a wider public.)[80]

Paradoxically, there is a point where the visibility seekers begin to find the attention of the media a hindrance rather than a help. The Mellon family, for instance, one of the truly powerful economic groups in the United States, engaged publicity agents to get into the news when they were still on the rise. Once they were on the top, reaching the heights of such powerfuls as the Rockefellers, the Mellons engaged public relations experts to keep them out of the news, presumably because any reporting about their real might would be counter-productive. Intelligence agencies are usually not served with publicity either for the exercise of their power. Invisibility in the media is, in this sense, a privilege of the very powerful and the fate of the powerless. Marginal groups, the poor, the old, the insane, the imprisoned are not much in the news.

In our questionnaire we asked newsmen how it came about that the 12,000 people who die from hunger every day receive hardly any media attention while the kidnapping of a single important politician receives total attention. The answers we got tell us something about the Western news values, although it has to be added that our sample was not very big or representative. Eliminating more or less identical answers, we got the following responses:

1. Not 'hot' news.
2. Propaganda about world hunger is counter-productive.
3. Hunger is old hat, unless close to home.
4. Freshness of event lacking.
5. Everyday events are not news.
6. Hunger is normal. Deviation from normal makes for news interest.
7. Identification possible only with individuals not masses.
8. Inability to identify with unknown people.
9. They die gradually, not at specific place.
10. This is analogous to car accidents-plane crashes: the second are more dramatic.
11. Censorship.

12. Lack of Third World access to industrialized countries.
13. The media are not present, not concerned.
14. News judgment takes into account what public wants to know as well as what it needs to know.
15. It is true that newscasts do not cover this problem unless dramatic events occur. But it is covered in documentary programmes.
16. If the public would read it, press would publish about hunger every day. Would be suicide for paper.

There are presently one billion people, almost one quarter of mankind, who are undernourished.[81] However, when in January 1979 three imprisoned terrorists of the RAF went on hunger strike in the Stammheim prison in Germany this was international news. Their hunger strike was voluntary while one billion people starve involuntarily. The three made the news on 26 January 1979; the billion did not make the news. Through the media the three terrorists were offered a chance to rally public sympathy with their political demands, while the involuntary hungry were not. Or, to take another example: in November 1968 a man and a woman staged events in New York. The man, a relief worker, held a press conference, wherein he predicted that two million children would die in the following month in Biafra. The *New York Times* reported it on page 20 in five paragraphs. The television news programmes did not report it. The woman, who had no message and who would probably not even have minded not being noted by the media when she arrived at the airport, drew a crowd of fifty-five reporters and cameramen who had waited for three hours in the cold rain. The *New York Times* gave thirteen paragraphs to the arrival of the newly remarried Jacqueline (Kennedy) Onassis, starting on page one and illustrating it with two three-column pictures. The television news also showed her arrival in detail.[82] There can be little doubt that an average media consumer was more gratified with seeing a smiling Jackie on the television screen than to face the pictures of starving children. The news assemblers' dilemma 'should the people get what they want or what they ought to get?' is a real one. The interesting is often not important and the important not interesting.

In the case of the Vietnamese boat people and the fugitives from Kampuchea, however, suffering masses did make the headlines in the Western media in the late 1970s. But the reason why they made the news has, in our view, little to do with themselves. Immediately after the 'liberation' of Vietnam, Kampuchea and Laos in 1975, the Western news media left the area together with the American military. As far as Kampuchea was concerned, the three US television networks, ABC,

CBS and NBC covered, in the period April 1975 to January 1977, the ongoing genocide with a mere twenty seconds per month on average. For one of the most enormous mass annihilations in recent times – an estimated 1.2 million people died in the land of Pol Pot during this period – this is a lack of attention that cannot simply be explained away by pointing at the difficulty of getting access to the facts.[83] During this period there were enough fugitives to tell the story. On the other hand the exodus of some 300,000 Vietnamese and Chinese from South Vietnam and the stream of Kampuchean people into Thailand received massive coverage. One reason why this was so probably is that two great powers, China and the United States, with their propaganda machines, mobilized these occurrences to muster world opinion against Vietnam. China used this negative publicity to justify its 1979 invasion of North Vietnam and the United States to justify posthumously its Indochina venture. Other fugitives are less fortunate in that nobody sees a chance to make political capital out of them. There are for instance 400,000 fugitives in Somalia and 350,000 in Sudan, half of them children. Altogether there are in Africa alone some five million fugitives.[84] Worldwide, there are between twelve and fifteen million fugitives. As long as there is no powerful source to direct the Western media's attention to them, they are largely treated with silence, which, for many of them, amounts to starvation.

Starvation is a process, while a hunger strike is an event. One billion undernourished people are faceless masses, while three German terrorists are individuals. The fugitives in Africa are far away from where the media gather their news, while the Stammheim prison is situated in a media-rich environment. To become news with the Western media, occurrences have to be events rather than processes, they have to be about individuals rather than masses, and they have to take place where the media are. And most important of all, there has to be a powerful source that preshapes the occurrences for the media. Two conflicting sources are even better since conflict is something the media are attracted to. How one wants to describe such characteristics of Western news values is a matter of one's reference system. Jerry Mander calls them 'biases'. Confining himself to the medium of television, he listed thirty-three 'biases'. We will reproduce some of these blindspots (the term we prefer) here, since they are pertinent to the subject we treat:

– War is better television than peace. It is filled with highlighted moments, contains action and resolution, and delivers a powerful emotion: fear. Peace is amorphous and broad. The emotions connected with it are subtle, personal and internal. These are far more difficult to televise.

- Violence is better TV than nonviolence.
- When there is a choice between objective events (incidents, data) and subjective information (perspectives, thoughts, feelings), the objective event will be chosen. It is more likely to take visual form....
- Political movements with single charismatic leaders are also more suitable and efficient for television. When a movement has no leader or focus, television needs to create one....
- ...hierarchy is easier to report upon than democracy or collectivity. The former is focused and has a specific form: leaders and followers. Only the leaders need to be interviewed....
- Short subjects with beginnings and ends are simpler to transmit than extended and multifaceted information....
- Competition is inherently more televiseable than cooperation as it involves drama, winning, wanting and loss. Cooperation offers no conflict and becomes boring....
- Death is easier than life. It is specific, focused, highlighted, fixed, resolved and has a meaning aside from context. Life on the (other) hand, is fluid, ambiguous, process oriented, complex, multileveled, sensory, intuitive.[85]

If these 'biases' are inherent in television, reflecting news values of the medium, some logical deductions can be made which are most disturbing. For instance: a social movement of equals is presented by television in such a way that over time a restructuring of the movement into one of the hierarchical type is favoured. Alternatively, if there are two social movements fighting for the same cause but with different means, the one with violence, the other without, the media will cover the violent movement more extensively. The cause can in this way be associated with the violence, discouraging some media spectators from joining the cause, while encouraging others to do so. By giving more coverage to the violent than to the nonviolent movement the media in fact can predetermine the mobilization chances of the two movements. The 'bias' of the medium, the assignment of a greater news value to violence, can, in such a way, in effect intervene in the competition of the two movements for followers.

We know of no empirical evidence which would support this but the possibility is intriguing enough to warrant attention. The only case that readily comes to our mind is Northern Ireland where in 1976 the peace movement suddenly came into the news, for a while rivalling the terrorists for media attention. But as far as we are able to judge the example is not very helpful. The fact that the IRA is still going strong while the peace movement has practically ceased to exist cannot rightfully be blamed on the media. It was rather the case that the peace movement never really existed outside the media. The organizational basis of the movement was weak, only the massive attention which the media bestowed on the movement made it for a while look like a serious rival. That the peace movement did get so much publicity is, in our view, due mainly to the fact that it was something new, something different. When bad news — terrorism — is the rule, a sudden break in the chain of negative events can become big news. Usually the media do not report the normal, but when violence is normal, nonviolence may gain the status of the abnormal, which bestows news value on it. On the other hand the peace people might have suffered from the fact that peace is difficult to visualize. A man with a machinegun means violence on television, but a man without one has often no such clear meaning in the media.

Bernard Roshco has enumerated some important principles why bad news in general has a high news value:

Because the unexpected is inherently obtrusive, it is likely to be perceived by an observer. The more obtrusive the event, the greater its currency and the higher its news value.... High visibility heightens news value, and visibility is most quickly attained through breakdowns and failures that upset the public's expectation. Since there is always more news available than time or space for publishing it, there is economy in publishing news that emphasizes deviations from the norm. Presumably, the unreported is behaving unexceptionally and proceeding on its expected way.... Turning points and landmarks are newsworthy — that is note-worthy — whether that news be graded good or bad. Bad news, however, tends to have higher currency than good news because danger creates more suspense than success, and menacing events are more likely to rivet the attention of an audience than happy tidings. Yet, when bad news is the norm, sudden alteration in the flow of illtidings makes headlines.... 'Names' make the news by their achievements as well as their failures.... The political area illustrates why conflict is especially newsworthy: the issues are defined by the disputants; the outcome is in doubt. The combination presents reporters with visibility through summation... and visibility through obtrusiveness, which heightens currency. Also, as long as conflict lasts, it generates timely information, each new development resulting in another reportable event.[86]

Roshco's observation that there is economy in publishing news that emphasizes deviations from the norm, raises another problem. If people get more and more of their experiences from the media rather than from life itself, an imbalance in perception can come about in which deviations, conflict and anti-social behaviour become the main sensory input. Even small doses of bad news seem to have a detrimental effect. In a previous chapter (p. 113) we have already mentioned an experiment described by Stephen M. Holloway and Harvey A. Hornstein. Although the body of research they have produced is too small to allow far-reaching conclusions, the results are of such social significance that these experiments should be reproduced on a much wider scale. Basically their laboratory research consisted of exposing a group of test-persons waiting for the experiment to begin in the waiting room to background music intermixed with fictional but authentic-sounding newscasts. The content of the radio newscasts consisted of various types of good (pro-social) and bad (anti-social) news. Afterwards the test-persons were exposed to a series of decision-making tests and the responses to these tests were correlated to the type of news programmes they had heard in the waiting room. The people tested had no knowledge that the preceding newscasts were already part of the experiment. The test-persons then had to answer questions about moral and ethical dispositions of people in general (e.g. What percentage of people are basically honest?). The samples of people tested in various set-ups included younger and older groups of listeners, males and females. Yet the results were, as the authors point out, invariably the same:

The good news produces more favorable views of humanity's general moral disposition than bad news does − despite the fact that the news deals only with certain special cases and not at all with human nature on the grand scale. But something even more startling happens when people hear good or bad news. Not only do their beliefs change, so does their behavior.... In several experiments, we recruited people who were told simply that they were going to participate in a study of human decisionmaking....Those who heard good news were predisposed to think well of the stranger (with which they could interact, cooperatively or competitively in the following experiment). They tended to believe that he or she was going to behave cooperatively during the task, and they took the risk of behaving cooperatively themselves. Those who heard bad news had a very different image of the stranger. In general, they expected the stranger to behave competitively, and they acted accordingly by competing themselves. It requires only a small stretch of imagination to see what might be happening *outside* the laboratory when people hear bad news. They are likely to become more competitive and less cooperative. Therefore, competition, cooperation and feelings of 'we' and 'they' are partly the result of the information about human beings that we gather from the news....systematic interviews after the experiment had ended, revealed that most of the people hadn't even been aware of having heard a news story until the interviewer brought it to their attention. Yet these same news stories had affected their subsequent behavior, as we had learned when we asked these same young men to make their choice in the cooperation/competition task. Once again, good news produced disproportionately more cooperation than bad news. The fact that most of these men and women hardly registered what they were hearing is an extraordinary finding in itself, for it suggests that good or bad news influences our behavior unconsciously.[87]...As we expected, the people who heard good news that was attributed to some human deed were much more likely to behave cooperatively (and expect the stranger in the other room to cooperate) than were those who heard bad news that was attributed to some human deed. We found no such effect among those who had heard good and bad news of the same

character and consequences, which the stories attributed to 'acts of nature'....
It is now clear, for example, that newscasts have serious and immediate consequences that are completely unintended. Far from just imparting facts, news
stories about morality or immorality in action impress us, at least temporarily,
with corresponding views of human nature – views that tend to move us, quite
unconsciously, to behave in ways appropriate to such views. At worst, as we have
seen, newscasts can break down the kinds of group ties that cause people to help
and trust their fellows....To put the matter in the plainest terms, certain news
stories can demoralize and estrange us from one another. We believe that this
finding places a new and very heavy burden of responsibility on the news media.[88]

If we contrast these findings with a statement from the managing
director of one of the four big Western news agencies, the size of the
problem becomes evident. This is what Mr Long from Reuters said in an
interview:

...that all normal, sane, positive receives little attention in the media, all abnormal,
unusual and negative on the other hand receives widest dissemination – I would
agree with you on this on the whole. But I do not see how this could be changed,
at least not in the sector of 'hard' news.[89]

The result of this predilection for bad news can be distortion. A
predilection for good news would of course also be distortion and
perhaps even of a more serious nature. Where media output is not
counterbalanced by one's own first-hand experience, the negative
perspective can become predominant. Certain countries of the Third
World, for instance, only receive coverage in the major Western media
when there is a war, a disaster or an atrocity. All the news we get from
such places tends to be bad news.[90]

With such a one-sided perspective, how can Western news agencies
and Western media in general claim that they are objective? Objectivity
is a necessity for mass media that want to be believed by a mass public
which consists of segments of people that often stand in social conflict
with each other. To satisfy a heterogeneous public the media produce a
kind of news to which few people can object. C.P. Scott, the famous
editor of the *Manchester Guardian*, introduced a motto into journalism
which says 'Facts are sacred, opinions are free'. It boils down to a
division of newspapers into a section that contains facts, and one that
contains opinions (editorial opinions, letters to the editor, contributions
by columnists). Yet this distinction is an artificial one since there are no
facts without implicit opinions. The very fact that one fact is quoted
rather than another one is the result of a selection process based among
other things on (news) values, about which opinion can differ. A fact

only makes sense within an ideological or cultural context. To say that somebody has his birthday today gains significance only in those cultures where birthdays are registered and celebrated. If a newspaper in the Netherlands mentions on page one, accompanied by a small picture, that Prince Bernhard is celebrating his birthday on 29 June, this is such a 'fact'. Thousands of other people in the Netherlands are also celebrating their birthday without their picture appearing in the news. The fact that his birthday is mentioned on page one in some papers carries the implicit opinion that the monarchy in the Netherlands is an institution of which people should be reminded. Other papers not mentioning his birthday might conceivably do so because the editor thought that this particular person had been involved in enough scandals to be punished by silence. In such a way facts are used to form and express opinions. On a more general level, Phil Harris has described how the Western media produce objectivity:

Newsmen employ two strategies to ensure the *accuracy* of their accounts – first, the newsman can report those events which he himself knows to have occurred; second, the newsman can use sources who are recognized to be reliable....The interesting point about the use of sources is that it enables news media to claim impartiality and objectivity while manifesting partiality....The selection and quotation of the source is the main strategy by which a news reporter, bound by the principles of factuality and impartiality in his own formulations, can add political opinion or bias to a news story without ostensibly violating the formal rules of professional objectivity. International news media are thus regarded by subscribers as authoritative media for the provision of accurate interpretations of reality because they consistently provide accurate representations *of that part of reality which is covered.* [91]

Only within such a limited framework are the Western media objective. But the choice of news items, the selection process based on news values is not objective even if there is a relatively high degree of intersubjectivity between various media in regard to what item has news value. In the words of the Glasgow University Media Group: '...one must see the news as reflecting not the events in the world "out there", but as the manifestations of the collective cultural codes of those employed to do this selective and judgmental work for society'. [92] The preference of the news assemblers for bad news over good news is in this light also a product of their training. Blair Justice has done an experiment, offering students of journalism a set of twenty headlines, ten suggesting nonconflict news, ten suggesting conflict and violence news. This was done twice, once before and once after they had received professional training. The results demonstrated that the students first showed a preference for nonconflict stories, while after training precedence was given to conflict and violence stories, even though their personal preference in contrast to their professional news value allocation still went to the good news stories.[93] In this sense these future representatives of a free press had partly given up their personal freedom of choice and submitted themselves to the institutional codes of the profession. In regard to a particular kind of bad news, terrorism, David Hubbard has insisted that it is 'reported by a controlled press — controlled by the unconscious career needs of its editors and correspondents, and the economics in the form of the Nielson (audience share) ratings...'[94]

Bad news sells well because it plays on the fears and perhaps also on the sadism of the audience. But the social cost of marketing bad news can be high. Israel Charny, a psychologist, has pointed to some of the dangers:

Over and over again we have the experience of newscasts that tell us the latest of human destructiveness in an indifferent or bored-sounding mechanical (or sirupy and glib) reportage of the facts of one or another or many deaths and injuries of human beings; often enough there is even a covert excitement that conveys...fascination and passionate interest in still another piece of sadism and/or suicide. We conclude that most newscasts of man's violent ways subtly and penetratingly contribute to a kind of demoralization and hopelessness, perhaps, too to passivity and resignation in the face of violence, and...to the further violence that grows precisely out of the hopelessness that is never quite tolerable to the inner human spirit. Can it be otherwise? Is it possible for the newscaster to serve as agent of man's better hopes for himself even as he remains a journalist true to his fundamental commitment to convey accurately and without editorial interpretation the facts of what is going on?[95]

In theory, much could be changed in the way the media report on violence. Most bad news stories can at least in part be turned into less destructive stories if the focus of attention is shifted away from the aggressor. In a story on an act of terrorism, for instance, the media could, rather than focus on the terrorist and his demands alone, concentrate on offers from the public to act as substitutes for the hostages and other signs of solidarity shown by people. This is far from being the standard media practice, although there have been laudable attempts in this direction by some media. Martin E. Silverstein, a specialist in traumatology, has suggested in the same vein:

I think there is inappropriate attention on the stylized aspects of the terrorists and their actions and the stylized aspects of the police story; we've had enough of suspense. Let's take a look at the people who get hurt, and by the way, their injuries last a very long time.[96]

A more victim-centred approach in reporting, stressing the horror of violence, its aftermath, rather than the terror of the act of violence, could also reduce the chances of media-induced contagion of violence. Media research has shown that viewer aggressiveness after the portrayal of violence is much higher when the horror that follows violence, the pain of the victim, the pictures of blood and wounds are eliminated, as is the standard practice of the media. The stimulating, exciting effect of viewing violence in the media would, as this research suggests, be counteracted if the consequences of aggressive acts were shown with equal realism as the act of aggression.

The difficulty with such an approach is that it is disgusting and therefore not well suited to sell anything with. A government-commissioned Canadian study on violence in the communications industry, referring to fictional media violence, has pointed out why the showing of violence is so attractive:

...producers believe that violence possesses a greater degree of certainty in attracting audiences. The comparative success of violence-orientated films and television programs, in relation to their costs of production, has produced a built-in economic inertia for them to perpetuate....Violence as a theme appears to be attractive because it lends itself to a highly formulaic pattern and does not necessarily require good acting and a good story to connect sequences and hold audience interest and attention.[97]

In our view, the high news value of violence in nonfictional newscasts is based on the same audience-attracting and therefore economic principle. In our questionnaire we asked whether it was still true that crime and violence stories sell papers and programmes. Fifteen out of twenty-four respondents held that it was true, four did not believe so, and the rest had other opinions (e.g. our medium is financed by the tax-payer, not market-based).

If the high news value of violence and of bad news in general is a reflection of the audience interest, as it undoubtedly is, can and should the media make any changes in the way they report these things? If people are not given what they want but what is good for them, the Western media could find themselves in the position of the Soviet media whose duty it is '...to bring close to our people the Soviet way of life and to explain the programme of our party'. The Soviet Central Committee sees television playing 'an important role in communist

education of the Soviet man to spiritual and moral steadfastness'.[98]
The Western system of news values is in our view superior to the
communist system, because it reflects two things, the social power
structure (which the communist system does as well) and the desires of
the audience. But the desires of the audience are not automatically
co-extensive with the interests and the needs of the audience. The
members of Western audiences have not been asked what kind of media
material, what kind of news they want. They have been judged on the
basis of their consuming behaviour in regard to the material that is
offered. If the public knew other kinds of media material it might like
them better. And in choosing from the available media material, the
people's choices are not in the first line made on the basis of their
reasoning power but on the basis of their largely unconscious psychological desires. The fact that people vote with their buying and
consuming behaviour for a particular mass medium or programme is
indeed a sign that the medium fulfils some of the gratification needs of
the public, but these needs can be quite contrary to the requirement for
rationally understanding the world beyond the people's first hand
perception. In responding to people's interests, the media might not
respond to their best interest. They might respond to people's curiosity,
voyeurism, jealousy, envy, need for authoritarianism and many other
characteristics which are not very helpful for successfully coping with life
in an unbelievably complex world. For those who want to keep people
from being self-reliant, conscious, critical and demanding their rights,
the present system of news values might serve best. But for those who
want to increase people's self-determination, it is open to improvement.

Since the Western mass media depend for their existence in the
majority on big audiences, their desire to get a big market leads them
down the same road the advertisers of material products travel, addressing themselves more to the psychological weaknesses of the public than
to their faculties of reasoning. About the advertising scientists Jerry
Mander has written:

Like miners seeking new deposits of coal in the mountains, these social scientists
attempt to mine the internal wilderness of human beings....In its monthly
publication, *Investments in Tomorrow*, Stanford Research Institute literally
catalogs new areas where human feelings can be converted into needs....Fear is
one of the most desirable emotions for advertisers. Loneliness and self-doubt are
good ones. So is competition.[99]

If our choice of media and media content is made on the basis of such
weaknesses and not on the basis of our strengths and potential to

improve ourselves and the world around us, we are presented, with the present news values, with a view of reality which is often more escapist than emancipating. In the present news value system, reportorial resources are not – as we have tried to show with the Jackie Onassis-Biafra example – allocated to areas where the well-being of the greatest number of people is at stake, but to the adventures and caprices of some elite persons. The unique power of the mass media to give visibility to social phenomena, to serve as an early warning system in society, could be mobilized for better things than celebrity star cults. The logic of the present news value system, which assigns a higher place to destructive news than constructive news, which prefers personalities over masses, has led to perversions such as the following one.

Idi Amin, the monster of Kampala, responsible for the death of up to 600,000 people, is trying to sell his memoirs in London and is asking $50,000 for an exclusive interview.[100] There is good reason to believe that he will find a buyer on the news market. Lesser and bigger criminals have been able to do so. Richard Nixon received two million dollars for his memoirs and at least $600,000 for a series of interviews with David Frost. Some of his fellow criminals could also profit from their crimes. Howard Hunt, chief burglar in Watergate, got $450,000 for his story *Undercover*. John Dean made one million dollars with his version of the story in *Blind Ambition* to which more than $100,000 have to be added that he got from his lectures. H. R. Haldeman, Nixon's chief of staff, got $100,000 for his book *The Ends of Power* and $50,000 for a television interview. John Ehrlichman got $100,000 for his novel *The Company* plus $75,000 for movie rights to it. Spiro Agnew also used his bad name to make good money.[101] It is the moral indifference of the bad-news-is-good-news-principle which allows such obscene spectacles. It is a dangerous principle since it can, if massively applied, eat away the moral fabric of society. In a wider sense, however, this transformation of values which capitalist news production can bring about when the cultural and commodity nature of a product clash, gives the system also some flexibility. While Nixon could not be tried by a court he could at least be exposed by the press.

The news value of the negative also allows voices who oppose the dominant system to get a hearing. This has been well expressed by the Cohn-Bendits. Daniel Cohn-Bendit, a German student in Paris in 1968, had been styled by the media as the leader of the student movement. Turned into 'Dany le Rouge' he got for a time high news value and one publisher offered him 50,000 German marks in advance for a book of which not a single line had yet been written. The book which he wrote in collaboration with his brother (*Left Radicalism – Remedy for the Senility Sickness of Communism,* 1968) explains in the introduction why the authors were able to see their cooperation with an establishment publisher as an immediate contribution to the revolution:

> Within this merchant system the capitalists are prepared to bring about their own extinction (their extinction as capitalists, not as individuals) through the dissemination of revolutionary ideas, provided that these revolutionary ideas earn them profits in the short run. For this they pay fat monies, although they know precisely that this money is going to be used for Molotov-Cocktails. That is because they think the revolution is impossible. Reader, prove them the contrary! [102]

The moral indifference of the capitalist culture industry – (almost) anything is worth publishing as long as a profit can be expected – leads to a tolerance of deviant thought which allows a certain pluralism for which there is no room in more rigid social systems. Yet the relatively high tolerance for nonconformist ideas is not matched by a commensurate tolerance for nonconformist actions. It is this contradiction between what one is allowed to say and what one is allowed to do which Herbert Marcuse labelled 'repressive tolerance'.

In the field of Western news production the news value system therefore not only contains elements which narrow access to newsmaking to elites, but also some elements which broaden access. The news value system puts a premium on anything that is different, new, change-inducing, unexpected, disruptive, dramatic, unique, surprising and full of what is termed 'human interest'. If non-establishment events qualify to a significant extent for these criteria they have a chance of being reported. However, since these are all exceptional qualities, people who want to get access to news-making by way of these criteria can, as a rule, only get access to news-making by exception. While ordinary events produced by the social powerful are news, ordinary things done by ordinary people are not news. Extraordinary things done by extraordinary people are big news. Due to its moral value indifference, the news value system does not distinguish between the pro- or anti-social content of extraordinary news. And since it is so much easier to produce an extraordinary bad event than an extraordinary good event, the temptation to win access to news-making the easy way is real enough. Violence is perhaps the most widespread manner of engaging the attention of the media the easy way.

We see the genesis of contemporary insurgent terrorism, as it has manifested itself in the Western World since the late 1960s, primarily as the outgrowth of minority strategies to get into the news. The choice of this strategy to get grievances vented and redressed, is, in our view, probably due to the fact that the significance of parliaments as an intermediary between people and the executives has declined, or, formulated more cautiously, that the awareness of the distance between rulers and ruled in formal democracies has increased. New issues, developments and needs in fast-changing Western societies are no longer primarily discussed and tackled by the official body elected by the people, but outside it. This failure of parliamentary democracy to respond adequately to the challenges coming out of society has led to a wild growth of extra-parliamentary groups who seek redress for their problems by direct appeal to the public via the media rather than via the slow-working inflexible bureaucratic government machinery. Partly this is due to the refinement of election techniques which has led to a situation where parliaments are often occupied by persons who are primarily representing themselves and the relative small power group behind them. Partly it is also a case of system overload: there are so many groups in society that demand their 'rights' that the present parliamentary systems are unable to accommodate them all.

This state of affairs has brought politics to the streets again. It began with acts of civil disobedience, evolved, in the confrontation with the forces of law and order, into civil violence, and culminated in acts of terrorism. There are striking structural similarities between some nonviolent forms of public protest and terrorism. What is in our view the main characteristic of terrorism, the triangular relationship between terrorist actor, instrumental victim, and enemy or audience, can also be found in nonviolent protest. Take the following examples:

1. Demonstrators sit on the street to protest against the increase of public transport fares. A traffic jam occurs, inconveniencing private and public transport. The media routinely report the traffic situation and also the cause for the disruption. In this way the message of the demonstrators is amplified and other dissatisfied users of the public transport system are offered the chance to join them if they wish to put increased weight behind the demand for a reduction of fares. City counsellors ask questions in city hall, a vote is taken as to whether or not fares will be reduced. If we see the public trying to pass as instrumental victim, as a kind of hostage, the similarity to terrorism is apparent.

2. A group of exiles in a host country goes on hunger strike on the capital's main square to call public attention to recent repressive measures in their home country. In this case actor and instrumental victim are identical. The self-castigation evokes public curiosity, possibly concern and quite likely media attention.

3. Demonstrators drape a straw puppet with the American flag and set it on fire in a public place. The flag-clad straw puppet of Uncle Sam serves as a symbolic

instrumental victim to generate a message which meets the event needs of the media.

In all these situations the pattern is similar. A group of people, sometimes even a single individual, who wants to convey a message but is without access to the mass media, places itself or others in a situation where somebody can be instrumentalized as victim. The victimizer is either the demonstrating group itself (e.g. in a hunger strike), or an agent called by the group to the scene in the form of the security forces (who beat them up, disperse them with tear gas, arrest them, etc.). The media have in most cases been warned in advance of the happening about to take place and when the three are brought together, the actor, the acted-upon and the observer and amplifier, the scene has been set for creating an event which has a good chance of getting into the news. Since the Western media grant access to news-making to events that are abnormal, unusual, dangerous, new, disruptive or violent, groups without habitual access to news-making use these characteristics of the news value system to obtain access. By creating events that fit into the reporting needs of the mass media such groups can obtain space or time in the media. However, through repetitive use such events tend to lose their news value. Political actors with few power resources who want to retain the relatively minor attention they gain with such activities have to vary the form of the activities by introducing novel aspects. These novel aspects are often found in an escalation into violent activities and at the end of it stands terrorism. Yet when violence is used to communicate, the means often deflect public attention from the ends so that the message often does not get through. People then see in terrorism only the violence and no longer the communication. Very few groups have therefore managed to transform themselves from disruptive news-makers into habitual news-makers who are no longer primarily dependent on violence. A case in point are the Palestinians who by the late 1970s had managed to build up a chain of information bureaux in sixty-two countries to tell the story of the Palestinian plight.

The process we have tried to describe here has been well summarized by Bernard Roshco, although his words do not directly refer to terrorism:

The less newsworthy the status of the visibility-seekers, the more deviant they must act to become visible. To be few in number compounds their problem, since they must find a means of making their protest not only visible but also plausible. Yet, the fewer they are, the more unrelated to popularly accepted notions of reality their issue will seem. Especially under such circumstances, reporters tend to ignore the issue and emphasize the performance, which is far easier to become acquainted with....Essentially, a symbolic protest is news management by the socially invisible. An indicator of success in such protest is accession to a permanently newsworthy status, with its enlarged opportunities for making and managing news by means the public does not consider deviant.[103]

The use of violence to get access to a mass audience and to convey a message is not, however, the strategy of the invisible and powerless alone. When the media use violence stories to boost their circulation or the size of their viewing and listening audiences they are doing essentially the same, instrumentalizing violence for something else. When advertisers on television sponsor crime stories to attract a mass audience to the television screen so that more people are exposed to their commercials, violence also serves to convey a message. The major difference is that the media use somebody else's violence or fictional violence to get a message across, while the terrorists have to use real violence. Both advertisers and terrorists use the news value or audience-attracting power of violence.

In a penetrating analysis of media content, Daniel Boorstin in the early 1960s described the rise of the pseudo-event, 'the new kind of synthetic novelty which has flooded our experience'. He defined the pseudo-event as possessing the following characteristics:

1. It is not spontaneous, but comes about because someone has planned, planted, or incited it.
2. It is planted primarily (not always exclusively) for the immediate purpose of being reported or reproduced. Therefore, its occurrence is arranged for the convenience of the reporting or reproducing media. Its success is measured by how widely it is reported....The power to make a reportable event is thus the power to make experience.

Boorstin sees the origin of the pseudo-event (such as press conferences, etc.) in certain practices discovered and developed in the interwar years by public relations firms. He quotes from the 1923 study of Edward L. Bernays, *Crystallizing Public Opinion*: the counsel on public relations 'not only knows what news value is, but knowing it, he is in a position to *make news happen*. He is the creator of events'.[104]

In our view, the discovery of the strategic use of news values was one which advertising agencies and terrorists made somewhat independently from each other, with the latter perhaps unconsciously learning from the former. In both advertising and terrorism we find a recurrence of similar powerful symbols, for instance aircraft as background, and well-known personalities as objects. The use of revolutionary symbols by the Tupamaros or the Red Brigades also reminds us of the cultivation of brandnames by product makers. In regard to the Californian SLA terrorists, James Monaco has given us a description which underlines such similarities:

> You don't name your group the 'Symbionese' Liberation Army, you don't invent a seven-headed cobra symbol, you don't decide to capture Citizen Kane's grand-daughter, you don't hold her for ransom for food rather than money, unless you are painfully aware that politics in the mid-seventies is a matter of imagery and iconography. It is no longer important for something to have happened; it is mainly important for something to have been reported.[105]

We see many (not all) acts of insurgent terrorism, as witnessed in the Western world in the last decade, primarily as pseudo-events. Pseudo means false, meant to deceive. The acts were of course real enough in regard to their victims. But they were often pseudo-events because they were not staged for their local effects but for their mediated effects. Often such acts served a military as well as publicity purpose. In many cases, however, the military potential of terrorist groups was negligible — the Symbionese Liberation Army, for instance, consisted of nine members. In some cases the military potential was developed only as a result of the additional membership which publicity attracted to these movements. This might even have been true for some of the Palestinian terrorist movements. In other cases, such as in the Irish and perhaps even more so the Basque case, the military component has always been stronger. But in its military dimension as well terrorism is basically a psychological weapon.

Insurgent terrorism is not senseless violence but a symptom that something is wrong with communication. As Fereydoun Hoveyda has said: 'Where there are no effective non-violent forms of protest, violence on an international scale will continue'.[101] If insurgent terrorism is seen as communication by violence, efforts to curb it might be more successful if they aimed at lowering the threshold of communication rather than at heightening the level of repression. In our last section we will therefore turn to the issue of a 'Right to Communicate'.

TOWARDS A RIGHT TO COMMUNICATE

Throughout history until less than two hundred years ago anybody who was not dumb could at a public meeting raise his voice and make himself heard. Although not everybody had an equal social opportunity to speak at length to a mass audience, everybody had the technical resource (his voice) to at least interrupt the speaker. The maximum size of an audience was for most of human history about twenty thousand people; that was how far under optimal circumstances a voice would carry. Today it is possible that a single person like the Pope, aided by satellites and television, can reach simultaneously one billion people. In other words, through new communication techniques the power to move people has increased by a factor of 50,000. Since there is only one Pope and there are 4.3 billion more common people who never get such a chance, our relative communication power has through this technological advance in fact decreased by the same factor. Since the eighteenth century most people have obtained the formal right to speak, yet with the rise of the mass media the ability to communicate with mass audiences has in effect been curtailed for all but a few due to the new resource inequality. When there was only one communication resource, the human voice, the right to speak and the right to com- municate were coextensive. They no longer are since the size of the reachable audience for common speech and electronically amplified telecommunicated speech vary so greatly. The one-way communication technology of the mass media makes interruption, taking over the word from another speaker, virtually impossible.

In the eighteenth century the public sphere was conceptualized as a free market-place for ideas. The concentration process inherent in capitalism has narrowed this market in such a way that there are only a few sellers of ideas and many more buyers. The sellers are concentrated in a few places such as Fleet Street (London), Madison Avenue (New York) and Sunset Boulevard (Hollywood). As a meeting of UNESCO experts noted in 1978:

Today, too many of the ideas circulated in society are simply deposited in the minds of the majority and deliberately elaborated as products to be consumed by an anonymous mass of consumers and not dialoguers. In this way, too many peoples have been denied their right to speak their word and are submitted to a violence which, without being physical, is as dehumanizing as physical aggression itself.[107]

With the rise of the mass media a new division of the world population has come about, a division between suppliers of information and consumers of information. The purpose of communication is to elicit a response in the listener. As long as every listener can talk back to the speaker, the chance of mutual gain exists. Communication is a process of give and take, of speaking and listening with about equal time and strength. The telephone, with its two-way capability, allows such reciprocity. Yet when the number of receivers outstrips the number of senders something gets lost. Dallas Smythe, the nestor of North American communication researchers, has remarked that 'with a decrease in feedback goes a proportionate decrease in the humanity of communications'.[108]

In our questionnaire we asked journalists and editors what in their opinion were presently the greatest threats to the integrity of the media. On top came, as could be expected, 'Government censorship' with twenty-one mentions, followed by 'Public apathy' (sixteen mentions). In third place was ranked 'Press ownership concentration' (twenty mentions), followed by 'Pressures from advertisers' (eighteen mentions). In the fifth and sixth place appeared 'Third World demands for new information order' (fifteen mentions) and 'Terrorists' (fourteen mentions). Among other threats mentioned the following were volunteered: 'Journalistic apathy and self-restraint within the media', 'Economic problems', 'Trade union pressures from journalists and printers', 'Lack of qualified reporters', 'Government pressures' and the fact that 'Electronic media push printed media off the market'. Unrepresentative as this list is due to the small and unweighted sample, the appearance of 'public apathy' in second place is nevertheless striking. We are tempted to interpret it as an outcome of the passive receptive role into which the media structure places the audience. The present information order allows no real dialogue, and monologue quite naturally leads to a certain apathy on the side of those condemned to silence.

Can it be otherwise? Can dialogue be restored? In the last decade a discussion has come about, first among communication researchers and since 1974 also within UNESCO about a 'Right to Communicate'.[109] While the dimensions of the new concept are still disputed, it represents, in our view, a revival of the individual-freedom-of-speech-and-expression-discussion of the Enlightenment. One of the communication researchers participating in this new discussion, Henry R. Cassirer, has said:

When the mass media see themselves as 'distribution machines', they are incapable of functioning as communicators in society....Action is the acid test of the relevance of the media. But to act, man must be conscious of his condition and of the issues he faces. A basic function of communication is to heighten such consciousness, to sharpen awareness, to open the mind to oneself and others, and to focus on the tasks ahead. Society needs channels of democratic interaction through which people may express themselves, exert pressures, and participate in decision making....The challenge is clear: How to employ modern communications media so that they may not only go out to the people but also reflect their aspirations, so that they may truly constitute communication 'for the people, of the people, and by the people'.[110]

Yet are the mass media capable of democratization? Although some technical developments, such as the two-way potential of cable television, might be fully explored, the mass media remain in essence one-way channels. Mass access to mass communication as sender, not receiver, will remain a structural impossibility. As one observer put it with regard to the United States, '...there are 220 million Americans and there's only one CBS Evening News, and they can't all get on it'.[111] The visibility which the present information order grants to a few can never be available for the many since, as Ben Bagdikian has pointed out:

No news system can conduct a continuous survey of all the interrelations of the 3.5 billion human beings on earth and their 167 governments....There will never be enough professional reporters to record all potential news, since theoretically it would require one observer for every participant in human events. If this unpleasant ratio of half the world reporting the activities of the other half should come about, there would not be enough communication capacity for all the reports to be transmitted. If all the reports could be transmitted, they could not be printed. If they could be printed, the reader would never have the time to look at the results.[112]

In short, a truly democratic mass media system is a technical impossibility. The power to command mass audiences for one's message can never be granted to the masses themselves. Should the mass media therefore be destroyed? Should cinemas showing Hollywood movies be burned down, as happened in Iran when Ayatollah Khomeini's revolution against Western dominance set in?[113] The answer is that they will not be destroyed since everybody gaining power will try to use the media for his purposes.[114] Since they are unlikely to be destroyed, efforts should be directed to transform them. For better or worse the mass media have become the central means by which the majority of people form their interpretation about the nature and developments of the world beyond their direct individual perception. The mass media have the ability to define what millions of people experience. They have the unique power to direct mass attention to particular issues, to give visibility to certain social phenomena and as such they can be powerful instruments to solve social problems.

Such a unique resource should not be wasted but put to the best possible use. This is far from being the case. More often than not the Western media are consciously or unconsciously used to produce conformity, self-indulgence, consumerism, passivity, complacency and escapism. The selection mechanism of news is based on a system of news values which reflects more the partly irrational consuming behaviour of audiences than their rational choice on the basis of a reflected need to know. The criteria for disseminating one type of information rather than another should be set by something more rational than the imperfect market laws of commodity production under capitalism. The Western media, even when they are not government-controlled, are not free since they are subject to the necessity to maximize their profits to survive. In 1842 Karl Marx, himself a journalist at that time, wrote: 'The first freedom of the press consists in its not being a trade'.[115] The laws of the market are too close to the laws of the jungle to provide people with an adequate reflection of reality to enable them to cope in the best way possible with the world. The news is too influential in forming our experience to be left to an oligopolistic market.

In place of a commercial news concept, some communication specialists therefore propose a more constructive news concept. Robert K. Baker, for instance, has written that 'The purpose of communicating news should be to reduce uncertainty and to increase the probability that the audience will respond to conflict and change in a rational manner'.[116] Kaarle Nordenstreng, in turn, has suggested that 'news should consist of the systematic explication of the ultimate goals of society'.[117] Two other communication researchers, Claudio Aguirre-Bianchi and Göran Hedebro, have come forward with yet another formulation, which is more down-to-earth:

The leading principle should be that information is a social utility, and that it is a right for people to get to know their surrounding society better. Information should give them the tool with which they can handle this environment, and show ways in which they can influence it.[118]

Such appeals have fallen on fertile ground in the Third World, where developing nations cannot afford to content themselves with the status-quo orientation, the elite-character, the misrepresentations by implication, the overemphasizing of particular events and the silence on macro-social phenomena which characterize much of the Western news flow. In analogy to demands for a New International Economic Order, many leaders of the Third World demand a New International

Information Order (NIIO). In their Kuala Lumpur Declaration they postulated that:

People and individuals have the right to acquire an objective picture of reality by means of accurate and comprehensive information through a diversity of sources and means of information available to them, *as well as to express themselves through various means of culture and communication.* [119]

In the West, this Third World demand for a New International Information Order has been received with suspicious apprehension by most governments as well as by most of the mass media. The countries which demand an equal flow of information between nations are often internally less egalitarian than the nations that dominate them culturally with their communications. State control of the mass media is frequently very strong in these countries and Western observers fear not without reason that the freedom of the press is threatened by the initiatives of these countries in UNESCO. What the developed Western nations are prepared to concede is not a new information order but only, as the American delegate at an UNESCO meeting in Paris in 1978 put it, a 'more just and effective world information order'.[120] To bring this about the developed Western nations, with few exceptions, want to introduce more communication technology in the Third World and train more Third World journalists in the First World. These initiatives, however, tend in our view to strengthen the present information order rather than transform it. In the present discussion the positive elements introduced by Third World nations, those pointing to a democratization of the mass media, have been largely ignored in the Western reaction.

Yet this issue can no longer be treated with silence. In today's world, the norms and values propagated by the mass media have gained the all-encompassment which in former times was reserved for religion. The mass media provide, as George Gerbner has noted, symbols in which human beings see their inspiration and from which they gain their sense of life.[121] If the news of the mass media is as equally norm-setting as the law, the day will come when people want to have a say about the selection principles of news just as in the past they struggled to gain a say over the process of law-making. The right to create and disseminate information which determines the experience of millions of people cannot be left in the hands of private power groups but has to become a public right. In the political sphere constitutions regulate who gets access to power, under what conditions and with what impositions. In an analogous manner it should be determined who is going to get access to news-making, who should have at any given moment the right to make his experience the experiences of millions. To govern is not only the power to make and enforce laws but it is also, as Machiavelli noted, the power to make believe. The mass media make believe and it is only natural that people will try to control the make-believe-instruments as they have tried to control the law-making instruments. Where people have gained control over the law the terror of the law has ceased. When public control over the mass media is gained, the media might also cease to serve as instruments of terror. A right to communicate for aggrieved minorities, in turn, is likely to stop many of them from having recourse to terrorist violence.

These issues require, however, more thorough investigation than we could offer in this exploratory analysis.

APPENDIX:
SUMMARY OF
A DUTCH CASE STUDY

Note: The original institute publication of the COMT study Insurgent Terrorism and the Western News Media *included, as Part II, a Dutch case study of about 150 pages length. It has been published separately in Dutch by Intermediair Bibliotheek, Amsterdam and is therefore not included here. In its place a short summary is added as an appendix to this book. Readers unfamiliar with the Dutch language can consult the original COMT institute publication for the complete English text of the Dutch case study. Copies of the COMT publication have been deposited at the British Library in London and at the Library of Congress in Washington, DC.*

INTRODUCTION

The Dutch case study deals with six acts of terrorism staged by South Moluccans in the Netherlands between 1970 and 1978, and with the way the media reacted to them. It is based on a fairly comprehensive survey of the Dutch media, both written and audiovisual. Furthermore, eight structured interviews with Dutch media representatives and seven such interviews with representatives of the Dutch government who were involved in these incidents were conducted. The structure of the case study is as follows: first a historical and sociological analysis of the background and social origins of South Moluccan terrorism is given.

This is followed by a description of each of the six hostage incidents and a sketch of the consequences of these actions for the terrorists, the hostages, the Dutch government, the Dutch public and the South Moluccan community. In the next section we analyze, paralleling the present study, the terrorist uses of the media, the media uses of news on terrorism, the effects of media reporting on various groups and, finally, the issue of censorship and governmental information policy.

HISTORICAL BACKGROUND

The analysis of Dutch-South Moluccan relations from the sixteenth century until the arrival of some 12,500 South Moluccans in 1951 in the colonial mother country is mainly done in order to look at sources of political violence which have nothing to do with the media. It turns out that the use of South Moluccans as elite soldiers in the Dutch Indies since the nineteenth century preconditioned them to some extent to seek violent solutions to their problems. The identification of the South Moluccan soldiers with the colonial power made them choose the 'wrong' side when decolonization came. When the re-conquest of the Dutch Indies by the Dutch failed after the Second World War, many South Moluccans, fearful of Indonesian retribution, put their hope in a state of their own, the Republik Maluku Selatan (RMS — South Moluccan Republic), which was founded in haste on 25 April 1950 on Ambon, the mother island and cultural centre of the Spice Islands. The RMS lasted only half a year and was put down in the fall of 1950 after fierce resistance. A low-level guerrilla resistance continued until the 1960s, but achieved nothing in the end.

SOCIAL ORIGINS

Through a bungled decolonization policy of the Dutch government, some 4,000 homeless South Moluccan soldiers and their families were brought against their will to the Netherlands in early 1951, and for years this was considered as a temporary measure. On the day they arrived the elite soldiers were dismissed from the ranks of the Dutch Royal Army. Deprived of their military status, isolated in camps, forced into idleness and saddled with a language problem, uncomfortable in a cold climate, these people had nothing but hopes, memories and myths to live from. One of these myths was the RMS and as repatriation became more and more unlikely and integration into Dutch society largely failed, the RMS became their spiritual home, the one thing that gave sense to the lives of these displaced people. Supported by Dutch sympathizers who could not forget the days of colonial glory, they also saw themselves in biblical terms as an exiled nation to be led back to the promised land by their leaders. Their first leader, Dr Chris Soumokil, who had organized the guerrilla war on Ceram against Indonesia, had been caught in 1963 and was executed in 1965. While this put an end to most of the guerrilla activities on the Spice Islands, the RMS ideal continued to find devoted supporters in the Netherlands. When the young widow of Soumokil arrived in Holland in 1966, the sight of her stirred a group of young South Moluccans to a night attack with Molotov cocktails on the Indonesian embassy in The Hague. This marked the beginning of South Moluccan political violence in the Netherlands. Fifteen years had passed since their arrival and a second generation of South Moluccans was growing up, less restrained by Christian ethics and more exposed to the symbols of protest transmitted by the media — Che Guevara, the student movement, the Black Panthers, the Palestinians. Increasingly distrustful of their aging leaders who had sought redress for their grievances by democratic means, the younger generation had no more patience and many of them were willing to wage the struggle for the RMS with other, violent, means.

THE SIX MAJOR TERRORISTIC ACTS

In August 1970, on the eve of a state visit by the Indonesian President Suharto — the man the South Moluccans held responsible for the execution of Soumokil — thirty-three young South Moluccans occupied the Indonesian Residency near the Hague, taking more than thirty hostages and killing one policeman on guard. The aim was to force Indonesia to discuss the South Moluccan problem. The incident lasted only twelve hours and was solved when South Moluccan leaders arrived on the scene. The next incident, following a foiled plan to take the Dutch queen hostage in April 1975, took place in December and lasted about two weeks. It was triggered off by the granting of independence to Surinam in late November. The queen's dictum on this occasion that every people had a right to independence came down hard on many South Moluccans. Why Surinam, and why not the South Moluccas? Seven activists hijacked a train to highlight their claim to a country of their own and this incident, in turn, triggered off a second one by sympathizers who stormed the Indonesian Consulate in Amsterdam. Four hostages died in these double incidents of December 1975. The only political outcome was the installation of a mixed South Moluccan-Dutch commission which was charged with finding possible solutions to the conflict which arose from the fact that 'among South Moluccans in the Netherlands expectations and political ideals are fostered which the Dutch government cannot share but whose existence and serious-ness it acknowledges'. Too many hopes were put on this commission Köbben-Mantouw: the Dutch hoped that it would put an end to terrorism, while South Moluccans hoped that it would ultimately bring about the RMS. When nothing substantial came out of this commission, another ad hoc group (there had never been a terrorist movement) of young South Moluccans decided to stir public opinion with another double action in May 1977. Again, it involved the capture of a train and the occupation of a school with more than one hundred children. The terrorists demanded, among other things, the freeing of imprisoned South Moluccan activists and an end to Dutch support for the 'fascist dictatorship' of Indonesia. Although no hostages were killed, the double incident, dragging on for two weeks, ended in bloodshed, leaving two hostages and six terrorists dead when Dutch marines stormed the hostage sites. Identification with the six South Moluccan 'martyrs', and a sense of revenge, caused three more Moluccans in March 1978 to occupy the administrative centre of the province of Drente. This incident, lasting less than thirty hours and costing the lives of two hostages, received far less support from the South Moluccan community than the 1977 and especially the 1975 incidents.

THE ROLE OF THE MEDIA

The way the South Moluccan activists used the media revealed that they were less sophisticated than some other terrorists in countries like Germany or Italy. They used less than half of the possible uses we have identified in Table 1A (see Table 6).

The main media use of the South Moluccan terrorists was that the media offered them — after two decades of unsuccessful peaceful lobbying — a model of action. They adopted this model as well as they could as ad hoc groups from underprivileged backgrounds lacking the resources which other terrorists abroad could command.

Table 6
South Moluccan Terrorist Media Uses (1970–1978)

1. Learning terrorist techniques from the media
2. Forcing national and international opinion to listen to their grievances and demands
3. Obtaining confirmation that their reference group supports them
4. Target identification among the hostages
5. Utilization of the media for message and demand delivery
6. Demanding publicity by threatening violence against hostages
7. Staging visual events for threat emphasis
8. Basing tactics and reactions on intelligence obtained from media
9. Using the media to observe security forces' countermeasures
10. Using publicity as a rationalization for capitulation (substitute victory)

The media, in turn, used these incidents as gripping stories with endless opportunities to play on the identification mechanisms of the public. In at least one case, it seems, these acts of terrorism were used to get a higher market share in a competitive news market. For some reporters on the scene the incidents served as a source for scoops. In their battle to involve and inform the public and to do better than competing rivals, the media generally did not stand still to ask more fundamental questions such as whether the quantity of information about the incidents was really warranted by their social significance and in relation to the importance of other stories which had to yield to these hostage stories; whether the massive coverage did not invite others to try to gain publicity in a similar way; whether the public was not more intimidated than informed; and whether the media themselves were not becoming the instruments of the terrorists or the government opposing them?

The effects of media reporting on the media themselves were relatively minor (programme changes, police protection of journalists, etc.), compared to the effects on the hostages and their families. Among the latter there was one casualty indirectly caused by the role the media played. Out of the more than fifty hostages of the 1978 incident, radio Hilversum 3 identified some by name which gave the terrorists information about the relative political value of different hostages. One of the two main hostages got wounded when the marines attacked and subsequently succumbed to his injuries. While the medium radio did not pull the trigger of the terrorist's gun, it had indicated a target, reducing the survival chances of those named relative to the anonymous hostages.

The information policy of the Dutch authorities during these incidents led to a number of charges of censorship. The term censorship usually refers to a prohibition to publish, to distribute information. Yet the dissemination of information is only one stage of the news production process where the government can interfere. Denying access to the hostage sites as a news-rich area, which took place by cordoning off the hostage sites, is a form of interference, though it cannot be properly labelled censorship. At the press centres the government enjoyed a kind of news monopoly; its spokesmen could feed the media with pieces of information which served the purposes of the authorities while counterproductive information could be denied, downplayed, delayed or placed in a different light. This, too, is not censorship in the narrow sense of the term. Where this term does apply, at the third stage of the news-making process in which news is broadcast and published, comparatively little interference occurred from the side of the Dutch authorities. The media were asked to suppress some pieces of information but no serious pressure was applied to effect this and, indeed, on a number of occasions the media did not follow the advice of the government. It seems that the government held one more device in readiness to interfere with the dissemination of news in the form of jamming equipment which was meant to serve as a last stop to news which could harm the hostages or help the terrorists. Since only a minute part of the public (the terrorists and their hostages), was thereby potentially denied some information (the equipment was not used for this purpose in the end), the term censorship is somewhat misplaced here.

For the Dutch authorities the media were one of several policy instruments. A more important instrument were the South Moluccan leaders who were used (with decreasing success as the years went by) as mediators. Another instrument of decreasing utility were the telephone negotiations in which psychologically trained specialists used certain argumentation techniques as nonviolent weapons to bring about a negotiated settlement which, while containing face-saving elements, amounted really to a negotiated surrender. The media policy was the government's third, and probably least important instrument to influence the hostage situation. Since it was difficult for the government to know in advance what effect the release of certain news stories would have on the terrorists (the hostages were, in this regard, largely neglected), the authorities generally opted for a very restricted news policy. Being a party to the conflict with the terrorists and, at the same time, being the chief source of information for the public and the terrorists, put the government in a role in which conflicting demands were made. The public's right to know could clash with the hostages' right to survive and the terrorists' desire to succeed. Since the information the public received was, by and large, also the information the terrorists received, it was tempting for the government to reduce the state of information of the public to the one of the terrorists. With a government wanting in general to release as little information as possible and the media, in the name of the public, desiring as much information as possible, the conflict between the media and the government was inescapable.

In principle this is a healthy conflict in which two public institutions check and balance each other. In practice, however, the outcome often produces little public good. It is suggested that partial solutions to keep the conflict between media and government within limits will have to be sought on the procedural level rather than on a substantive level since the problem is basically unsolvable within the present information order. A solution will have to come from a changed understanding by the public as to what is important to be made known. As terroristic incidents become more frequent and as the links between some types of terrorism and the media become more apparent, pressures are likely to develop from groups affected by media-induced effects. Censorship by the government and self-censorship by the media are both negative approaches to the problem of harmful news. Yet so far no viable institutional carrier has appeared on the scene who could be entrusted with deciding what should be public news. It will probably take a long time to make the public media more responsible to the public in general and to those sections most affected by harmful news in particular.

NOTES

CHAPTER 1

1. Cit. Bernard Johnpoll. 'Terrorism and the Mass Media in the United States'. In: Yonah Alexander and Seymour Maxwell Finger (eds.). *Terrorism: Interdisciplinary Perspectives*. New York, John Jay Press, 1977, p. 160.

2. Arnold Gehlen. 'Die gewaltlose Lenkung'. In: Oskar Schatz (ed.). *Die elektronische Revolution. Wie gefährlich sind die Massenmedien?* Graz, Styria, 1975, p. 49.

3. Eugene H. Methvin. 'Terrorism and the Rise of Megamedia in "The Global Village".' Unpubl. Paper, 1976, p. 8.

4. Cit. Friedrich Hacker. *Terror. Mythos, Realität, Analyse.* Reinbek, Rowohlt, 1975, p. 259.

5. Cit. Barbara Tuchman. *The Proud Tower.* New York, Bantam Books, 1972, p. 118, quoted in H. H. A. Cooper. 'Terrorism and the Media'. In: Y. Alexander and S. M. Finger, op. cit. (note 1), p. 144.

6. Herostratus, a Greek, sought to immortalize his name by putting the Artemis temple in Ephesus on fire (356 BC).

7. For an exposition of this process, see: Anne van der Meiden and H. van Ommen. *Ik herinner mij niet u iets gevraagd te hebben. Over journalistieke vrijheid en publieksvrijheid.* 's-Gravenhage, Boekencentrum, 1975, pp. 99–100.

8. Henry Varenne. *De Ravachol à Caserio.* Paris, 1895, quoted in Ze'ev Iviansky. 'Individual Terror: Concept and Typology'. *Journal of Contemporary History*, Vol. 12, 1977, p. 48.

9. The term 'expressive' violence is not used here as a concept. Monica D. Blumenthal et al. (*Justifying Violence: Attitudes of American Man.* Ann Arbor, Institute for Social Research, University of Michigan, 1972, p. 13) distinguish between 'expressive violence' which 'arises primarily in response to feelings of

hate or rage', and 'instrumental violence', which is 'violence used to some end'.
Terrorism as we see it would be 'instrumental' in Blumenthal's terminology.
  10. This typology is taken from Jeremy Tunstall. *The Media are American.
Anglo-American Media in the World*. London, Constable, 1977, p. 25.
  11. John Tebbel. *The Media in America*. New York, Mentor Book, 1976,
p. 310.
  12. Jeremy Tunstall, op. cit. (note 10), p. 98.
  13. J. Guillaume (ed.). *L'Internationale. Documents et Souvenirs, 1864–1887*.
Paris, 1910, Vol. 2, p. 225, quoted in Ze'ev Iviansky, op. cit. (note 8), p. 45.
  14. David Rapaport. *The Politics of Atrocity*. In: Y. Alexander and S. M.
Finger, op. cit. (note 1), p. 47.
  15. Cit. Geoffrey Fairbairn. *Revolutionary Guerrilla Warfare. The Countryside
Version*. Harmondsworth, Penguin, 1974, p. 284.
  16. Programma Ispolnitelnago Komiteta, 1879; cit. *Encyclopaedia of the
Social Sciences*, Vol. 14. New York, Macmillan, 1936, p. 578.
  17. *Freiheit*, 13 September 1884 and 25 July 1885. Repr. in: Walter Laqueur
(ed.). *The Terrorism Reader*. New York, New American Library, 1978, p. 100
and p. 105.
  18. Jean Maitron. *Historie du Movement Anarchiste en France, 1880–1914*.
Paris, 1955. Partly repr. in: W. Laqueur, op. cit. (note 17), p. 97.
  19. Peter Kropotkin. 'The Spirit of Revolt', cit. Ze'ev Iviansky, op. cit. (note
8), p. 45.
  20. Cit. Jacques Ellul. *Propaganda. The Formation of Men's Attitudes*. New
York, Vintage Books, 1973, p. x.
  21. Cit. Marius H. Livingston (ed.). *International Terrorism in the Contemporary World*. Westport, Conn., Greenwood Press, 1978, p. xv.
  22. Peter R. Knauss and D. A. Strickland. 'Political Disintegration and Latent
Terror'. In: Michael Stohl (ed.). *The Politics of Terrorism*. New York, Marcel
Decker, 1979, p. 91.
  23. For a discussion of definitional problems see our *A Research Guide to
Political Terrorism*. Leiden and Amsterdam, COMT, 1982.
  24. *Encyclopaedia of the Social Sciences*. New York, Macmillan, 1936. Vol.
14, p. 576.
  25. Tony Schwartz. *The Responsive Chord*. New York, Anchor Press, 1974,
pp. 41–42.
  26. Klaus Commer. 'Nicht mehr heiter, aber weiter'. *Funk Korrespondenz*,
No. 37, 14 September 1972, p. 13. Richard Clutterbuck (*Guerrillas and Terrorists*. London, Faber and Faber, 1977, p. 82) gives a lower estimate, 500 million.
  27. Cit. Oliver Thomson. *Mass Persuasion in History. An Historical Analysis
of the Development of Propaganda Techniques*. Edinburgh, Paul Harris Publ.,
1977, p. 112.
  28. Terence H. Qualter. *Propaganda and Psychological Warfare*. New York,
Random House, 1962, p. 117.
  29. Friedrich Hacker, op. cit. (note 4), p. 213.
  30. Lawrence Durrell. *Bitter Lemons*. London, 1959, p. 224, quoted in
David Rapaport. 'The Politics of Atrocity'. In: Y. Alexander and S. M. Finger,
op. cit. (note 1), p. 52.
  31. Cit. Geoffrey Fairbairn, op. cit. (note 15), p. 287n.
  32. The discussion of Maoist doctrine is based on Franz Wördemann. 'Mobilität,

Technik und Kommunikation als Strukturelemente des Terrorismus'. In: Manfred Funke (ed.). *Terrorismus. Untersuchungen zur Strategie und Struktur revolutionärer Gewaltpolitik.* Bonn, Bundeszentrale für politische Bildung, 1977, p. 152. Wördemann himself draws from Brian M. Jenkins. *High Technology Terrorism and Surrogate War – The Impact of New Technology on Low Level Violence.* Santa Monica, Rand, 1975, p. 4.

33. Cit. Harold Jacobs (ed.). *Weatherman.* San Francisco, Ramparts Press, 1970, p. 438. In his Bolivian period, however, Guevara and his guerrilleros used organized terror to neutralize the peasant resistance to their attempts to liberate them (E. Che Guevara. *Boliviaans dagboek.* Polak & van Gennep, 1968, p. 129 and p. 148, cit. A. J. F. Köbben. 'Weerstanden tegen mobilisering'. *Sociologische Gids*, Vol. 18, No. 2, March/April 1971, p. 126).

34. Ulrike Pesch. 'Diplomaten-Entführung als terroristisches Kampfmittel'. In: M. Funke, op. cit. (note 32), p. 101. For an analysis of Castro's communication strategy, see: Richard Monk. 'The Use of Foreign Mass Media as an Effective Nonviolent Strategy by Participants in Internal Wars'. Unpubl. Paper, Uppsala, ISA, 1978.

35. Fritz R. Allemann. 'Terrorismus in Lateinamerika – Motive und Erscheinungsformen'. In: M. Funke, op. cit. (note 32), pp. 174–175.

36. Carlos Marighela. *For the Liberation of Brazil.* Harmondsworth, Pelican, 1971, p. 77.

37. Ibid., pp. 87–90. Our emphasis.

38. Eugene H. Methvin. 'Objectivity and the Tactics of Terrorists'. *The Washington Star-News*, 24 February 1974; Carlos Marighela, op. cit. (note 36), pp. 34–35.

39. Cit. Lester A. Sobel (Comp.). *Political Terrorism.* New York, Facts on File, 1975, pp. 5–6.

40. João Quartim. 'Leninism or Militarism'. In: James Kohl and John Litt (eds.). *Urban Guerrilla Warfare in Latin America.* Cambridge, Mass., MIT Press, 1974, p. 151.

41. US Congress, House Committee on Internal Security. *Political Kidnappings, 1968–1973.* 93rd Cong., 1st Sess. Washington, DC, GPO, 1973, p. 11.

42. James Kohl and John Litt, op. cit. (note 40), p. 137.

43. João Quartim, op. cit. (note 40), pp. 150–151.

44. Robert Moss. 'Uruguay: Terrorism versus Democracy'. In: *Conflict Studies*, No. 14, London, Institute for the Study of Power and Conflict, 1971, p. 3; Peter Chippindale and Ed Harriman. *Juntas United!* London, Quartet Books, 1978, pp. 136–138; *NRC-Handelsblad*, 8 March 1980, p. 5.

45. Robert Moss, op. cit. (note 44), p. 7.

46. Ernest Evans. 'American Response to International Terrorism'. In: Y. Alexander and S. M. Finger, op. cit. (note 1), p. 108.

47. Richard Clutterbuck. *Kidnap and Ransom: The Response.* London, Faber & Faber, 1978, p. 58.

48. Jan Schreiber. *The Ultimate Weapon: Terrorists and World Order.* New York, William Morrow & Co., 1978, pp. 113–114.

49. For excerpts from the transcripts of the interrogation of the kidnapped US police instructor Dan Mitrione, distributed by the Liberation News Service, see: US Congress, Senate. Committee on the Judiciary. Subcommittee to Investigate the Administration of the Internal Security Act and Other Internal Security

Laws. *Hearings. Terroristic Activity, Part 5: Hostage Defense Measures* (25 July 1975). 94th Cong., 1st Sess. Washington, DC, GPO, 1975, pp. 277–278.

50. Robert Moss, op. cit. (note 44), p. 7.

51. US Congress, House Committee on Foreign Affairs. Subcommittee on The Near East and South Asia. *Hearings. International Terrorism*, 11, 18, 19 and 24 June 1974. 93rd Cong., 2nd Sess. Washington, DC, GPO, 1974, pp. 43–44.

52. Robert Moss, op. cit. (note 44), p. 7.

53. Peter Chippindale and Ed Harriman, op. cit. (note 44), p. 138.

54. US Congress, House Committee on Internal Security. *Terrorism. A Staff Study.* 93rd Cong., 2nd Sess. Washington, DC, GPO, 1974, p. 14.

55. Yonah Alexander. 'Terrorism and the Media in the Middle East'. In: Y. Alexander and S. M. Finger, op. cit. (note 1), p. 169.

56. *Volkskrant* (Amsterdam), 24th March 1979, p. 6.

57. Peter Chippindale and Ed Harriman, op. cit. (note 44), p. 9 and p. 13; *Volkskrant*, 25 October 1979, p. 9.

58. *Volkskrant*, 11 November 1978, p. 3.

59. *Volkskrant*, 8 April 1978, p. 5; ibid., 22 August 1978, p. 5; ibid., 20 December 1978, p. 3; ibid., 2 January 1979, p. 3.

60. Peter Chippindale and Ed Harriman, op. cit. (note 44), p. 51.

61. Lauran Paine. *The Terrorists.* London, Robert Hale & Co., 1975, p. 31.

62. Groups and individuals linked with Dr George Habash's Popular Front came from the Netherlands, Brazil, France, Venezuela, Britain, Colombia, Turkey, Algeria, Egypt, Libya, Jordan, Lebanon, Italy and Germany. Charles A. Russell, Chief of acquisitions and analysis division in the US Air Force's Directorate of Counterintelligence, cit. *New York Times*, 26 June 1978, p. A-9.

63. Seth Tillman, staff member of the US Senate Committee on Foreign Relations, 5 March 1974, cit. Lester A. Sobel (Comp.), op. cit. (note 39), p. 3.

64. Cit. J. Bowyer Bell. *A Time of Terror. How Democratic Societies Respond to Revolutionary Violence.* New York, Basic Books, 1978, p. 168.

65. Cit. Gerard McKnight. *The Mind of the Terrorist.* London, 1974, p. 168, quoted from Jan Schreiber. *The Ultimate Weapon. Terrorists and World Order.* New York, William Morrow & Co., 1978, p. 13.

66. US Congress, House Committee on Internal Security. *Terrorism. A Staff Study.* op. cit. (note 54), p. 30.

67. *Al-Hawadeth* (Beirut), 11 April 1969, cit. Yonah Alexander, op. cit. (note 55), p. 187.

68. Cit. Franz Wördemann. *Terrorismus. Motive, Täter, Strategien.* München, Piper, 1977, p. 139.

69. David Phillips. *Skyjack. The Story of Air Piracy.* London, Harrap, 1973, p. 144.

70. Philip Goodhard. *The Climate of Collapse. The Terrorist Threat to Britain and her Allies.* Richmond, Surrey, Foreign Affairs Publ. Co., 1975, p. 3; Richard Clutterbuck, op. cit. (note 26), p. 82.

71. Cit. P. Goodhard, op. cit. (note 70), p. 3.

72. Cit. Franz Wördemann, op. cit. (note 68), p. 152.

73. Klaus Commer, op. cit. (note 26), pp. 13–14.

74. *Newsweek*, 18 September 1972, p. 24.

75. Abu Ijad. *Heimat oder Tod.* Düsseldorf, Econ Verlag, 1979; cit. *Neue Zürcher Zeitung*, 13 August 1979, p. 19.

76. Cit. Christopher Dobson and Ronald Paine. *The Carlos Complex. A Pattern of Violence*. London. Hodder and Stoughton, 1977, p. 15.

77. *Newsweek*, 18 September 1972, p. 35.

78. Friedrich Hacker, op. cit. (note 4), p. 168.

79. Cit. Neil Hickey. 'Terrorism and Television. The Medium in the Middle'. *TV Guide*, Vol. 24, No. 32, 7 August 1976, p. 10.

80. Cit. J. Bowyer Bell. 'Terror: An Overview'. In: Marius H. Livingston (ed.). *International Terrorism in the Contemporary World*. Westport, Conn., Greenwood Press, 1978, p. 38.

81. Ibid.

82. John Laffin. 'Murder Incorporated'. *The Spectator*, 30 August 1975.

83. William J. Drummond and Augustine Zycher. 'Arafat's Press Agents'. In: *Harper's*, March 1976, p. 26.

84. Walter Laqueur. *Terrorism*. London, Weidenfeld and Nicolson, 1977, p. 261; William J. Drummond and Augustine Zycher, op. cit. (note 83), p. 30.

85. US Congress, House Committee on Internal Security. *Terrorism. A Staff Study*, op. cit. (note 54), p. 44.

86. J. Schreiber, op. cit. (note 48), p. 114.

87. *Der Spiegel*, No. 32, 7 August 1978, p. 78 (interview with Hans-Joachim Klein).

88. Christopher Dobson and Ronald Paine, op. cit. (note 76), p. 89.

89. Neil Hickey. 'Terrorism and Television'. *TV Guide*, Vol. 24, No. 31, 31 July 1976, p. 6.

90. Christopher Dobson and Ronald Paine, op. cit. (note 76), p. 113.

91. Andrew Kopkind. 'Publish and Perish'. *More*, April 1978, p. 13.

92. See: Jeremy Tunstall, op. cit. (note 10).

93. George Gerbner et al. *Violence Profile No. 7*. Philadelphia, Annenberg School of Communication, 1976, cit. John A. Pandiani. 'Crime Time TV: If all we knew is what we saw....' In: *Contemporary Crises*, Vol. 2, No. 4, October 1978, p. 452.

94. Cit. Frank Mankiewicz and Joel Swerdlow. *Remote Control. Television and the Manipulation of American Life*. New York, Times Book, 1978, p. 34.

95. Vincent Bugliosi. *The Manson Murders*. London, The Bodley Head, 1975, pp. 78ff. quoted in Franz Wördemann, in M. Funke, op. cit. (note 32), p. 150.

96. Cit. H. H. A. Cooper. 'Terrorism and the Media'. In: Y. Alexander and S. M. Finger, op. cit. (note 1), p. 149.

97. Friedrich Hacker, op. cit. (note 4), p. 271.

98. Cit. Neil Hickey, op. cit. (note 89), p. 6.

99. Neil Hickey, op. cit. (note 79).

100. J. Bowyer Bell, op. cit. (note 64), p. 11.

101. Ibid., p. 23.

102. J. Schreiber, op. cit. (note 48), p. 34.

103. F. Thomas Schornhorst. 'The Lawyer and the Terrorist: Another Ethical Dilemma'. In: *Indiana Law Journal*, Vol. 53, No. 4, 1978, p. 683.

104. Ibid., pp. 685–686.

105. Philip J. Troustine. 'We Interrupt This Program. Indiana Kidnapper Directs Live Newscasts with Shotgun'. *More*, June 1977, pp. 14–21.

106. Frank Mankiewicz and Joel Swerdlow, op. cit. (note 94), pp. 103–105.

107. Cit. Eugene H. Methvin. *The Rise of Radicalism. The Social Psychology*

of Messianic Extremism. New Rochelle, N Y , Arlington House, 1973, pp. 506–509.

108. Jerry Rubin. *Do it. Scenarios of the Revolution.* New York, Ballantine Books, 1970, pp. 107–108.

109. Cit. David C. Rapoport. *Assassination and Terrorism.* Toronto, Canadian Broadcasting Corporation, 1971, p. 54.

110. Jerry Mander. *Four Arguments for the Elimination of Television.* New York, William Morrow & Co., 1978, p. 31.

111. Cit. ibid., p. 320.

112. Ibid., pp. 31–32.

113. US Congress, Senate. Committee on the Judiciary. *Report: The Weather Underground.* 94th Cong., 1st Sess. Washington, DC, GPO, 1975, p. 40; Philip A. Karber. 'Urban Terrorism: Baseline Data and Conceptual Framework'. In: *Social Science Quarterly*, Vol. 52, December 1971, p. 531.

114. Cit. Philip A. Karber, op. cit. (note 113), p. 531.

115. US Congress, Senate. Committee on the Judiciary. Subcommittee to Investigate the Administration of the Internal Security Act and Other Internal Security Laws. *Hearings. Terroristic Activity. Part 5: Hostage Defense Measures. Testimony of Brooks McClure, Foreign Service Officer, 25 July 1975.* 94th Cong., 1st Sess. Washington, DC, GPO, 1975, pp. 274–275.

116. William P. Yarborough. 'Terrorism – The Past as an Indicator of the Future'. In: Marius H. Livingston (ed.), op. cit. (note 21), p. 459.

117. Francis M. Watson. *Political Terrorism: The Threat and the Response.* Washington, Robert B. Luce Co., 1976, pp. 174–175.

118. 'Prairie Fire – Political Statement of the Weather Underground, 1974'. Partly repr. in Walter Laqueur (ed.), op. cit. (note 17), p. 174.

119. Gabrielle Schang and Ron Rosenbaum. 'Now the Urban Guerrillas have a Real Problem. They're Trying to Make it in the Magazine Business'. *More*, November 1976, pp. 16–20.

120. Desmond Smith. 'Scenario Reality. A New Brand of Terrorism'. *The Nation*, 30 March 1974, p. 392.

121. Cit. Hank Messick and Burt Goldblatt. *Kidnapping. The Illustrated History.* New York, Dial Press, 1974, p. 159.

122. David Shaw. 'Editors Face Terrorist Demand Dilemma'. *Los Angeles Times*, 15 September 1976; Randy I. Bellows. 'Hijacking the 1st Amendment'. *More*, June 1977, p. 16.

123. Vin McLellan and Paul Avery. *The Voices of Guns.* New York, G. P. Putnam, 1977, p. 22.

124. Hank Messick and Burt Goldblatt, op. cit. (note 121), p. 166.

125. Cit. *Time.* 29 April 1974, p. 14.

126. Desmond Smith, op. cit. (note 120), pp. 392–393.

127. Remarks made by Brian M. Jenkins before a Conference on Terrorism and the Media. Florence, 16–18 June 1978, p. 5.

128. See: James Monaco. 'The Mythologizing of Citizen Patty'. In: James Monaco (ed.). *Celebrity. The Media as Image Makers.* New York, Delta Books, 1978, pp. 65–78.

129. For a list of the movies and books, see: ibid., pp. 77–78.

130. Askia Muhammad. 'Civil War in Islamic America'. *The Nation*, Vol. 224, No. 23, 11 June 1977, p. 721; Randy I. Bellows, op. cit. (note 122), p. 16.

131. Hank Siegel. 'Looking at the Media from the Other End of the Gun'. In: Marie Snider (ed.). *Media and Terrorism. The Psychological Impact.* Seminar, 3–4 March 1978. Newton, Kansas, Prairie View, 1978, pp. 45–46.

132. Cit. Charles Fenyvesi, in: *The Media and Terrorism. A Seminar Sponsored by The Chicago Sun-Times and Chicago Daily News.* Chicago, Field Enterprises, 1977, p. 28.

133. Hank Siegel, op. cit. (note 131), p. 44.

134. Charles Fenyvesi, op. cit. (note 132), p. 29.

135. Ibid., p. 29.

136. Ibid., p. 29.

137. Cit. *New York Times*, 19 March 1977, p. 3.

138. *Quick* (Germany), 2 March 1978, p. 138.

139. US Congress, Senate. Committee on the Judiciary. Subcommittee to Investigate the Administration of the Internal Security Act and Other Internal Security Laws. *Hearings. Terroristic Activity. Part 5: Hostage Defense Measures. Testimony of Brooks McClure, Foreign Service Officer,* op. cit. (note 115), p. 274.

140. Ibid., pp. 275–276.

141. J. Bowyer Bell. *IPI-Report*, Vol. 25, No. 6, June 1976, p. 4.

142. Cit. Michael Moodie. 'The Patriotic Game. The Politics of Violence in Northern Ireland'. In: Marius H. Livingston (ed.), op. cit. (note 21), p. 98.

143. Peter Taylor. 'Reporting Northern Ireland'. *Index on Censorship*, Vol. 7, No. 6, November–December 1978, p. 8.

144. Denis Hamill. 'Belfast Beat: Cityside Reporting under the Gun'. *More*, November 1977, pp. 41–42.

145. US Congress, Senate. Committee on Governmental Affairs. *An Act to Combat International Terrorism. Report to accompany S. 2236.* 95th Cong., 2nd Sess. Report No. 95–908. Washington, DC, GPO, 1978, p. 126.

146. *Index on Censorship*, Vol. 7, No. 6, November–December 1978, p. 67.

147. *Volkskrant*, 27 February 1978, p. 5.

148. *Volkskrant*, 21 September 1977, p. 3; ibid., 24 October 1977, p. 4.

149. *Volkskrant*, 24 October 1977, p. 3.

150. *Volkskrant*, 3 October 1977, p. 7.

151. The term is from the imprisoned writer Peter Paul Zahl; cit. *Der Spiegel*, 11 December 1978, p. 62.

152. Cit. Boudewijn Chorus. *Als op ons geschoten wordt....* Groningen, Pamphlet, 1978, p. 67.

153. Cit. *Der Spiegel*, No. 32, 7 August 1978, p. 70.

154. Werner Kahl. 'Akteure und Aktionen während der Formationsphase des Terrorismus'. In: Manfred Funke, op. cit. (note 32), p. 273.

155. Ibid., p. 276.

156. Jillian Becker. *Hitler's Children.* London, Panther, 1978, p. 363.

157. Arthur Koestler. *The Ghost in the Machine.* London, Hutchinson, 1967, p. 243.

158. Ibid., p. 251.

159. Horst Mahler. 'Der Foltervorwurf – eine Propagandalüge'. *Der Spiegel*, 11 December 1978, pp. 62–65.

160. Melvin Lasky. 'Ulrike Meinhof & the Baader-Meinhof Gang'. *Encounter*, Vol. 44, No. 6, June 1975, p. 10.

161. Spiegel-Gespräch im Untergrund: 'Opec-Terrorist Klein packt aus'. *Der Spiegel*, No. 32, 7 August 1978, p. 81.
162. Walter Althammer. *Gegen den Terror. Texte/Dokumente.* Stuttgart, Verlag Bonn Aktuell, 1978, p. 67.
163. Spiegel-Gespräch im Untergrund, op. cit. (note 161), p. 81.
164. Ibid.
165. Horst Mahler, op. cit. (note 159), p. 65.
166. Gerd Langguth. 'Guerilla und Terror als linksextremistische Kampfmittel. Rezeption und Kritik'. In: Manfred Funke (ed.). *Extremismus im demokratischen Rechtsstaat.* Bonn, Bundeszentrale für politische Bildung, 1978, pp. 119–120.
167. Cit. *Der Stern*, 1 June 1978, quoted by Reinhard Rupprecht. 'Il Caso della Germania Federale – I'. In: *Affari Esteri*, Anno X, No. 30, July 1978, p. 473.
168. M. Baumann. *Wie alles anfing.* München, Trikontinent, n. d., p. 129; cit. Iring Fetcher. *Terrorismus und Reaktion.* Köln, Europäische Verlagsanstalt, 1977, p. 19.
169. Klaus Bresser. 'Wenn der Terror Programm macht. Das Fernsehen und der Fall Schleyer'. In: *Fünkchen. WDR im Team*, No. 34, 1977, p. 1.
170. Cit. Melvin J. Lasky, op. cit. (note 160), p. 15.
171. Spiegel-Gespräch im Untergrund, op. cit. (note 161), p. 79.
172. Reinhard Rupprecht, op. cit. (note 167), p. 473.
173. Dennis Redmont. *Covering Terrorism.* Rome, Associated Press, 1978 (Article).
174. Richard Clutterbuck, op. cit. (note 47), p. 63.
175. Video tape from H. M. Schleyer, 14 September 1977, cit. Walter Althammer, op. cit. (note 162), p. 144.
176. Horst Mahler, op. cit. (note 159), p. 65.
177. *Time*, 28 March 1977, p. 13; *Newsweek*, 22 May 1978, p. 35.
178. Cit. Walter Laqueur, op. cit. (note 84), p. 66.
179. *Domenica del Corriere*, Anno 81, No. 13, 28 March 1979, p. 13.
180. Aaron Latham. 'The Bravest Journalist in the World'. *Esquire*, Vol. 89, No. 8, 9 May 1978, p. 51.
181. Ibid., pp. 51–52.
182. Sabino Acquaviva. 'Il Caso Dell'Italia – II'. In: *Affari Esteri*, Anno X, No. 39, July 1978, pp. 466–467.
183. Dennis Redmont, op. cit. (note 173), s. p.
184. *Bünder Zeitung* (Switzerland), 10 March 1978, p. 40.
185. Private information.
186. Aaron Latham, op. cit. (note 180), pp. 48–49.
187. Andrew Kopkind, op. cit. (note 91), p. 15.
188. *Der Spiegel*, No. 31, 1977, p. 100.
189. For analyses of the media in the Moro affair, see: Yves de la Haye. 'Petit traité des media en usages terroristes'. In: Gilles Lipovetsky (Comp.). 'Territoires de la Terreur'. *Silex* (Grenoble), No. 10, 1978, pp. 117–125, and: Alessandro Silj. *Brigate Rosse – Stato, lo scontro spettacolo nella regia della stampa quotidiana.* Firenze, Vallecchi, 1978.
190. *Volkskrant*, 23 May 1978, p. 5.
191. *Volkskrant*, 11 October 1978, p. 3.

192. For an elaboration of this notion, see: J. Mander, op. cit. (note 110), pp. 200–205.

193. The suggestion for a content analysis of terrorism was first made by Philip A. Karber, op. cit. (note 113), p. 533.

194. Bruce L. Smith, Harold D. Lasswell and Ralph D. Casey. *Propaganda, Communication, and Public Opinion*. Princeton, NJ, Princeton University Press, 1946, p. 121.

CHAPTER 2

1. To our knowledge only two studies, which were both inaccessible to us, address this problem. They are: Philip A. Karber. 'Newspaper Coverage of Domestic Bombings: Reporting Patterns of American Violence'. *Bomb Incident Bulletin*, March 1973; Edward F. Mickolus. *Assessing the Degrees of Error in Public Reporting of Transnational Terrorism.* Washington, DC, Central Intelligence Agency, Office of Political Research, 1976.

2. David Phillips. *Skyjack. The Story of Air Piracy.* London, Harrap, 1973, p. 44.

3. The reader interested in a broader discussion of these questions can find it in another study of ours, *A Research Guide to Political Terrorism*. Leiden and Amsterdam, COMT, 1982.

4. Cit. Ovid Demaris. *Brothers in Blood. The International Terrorist Network.* New York, Charles Scribner's Sons, 1977, pp. 386–387.

5. Peter W. Sandman, David M. Rubin and David B. Sachsman. *Media. An Introductory Analysis of American Mass Communications.* Englewood Cliffs, Prentice Hall, 1976, p. 165.

6. Our sample consisted of seven Dutch respondents and seventeen other West- and South-European ones; the remaining three were from Japan, the United States and South Africa respectively. Two of the twenty-seven respondents worked for news agencies, two for weekly papers or magazines, eight for daily newspapers and fifteen for radio or television stations. The functions of the respondents varied from journalist to director. One was an official of an Italian news agency, another was a counsellor of a Belgian broadcasting station, a third a reporter of a Turkish broadcasting station, a fourth was a Dutch television editor, the fifth was a Danish television news director and the sixth a British newspaper editor. The functions of the remaining twenty-one are mentioned between brackets in Table 2C.

7. Horst Herold. 'Krise des Sicherheitsgefühls, nicht der Sicherheitslage'. *Frankfurter Rundschau*, 3 May 1979, p. 10.

8. Edward C. Epstein. 'The Uses of Terrorism: A Study in Media Bias'. *Stanford Journal of International Studies*, Vol. 12, Spring 1977, pp. 68–71.

9. Peter M. Sandman et al., op. cit. (note 5), 1976, pp. 420–421.

10. Lord Hill. *Behind the Screen*. London, Sidgwick & Jackson, 1974, p. 207.

11. Memorandum from Chief Assistant to Editor, Television News to News-room Staff, cit. Philip Schlesinger. *Putting 'Reality' Together. BBC News.* London, Constable, 1978, pp. 229–230.

12. *Elseviers Magazine*, 8 September 1979, p. 45; Philip Schlesinger, op. cit. (note 11), p. 230.

13. H. Molotch and M. Lester. 'News as Purposive Behavior – On the Strategic Use of Routine Events, Accidents and Scandals'. *American Sociological Review*, Vol. 39, No. 1, 1974, p. 105.

14. For the Dutch situation, see: A. W. M. Coenen and J. J. M. van Dijk. *Misdaadverslaggeving in Nederlandse Dagbladen tussen 1966 en 1974.* The Hague, WODC, 1976; for a US study bearing out the hypothesis that there is no con-sistent relationship between crime rates and the amount of crime news, see: F. James Davis. 'Crime News in Colorado Newspapers'. *The American Journal of Sociology*, Vol. 57, 1951–52, pp. 325–330.

15. Peter M. Sandman et al., 1976, op. cit. (note 5), p. 412.

16. Yves de la Haye. 'Petit traité des media en usages terroristes'. In: Gilles Lipovetsky (Comp.) 'Territoires de la Terreur'. *Silex* (Grenoble), No. 10, 1978, p. 119.

17. Gaspare Barbiellini Amidei. 'Responsibilità dei news media – II'. *Affari Esteri*, Anno X, July 1978, pp. 428–429.

18. For empirical data on this relationship, see: George Gerbner, Larry Gross, Marilyn Jackson-Beeck, Suzanne Jeffries-Fox and Nancy Signorielli. 'Violence on the Screen. Cultural Indicators: Violence Profile No. 9'. *Journal of Communication*, Summer 1978, pp. 176–207.

19. Horst Herold, op. cit. (note 7), p. 10.

20. Erich Fromm. *Anatomie der menschlichen Destruktivität.* Stuttgart, 1974, p. 221, cit. Eric Ertl. 'Geisel-Dramen. Ueber den Unterhaltungswert der Gewalt'. *Medium*, Jg. 5, Heft 6, 1976, p. 6.

21. Cit. Oliver Thomson. *Mass Persuasion in History. An Historical Analysis of the Development of Propaganda Techniques.* Edinburgh, Paul Harris Publ., 1977, p. 30.

22. Cit. H. H. A. Cooper. 'Terrorism and the News Media'. In: Y. Alexander and S. M. Finger. *Terrorism: Interdisciplinary Perspectives.* New York, John Jay Press, 1977, p. 147.

23. Bob Ferrante, 'WGBH-TV, Boston', cit. *More*, June 1977, p. 20.

24. Cit. Charles B. Seib. 'The Hanafi Episode: A Media Event'. *Washington Post*, 18 March 1977, p. A-27.

25. *Volkskrant*, 2 June 1979, p. 1.

26. David Phillips op. cit. (note 2), p. 76; James A. Arey. *The Sky Pirates.* London, Ian Allan, 1973, pp. 178–180.

27. David Phillips, op. cit. (note 2), pp. 187–188.

28. Eric Ertl, op. cit. (note 20), p. 6; Boudewijn Chorus. *Als op ons geschoten wordt...* Groningen, Pamphlet, 1978, p. 89.

29. Eric Ertl, op. cit. (note 20), p. 6.

30. Iring Fetscher. 'TV bracht terrorisme in de huiskamers'. *Het Parool*, 31 December 1979, p. 21.

31. Edward Jay Epstein. *Between Fact and Fiction: The Problem of Journalism.* New York, Vintage Books, 1975, p. 204.

32. Frank Mankiewicz and Joel Swerdlow. *Remote Control. Television and*

Manipulation of American Life. New York, Times Books, 1978, p. 77.

33. Neil Hickey. 'Terrorism and Television'. *TV Guide,* Vol. 24, No. 31, 31 July 1976, p. 6. Hickey offers no empirical evidence. Some confirmation for his statement, albeit indirect, seems to be offered by a Canadian study analyzing the news on television and in the written press. This study, which scrutinized almost 13,000 news items, found that physical violence constituted 47.9 percent of all violence-and-conflict items on television but only 38.8 percent in papers. Television was found to focus generally more on actual or threatened violence while newspapers carried comparatively more conflict items (*Ontario Royal Commission on Violence in the Communications Industry.* Ontario, Ministry of Government Services, 1977, Vol. 3, pp. 603–604). Assuming that this preference of television is based on the visual attractiveness of physical violence compared to the medium's difficulty in portraying conflict, it could be said that television news favours violence for reasons characteristic to the medium's nature.

34. David Phillips, op. cit. (note 2), p. 116.

35. J. Bowyer Bell. 'Terrorist Scripts and Live-action Spectaculars'. *Columbia Journalism Review,* May/June 1978, p. 50.

36. Walter Laqueur. 'The Futility of Terrorism'. *Harper's,* Vol. 252, No. 1510, March 1976, p. 104.

37. H. Molotch and M. Lester, op. cit. (note 13), p. 106.

38. Friedrich Hacker. *Terror: Mythos, Realität, Analyse.* Reinbek, Rowohlt, 1975, p. 227.

39. William R. Catton, Jr. 'Militants and the Media: Partners in Terrorism?' *Indiana Law Journal,* Vol. 53, No. 4, 1978, p. 713.

40. Ontario Royal Commission, op. cit. (note 33), p. 645.

41. Ben H. Bagdikian. *The Information Machines. Their Impact on Men and the Media.* New York, Harper & Row, 1971, p. 46.

42. Gayle Durham Hollander. 'Developments in Soviet Radio and Television News Reporting'. In: Jeremy Tunstall (ed.). *Media Sociology. A Reader.* London, Constable, 1974, p. 253; see also: Jacques Ellul. *Propaganda. The Formation of Men's Attitudes.* New York, Vintage Books, 1973, p. 113n.

43. Hendrick Smith. 'The Russians', cit. Peter Hofstede and Rein van Rooij. *Over Televisie.* Hilversum, Televizier, 1978, p. 87; James A. Arey, op. cit. (note 26), pp. 191–192.

44. H. Molotch and M. Lester, op. cit. (note 13), p. 105.

45. Bernard Roshco. *Newsmaking.* Chicago, University of Chicago Press, 1975, p. 62.

46. James B. Lemert. 'Content Duplication by the Networks in Competing Evening Newscasts'. *Journalism Quarterly,* Vol. 51, No. 2, Summer 1974, pp. 238–250.

47. Cit. Philip Schlesinger, op. cit. (note 11), p. 117.

48. Johan Galtung and Mari Holmboe Ruge. 'The Structure of Foreign News'. (1965). Repr. in: J. Tunstall (ed.), op. cit. (note 42), pp. 259–298.

49. Giovanni Bechelloni. 'Il Colpo di Stato in diretta'. Repr. in: A. Silj. *Brigate Rosse.* Firenze, Vallecchi, 1978, pp. 220–222.

50. Brian Jenkins. 'International Terrorism: A Balance Sheet'. *Survival,* July/August 1975. Repr. in: *Terrorisme als vorm van politiek geweld.* Katholieke Hogeschool Tilburg, 1977, p. 13.

51. Charles B. Seib. 'The Hanafi Episode: A Media Event'. *Washington Post*, 18 March 1977, p. A-27.

52. A. Kamsteeg. 'Terrorisme: groeiend probleem voor de westerse wereld'. *Nederlands Dagblad*, 26 May 1977.

53. Charles B. Seib, op. cit. (note 51), p. A-27.

54. William R. Catton, Jr., op. cit. (note 39), p. 719.

55. Computations from Herbert A. Terry. 'Television and Terrorism: Professionalism not quite the answer'. *Indiana Law Journal*, Vol. 53, No. 4, 1978, p. 754.

56. Marvin Barrett. *Rich News, Poor News.* New York, Thomas Y. Crowell, 1978, p. 98.

57. David Anable. 'Media, The Reluctant Participant in Terrorism'. In: Marie Snider (ed.), *Media and Terrorism. The Psychological Impact.* Seminar, 3–4 March 1978. Newton, Kansas, Prairie View, 1978, p. 18.

58. Charles Fenyvesi, a reporter and hostage, in: Chicago Sun-Times and Chicago Daily News. *The Media and Terrorism. A Seminar.* Chicago, Field Enterprises Inc., 1977, p. 28.

59. Marvin Barrett, op. cit. (note 56), p. 99.

60. Cit. Charles Fenyvesi, op. cit. (note 58), pp. 27–28.

61. David Phillips, op. cit. (note 2), p. 116.

62. Private information from Japanese editor.

63. Franz Wördemann. 'Mobilität, Technik und Kommunikation als Strukturelemente des Terrorismus'. In: Manfred Funke (ed.). *Terrorismus. Untersuchungen zur Strategie und Struktur revolutionärer Gewaltpolitik.* Bonn, Bundeszentrale für politische Bildung, 1977, p. 154.

64. Cit. Franz Wördemann. *Terrorismus. Motive, Täter, Strategien.* München, Piper, 1977, p. 150.

65. Ibid.

66. Jillian Becker. *Hitler's Children.* London, Panther, 1978, p. 39.

67. Iring Fetscher. *Terrorismus und Reaktion.* Köln, Europäische Verlagsanstalt, 1977, p. 104.

68. Werner Kahl. 'Akteure und Aktionen während der Formationsphase des Terrorismus'. In: Manfred Funke (ed.), op. cit. (note 63), p. 281.

69. Data adapted from Table I of the report by Gert Ellinghaus and Günther Rager. 'Arbeitsmaterialien zu einer vergleichenden Untersuchung der Presseberichterstattung über die Entführung des Berliner CDU-Vorsitzenden Peter Lorenz'. In: *Funk Report*, Jg. 11, 8/75, 16 May 1975, p. vii.

70. Ibid., pp. iii–iv.

71. Private information.

72. A. Silj. op. cit. (note 49), p. 66.

73. The percentages have been calculated on the basis of the data gathered by A. Silj, ibid., p. 50.

74. Cit. Yves de la Haye, op. cit. (note 16), p. 118.

75. A. Silj, op. cit. (note 49), p. 40.

76. Ibid., p. 212.

77. Ibid., p. 9.

78. Sandro Curzi. *La Repubblica*, 18 April 1978; cit. A. Silj, op. cit. (note 49), p. 210.

79. Private information.

80. Communiqué No. 11, cit. A. Silj, op. cit. (note 49), p. 217.

81. Giovanni Bechelloni, op. cit. (note 49), p. 220.

82. A. Silj, op. cit. (note 49), p. 43 and pp. 8—9.

83. Peter M. Sandmann et al., op. cit. (note 5), 1976, p. 420.

84. Anthony Smith. *The Politics of Information. Problems of Policy in Modern Media*. London, Macmillan, 1978, p. 107.

85. Colin Seymour-Ure. *The Political Impact of Mass Media*. London, Constable, 1974, p. 46.

86. Cit. Philip Schlesinger, op. cit. (note 11), p. 221.

87. *Daily Express*, 11 November 1971; cit. Steve Chibnall. *Law-and-Order-News. An Analysis of Crime Reporting in the British Press*. London, Tavistock, 1977, p. 41.

88. Lord Hill in a letter to Home Secretary, Mr Maudling, 23 November 1975, cit. Philip Schlesinger, op. cit. (note 11), p. 212.

89. This is a conclusion of Philip Elliott. *Reporting Northern Ireland: A Study of News in Britain, Ulster and the Irish Republic*. Leicester, Centre for Mass Communication Research, 1976, p. V—16. The study has been published by UNESCO in a book titled, *Ethnicity and the Media*.

90. Ibid., p. V—17.

91. Ibid.

92. Cit. Peter Hofstede and Rein van Rooij, op. cit. (note 43), pp. 87—88.

93. James Kohl & John Litt (eds.). *Urban Guerrilla Warfare in Latin America*. Cambridge, Mass., MIT Press, 1974, p. 1.

94. Stuart Hall. 'A World at One with Itself'. In: Stanley Cohen and Jock Young (eds.). *The Manufacture of News. Social Problems, Deviance and the Mass Media*. London, Constable, 1973, p. 92.

95. According to data compiled by RAND, there were 1,017 persons killed and 2,509 wounded or injured (terrorists included) in 1,019 recorded incidents of international terrorism in the ten year period 1968—1977. Brian M. Jenkins. *International Terrorism: Trends and Potentialities*. Santa Monica, Rand, May 1978 (Rand P—6117), p. 11. In the past 25 years more than 70,000 people died in Guatemala through political violence, most of them by state or state-tolerated terrorism. In the first four months of 1979 alone there were, according to a conservative estimate of Amnesty International, 1,000 political murders. *Volkskrant*, 10 October 1979, p. 6.

96. David Rapoport. 'The Politics of Atrocity'. In: Y. Alexander and S. M. Finger (eds.), op. cit. (note 22), p. 46.

97. James Kohl and John Litt (eds.), op. cit. (note 93), p. 23.

98. Boudewijn Chorus, op. cit. (note 28), p. 112.

99. Steve Chibnall, op. cit. (note 87), pp. 104—105.

100. Francis M. Watson. *Political Terrorism*. Washington, Robert B. Luce Co., 1976, p. 31; US Congress, Senate. Committee on the Judiciary. Subcommittee to Investigate the Administration of the Internal Security Act and Other Internal Security Laws. *Hearings. Terroristic Activity. Part 3*. 93rd Cong., 2nd Sess., Washington, DC, GPO, 1975, p. 173.

101. A. Silj, op. cit. (note 49), p. 236; Yves de la Haye, op. cit. (note 16), p. 118.

102. For a discussion of the varying uses of the photo, see: A. Silj, op. cit. (note 49), pp. 11—14. See also: Gaspare Barbiellini Amidei. 'Responsibilità dei

news media – II'. *Affari Esteri*, Anno X, No. 39, July 1978, p. 31.

103. *Al-Hawadeth*, 11 April 1969; cit. Y. Alexander. 'Terrorism and the Media in the Middle East'. In: Y. Alexander and S. M. Finger (eds.), op. cit. (note 22), p. 187.

104. Edward Jay Epstein. *Between Fact and Fiction: The Problem of Journalism*. New York, Vintage Books, 1975, pp. 34, 41 and 76.

105. In 1969–70 at least ten policemen were killed by identified Panthers. Eugene H. Methvin. *The Rise of Radicalism. The Social Psychology of Messianic Extremism*. New Rochelle, NY, Arlington House, 1973, p. 511.

106. Interview by Robert Friedmann with Lt. Frank Bolz, Head of the New York City Police Department's Hostage Negotiating Squad. *More*, June 1977, p. 19.

107. Ibid., p. 20.

108. Melvin J. Lasky. 'Ulrike Meinhof & the Baader-Meinhof Gang'. *Encounter*, Vol. 44, No. 6, June 1975, p. 18.

109. Richard Francis. *Broadcasting to a Community in Conflict – the Experience in Northern Ireland*. London, BBC, 1977, p. 13.

110. Philip Schlesinger, op. cit. (note 11), p. 228.

111. Ibid., p. 229.

112. *NRC-Handelsblad*, 13 July 1979, p. 5.

113. *Fernseh-Informationen*, No. 6, March 1975, p. 114.

114. Paul H. Weaver. 'The New Journalism and the Old'. In: John C. Merrill and Ralph D. Barney (eds.). *Ethics and the Press. Readings in Mass Media Morality*. New York, Hastings House, 1975, pp. 100–101. The question is not merely hypothetical. Journalists do go to jail for protecting their sources. An example is the station manager of KPFK in Santa Monica, Calif., who was imprisoned for refusing to give the authorities an original tape of a communiqué from the Symbionese Liberation Army. US Congress, Senate. Committee on the Judiciary. Subcommittee to Investigate the Administration of the Internal Security Act and Other Internal Security Laws. *Hearings. Terroristic Activity. Part 5: Hostage Defense Measures. 25 July 1975. Testimony of Brooks McClure*. 94th Cong., 1st Sess., Washington, DC, GPO, 1975, p. 274.

115. Philip Knightly. *The First Casualty. From the Crimea to Vietnam. The War Correspondent as Hero, Propagandist and Myth Maker*. London, André Deutsch, 1976.

116. Jerry Mander. *Four Arguments for the Elimination of Television*. New York, William Morrow & Co., 1978, pp. 293–294.

117. Russell Warren Howe. 'Asset Unwitting: Covering the World for the CIA. Correspondent Tells of Employment by Secretly Funded Agency News Service'. *More*, May 1978, p. 27.

118. Edward Mickolus. 'Transnational Terrorism'. In: Michael Stohl (ed.), *The Politics of Terrorism*. New York-Basel, Marcel Dekker, Inc, 1979, p. 188. The author, working for the CIA, has been in a position to compare reported incidents with classified data for the period 1968–1975.

119. Cit. Philip Elliott, op. cit. (note 89), p. V–5.

120. Denis Hamill. 'Belfast Beat: Cityside Reporting under the Gun', *More*, November 1977, p. 40.

121. G. L. C. Cooper. 'Some Aspects of Conflict in Ulster'. *Military Review*, Vol. 53, No. 9, September 1973, pp. 86–96; cit. P. N. Grabosky. 'The Urban

Context of Political Terrorism'. In: M. Stohl (ed.), op. cit. (note 118), p. 70.

122. A. Stephen. 'A Reporter's Life in Ulster'. *The Observer*, 29 February 1976, cit. Steve Chibnall, op. cit. (note 87), p. 181 and p. 177.

123. Philip Elliott, op. cit. (note 89), p. V−8.

124. Robert Fisk. 'The Effects of Social and Political Crime on the Police and British Army in Northern Ireland'. In: Marius H. Livingston (ed.). *International Terrorism in the Contemporary World*. Westport, Conn., Greenwood Press, 1978, p. 87.

125. Philip Elliott, op. cit. (note 89), p. V−6.

126. *The Sunday Times*, 13 March 1977; cit. Philip Schlesinger, op. cit. (note 11), p. 241. There have also been charges that the Army, warned by an informed journalist about an impending explosion of an IRA bomb, failed to respond in time, the implication being that the Army did this to discredit the terrorists by 'exposing' their small concern for innocent casualties (Dennis Hamill, op. cit. (note 120), p. 43); see also 'Freedom Struggle by the Provisional IRA'. N. d., n. p. Reprinted in Walter Laqueur (ed.). *The Terrorism Reader*. New York, New American Library, 1978, p. 132. Cases where security forces were involved in terrorist bombings which were attributed publicly to insurgent terrorists are not infrequent. For CIA involvement in such tactics, see: Philip Agee. *Inside the Company: CIA Diary*. New York, Bantam Books, 1975. For FBI involvement in bombings to discredit dissenters, see: National Advisory Committee on Criminal Justice Standards and Goals. *Disorders and Terrorism*. Washington, DC, US Department of Justice, 1976, pp. 546 and 548. For a recent case where the authorities were said to be involved in a bombing attributed to the other side, see: Jan Keulen. 'Via Bomaanslag op "fascistisch" café.' "Schokcommando" van politie beoogde coup in Spanje'. *Volkskrant*, 13 June 1979, p. 6. The account refers to the 26 May 1979 bombing of the cafeteria 'California 47' in Madrid, resulting in eight dead and many more wounded people. A special unit of the Spanish police, the G-2, was said to be responsible for the attack on the premises frequented by members of the fascist Fuerza Nueva. The police, however, sought to blame the bombing on elements from the anti-fascist GRAPO. The Dutch journalist who reported the anti-police version of the story was expelled from Spain.

127. Robert Fisk, op. cit. (note 124), pp. 87−88.

128. Richard Clutterbuck. *Kidnap and Ransom: The Response*. London, Faber & Faber, 1978, pp. 135−136.

129. *Volkskrant*, 4 June 1977; Sir Robert Mark. 'Il Caso della Gran Bretagna'. *Affari Esteri*, Anno X, July 1978, p. 448.

130. Chujo Watanabe. 'Il Caso del Giapone'. *Affari Esteri*, Anno X, No. 39, July 1978, p. 504.

131. J. Chester Stern. 'News Media Relations During A Major Incident'. *The Police Journal*, No. 4, October 1976, pp. 257 and 260.

132. Private information. For a publicly admitted instance of attempted media manipulation in the case of the RAF occupation of the German embassy in Stockholm, see: Hans Bausch, 'Intendant Süddeutscher Rundfunk, ARD'. In: European Broadcasting Union, *Proceedings of the 37th Meeting of the Television Programme Committee*. London, 14−17 April 1978, p. 15.

133. John L. Hulteng. *The Messenger's Motives....Ethical Problems of the News Media*. Englewood Cliffs, Prentice Hall, 1976, pp. 91−92.

134. *Index on Censorship*, Vol. 7, No. 6, November–December 1978, pp. 52-54; *Volkskrant*, 10 October 1979, p. 6 and 8 February 1980, p. 9.

135. Onne Reitsma en Cees Labeur. *De Gijzeling. Honderd Uren Machteloze Kracht.* Amsterdam, Bonaventura, 1974, p. 76.

136. Peter Hall. 'Fahndungsfilme des Bundeskriminalamtes im bundesdeutschen Fernsehen'. *Medium*, Jg. 8, Heft 1, 1978, p. 7.

137. Steven S. Rosenfeld. *Washington Post*, 21 November 1975.

CHAPTER 3

1. The largest existing bibliography on this topic, amounting to some 3,000 titles, is: Ontario Royal Commission on Violence in the Communications Industry. Vol 2: *Violence and the Media: A Bibliography.* Ontario, Ministry of Governmental Services, 1976.

2. Milton Shulman. *The Ravenous Eye.* London, Coronet Books, 1975, p. 167.

3. Dennis Howitt and Guy Cumberbatch. *Massamedia en geweld.* Utrecht, Het Spectrum, 1977, p. 196.

4. Halina J. Czerniejewski. 'Guidelines For the Coverage of Terrorism'. *The Quill*, July–August 1977, p. 21; National Advisory Committee on Criminal Justice Standards and Goals. *Disorders and Terrorism. Report of the Task Force on Disorders and Terrorism.* Washington, DC, GPO, 1976, p. 388.

5. A. S. Spoor, *NRC-Handelsblad*, cit. *Volkskrant*, 14 December 1978, p. 6.

6. Michael Sommer. 'Nation's Police Chiefs, Media Differ on Terrorism Coverage, year-long study shows'. California State University, Northridge, University News Bureau. Release of 17 August 1978. The sample consisted of 30 police chiefs from the United States' 30 most populated cities, some 150 vidnews editors, 257 radio news directors and 76 newspaper editors (*Daily Variety*, 17 August 1978, p. 2).

7. John Weisman. 'When Hostages' Lives Are At Stake....Should a TV Reporter Push or Pull Back?' *TV Guide*, 26 August 1978, p. 5.

8. Private information.

9. Cit. John Weisman, op. cit. (note 7), p. 9.

10. *Variety*, 23 November 1977, p. 95.

11. Abraham N. Miller. In: 'Terrorism and the Media'. A Special Issue of *Terrorism: An International Journal*, Vol. 2, Nos. 1–2, 1979, p. 84.

12. J. Chester Stern. 'News Media Relations During a Major Incident'. *The Police Journal*, No. 4, October 1976, p. 256.

13. Gitta M. Bauer, in: *Terrorism*, Vol. 2, Nos. 1–2, 1979, pp. 134–135.

14. *Terrorism*, Vol. 2, Nos. 1–2, 1979, p. 92.

15. Robert Kleiman, in: *Terrorism*, Vol. 2, Nos. 1–2, 1979, p. 117; Gitta M. Bauer, ibid., p. 135.

16. Jane Levere. 'Guidelines for Covering Terrorists Debated'. *Editor and Publisher*, 3 December 1977, p. 35.

17. J. Chester Stern, op. cit. (note 12), p. 258.

18. Michael T. McEwen, in: Oklahoma Publishing Company and The University of Oklahoma. Seminar. Terrorism: Police and Press Problems. Oklahoma, mimeo transcript, 14 April 1977, p. 35.

19. David Phillips. *Skyjack*. London, Harrap, 1973, pp. 223–224.

20. Thomas M. Ashwood, Chairman, Airlines Pilot Association, International. In: *Terrorism*, Vol. 2, Nos. 1–2, 1979, p. 92.

21. US Congress, House Committee on the Judiciary. Subcommittee to Investigate the Administration of the Internal Security Act and Other Internal Security Laws. *Hearings. Terroristic Activity, Part 7: Testimony of A. E. McCree, Sergeant, Los Angeles Police Department.* 94th Cong., 1st Sess., Washington, DC, GPO, 1975, pp. 509–510.

22. Lt. Frank Bolz, head of the New York City Police Department's Hostage Negotiating Squad, in interview with Robert Friedman. *More*, June 1977, p. 19.

23. Paul Wilkinson. 'Terrorism and the Media'. *Journalism Studies Review*, No. 3, June 1978, p. 3.

24. William H. Davidson, Security Committee, Canadian Airline Pilots Association, in: *Terrorism*, Vol. 2, Nos. 1–2, 1979, p. 95.

25. Private information.

26. Sven Papcke. 'Terrorismus und Verfeindungstendenzen in der Bundesrepublik Deutschland'. Unpubl. paper, 1979, p. 1.

27. M. Cherif Bassiouni. 'Prolegomenon to Terror Violence'. *Creighton Law Review*, Vol. 12, No. 3, Spring 1979, p. 746n.

28. Richard Clutterbuck. *Guerrillas and Terrorists*. London, Faber, 1977, pp. 13–14.

29. The enumeration is Roger Mudd's, a CBS anchorman, in the March 1971 issue of *The Quill*, cit. *Orbis*, Vol. 21, No. 3, Fall 1977, p. 730n.

30. Brian Crozier, Director of the Institute for the Study of Conflict, London, in: US Congress, Senate. Committee on the Judiciary. Subcommittee to Investigate the Administration of the Internal Security Act and Other Internal Security Laws. *Hearings. Terroristic Activity, Part 4: International Terrorism. 14 May 1975.* 94th Cong., 1st Sess., Washington, DC, GPO, 1975, p. 189.

31. Cit. Philip Elliott. *Reporting Northern Ireland.* Leicester, Centre for Mass Communication Research, 1976, p. I–13.

32. M. Cherif Bassiouni, in: *The Media and Terrorism.* A Seminar sponsored by The Chicago Sun-Times, Chicago, Field Enterprises, 1977, p. 36.

33. Cit. Frank Mankiewicz and Joel Swerdlow. *Remote Control.* New York, Times Books, 1978, pp. 103–104.

34. Peter Hofstede and Rein van Rooij. *Over Televisie.* Hilversum, Televizier, 1978, p. 145.

35. *Der Spiegel*, 32. Jg., No. 38, 18 September 1978, p. 150.

36. H. H. A. Cooper. 'Terrorism and the Media'. In: Y. Alexander and S. M. Finger (eds.). *Terrorism.* New York, John Jay Press, 1977, p. 149.

37. Cit. F. Mankiewicz and J. Swerdlow, op. cit. (note 33), p. 279.

38. This hypothesis has been suggested by Denis McQuail. 'A View of the Effect of Mass-Media in Political Matters'. Unpubl. paper, 1979, p. 6.

39. From *Marshall Today*, quoted by J. Chester Stern, op. cit. (note 12), p. 259.

40. Just how massive such opinion changes can be has recently been demonstrated in a different context in the German Federal Republic where the American television series 'Holocaust', which dealt with the extermination of Jews in World War II, produced an opinion change in regard to the question whether the prosecution of war crimes should be subject to a time limitation. Before 'Holocaust', 32 percent of the population wanted to see no limitation to the prosecution. After the series, 47 percent were of the same opinion. Poll by the Wickert Institute, cit. *Volkskrant*, 29 January 1979, p. 4.

41. Yves de la Haye. 'Petit traité...'. In: Gilles Lipovetsky (comp.) 'Territoires de la Terreur'. *Silex* (Grenoble), No. 10, 1978, p. 117.

42. Cit. Philip Abott Luce. 'Contemporary Terrorism Within the United States: Relationships Between External Communist Ideology and Internal Communist Terrorism' (1976). Repr. in: US Congress, Senate. Committee on the Judiciary. Subcommittee to Investigate the Administration of the Internal Security Act and Other Internal Security Laws. *Hearings. Terroristic Activity. Part 9: Interlocks Between Communism and Terrorism. 7 May 1976.* 94th Cong., 2nd Sess. Washington, DC, GPO, 1976, p. 717.

43. Philip A. Karber. 'Urban Terrorism: Baseline Data and Conceptual Framework'. *Social Science Quarterly*, Vol. 52, December 1971, p. 532.

44. Jacques Ellul. 'With a View Toward Assessing the Facts'. In: John C. Merrill and Ralph D. Barney (eds.). *Ethics and the Press. Readings in Mass Media Morality.* New York, Hastings, 1975, p. 155; Jerry Mander. *Four Arguments...* New York, William Morrow & Co., 1978, p. 207; Peter Hofstede and Rein van Rooij, op. cit. (note 34), p. 64.

45. Even terrorist movements which have been in the news for years, like the Palestinian Liberation Organization, have to cope with the problem of retention. An American opinion poll revealed that in January 1975, 52 percent of the American public said that they had heard about the PLO. One year later the figure had increased to 63 percent (Cit. Y. Alexander. 'Terrorism, the Media and the Police'. *Journal of International Affairs*, Vol. 32, No. 1, Spring/Summer 1978, p. 104). The American public is in general much less well informed about foreign affairs than comparable publics in Western Europe. The increase in retention was, in this case, probably not due to terroristic activities of the PLO, but to other factors such as the US peace efforts in the Middle East.

46. J. Schreiber. *The Ultimate Weapon.* New York, William Morrow & Co., 1978, p. 41.

47. Richard Clutterbuck. *Kidnap and Ransom: The Response.* London, Faber & Faber, 1978, p. 38, p. 44.

48. F. Mankiewicz and J. Swerdlow, op. cit. (note 33), p. 287.

49. Cit. *More*, June 1977, p. 20.

50. *Newsweek*, 29 April 1974.

51. Friedrich Hacker. *Terror.* Reinbeck, Rowohlt, 1975, pp. 307–308.

52. The Gallup Opinion Index, *Report No. 144*, July 1977, p. 13.

53. Leonard Berkowitz. 'Studies of the Contagion of Violence'. In: Herbert Hirsch and David C. Perry (eds.). *Violence as Politics.* New York, Harper & Row, 1973, p. 42.

54. Stephen M. Holloway and Harvey A. Hornstein. 'How Good News Makes Us Good'. *Psychology Today*, December 1976, p. 76.

55. Dieter Stolte. 'Das Fernsehen als Medium und Faktor in Krisenzeiten'.

Funk Korrespondenz, No. 2, 11 January 1979, pp. 1–2.

56. Peter Christian Hall. 'Zwischen Gedenken und Denkverbot. Wie sich das Fernsehen aus Betroffenheit zum Entspannungsmedium degradiert'. *Kirche und Rundfunk/epd*, No. 82, 22 October 1977, p. 7.

57. Klaus Bresser. 'Wenn der Terror Programm macht'. *Fünkchen. WDR im Team*, No. 34, 1977, p. 2.

58. During the Moro kidnapping, the head of a police section in Rome was quoted as saying that 'we cannot afford to catch him (Moro) alive'. The journalist who interviewed him could not get her report published by the press agency for which she was then working. Johan Galtung. 'On Violence in General. And Terrorism in Particular'. Geneva, UN University (unpubl. paper), 1978. p. 26.

59. Yves de la Haye, op. cit. (note 41), p. 117.

60. *Washington Post*; cit. by Charles Fenyvesi, editor of the National Jewish Monthly, in: *Terrorism*, Vol. 2, Nos. 1–2, 1979, p. 99.

61. *Boston Globe*; cit. James Monaco. 'The Mythologizing of Citizen Patty'. In: J. Monaco (ed.). *Celebrity*. New York, Delta Book, 1978, p. 65.

62. Cit. Ontario Royal Commission on Violence in the Communications Industry. Vol 5: *Learning from the Media*. Ontario, Ministry of Government Services, 1976, pp. 76–77.

63. F. Mankiewicz and J. Swerdlow, op. cit. (note 33), pp. 46–47.

64. J. Schreiber, op. cit. (note 46), p. 21.

65. Walter Althammer. *Gegen den Terror*. Stuttgart, Verlag Bonn Aktuell, 1978, p. 77.

66. Milton Shulman, op. cit. (note 2), p. 196.

67. Joseph Klapper. *The Effects of Mass Communication*. New York, The Free Press, 1960, p. 165.

68. H. J. Eysenck and D. K. B. Nias. *Sex, Violence and the Media*. London, Maurice Temple Smith, 1978, p. 200. James Halloran, pointing to some Australian studies, however, writes that 'Where distinctions have been made with regard to types of violence portrayed and types of response produced...a more subtle form of catharsis appears to be a possibility'. (James Halloran. 'The Effects of the Media Portrayal of Violence and Aggression' (1968), in: Jeremy Tunstall (ed.). *Media Sociology*. London, Constable, 1974, p. 318).

69. The division of research into three phases has been suggested by Denis McQuail. 'The Influence and Effects of Mass Media'. In: James Curran et al. (eds.). *Mass Communication and Society*. London, Edward Arnold, 1977, pp. 72–74.

70. Cit. *More*, June 1977, p. 20.

71. Cit. Marvin Barrett. *Rich News, Poor News*. New York, Thomas Y. Crowell, 1978, p. 112.

72. George Comstock and George Lindsey. *Television and Human Behavior: The Research Horizon, Future and Present*. Santa Monica, RAND, 1975, pp. 26–29.

73. Peter Hofstede and Rein van Rooij, op. cit. (note 34), p. 68.

74. Paul Lazarsfeld. 'Zwei Wege der Kommunikationsforschung'. In: O. Schatz (ed.). *Die elektronische Revolution*. Graz, Styria, 1975, p. 208.

75. This has been calculated on the basis of Nielson Index figures. Michael B. Rothenberg. 'Effects of Television Violence on Children and Youth'. *Journal of the American Medical Association*, Vol. 234, No. 10, 8 December 1975, p. 1043.

76. *Volkskrant*, 9 November 1977, p. 9.

77. Fred Czarra and Joseph Heaps. *Censorship and the Media. Mixed Blessing or Dangerous Threat?* Boston, Allyn & Bacon, 1976, p. 51.

78. For a documentation on the massive US programme exports, see: K. Nordenstreng and T. Varis. *Television Traffic — A One-way Street?* Paris, UNESCO, 1974.

79. F. Mankiewicz and J. Swerdlow, op. cit. (note 33), p. 257.

80. Ibid., p. 36.

81. *ARD Tagesschau* (GFR), Saturday, 24 February 1979.

82. H. J. Eysenck and D. K. B. Nias, op. cit. (note 68), p. 184.

83. Cit. F. Mankiewicz and J. Swerdlow, op. cit. (note 33), p. 111.

84. Denis McQuail. 'The Influence and Effects of Mass Media'. In: James Curran et al. (eds.), op. cit. (note 69), p. 83.

85. Mary Burnet. *The Mass Media in a Violent World.* Paris, UNESCO, 1971, p. 17.

86. For a discussion of the scholarly evidence, see: F. Mankiewicz and J. Swerdlow, op. cit. (note 33), pp. 28—44.

87. Jürgen vom Scheidt. *Innenwelt-Verschmutzung.* Zürich, Ex Libris, 1973, p. 206.

88. F. Mankiewicz and J. Swerdlow, op. cit. (note 33), p. 49.

89. Cit. ibid., p. 44.

90. Television Research Committee. *Second Progress Report and Recommendations.* Leicester, 1968, p. 38, cit. Milton Shulman, op. cit. (note 2), p. 167.

91. Albert Bandura. 'Social-Learning Theory of Identificatory Processes'. In: D. Goslin (ed.). *Handbook of Socialization Theory and Research.* 1969, pp. 213—262; cit. William R. Catton, Jr. 'Militants and the Media: Partners in Terrorism?' *Indiana Law Journal*, Vol. 53, No. 4, Summer 1978, p. 714.

92. D. P. Phillips. 'The Influence of Suggestion on Suicide. Substantive and Theoretical Implications of the Werther Effect'. *American Sociological Review*, 1974, 39, pp. 340—354, cit. Leonard Berkowitz. *A Survey of Social Psychology.* Hinsdale, Ill., The Dryden Press, 1975, p. 324.

93. Bob Roshier. 'The Selection of Crime News by the Press' In: Stanley Cohen and Jack Young (eds.). *The Manufacture of News. Social Problems, Deviance and the Mass Media.* London, Constable, 1977, p. 30.

94. The Gallup Opinion Index, *Report No. 141,* April 1977, p. 13.

95. J. D. Halloran, R. L. Brown and D. C. Chaney. *Television and Delinquency.* Leicester, University Press, 1970, p. 178.

96. Melvin Heller and Samuel J. D. Polsky. *Studies in Violence and Television.* New York, American Broadcasting Company, 1976, pp. 96, 123, 129.

97. F. Mankiewicz and J. Swerdlow, op. cit. (note 33), p. 23.

98. Douglas Cater and Stephen Strickland. *TV Violence and the Child. The Evolution and Fate of the Surgeon General's Report.* New York, Russell Sage Foundation, 1976, p. 72 (reviewing: US Surgeon General. Television and Growing Up: The Impact of Televised Violence. Report to the Surgeon General, United States Public Health Service. From the Surgeon General's Scientific Advisory Committee on Television and Social Behavior. Washington, DC, GPO, 1972).

99. Michael B. Rothenberg, op. cit. (note 75), p. 1043.

100. H. J. Eysenck and D. K. B. Nias, op. cit. (note 68), p. 252.

101. Ibid., p. 252.

102. Report in the *New York State Journal of Medicine*, 1 July 1971, cit. Milton Shulman, op. cit. (note 2), pp. 202–203.

103. 'Contagion' has been defined as 'the spread of a particular type of behavior through time and space as the result of a prototype or model performing the behavior and either facilitating that behavior in the observer or reducing the observer's inhibitions against performing that same behavior'. Manus I. Midlarsky. 'Analyzing Diffusion and Contagion Effects: The Urban Disorders of the 1960s'. *The American Political Science Review*, Vol. 72, No. 3, September 1978, p. 1006.

104. Cit. Leonard Berkowitz, op. cit. (note 92), p. 41.

105. US Congress, Senate. Committee on Government Operations. Subcommittee on Investigations. *Hearings. Riots, Civil and Criminal Disorders*. Washington, DC, GPO, 1967, p. 3, cit. National Advisory Committee on Criminal Justice Standards and Goals, op. cit. (note 4), p. 23.

106. Benjamin D. Singer; cit. F. Mankiewicz and J. Swerdlow, op. cit. (note 33), p. 111.

107. Cit. Hans Bausch, in: European Broadcasting Union. 36th Meeting of the Television Programme Committee. Professional Discussion on 'Violence in Television Programmes', op. cit., p. 27.

108. The Gallup Opinion Index, *Report No. 144*, July 1977, p. 13.

109. James P. Needham. *Neutralization of Prison Hostage Situations*. Huntsville, Texas, Houston State University, 1977, p. 45.

110. Michael Sommer, op. cit. (note 6). For information on sample see note 6 of this chapter.

111. Cit. *Volkskrant*, 26 October 1977, p. 5.

112. Edward Heyman. 'Imitation by Terrorists. Quantitative Approaches to the Study of Diffusion Patterns in Transnational Terrorism'. Unpubl. paper. University of North Carolina at Chapel Hill, 1978, p. 9.

113. Ibid., p. 10.

114. Cherif M. Bassiouni, op. cit. (note 32), p. 36.

115. Jillian Becker. *Hitler's Children*. London, Panther, 1978, pp. 57–58.

116. Y. Alexander, op. cit. (note 45), p. 105; *Volkskrant*, 18 May 1978, p. 11.

117. *Washington Post*, 10 October 1975; *Congressional Record*, Tuesday, 23 September 1975, p. H 8966.

118. F. Mankiewicz and J. Swerdlow, op. cit. (note 33), p. 85n.

119. Cit. Peter Sandman et al. *Media*. Englewood Cliffs, Prentice Hall, 1976, p. 421.

120. H. J. Eysenck and D. K. B. Nias, op. cit. (note 68), p. 66; Friedrich Hacker, op. cit. (note 51), pp. 257–258.

121. Marcia McKnight Trick. 'Chronology of Incidents of Terroristic, Quasi-Terroristic and Political Violence in the United States: January 1965 to March 1976'. In: National Advisory Committee on Criminal Justice Standards and Goals, op. cit. (note 4), pp. 515, 589, 583–594; James Monaco (ed.), op. cit. (note 61), p. 68.

122. Marcia McKnight Trick, op. cit. (note 121), p. 580.

123. Hank Messick and Burt Goldblatt. *Kidnapping. The Illustrated History*. New York, Dial Press, 1974, p. 168, p. 172.

124. F. Mankiewicz and J. Swerdlow, op. cit. (note 33), pp. 13–14; Ontario Royal Commission on Violence in the Communications Industry. Vol. 5:

Learning from the Media. Ontario, Ministry of Governmental Services, 1976, pp. 79–80.

125. David Phillips, op. cit. (note 19), p. 72.

126. Sandra Stencel. 'International Terrorism'. *Editorial Research Reports*, 2 December 1977, pp. 922–923.

127. Leonard Berkowitz, op. cit. (note 92), p. 44, figure 12.

128. James Arey. *The Sky Pirates*. London, Ian Allan, 1973, p. 75; D. Phillips, op. cit. (note 19), p. 265n.

129. James Arey, op. cit. (note 128), p. 181.

130. Irwin Arieff. 'TV Terrorists: The News Media Under Siege'. *Videography*, May 1977, p. 45.

131. James Arey, op. cit. (note 128), p. 311; Friedrich Hacker, op. cit. (note 51), p. 266.

132. Marcia McKnight Trick, op. cit. (note 121), p. 563.

133. Ibid., p. 564.

134. Ibid., p. 564.

135. Ibid., p. 564.

136. Ibid., p. 564.

137. Federal Aviation Administration. *Civil Aviation Security Service. Domestic and Foreign Aircraft Hijackings*. Washington, DC, FAA, 1978, p. 36.

138. Marcia McKnight Trick, op. cit. (note 121), p. 564.

139. Ibid., p. 564.

140. Ibid., p. 566.

141. Federal Aviation Administration, op. cit. (note 137), p. 38.

142. Ibid., p. 38.

143. Ibid., p. 38.

144. Marcia McKnight Trick, op. cit. (note 121), p. 568.

145. Federal Aviation Administration, op. cit. (note 137), p. 39.

146. Marcia McKnight Trick, op. cit. (note 121), p. 568.

147. Ibid., p. 568.

148. Ibid., p. 568.

149. James Arey, op. cit. (note 128), p. 402.

150. Marcia McKnight Trick, op. cit. (note 121), p. 568.

151. Ibid., p. 568.

152. Ibid., p. 570.

153. Federal Aviation Administration, op. cit. (note 137), p. 42.

154. Ibid., p. 48.

155. Ibid., p. 54.

156. Ibid., p. 54.

157. Ibid., p. 68.

158. Remarks made by Brian Jenkins before Conference on Terrorism and the Media. Florence, Italy, 15–18 June 1978, p. 3; private information.

159. Brian M. Jenkins. 'International Terrorism: Trends and Potentialities'. In: US Congress, Senate. Committee on Governmental Affairs. *An Act to Combat International Terrorism. Report to Accompany S. 2236*. Report No. 95–908. 95th Cong., 2nd Sess. Washington, DC, GPO, 1978, p. 247; Mary Burnet, op. cit. (note 85), p. 32.

160. Horst Mahler in interview with Annet Bleich. 'De muren die ons denken gevangen hielden liggen in puin'. *De Groene Amsterdammer*, 5 September 1979, p. 9.

161. J. Mander, op. cit. (note 44), pp. 167–168.

162. Cit. Boudewijn Chorus. 'Als op ons geschoten wordt...' Groningen Pamphlet, 1978, p. 67.

163. Steve Chibnall. *Law and Order News.* London, Tavistock, 1977, pp. 26–27.

164. Charles Fenyvesi, in: *Terrorism*, Vol. 2, Nos. 1–2, 1979, p. 100.

165. Cit. Irwin Arieff, op. cit. (note 130), p. 45.

166. Cit. Sidney Kobre. *The Yellow Press and the Gilded Age of Journalism*, Tallahassee, Florida State University Press, 1964, p. 541, as quoted in: Ontario Royal Commission on Violence in the Communications Industry. Vol. 5: *Learning from the Media*. Ontario, Ministry of Governmental Services, 1976, p. 77.

167. Het Dossier. 'De moord op Robert Kennedy'. NOS, Nederland I, 17 July 1979.

168. *The British Media and Ireland.* London, The Campaign for Free Speech on Ireland, ca. 1978, p. 38.

169. Silvio van Rooy. 'Zur Deutung des grossstädtischen Kleinkrieges'. Groningen, unpubl. paper, 1978, p. 12.

170. F. Wördemann, in: M. Funke (ed.), *Terrorismus*, Bonn, 1977, pp. 155–156; Philip Elliott, op. cit. (note 31), p. II–3.

171. *Television/Radio Age*, Vol. XXV, No. 7, 24 October 1977, p. 74.

172. Robert Kleiman, editorial board, *New York Times*, in: *Terrorism*, Vol. 2, Nos. 1–2, 1979, p. 116.

173. Remarks made by Brian Jenkins before Conference on Terrorism and the Media, Florence, Italy, 16–18 June 1978, p. 4.

174. Chalmers Johnson. 'Perspectives on Terrorism'. In: W. Laqueur (ed.). *The Terrorism Reader.* New York, New American Library, 1978, p. 278.

CHAPTER 4

1. Cit. Leon V. Sigal. *Reporters and Officials. The Organization and Politics of Newsmaking.* Lexington, Mass., D.C. Heath, 1973, p. 88.

2. Cit. Theodore Peterson. 'The Social Responsibility Theory of the Press'. In: Fred S. Siebert, Theodore Peterson and Wilbur Schramm (eds.). *Four Theories of the Press. The Authoritarian, Libertarian, Social Responsibility and Soviet Communist Concepts of what the Press Should Be and Do.* Urbana, University of Illinois Press, 1976, p. 73.

3. Cit. J. K. Hvistendahl. 'An Ethical Dilemma: Responsibility for "Self-Generating" News'. In: John C. Merrill and Ralph D. Barney (eds.). *Ethics and the Press. Readings in Mass Media Morality.* New York, Hastings House, 1975, p. 188.

4. Bernard Johnpoll. 'Terrorism and the Mass Media in the United States'. In: Y. Alexander and S. M. Finger (eds.). *Terrorism.* New York, John Jay Press, 1977, pp. 159–160.

5. William J. Drummond and Augustine Zycher. 'Arafat's Press Agents', *Harper's*, March 1976, p. 26.

6. *Volkskrant*, 28 March 1979, p. 5. For background on this story, see: Howard Morland. 'The H-Bomb "Secret"'. *The Progressive*, Vol. 43, No. 5, 1979, pp. 24—27; and *Haagse Courant*, 3 October 1979, p. 1.

7. *Volkskrant*, 18 September 1979, p. 9.

8. *Volkskrant*, 7 August 1979, p. 7. If the long-term effects are included the combined death figures surpass 200,000 and another 370,000 suffered in varying degrees from the radiation effects.

9. The example is J. K. Hvistendahl's, op. cit. (note 3), p. 189.

10. *Weltwoche* (Zurich), 47 Jg. No. 32, 8 August 1979, p. 2. The number of people dying from suicide is much higher than the number of victims of insurgent terrorism. In seventeen European countries suicide is one of the five main causes of death. *Volkskrant*, 14 November 1979, p. 3 (figures for 1973 from the World Health Organization).

11. Suicide is self-directed violence and as such more of a private affair; terrorism threatens others which makes it a public concern. Consequently, terrorism tends to have a high news value and suicide, exceptions excluded, a low one. It is much easier for the media to be responsible and restrictive in an area that is peripheral to their own and the public's interests.

12. Peter M. Sandman et al. *Media.* Englewood Cliffs, Prentice Hall, 1976, p. 165.

13. Jordan J. Paust. 'International Law and Control of the Media: Terror, Repression and the Alternatives'. *Indiana Law Journal*, Vol. 53, No. 4, 1978, p. 632.

14. Paul Wilkinson. *Terrorism and the Liberal State.* London, Macmillan, 1977, p. 176.

15. Cees Hamelink. *De mythe van de vrije informatie.* Baarn, Anthos, 1978, p. 16.

16. James Kohl and John Litt (eds.). *Urban Guerrilla Warfare in Latin America.* Cambridge, Mass., MIT Press, 1974, p. 186.

17. Cit. Jordan J. Paust, op. cit. (note 13), pp. 644—645.

18. US Congress, House Committee on Internal Security. *Terrorism. A Staff Study.* 93rd Cong., 2nd Sess. Washington, DC, GPO, 1974, p. 16.

19. *Washington Post*, 6 May 1976; cit. H. H. A. Cooper. 'Terrorism and the Media'. In: Y. Alexander and S. M. Finger, op. cit. (note 4), p. 149.

20. *Volkskrant*, 28 July 1979, p. 5.

21. *IPI-Report*, Vol. 26, No. 6, July 1977, p. 3.

22. In 1978 half of the world's known total of arrested and missing journalists were of Latin American origin. Of the 162 Latin Americans, Argentina accounted for 89, more than a quarter of the world's total. *Volkskrant*, 24 March 1979, p. 6. Cf. also Jordan J. Paust, op. cit. (note 13), pp. 641—642.

23. Remarks made by Brian Jenkins before Conference on Terrorism and the Media. Florence, Italy, 16—18 June 1978, p. 5.

24. Jordan J. Paust, op. cit. (note 13), p. 661.

25. Private communication; cf. also: William J. Drummond and Augustine Zycher, op. cit. (note 5), p. 26.

26. Private communication.

27. Jordan J. Paust, op. cit. (note 13), p. 641.

28. *Guidelines in relation to directions of (a) 1 October 1971 and (b) 18 October 1976 to Radio Telefis Eireann under Section 31 of Broadcasting Authority Act, 1960.* Dublin, Stationery Office, 1979, p. 2.

29. *Volkskrant,* 18 June 1979, p. 3.

30. *NRC-Handelsblad,* 26 April 1979, p. 2.

31. Francis M. Watson. *Political Terrorism.* Washington, Robert B. Luce Co., 1976, p. 93.

32. For a discussion on how the *Washington Post* handled government misinformation during the Hanafi incident, see: Leonard Downie, Jr., Assistant Managing Editor, in: *The Media and Terrorism: A Seminar sponsored by the Chicago Sun-Times and Chicago Daily News.* Chicago, Field Enterprises, 1977, p. 21.

33. *Volkskrant,* 23 May 1978, p. 5.

34. Gaspare Barbiellini Amidei. 'Responsibilità dei news media – II'. *Affari Esteri,* Anno X, No. 39, July 1978, p. 427.

35. Cit. Jerry Walker. 'Psychologist Proposes Terrorist News Guides'. *Editor and Publisher,* 17 September 1977, p. 12.

36. Vic Cantone. 'Hostage News Guide Proposal by Police Chief'. *Editor and Publisher,* 3 December 1977, p. 15.

37. *Christian Science Monitor,* 5 December 1977, p. 47; cit. Walter B. Jaehnig. 'Journalists and Terrorism: Captives of the Libertarian Tradition'. In: *Indiana Law Journal,* Vol. 53, No. 4, Summer 1978, p. 728n.

38. Herbert A. Terry. 'Television and Terrorism: Professionalism not quite the Answer'. *Indiana Law Journal,* Vol. 53, No. 4, Summer 1978, p. 758.

39. National Advisory Committee on Criminal Justice Standards and Goals. *Disorders and Terrorism.* Washington, DC, GPO, 1976, p. 366.

40. Ibid., p. 387.

41. Ibid., pp. 387–388.

42. Boudewijn Chorus. 'Als op ons geschoten wordt...'. Groningen, Pamphlet, 1978, p. 112.

43. Gunther Hoffmann. 'Bemerkungen eines Bonner Journalisten zur Nachrichtenlenkung'. *Medium,* Jg. 7, Heft 11, 1977, p. 3.

44. R. Clutterbuck. *Kidnap and Ransom: The Response.* London, Faber & Faber, 1978, p. 154.

45. J. Kurt Klein. 'Der deutsche Terrorismus in den Perspektiven der Konfliktforschung'. Letter of Klaus Bölling to editors-in-chief, 8 September 1977. Repr. in: *Beiträge zur Konfliktforschung,* Jg. 7, No. 7, 1977, p. 147; Reinhard Rupprecht. 'Il Caso della Germania Federale – I'. *Affari Esteri,* Anno X, No. 39, July 1978, p. 473.

46. Reinhard Rupprecht, op. cit. (note 45), p. 475.

47. J. Kurt Klein, op. cit. (note 45), pp. 152–153.

48. Armin Gruenewald. 'Governo e Stampa: Sicurezza nazionale e diritto del publico ad essere informato'. *Affari Esteri,* Anno X, No. 39, July 1978, pp. 443–444.

49. David Anable. 'Media, The Reluctant Participant in Terrorism'. In: M. Snider (ed.). *Media and Terrorism.* Newton, Kansas, 1978, pp. 18–19.

50. Private information.

51. Klaus Bresser. 'Wenn der Terror Programm macht'. *Fünkchen – WDR im Team,* No. 34, 1977, p. 2.

52. Reinhard Rupprecht, op. cit. (note 45), p. 475.

53. R. Clutterbuck, op. cit. (note 44), p. 154.

54. Dennis Redmont. *Covering Terrorism.* Rome, Associated Press, 1978; Gitta M. Bauer (Springer Foreign News Service), in: *Terrorism*, Vol. 2, Nos. 1–2, 1979, p. 134.

55. Heinrich von Nussbaum. 'Das Verhältnis Politiker/Journalist hat sich verändert. Ein Interview mit Horst Schättle (ZDF) über die Nachrichtensperre der letzten Wochen'. *epd/Kirche und Rundfunk*, No. 86, 5 November 1977, p. 1.

56. Gitta M. Bauer, op. cit. (note 54), p. 136; Klaus Bresser, op. cit. (note 51), p. 2.

57. Heinz Werner Hübner. 'WRD-Fernsehdirektor Hübner zur Nachrichtensperre'. *Hörfunk, Fernsehen, Film*, Jg. 27, Heft, 10, 1977, p. 7.

58. Reinhard Rupprecht, op. cit. (note 45), p. 472.

59. Letter of government spokesman to editors-in-chief, 15 September 1977; repr. in: J. Kurt Klein, op. cit. (note 45), p. 153.

60. Karl-Otto Saur. 'Die Katerstimmung nach der Nachrichtensperre'. *epd/Kirche und Rundfunk*, No. 98, 17 December 1977, p. 2. According to a public opinion poll taken immediately after the Schleyer kidnapping, 72 percent of the population opposed giving in to the terrorists' demands; in a second poll, taken a few days later, 60 percent opposed the exchange of prisoners for Schleyer. *Volkskrant*, 12 September 1977, p. 5.

61. Brian M. Jenkins. 'International Terrorism. Trends and Potentialities'. In: US Congress, Senate. Committee on Government Affairs. *An Act to Combat International Terrorism. Report to accompany S. 2236.* Washington, DC, GPO, 1978, p. 256.

62. *Volkskrant*, 27 March 1979, p. 23; ibid., 26 August 1978, p. 8.

63. *Vrij Nederland* (Amsterdam), 14 October 1978, p. 8.

64. *Volkskrant*, 17 May 1978, p. 5.

65. J. Bowyer Bell. 'Terrorist Scripts and Live-action Spectaculars'. *Columbia Journalism Review*, May–June 1978, p. 50.

66. Steve Chibnall. *Law and Order News.* London, Tavistock, 1977, p. 102.

67. Ibid., pp. 95–96.

68. Ibid., p. 102.

69. R. Clutterbuck, op. cit. (note 44), p. 75, p. 135. In general, the case for guidelines in cases of criminal kidnappings is a strong one. The Commissioner of the Metropolitan Police in London, Sir Robert Mark, offered the following justification for a voluntary agreement between press and police:

– the need to save the life of the victim,

– to ease the distress of his or her family,

– to avoid action provoking the kidnapper into panic action, possibly the murder of his victim,

– to avoid blocking communication between the kidnappers and those on whom he is making demands,

– to avoid through excessive publicity encouraging exploitation of the situation by bogus kidnappers. There is, too, the likelihood that publicity will inevitably hamper the police and thus to some extent the kidnappers.

– *IPI-Report* (Monthly Bulletin of the International Press Institute), Vol. 25, No. 6, June 1976, p. 4.

70. Peter Harland. 'Terror and the Press' *IPI-Report*, Vol. 26, No. 10, November 1977, p. 7.

71. Peter Taylor. 'Reporting Northern Ireland'. In: *The British Media and Ireland*. London, The Campaign for Free Speech on Ireland, ca. 1978, pp. 22–23.

72. David Elstein. 'Why Can't we Broadcast the Truth?' In: *The British Media and Ireland*, op. cit. (note 71), pp. 14–15.

73. Ibid., p. 14.

74. Cit. Philip Schlesinger. *Putting 'Reality' Together*. London, Constable, 1978, p. 214.

75. Peter Taylor. 'Reporting Northern Ireland'. *Index on Censorship*, Vol. 7, No. 6, November–December 1978, p. 5.

76. David Elstein, op. cit. (note 72), pp. 14–15.

77. David Madden. 'Banned, Censored and Delayed. A Chronology of some TV Programmes dealing with Northern Ireland'. In: *The British Media and Ireland*, op. cit. (note 71), pp. 17–20.

78. Philip Schlesinger. 'The BBC and Northern Ireland'. In: *The British Media and Ireland*, op. cit. (note 71), p. 10; David Elstein, op. cit. (note 72), p. 15.

79. *Volkskrant*, 28 August 1979, p. 1.

80. *Volkskrant*, 8 October 1979, p. 5.

81. *An Phoblacht-Republican News*, 12 May 1979; cit. *State Research Bulletin*, No. 12, June–July 1979, p. 98.

82. Cit. *The British Media and Ireland*, op. cit. (note 71), p. 42.

83. Ibid., p. 3.

84. In the 1978 BBC radio programme *You The Jury*, the verdict of a 2:1 majority was that the public was not told the truth about Northern Ireland. David Elstein, op. cit. (note 72), p. 14.

85. Private communication.

86. Joseph T. Klapper. *The Effects of Mass Communication*. New York, The Free Press, 1960, p. 141.

87. Friedrich Hacker. *Terror*. Reinbeck, Rowohlt, 1975, p. 307.

88. Virgil Dominic, WJW-TV, Cleveland; cit. *More*, June 1977, p. 20.

89. *Who's Who*, 15 March 1977, cit. *Television/Radio Age*, Vol. XXV, No. 7, 24 October 1977, p. 38.

90. Cit. Peter F. Gallasch. 'Informatoren oder Komplizen in den Funkhäusern? Terrorismus und elektronische Medien – Modellfall Geiselnahme Beilen'. *Funk Korrespondenz*, No. 3, 14 January 1976, p. 1.

91. Herbert A. Terry, op. cit. (note 38), p. 768n.

92. Lee Hanna, Vice President and General Manager of WMAQ-TV, Chicago, in: *The Media and Terrorism. A Seminar sponsored by the Chicago Sun-Times and Chicago Daily News*, op. cit. (note 32), p. 23.

93. For an overview of some conferences, see: Y. Alexander. 'Terrorism, the Media and the Police'. *Journal of International Affairs*, Vol. 32, No. 1, 1978, pp. 110–111.

94. *Television/Radio Age*, Vol. XXV, No. 7, 24 October 1977, p. 75. The size of the sample is not given.

95. Herbert A. Terry, op. cit. (note 38), p. 767.

96. Cit. *Television/Radio Age*, Vol. XXV, No. 7, 24 October 1977, p. 38.

97. The CBS Rules on Terrorist Coverage are reprinted in *More*, June 1977, p. 21. On the reception of these CBS standards by other media and the police,

see: Michael Sommer. 'C.B.S. News Guidelines on Terrorism Coverage Win Favor with Nation's Police Chiefs, T.V. News Directors, Survey Reveals'. Northridge, California State University. Department of Journalism Release, 31 October 1977.

98. *UPI Reporter*, 12 May 1977. Statement of Paul G. Eberhart, Managing Editor.

99. *RTNDA Communicator*, May 1977, p. 10.

100. *The Media and Terrorism. A Seminar Sponsored by the Chicago Sun-Times and Chicago Daily News*, op. cit. (note 32), p. 38.

101. Repr. in *Terrorism*, Vol. 2, Nos. 1–2, 1979, p. 145. In our questionnaire we asked whether experienced journalists were regularly assigned to the task of covering terroristic events. Fourteen respondents answered Yes, twelve No. The specialization of journalists assigned to such stories was either crime reporters (six mentionings), political journalists (three mentionings), military journalists (two mentionings) and others (six mentionings, e.g. social science journalist). When asked what their impression of media reporting on terrorism was, eleven respondents answered that it was, in their view, adequate, twelve thought it could be improved and two thought it should be improved drastically.

102. Cit. *Television/Radio Age*, Vol. XXV, No. 7, 24 October 1977, p. 39.

103. Hank Siegel. 'Looking at the Media from the Other End of the Gun'. in: Marie Snider (ed.), op. cit. (note 49), p. 48.

104. In response to a related question in our questionnaire, asking whether there were any limits that should not be transgressed when presenting pictorial material (still photos, motion pictures) on terrorism, ten mentions were given for 'no pictures of humiliated victims', twelve to 'no pictures of executions', seven to 'no pictures of triumphant terrorists'. Other mentions included 'no abhorrent pictures in general' and 'no information useful for terrorists', 'no anti-terrorist measures'.

105. Richard Francis. *Broadcasting to a Community in Conflict*. London, BBC, 1977, pp. 14–15.

106. Chujo Watanabe. 'Il Caso del Giapone'. *Affari Esteri*, Anno X, No. 39, July 1978, p. 504.

107. Lou Rothbart, News Director, KTLA-TV, Los Angeles; cit. *More*, June 1977, p. 20.

108. In seven cases physical threats from the side of the security forces were mentioned by our respondents. Other complaints were denial of access to the site of action (sixteen mentions), removal of photographic material (nine mentions). Other problems mentioned included 'Denial of information', 'Incomplete and too slow information', 'Discrimination between different media', 'Threat of legal action'. Asked about their experiences with government information policy during terrorist incidents, seven respondents answered 'positive', sixteen 'mixed' and two 'negative'. Eight of the respondents said that there was a special forum in their country where representatives of the media and the government meet to discuss points of friction in regard to the handling of news on acts of terrorism. Nineteen respondents answered that there was, to their knowledge, no such forum. Asked whether these fora worked satisfactorily, the answers were as often positive as negative.

109. Edward Mickolus. 'Transnational Terrorism'. In: M. Stohl (ed.). *The Politics of Terrorism*. New York-Basel, Marcel Dekker Inc., 1979, pp. 166–167.

110. The Gallup Opinion Index, *Report No. 144*, July 1977, p. 13.

111. Cit. Paul Madden, op. cit. (note 77), p. 17. In our own survey, ten respondents said that their medium had conducted interviews with terrorists in the underground while fourteen had not conducted any such interviews. Interviews with imprisoned terrorists were mentioned in seven cases; fifteen respondents said their medium had not conducted such interviews. Nine respondents said that there were legal constraints for interviews with terrorists in their country, while thirteen knew of no such restriction. Asked whether their medium had ever published or broadcast letters, communiqués or (video-) tapes from terrorists without prior consultation with the government, thirteen respondents answered Yes and twelve No. Seven respondents also mentioned that their medium had conducted interviews with terrorists during hostage situations; in only one case had the government been consulted prior to the interview. Twenty respondents answered that they had not conducted such interviews.

112. Tom Paine. *The Rights of Man*. 1794, Part II, p. 26, cit. Jordan J. Paust, op. cit. (note 13), p. 676.

113. James Ring Adams, editorial page writer, *Wall Street Journal*, in: *Terrorism*, Vol. 2, Nos. 1–2, pp. 127–128.

114. Cit. Jerome A. Barron. 'Access to the Press – A New First Amendment Right'. In: David G. Clark and Earl R. Hutchinson (eds.). *Mass Media and the Law, Freedom and Restraint*. New York, Wiley-Interscience, 1970, p. 457.

CHAPTER 5

1. Bob Gottlieb. 'Information Wars'. *More*, May 1978, p. 34.

2. Cit. Jerry Mander. *Four Arguments....* New York, William Morrow & Co., 1978, p. 19.

3. Earl L. Vance. 'Freedom of the Press for Whom?' *Virginia Quarterly Review*, 21, Summer 1945, pp. 340–354, cit. Herbert I. Schiller. *Communication and Cultural Domination*. White Plains, NY, M. W. Sharpe, 1976, p. 41.

4. Cit. Denis McQuail. 'The Influence and Effects of Mass Media'. In: James Curran et al. (eds.). *Mass Communication and Society*. London, Edward Arnold, 1977, p. 91.

5. Cit. ibid., p. 90.

6. Cit. Ben H. Bagdikian. *The Information Machines*. New York, Harper & Row, 1971, p. xiii.

7. Paula B. Johnson, David O. Sears and John B. McConahay. 'Black Invisibility, the Press, and the Los Angeles Riot'. *American Journal of Sociology*, Vol. 76, January 1971, p. 706, cit. Bernard Roshco. *Newsmaking*. Chicago, University of Chicago Press, 1975, p. 97.

8. Walter Laqueur. *Terrorism*. London, Weidenfeld and Nicolson, 1977, p. 21.

9. George Habash in interview with Oriana Fallaci. *Life*, 22 June 1970, cit. Abraham H. Miller, in: *Terrorism*, Vol. 2, Nos. 1–2, 1979, p. 81.

10. Ben. H. Bagdikian, op. cit. (note 6), p. 295.

11. Jerry Mander, op. cit. (note 2), p. 32.

12. Ibid., p. 32.

13. Friedrich Hacker. *Terror*. Reinbek, Rowohlt, 1975, p. 220–221.

14. *Time*, 28 March 1977, p. 39.

15. Anonymous contributor to the seminar *The Media and Terrorism*. Chicago, Field Enterprises, 1977, p. 35.

16. European Broadcasting Union. 37th Meeting of the Television Programme Committee. Report on Part 2 of the Agenda. London, 14–17 April 1978, p. 31.

17. David Anable. 'Media, the Reluctant Participant in Terrorism'. Mimeo, 1978, p. 2.

18. Wolfgang Salewski, in: *Das Parlament* (Bonn), No. 3, 21 January 1978, p. 5.

19. Heinrich von Nussbaum. 'UN-Ordnung mit System'. *Medium*, 9 Jg., February 1979, p. 9.

20. Data from Robert H. Kupperman, in: *Terrorism*, Vol. 2, Nos. 1–2, 1979, p. 59.

21. The Dutch data have been calculated by Cees J. Hamelink, in: *Mare* (Leiden), No. 17, 21 December 1978, p. 11; the American data are based on research by CBS and are taken from Tony Schwartz. *The Responsive Chord*. New York, Anchor Press, 1974, p. 52.

22. *Der Spiegel*, 33 Jg., No. 30, 23 July 1979, p. 77.

23. Ben H. Bagdikian, op. cit. (note 6), pp. xii–xiii.

24. George Gerbner and Larry Gross, in: *Psychology Today*, 1975, cit. Jerry Mander, op. cit. (note 2), p. 225.

25. Niklas Luhman. 'Veränderungen im System gesellschaftlicher Kommunikation und die Massenmedien'. In: Oskar Schatz (ed.). *Die elektronische Revolution*. Graz, Styria, 1975, pp. 28–29.

26. In the description of the two models we follow Stanley Cohen and Jack Young (eds.). *The Manufacture of News*. London, Constable, 1973, p. 10.

27. Dallas W. Smythe. 'Communications: Blindspot of Western Marxism'. *Canadian Journal of Political and Social Theory*, Vol. 1, No. 3, Fall 1977, p. 20.

28. F. Mankiewicz and J. Swerdlow. *Remote Control*. New York, Times Books, 1978, p. 74. Another source says that more than 60 percent of all Americans get most of their news from TV, while about one third get all of it from TV. Ernie Schulz. 'Censorship Is No Solution to Coverage of Terrorist-Hostage Situations'. *RTNDA Communicator*, July 1977, p. 7.

29. A 1973 survey on the US public found that 48 percent of those interviewed found television the most credible among the four major media, followed by newspapers with 21 percent and magazines and radio with 10 and 8 percent respectively. Roper Organization Poll, cit. John Tebbel. *The Media in America*. New York, Mentor Book, 1976, p. 407.

30. Theodore Peterson. 'The Social Responsibility Theory of the Press'. In: Fred S. Siebert, Theodore Peterson and Wilbur Schramm. *Four Theories of the Press*. Urbana, University of Illinois Press, 1976, p. 78; Iel Ross. 'Information: Monopolies in the United States'. IPS Feature. Bogota, IPS, 4 July 1979, telex; cit. Claudio Aguirre-Bianchi and Göran Hedebro. 'Communication Alternatives and the NIIO in Latin America'. Königstein, IPRA, 1979 (unpubl. paper), p. 2.

31. Steve Chibnall. *Law and Order News*. London, Tavistock, 1977, p. 226.

32. These three points are taken from a list of five offered by Denis McQuail, in: James Curran et al. (eds.), op. cit. (note 4), p. 90. The two other points mentioned by McQuail are: 'Fourth, the mass media can help to bring certain kinds of public into being and maintain them. Fifth, the media are a vehicle for offering rewards and gratifications. They can divert and amuse and they can flatter' (ibid.).

33. Jonathan H. Turner. *The Structure of Sociological Theory.* Homewood, Ill., The Dorsey Press, 1974, p. 322, p. 330, pp. 324–325.

34. The analogy law-news has been elaborated by a certain Mr Alexander in a presentation to the 1978 International Sociological Association conference in Uppsala. Our representation of his views is based on T. Szecskö. 'Report of the Symposium 7'. Uppsala, unpubl. paper, 1978, pp. 21, 25.

35. H. Molotch and M. Lester. 'News as Purposive Behavior'. *American Sociological Review*, Vol. 39, No. 1, 1974, pp. 111, 101, 111.

36. Ibid., p. 105.

37. Jerry Mander, op. cit. (note 2), pp. 19, 143. On the other hand this is also very cheap. If 30 million people's attention for one minute costs $120,000 this is only 0.4 cents per person. On an hourly basis this is 24 cents, which is far below the US minimum wage. If viewing television commercials is considered as work, namely learning consumption behaviour, this is an extremely low pay. The pay, however, does not go to the viewer but to the medium which makes it some sort of voluntary slavery. An American child has by the time it reaches high school watched 650,000 commercials, which is some 3,000 hours, or, if translated into a 40 hours work week, 75 weeks (Arthur Asa Berger. *Television as an Instrument of Terror. Essays on Media, Popular Culture and Everyday Life.* New Brunswick, NJ, Transaction Books, 1979, p. 89).

38. Jerry Mander, op. cit. (note 2), p. 19; Jeff Greenfield. 'TV is Not the World'. *Columbia Journalism Review*, May/June 1978, p. 28.

39. Ben H. Bagdikian, op. cit. (note 6), p. 287.

40. Peter Hofstede and Rein van Rooij. *Over Televisie.* Hilversum, Televizier, 1978, pp. 10–11.

41. Richard Clutterbuck. *Kidnap and Ransom.* London, Faber and Faber, 1978, p. 143; *Der Spiegel*, 33 Jg., No. 49, 3 December 1979, p. 282; *Volkskrant*, 4 February 1980, p. 15.

42. Jeremy Tunstall. *The Media are American. Anglo-American Media in the World.* London, Constable, 1977, pp. 264–265.

43. Cit. Leonard H. Marks, in address to the annual conference of the International Institute of Communications, Dubrovnik, 11–14 September 1978.

44. Cit. Herbert I. Schiller. *Communication and Cultural Domination.* New York, International Arts and Sciences Press, 1976, p. 24.

45. Zbigniew Brzezinski. *La Révolution technétronique.* Paris, Calmann-Levy, 1971, cit. Armand and Michèle Mattelard. 'Une culture pour gérer la crise'. *Le Monde diplomatique*, October 1979, p. 8.

46. Jeremy Tunstall, op. cit. (note 42), pp. 17–18.

47. Ibid., p. 92.

48. Victor Perlo. *El Imperialismo Norteamericano.* Buenos Aires, Editorial Platina, 1961, p. 149.

49. Ekkehart Krippendorff. *Die Amerikanische Strategie. Entscheidungsprozess und Instrumentarium der Amerikanischen Aussenpolitik.* Frankfurt a.M., Suhrkamp, 1970, p. 315.

50. *Volkskrant*, 16 March 1974.
51. Jeremy Tunstall, op. cit. (note 42), p. 92.
52. Paul Brennan and Michael Symons. 'View from the Other Side'. *New Journalist* (European Edition), No. 16, September 1976, p. 2.
53. K. Nordenstreng and T. Varis. *Television Traffic – A One-way Street?* Paris, UNESCO, 1974, pp. 31ff., cit. Friedrich Knilli. 'Zur Sprache der Lautsprecher in Österreich'. In: Oskar Schatz (ed.), op. cit. (note 25), p. 159.
54. Ata Gil. 'Les chances d'un rééquilibrage Nord-Sud'. *Le Monde diplomatique*, January 1979, p. 18.
55. Paul Brennan and Michael Symons, op. cit. (note 52), p. 2.
56. Heinrich von Nussbaum, op. cit. (note 19), p. 11.
57. *Der Spiegel*, 33 Jg., No. 30, 23 July 1979, p. 79.
58. Statement of John E. Reinhardt, USIA Director, in: US Congress, Senate. Committee on Foreign Relations. Subcommittee on International Operations. *Hearings. International Communications and Information.* 95th Cong., 1st Sess. Washington, DC, GPO, 1977, p. 223.
59. Cit. *NRC-Handelsblad*, 21 June 1979, p. 7.
60. Jörg Becker. 'The Federal Republic of Germany's Policy after the Unesco Media Declaration, November 1978'. Königstein, IPRA, 1979 (unpubl. paper), p. 7.
61. Alan Wells. *Picture-Tube Imperialism? The Impact of U.S. Television in Latin America.* New York, Orbis, 1972, p. 186, Table XIX.
62. *Volkskrant*, 24 July 1976, p. 23, reporting data presented at a UNESCO conference in San Jose, Costa Rica.
63. Ben H. Bagdikian, op. cit. (note 6), p. 296.
64. International Research Associates. *A Survey of World Advertising Expenditures in 1970.* New York, IRA, 1972, p. 2.
65. Cit. Claudio Aguirre-Bianchi and Göran Hedebro, op. cit. (note 30), p. 2.
66. Cees Hamelink. 'The New Information Order and the Industrial State' *Peace and the Sciences*, 1/78, p. 7.
67. Peter M. Sandman, David M. Ruben and David B. Sachsman. *Media. An Introductory Analysis of American Mass Communications.* Englewood Cliffs, Prentice Hall, 1972, p. 304.
68. *The New York Times Book Review*, 30 November 1975, p. 20.
69. The 1967 CIESPAL study is quoted in Joaquin G. Santana. 'AP, UPI, ABC, NBC, CBS: Siglas de la penetracion'. *Meridiano 80* (Havana), Ano 1, Agosto 1975, p. 26.
70. Albert Lee Hester. 'The Associated Press and News from Latin America: A Gatekeeper and News-Flow Study'. Unpubl. diss., University of Wisconsin, 1972, p. 74.
71. Ata Gil., op. cit. (note 54), p. 17.
72. Cit. Jörg Becker. 'Medienkonflikte bei WARC 1979'. *epd/Entwicklungspolitik*, 15–79, p. 17.
73. Cit. Daniel J. Boorstin. 'From News Gathering to News Making: A Flood of Pseudo-Events'. In: James Combs et al. (eds.). *Drama in Life. The Uses of Communication in Society.* New York, Hastings House, 1976, p. 181.
74. J. Tunstall, op. cit. (note 42), p. 199.
75. Ben H. Bagdikian, op. cit. (note 6), p. 90.
76. Anthony Smith. *The Politics of Information.* London, Macmillan, 1978, p. 145.

77. Richard Hoggart in Foreword to Glasgow University Media Group. *Bad News. Vol. 1*. London, Routledge & Kegan Paul, 1978, pp. ix–x.

78. Leon V. Sigal. *Reporters and Officials*. Lexington, Mass., D. C. Heath, 1973, p. 189.

79. *Volkskrant*, 8 September 1979, p. 17.

80. Eugene H. Methvin. 'Mass Media and Mass Violence'. In: Renatus Hartogs and Eric Artzt (eds.). *Violence: Causes and Solutions*. New York, Dell, 1970, p. 81.

81. Ruth Leger Sivard. *World Military and Social Expenditures 1978*. Leesburg, Va., WMSE Publ., 1978, p. 18.

82. Robert Stein. 'Telling It Like It Is'. *Television Quarterly*, Winter 1973, p. 49, cit. Bernard Roshco, op. cit. (note 7), pp. 12–13.

83. William P. Hoar. 'The Human Cost of Betrayal'. *American Opinion*, Vol. 20, October 1977, p. 6.

84. *Volkskrant*, 20 November 1979, p. 13.

85. Jerry Mander, op. cit. (note 2), pp. 323–328.

86. Bernard Roshco, op. cit. (note 7), pp. 16–17.

87. This finding is not that new; it was already discussed in Vance Packard, *The Hidden Persuaders*. New edition, Harmondsworth, Pelican, 1957. In a recent experiment 50 US department stores have mixed into the background music the almost inaudible message 'I'm not a thief, I'm not shoplifting' which is constantly repeated. The result was that shoplifting in these stores dropped by 37 percent. The same technique, developed by Hal. C. Becker, is also used to stimulate some hockey and football teams. *Der Spiegel*, 33. Jg., No. 38, 17 September 1979, p. 281.

88. Stephen M. Holloway and Harvey A. Hornstein. 'How Good News Makes Us Good'. *Psychology Today*, December 1976, pp. 76, 78, 106, 108.

89. Long, Managing Director of Reuters, in interview with Eberhard Rondholz, WRD III, 4 January 1977, cit. Heinrich von Nussbaum, op. cit. (note 19), p. 9.

90. Cf., for instance, Frans Bergsma. 'News Values in Foreign Affairs on Dutch Television'. *Gazette. International Journal for Mass Communications Studies*. Reprint, n.d. (ca. 1978), pp. 207–222. This study found confirmation for the Galtung/Ruge hypotheses that:
(1) The more distant socioculturally the nations, the more negative the events (reported); (2) the less powerful the nations the more negative the events (reported); (3) the poorer the nations the more negative the events (reported).

91. Phil Harris. 'International News Media. Authority and Dependence', *Instant Research on Peace and Violence*, Vol. VI, No. 4, 1976, p. 153.

92. Glasgow University Media Group. *Bad News. Vol. 1*. op. cit. (note 77), pp. 13–14.

93. Cit. Eugene H. Methvin. 'Mass Media and Mass Violence'. In: Renatus Hartogs and Eric Artzt (eds.), op. cit. (note 80), p. 79.

94. Cit. Neil Hickey. 'Terrorism and Television. The Medium in the Middle'. *TV Guide*, Vol. 24, No. 32, 7 August 1976, p. 12.

95. Israel W. Charny. 'We Need a *Human* Language for Reporting the Tragedies of Current Violent Events'. *International Journal of Group Tensions*, Vol. 2, No. 3, 1972, p. 53.

96. Martin Elliot Silverstein, in: *Terrorism*, Vol. 2, Nos. 1–2, 1979, p. 106.

97. Ontario Royal Commission on Violence in the Communications Industry.

Vol. 5: *Learning from the Media.* Ontario, Ministry of Governmental Services, 1976, p. 14; cit. ibid., Vol. 7, p. 172.

98. The first quote is from the vice-director of television programming, Trisow; cit. *Der Spiegel*, 33. Jg., No. 30, 23 July 1979, p. 79.

99. J. Mander, op. cit. (note 2), pp. 129—130.

100. *Volkskrant*, 30 June 1979, p. 17.

101. *Volkskrant*, 10 May 1978, p. 17.

102. Gabriel Cohn-Bendit and Daniel Cohn-Bendit. *Linksradikalismus — Gewaltkur gegen die Alterskrankheit des Kommunismus.* Reinbek, Rowohlt, 1968; cit. Günther Hoherz (Comp.). *Terrorismus und Gewalt.* Bonn, Deutscher Bundestag, Wissenschaftliche Dienste. Bibliographien, No. 43, July 1975, p. 68.

103. Bernard Roshco, op. cit. (note 7), p. 100.

104. Daniel J. Boorstin, op. cit. (note 73), pp. 181—183.

105. James Monaco. 'The Mythologizing of Citizen Patty'. In: J. Monaco (ed.). *Celebrity.* New York, Delta Book, 1978, p. 67.

106. Fereyoun Hoveyda. 'International Terrorism at the United Nations'. *Terrorism*, Vol. 1, No. 1, 1977, p. 83.

107. UNESCO. Towards a Definition of the Right to Communicate: An Expert Meeting. Stockholm, 8—12 May 1978, Draft Report, p. 7.

108. Cit. Oliver Thomson. *Mass Persuasion in History.* Edinburgh, Paul Harris Publ., 1977, p. 28.

109. For an overview, see: L. S. Harms and Jim Richstad (eds.). *Evolving Perspectives on The Right to Communicate.* Honolulu, East-West Center, 1977.

110. Henry R. Cassirer. 'It's a Long Way to Communication'. In: L. S. Harms and Jim Richstad (eds.), op. cit. (note 109), pp. 60—61.

111. William J. Small, CBS News Senior Vice-President-Director, in: *The Media and Terrorism. A Seminar Sponsored by The Chicago Sun-Times and Chicago Daily News.* Chicago, Field Enterprises, 1977, p. 35.

112. Ben H. Bagdikian, op. cit. (note 6), p. 88.

113. It is interesting to note how the Iranian revolution managed to beat the hierarchical information order under the Shah. The revolutionary messages of Ayatollah Khomeini were telephoned from France to Teheran, multiplied on simple cassette tapes, and replayed by his followers in the streets with transistor recorders. Once the revolution had won the official information machines were taken over by the news regime. A strong case can in our view be made that the collapse of the Chilean revolution under Allende was attributable to the failure to gain control over the mass media. They were the main spearheads of the CIA destabilization campaign. See: Alex P. Schmid. 'The Northamerican Penetration of the Latin American Knowledge Sector — Some Aspects of Communication and Information Dependence'. In: Luis Herrera and Raimo Väyrynen (eds.). *Peace, Development, and New International Economic Order.* Tampere, International Peace Research Association, 1979, p. 344.

114. Proof for this can also be found in post-revolutionary Iran. After first expelling a number of journalists for not 'correctly' reporting the revolution, the new leaders began, during the first phase of the occupation of the US embassy, to cajole the foreign, especially the US correspondents. Iran TV was given the order to provide American journalists with every conceivable support. Ayatollah Khomeini insisted, however, that his interviews with US television networks could only be

broadcast in prime time. *Der Spiegel*, 33. Jg., No. 49, 3 December 1979, pp. 159–160.

115. *Rheinische Zeitung*, 19 May 1842, cit. Steve Chibnall, op. cit. (note 31), p. 206.

116. Robert K. Baker. 'Functions and Credibility'. In: John C. Merrill and Ralph D. Barney (eds.). *Ethics and the Press*. New York, Hastings House, 1975, p. 179.

117. Cit. Oliver Thomson, op. cit. (note 108), p. 3.

118. Claudio Aguirre-Bianchi and Göran Hedebro, op. cit. (note 30), p. 8.

119. Cit. Kaarle Nordenstreng (President of the International Organization of Journalists). 'Struggle Around "New International Information Order"', unpubl. paper, 1979, p. 15. Our emphasis.

120. Cit. Jörg. Becker, op. cit. (note 72), p. 3.

121. Cit. Peter Hofstede and Rein van Rooij, op. cit. (note 40), p. 118.

SELECTED BIBLIOGRAPHY

Acquaviva, Sabino. 'Il Caso dell' Italia – II'. *Affari Esteri*, Anno X, No. 39, July 1978.

Agee, Philip. *Inside the Company: CIA Diary*. New York, Bantam Books, 1975.

Aguirre-Bianchi, Claudio and Göran Hedebro. 'Communication Alternatives and the NIIO in Latin America'. Königstein, IPRA, 1979 (unpubl. paper).

Alexander, Yonah. 'Terrorism and the Media in the Middle East'. In: Y. Alexander and S. M. Finger (eds.), 1977.

Alexander, Yonah. 'Terrorism, the Media and the Police'. *Journal of International Affairs*, Vol. 32, No. 1, Spring/Summer 1978.

Alexander, Yonah and Seymour Maxwell Finger (eds.). *Terrorism: Interdisciplinary Perspectives*. New York, John Jay Press, 1977.

Alleman, Fritz R. 'Terrorismus in Lateinamerika – Motive und Erscheinungs-formen'. In: M. Funke (ed.), 1977.

Althammer, Walter (ed.). *Gegen den Terror. Texte/Dokumente*. Stuttgart, Verlag Bonn Aktuell, 1978.

Anable, David. 'Media, The Reluctant Participant in Terrorism'. In: Marie Snider (ed.), 1978.

Arey, James A. *The Sky Pirates*. London, Ian Allan, 1973.

Arieff, Erwin. 'TV Terrorists: The News Media Under Siege'. *Videography*, May 1977.

Bagdikian, Ben H. *The Information Machines. Their Impact on Men and the Media*. New York, Harper & Row, 1971.

Baker, Robert K. 'Functions and Credibility'. In: John C. Merrill and Ralph D. Barney (eds.), 1975.

Barbiellini Amidei, Gaspare. 'Responsibilità dei news media – II'. *Affari Esteri*, Anno X, No. 39, July 1978.

Barrett, Marvin. *Rich News, Poor News*. New York, Thomas Y. Crowell, 1978.

271

Barron, Jerome A. 'Access to the Press – A New First Amendment Right'. In: David G. Clark and Earl R. Hutchinson (eds.), 1970.

Bassiouni, M. Cherif. 'Prolegomenon to Terror Violence'. *Creighton Law Review*, Vol. 12, No. 3, Spring 1979.

Baumann, M. *Wie alles anfing*. München, Trikontinent, 1975.

Bechelloni, Giovanni. 'Il Colpo di Stato in diretta'. Repr. in: A. Silj, 1978.

Becker, Jillian. *Hitler's Children*. London, Panther, 1978.

Becker, Jörg. 'Medienkonflikte bei WARC 1979'. *epd/Entwicklungspolitik*, 15/79.

Becker, Jörg. 'The Federal Republic of Germany's Policy after the Unesco-Media Declaration, November 1978'. Königstein, IPRA, 1979 (unpubl. paper).

Bell, J. Bowyer. 'Terror: An Overview'. In: Marius H. Livingston (ed.), 1978.

Bell, J. Bowyer. 'Terrorist Scripts and Live-action Spectaculars'. *Columbia Journalism Review*, May/June 1978.

Bell, J. Bowyer. *A Time of Terror. How Democratic Societies Respond to Revolutionary Violence*. New York, Basic Books, 1978.

Bellows, Randy I. 'Hijacking the 1st Amendment'. *More*, June 1977.

Berger, Arthur Asa. *Television as an Instrument of Terror. Essays on Media, Popular Culture and Everyday Life*. New Brunswick, NJ, Transaction Books, 1979.

Berkowitz, Leonard. 'Studies of the Contagion of Violence'. In: H. Hirsch and D. C. Perry (eds.), 1973.

Berkowitz, Leonard. *A Survey of Social Psychology*. Hinsdale, Ill., Dryden Press, 1975.

Blumenthal, Monica D. et al. *Justifying Violence: Attitudes of American Men*. Ann Arbor, Institute for Social Research, University of Michigan, 1972.

Boorstin, Daniel J. 'From News Gathering to News Making: A Flood of Pseudo-Events'. In: James Combs et al. (eds.), 1976.

Brennan, Paul and Michael Symons. 'View from the Other Side'. *New Journalist* (European Edition), No. 16, September 1976.

Bresser, Klaus. 'Wenn der Terror Programm macht. Das Fernsehen und der Fall Schleyer'. *Fünkchen. WDR im Team*, No. 34, 1977.

British Media and Ireland, The. London, The Campaign for Free Speech on Ireland, 1978.

Brzezinski, Zbigniew. *La Révolution technétronique*. Paris, Calmann-Levy, 1971.

Bugliosi, Vincent. *The Manson Murders*. London, The Bodley Head, 1975.

Burnet, Mary. *The Mass Media in a Violent World*. Paris, UNESCO, 1971.

Cantone, Vic. 'Hostage News Guide proposed by Police Chief'. *Editor and Publisher*, 3 December 1977.

Cassirer, Henry R. 'It's a Long Way to Communication'. In: L. S. Harms and Jim Richstad (eds.), 1977.

Catton, William R., Jr. 'Militants and the Media: Partners in Terrorism?' *Indiana Law Journal*, Vol. 53, No. 4, 1978.

Charny, Israel W. 'We Need a *Human* Language for Reporting the Tragedies of Current Violent Events'. *International Journal of Group Tensions*, Vol. 2, No. 3, 1972.

Chibnall, Steve. *Law-and-Order News. An Analysis of Crime Reporting in the British Press*. London, Tavistock, 1977.

Chicago Sun-Times and *Chicago Daily News. The Media and Terrorism: A*

Seminar. Chicago, Field Enterprises, 1977.

Chippindale, Peter and Ed Harriman. *Juntas United!* London, Quartet Books, 1978.

Clark, David G. and Earl R. Hutchinson (eds.). *Mass Media and the Law, Freedom and Restraint.* New York, Wiley-Interscience, 1970.

Clutterbuck, Richard. *Guerrillas and Terrorists.* London, Faber, 1977.

Clutterbuck, Richard. *Kidnap and Ransom: The Response.* London, Faber & Faber, 1978.

Coenen, A. W. M. and J. J. M. van Dijk. *Misdaadverslaggeving in Nederlandse Dagbladen tussen 1966 en 1974.* The Hague, WODC, 1976.

Cohen, Stanley and Jock Young (eds.). *The Manufacture of News. Social Problems, Deviance and the Mass Media.* London, Constable, 1973.

Cohn-Bendit, Gabriel and Daniel Cohn-Bendit. *Linksradikalismus – Gewaltkur gegen die Alterskrankheit des Kommunismus.* Reinbek, Rowohlt, 1968.

Chorus, Boudewijn. *Als op ons geschoten wordt.... Gewapend verzet in de BRD.* Groningen, Pamphlet, 1978.

Combs, James et al. (eds.). *Drama in Life. The Uses of Communication in Society* New York, Hastings House, 1976.

Commer, Klaus. 'Nicht mehr heiter, aber weiter'. *Funk-Korrespondenz*, No. 37, 14 September 1972.

Comstock, George and George Lindsey. *Television and Human Behavior: The Research Horizon, Future and Present.* Santa Monica, Rand, 1975.

Cooper, G. L. C. 'Some Aspects of Conflict in Ulster'. *Military Review*, Vol. 53, No. 9, September 1973.

Cooper, H. H. A. 'Terrorism and the Media'. In: Y. Alexander and S. M. Finger (eds.), 1977.

Curran, James et al. (eds.). *Mass Communication and Society.* London, Edward Arnold, 1977.

Czerniejewski, Halina J. 'Guidelines For the Coverage of Terrorism'. *The Quill*, July–August 1977.

Davis, F. James. 'Crime News in Colorado Newspapers'. *The American Journal of Sociology*, Vol. 57, 1951–52.

Demaris, Ovid. *Brothers in Blood. The International Terrorist Network.* New York, Charles Scribner's Sons, 1977.

Dobson, Christopher and Ronald Paine. *The Carlos Complex. A Pattern of Violence.* London, Hodder and Stoughton, 1977.

Drummond, William J. and Augustine Zycher. 'Arafat's Press Agents'. *Harper's*, March 1976.

Ellinghaus, Gert and Günther Rager. 'Arbeitsmaterialien zu einer vergleichenden Untersuchung der Presseberichterstattung über die Entführung des Berliner CDU-Vorsitzenden Peter Lorenz'. *Funk Report*, Jg. 11, 8/75, 16 May 1975.

Elliott, Philip. *Reporting Northern Ireland: A Study of News in Britian, Ulster and the Irish Republic.* Leicester, Centre for Mass Communication Research, 1976 (published by UNESCO in a book titled: *Ethnicity and the Media*).

Ellul, Jacques. *Propaganda. The Formation of Men's Attitudes.* New York, Vintage Books, 1973.

Ellul, Jacques. 'With a View Toward Assessing the Facts'. In: John C. Merrill and Ralph D. Barney (eds.), 1975.

Elstein, David. 'Why Can't we Broadcast the Truth?' In: *The British Media and Ireland*, 1978.

Epstein, Edward C. 'The Uses of Terrorism: A Study in Media Bias'. *Stanford Journal of International Studies*, Vol. 12, Spring 1977.

Epstein, Edward Jay. *Between Fact and Fiction: The Problem of Journalism*. New York, Vintage Books, 1975.

Ertl, Eric. 'Geisel-Dramen. Ueber den Unterhaltungswert der Gewalt'. *Medium*, Jg. 5, Heft 6, 1975.

Evans, Ernest. 'American Response to International Terrorism'. In Y. Alexander and S. M. Finger (eds.), 1977.

Eysenck, H. J. and D. K. B. Nias. *Sex, Violence and the Media*. London, Maurice Temple Smith, 1978.

Fairbairn, Geoffrey. *Revolutionary Guerrilla Warfare. The Countryside Version*. Harmondsworth, Penguin, 1974.

Fetcher, Iring. *Terrorismus und Reaktion*. Köln, Europäische Verlagsanstalt, 1977.

Fisk, Robert. 'The Effects of Social and Political Crime on the Police and British Army in Northern Ireland'. In: Marius H. Livingston (ed.), 1978.

Francis, Richard. *Broadcasting to a Community in Conflict – The Experience in Northern Ireland*. London, BBC, 1977.

Friedman, Robert. 'Interview with Lt. Frank Bolz, Head of the New York City Police Department's Hostage Negotiating Squad'. *More*, June 1977.

Fromm, Erich. *The Anatomy of Human Destructiveness*. New York, Holt, Rinehart and Winston, 1973.

Funke, Manfred (ed.). *Terrorismus. Untersuchungen zur Strategie und Struktur revolutionärer Gewaltpolitik*. Bonn, Bundeszentrale für politische Bildung. 1977.

Funke, Manfred (ed.). *Extremismus im demokratischen Rechtsstaat*. Bonn, Bundeszentrale für politische Bildung, 1978.

Gallasch, Peter F. 'Informatoren oder Komplizen in den Funkhäusern? Terrorismus und elektronische Medien – Modellfall Geiselnahme Beilen'. *Funk-Korrespondenz*, No. 3, 14 January 1976.

Galtung, Johan and Mari Holmboe Ruge. 'The Structure of Foreign News (1965)'. Repr. in: J. Tunstall (ed.), 1974.

Galtung, Johan. 'On Violence in General. And Terrorism in Particular'. Geneva, UN University (unpubl. paper), 1978.

Gehlen, Arnold. 'Die gewaltlose Lenkung'. In: Oskar Schatz (ed.), 1975.

Gerbner, George, Larry Gross, Marilyn Jackson-Beeck, Suzanne Jeffries-Fox and Nancy Signorielli. 'Violence on the Screen. Cultural Indicators: Violence Profile No. 9'. *Journal of Communication*, Summer 1978.

Glasgow University Media Group. *Bad News. Vol. 1*. London, Routledge & Kegan Paul, 1978.

Goodhart, Philip. *The Climate of Collapse. The Terrorist Threat to Britain and her Allies*. Richmond, Surrey, Foreign Affairs Publ. Co., 1975.

Gottlieb, Bob. 'Information Wars'. *More*, May 1978.

Grabosky, P. N. 'The Urban Context of Political Terrorism'. In: M. Stohl (ed.), 1979.

Greenfield, Jeff. 'TV is not the World'. *Columbia Journalism Review*, May/June 1978.

Gruenewald, Armin. 'Governo e Stampa: Sicurezza nationale e diritto del publico ad essere informato'. *Affari Esteri*, Anno X, No. 39, July 1978.

Guillaume, J. (ed.). *L'Internationale, Documents et Souvenirs, 1864–1887. Vol. 2.* Paris, 1910.

Hacker, Friedrich. *Terror. Mythos, Realität, Analyse.* Reinbek, Rowohlt, 1975.

Hall, Peter Christian. 'Zwischen Gedenken und Denkverbot. Wie sich das Fernsehen aus Betroffenheit zum Entspannungsmedium degradiert'. *Kirche und Rundfunk/epd*, No. 82, 22 October 1977.

Hall, Peter. 'Fahndungsfilme des Bundeskriminalamtes im bundesdeutschen Fernsehen'. *Medium*, Jg. 8, Heft 1, 1978.

Hall, Stuart. 'A World at One with Itself'. In: Stanley Cohen and Jock Young (eds.), 1973.

Halloran, James. 'The Effects of the Media Portrayal of Violence and Aggression (1968)'. In: Jeremy Tunstall (ed.), 1974.

Hamelink, Cees. *De mythe van de vrije informatie.* Baarn, Anthos, 1978.

Hamelink, Cees. 'The New Information Order and the Industrial State'. *Peace and the Sciences*, 1/78.

Hamill, Denis. 'Belfast Beat: Cityside Reporting under the Gun'. *More*, November 1977.

Harland, Peter. 'Terror and the Press'. *IPI-Report*, Vol. 26, No. 10, November 1977.

Harms, L. S. and Jim Richstad (eds.). *Evolving Perspectives in The Right to Communicate.* Honolulu, East-West Center, 1977.

Harris, Phil. 'International News Media, Authority and Dependence'. *Instant Research on Peace and Violence*, Vol. VI, No. 4, 1976.

Hartogs, Renatus and Eric Artzt (eds.). *Violence: Causes and Solutions.* New York, Dell, 1970.

Haye, Yves de la. 'Petit traité des media en usages terroristes'. *Silex*, No. 10, 1978.

Hester, Albert Lee. 'The Associated Press and News From Latin America: A Gate-keeper and News-Flow Study'. University of Wisconsin, unpubl. diss., 1972.

Heyman, Edward. 'Imitation by Terrorists. Quantitative Approaches to the Study of Diffusion Patterns in Transnational Terrorism'. University of North Carolina at Chapel Hill, unpubl. paper, 1978.

Hickey, Neil. 'Terrorism and Television'. *TV Guide*, Vol. 24, No. 31, 31 July 1976.

Hickey, Neil. 'Terrorism and Television. The Medium in the Middle'. *TV Guide*, Vol. 24, No. 32, 7 August 1976.

Hill, Lord. *Behind the Screen.* London, Sidgwick & Jackson, 1974.

Hirsch, Herbert and David C. Perry (eds.). *Violence as Politics.* New York, Harper & Row, 1973.

Hofstede, Peter and Rein van Rooij. *Over Televisie.* Hilversum, Televizier, 1978.

Hoffman, Gunther. 'Bemerkungen eines Bonner Journalisten zur Nachrichtenlenkung'. *Medium*, Jg. 7, Heft 11, 1977.

Hollander, Gayle Durham. 'Developments in Soviet Radio and Television News Reporting'. In: Jeremy Tunstall (ed.), 1974.

Holloway, Stephen M. and Harvey A. Hornstein. 'How Good News Makes Us Good'. *Psychology Today*, December 1976.

Hoveyda, Fereyoun. 'International Terrorism at the United Nations'. *Terrorism*, Vol. 1, No. 1, 1977.

Howitt, Dennis and Guy Cumberbatch. *Massamedia en geweld*. Utrecht, Het Spectrum, 1977.

Hübner, Heinz Werner. 'WRD-Fernsehdirektor Hübner zur Nachrichtensperre'. *Hörfunk, Fernsehen, Film*, Jg. 27, Heft 10, 1977.

Hulteng, John L. *The Messenger's Motives...Ethical Problems of the News Media*. Englewood Cliffs, Prentice Hall, 1976.

Hvistendahl, J. K. 'An Ethical Dilemma: Responsibility for "Self-Generating" News'. In: John C. Merrill and Ralph D. Barney (eds.), 1975.

International Research Associates. *A Survey of World Advertising Expenditures in 1970*. New York, IRA, 1972.

Iviansky, Ze'ev. 'Individual Terror: Concept and Typology'. *Journal of Contemporary History*, Vol. 12, No. 1, 1977.

Jacobs, Harold (ed.). *Weatherman*. San Francisco, Ramparts Press, 1970.

Jaehnig, Walter B. 'Journalists and Terrorism: Captives of the Libertarian Tradition'. *Indiana Law Journal*, Vol. 53, No. 4, Summer 1978.

Jenkins, Brian M. 'International Terrorism: A Balance Sheet'. *Survival*, July/August 1975. (Repr. in: *Terrorisme als vorm van politiek geweld*. Katholieke Hogeschool Tilburg, 1977.)

Jenkins, Brian M. *High Technology Terrorism and Surrogate War – The Impact of New Technology on Low Level Violence*. Santa Monica, Rand, 1975.

Jenkins, Brian M. *International Terrorism: Trends and Potentialities*. Santa Monica, Rand, May 1978. (Rand P-6117; repr. in: US Congress, Senate. Committee on Government Affairs, 1978.)

Johnpoll, Bernard. 'Terrorism and the Mass Media in the Unites States'. In: Y. Alexander and S. M. Finger (eds.), 1977.

Johnson, Chalmers, 'Perspectives on Terrorism'. In: W. Laqueur (ed.), 1978.

Kahl, Werner. 'Akteure und Aktionen während der Formationsphase des Terrorismus'. In: M. Funk (ed.), 1977.

Karber, Philip A. 'Urban Terrorism: Baseline Data and Conceptual Framework'. *Social Science Quarterly*, Vol. 52, December 1971.

Karber, Philip A. 'Newspaper Coverage of Domestic Bombings: Reporting Patterns of American Violence'. *Bomb Incident Bulletin*, March 1973.

Klapper, Joseph T. *The Effects of Mass Communication*. New York, The Free Press, 1960.

Klein, J. Kurt. 'Der deutsche Terrorismus in den Perspektiven der Konfliktforschung'. *Beiträge zur Konfliktforschung*, Jg. 7, No. 7, 1977.

Knauss, Peter R. and D. A. Strickland. 'Political Disintegration and Latent Terror'. In: Michael Stohl (ed.), 1979.

Knightly, Philip. *The First Casualty. From the Crimea to Vietnam. The War Correspondent as Hero, Propagandist and Myth Maker*. London, André Deutsch, 1976.

Knilli, Friedrich. 'Zur Sprache der Lautsprecher in Österreich'. In: O. Schatz (ed.), 1975.

Kobre, Sidney. *The Yellow Press and the Gilded Age of Journalism*. Tallahassee, Florida State University Press, 1964.

Koestler, Arthur. *The Ghost in the Machine*. London, Hutchinson, 1967.

Kohl, James and John Litt (eds.). *Urban Guerrilla Warfare in Latin America*.

Cambridge, Mass., MIT Press, 1974.

Kopkind, Andrew. 'Publish and Perish'. *More*, April 1978.

Krippendorff, Ekkehart. *Die Amerikanische Strategie. Entscheidungsprozess und Instrumentarium der Amerikanischen Aussenpolitik.* Frankfurt a.M., Suhrkamp, 1970.

Langguth, Gerd. 'Guerrilla und Terror als linksextremistische Kampfmittel. Rezeption und Kritik'. In: M. Funke (ed.), 1978.

Laqueur, Walter. 'The Futility of Terrorism'. *Harper's*, Vol. 252, No. 1510, March 1976.

Laqueur, Walter. *Terrorism.* London, Weidenfeld and Nicolson, 1977.

Laqueur, Walter (ed.). *The Terrorism Reader.* New York, New American Library, 1978.

Lasky, Melvin I. 'Ulrike Meinhof & the Baader-Meinhof Gang'. *Encounter*, Vol. 44, No. 6, June 1975.

Lazarsfeld, Paul. 'Zwei Wege der Kommunikationsforschung'. In: O. Schatz (ed.), 1975.

Lemert, James B. 'Content Duplication by the Networks in Competing Evening Newscasts'. *Journalism Quarterly*, Vol. 51, No. 2, Summer 1974.

Levere, Jane. 'Guidelines for Covering Terrorists Debated'. *Editor and Publisher*, 3 December 1977.

Livingston, Marius H (ed.). *International Terrorism in the Contemporary World.* Westport, Conn., Greenwood Press, 1978.

Luhman, Niklas. 'Veränderungen im System gesellschaftlicher Kommunikation und die Massenmedien'. In: Oskar Schatz (ed.), 1975.

Madden, Paul. 'Banned, Censored and Delayed. A Chronology of Some TV Programmes Dealing with Northern Ireland'. In: *The British Media and Ireland*, 1978.

Maitron, Jean. *Histoire du Movement Anarchiste en France, 1880–1914.* Paris, Société Universitaire d'éditions de librairie, 1955.

Mander, Jerry. *Four Arguments for the Elimination of Television.* New York, William Morrow & Co., 1978.

Mankiewicz, Frank and Joel Swerdlow. *Remote Control. Television and the Manipulation of American Life.* New York, Times Books, 1978.

Marighela, Carlos. *For the Liberation of Brazil.* Harmondsworth, Pelican, 1971.

Mark, Sir Robert. 'Il Caso della Gran Bretagna'. *Affari Esteri*, Anno X, No. 39, July 1978.

McKnight, Gerard. *The Mind of the Terrorist.* London, Michael Joseph, 1974.

McLellan, Vin and Paul Avery. *The Voices of Guns.* New York, G. P. Putnam, 1977.

McQuail, Denis. 'The Influence and Effects of Mass Media'. In: James Curran et al. (eds.), 1977.

McQuail, Denis. 'A View of the Effect of Mass-Media in Political Matters'. Unpubl. paper, 1979.

Meiden, Anne van der and H. van Ommen. *Ik Herinner mij niet u iets gevraagd te hebben, Over journalistieke vrijheid en publieksvrijheid.* 's-Gravenhage, Boekencentrum, 1975.

Merrill, John C. and Ralph D. Barney (eds.). *Ethics and the Press. Readings in Mass Media Morality.* New York, Hastings House, 1975.

Messick, Hank and Burt Goldblatt. *Kidnapping. The Illustrated History.* New York, Dial Press, 1974.

Methvin, Eugene H. 'Mass Media and Mass Violence'. In: Renatus Hartogs and Eric Artzt (eds.), 1970.

Methvin, Eugene H. *The Rise of Radicalism. The Social Psychology of Messianic Extremism.* New Rochelle, NY, Arlington House, 1973.

Methvin, Eugene H. 'Terrorism and the Rise of Megamedia in "The Global Village"'. Unpubl. paper, 1976.

Mickolus, Edward F. *Assessing the Degrees of Error in Public Reporting of Transnational Terrorism.* Washington, DC, Central Intelligence Agency, Office of Political Research, 1976.

Mickolus, Edward. 'Transnational Terrorism'. In: Michael Stohl (ed.), 1979.

Midlarsky, Manus I. 'Analyzing Diffusion and Contagion Effects: The Urban Disorders of the 1960s'. *The American Political Science Review*, Vol. 72, No. 3, September 1978.

Molotch, Harvey and Marilyn Lester. 'News as Purposive Behavior — On the Strategic Use of Routine Events, Accidents and Scandals'. *American Sociological Review*, Vol. 39, No. 1, 1974.

Monaco, James. 'The Mythologizing of Citizen Patty'. In: James Monaco (ed.). *Celebrity. The Media as Image Makers.* New York, Delta Book, 1978.

Monk, Richard. 'The Use of Foreign Mass Media as an Effective Nonviolent Strategy by Participants in Internal Wars'. Uppsala, Sociology World Conference, 1978. (Unpubl. paper 78508548 ISA 1978 2141.)

Moodie, Michael. 'The Patriotic Game. The Politics of Violence in Northern Ireland'. In: Marius H. Livingston (ed.), 1978.

Moss, Robert. *Uruguay: Terrorism versus Democracy.* London, Institute for the Study of Power and Conflict, Conflict Studies, No. 14, 1971.

Muhammad, Askia. 'Civil War in Islamic America'. *The Nation*, Vol. 224, No. 23, 11 June 1977.

Needham, James P. 'Neutralization of Prison Hostage Situations'. Huntsville, Texas, Houston State University, 1977.

Nordenstreng, Kaarle and Tapio Varis. *Television Traffic — A One-way Street?* Paris, UNESCO, 1974.

Nordenstreng, Kaarle. 'Struggle Around "New International Information Order"'. Unpubl. paper, 1979.

Nussbaum, Heinrich von. 'Das Verhältnis Politiker/Journalist hat sich verändert. Ein Interview mit Horst Schättle (ZDF) über die Nachrichtensperre der letzten Wochen'. *epd/Kirche und Rundfunk*, No. 86, 5 November 1977.

Nussbaum, Heinrich von. 'UN — Ordnung mit System'. *Medium*, 9 Jg., February 1979.

Oklahoma Publishing Company and the University of Oklahoma. Seminar. 'Terrorism: Police and Press Problems'. Oklahoma, mimeo transcript, 14 April 1977.

Ontario Royal Commission on Violence in the Communication Industry. *Vol 2: Violence and the Media: A Bibliography.* (approx. 3,000 titles). *Vol. 5: Learning from the Media.* Ontario, Ministry of Government Services, 1976.

Paine, Lauran. *The Terrorists.* London, Robert Hale & Co., 1975.

Pandiani, John A. 'Crime Time TV: If All We Knew Is What We Saw'. *Contemporary Crises*, Vol. 2, No. 4, October 1978.

Papcke, Sven. 'Terrorismus und Verfeindungstendenzen in der Bundesrepublik Deutschland'. Unpubl. paper, 1979.

Paust, Jordan J. 'International Law and Control of the Media: Terror, Repression and the Alternatives'. *Indiana Law Journal*, Vol. 53, No. 4, 1978.

Perlo, Victor. *El Imperialismo Norteamericano*. Buenos Aires, Editorial Platina, 1961.

Pesch, Ulrike. 'Diplomaten-Entführung als terroristisches Kampfmittel'. In: M. Funke (ed.), 1977.

Peterson, Theodore. 'The Social Responsibility Theory of the Press' In: Fred S. Siebert et al., 1976.

Philips, David. *Skyjack. The Story of Air Piracy*. London, Harrap, 1973.

'Prairie Fire – Political Statement of the Weather Underground' (1974). Partly repr. in: W. Laqueur (ed.), 1978.

Qualter, Terence H. *Propaganda and Psychological Warfare*. New York, Random House, 1962.

Quartim, Joâo. 'Leninism or Militarism'. In: J. Kohl and J. Litt (eds.), 1974.

Rapoport, David C. *Assassination and Terrorism*. Toronto, Canadian Broadcasting Corporation, 1971.

Rapoport, David. 'The Politics of Atrocity'. In: Y. Alexander and S. M. Finger (eds.), 1977.

Redmont, Dennis. *Covering Terrorism*. Rome, Associated Press, 1978.

Reitsma, Onno en Cees Labeur. *De Gijzeling. Honderd Uren Machteloze Kracht*. Amsterdam, Bonaventura, 1974.

Roshco, Bernard. *Newsmaking*. Chicago, University of Chicago Press, 1975.

Rothenberg, Michael B. 'Effects of Television Violence on Children and Youth'. *Journal of the American Medical Association*, Vol. 234, No. 10, 8 December 1975.

Rubin, Jerry. *Do It. Scenarios of the Revolution*. New York, Ballantine Books, 1970.

Rupprecht, Reinhard. 'Il Caso della Germania Federale – I'. *Affari Esteri*, Anno X, No. 39, July 1978.

Sandman, Peter M., David M. Rubin and David B. Sachsman. *Media. An Introductory Analysis of American Mass Communications*. Englewood Cliffs, Prentice Hall, 1976.

Santana, Joaquin G. 'AP, UPI, ABC, NBC, CBS: Siglas de la penetración'. *Meridiano 80* (Havana), Ano 1, Agosto 1975.

Saur, Karl-Otto. 'Die Katerstimmung nach der Nachrichtensperre'. *epd/Kirche und Rundfunk*, No. 98, 17 December 1977.

Schang, Gabrielle and Ron Rosenbaum. 'Now the Urban Guerrillas have a Real Problem. They're Trying to Make it in the Magazine Business'. *More*, November 1976.

Schatz, Oskar (ed.). *Die elektronische Revolution. Wie gefährlich sind die Massenmedien?* Graz, Styria, 1975.

Schlesinger, Philip. *Putting 'Reality' Together. BBC News*. London, Constable, 1978.

Schlesinger, Philip. 'The BBC and Northern Ireland'. In: *The British Media and Ireland*, 1978.

Schiller, Herbert I. *Communication and Cultural Domination*. White Plains, NY, M. E. Sharpe, 1976.

Schmid, Alex Peter. 'The Northamerican Penetration of the Latin American Knowledge Sector – Some Aspects of Communication and Information Dependence'. In: Luis Herrera and Raimo Väyrynen (eds.) *Peace, Development, and New International Economic Order.* Tampere, International Peace Research Association, 1979.

Schmid, Alex P. *A Research Guide to Political Terrorism.* Leiden and Amsterdam, COMT, 1982.

Schornhorst, F. Thomas. 'The Lawyer and the Terrorist: Another Ethical Dilemma'. *Indiana Law Journal,* Vol. 53, No. 4, 1978.

Schreiber, Jan. *The Ultimate Weapon: Terrorists and World Order.* New York, William Morrow & Co., 1978.

Schulz, Ernie. 'Censorship is no Solution to Coverage of Terrorist-Hostage Situations'. *RTNDA Communicator,* July 1977.

Schwartz, Tony. *The Responsive Chord.* New York, Anchor Press, 1974.

Seymour-Ure, Colin. *The Political Impact of Mass Media.* London, Constable, 1974.

Shulman, Milton. *The Ravenous Eye.* London, Coronet Books, 1975.

Siebert, Fred S., Theodore Peterson and Wilbur Schramm (eds.). *Four Theories of the Press. The Authoritarian, Libertarian, Social Responsibility and Soviet Communist Concepts of what the Press Should Be and Do.* Urbana, University of Illinois Press, 1976.

Siegel, Hank. 'Looking at the Media from the Other End of the Gun'. In: Marie Snider (ed.), 1978.

Sigal, Leon V. *Reporters and Officials. The Organization and Politics of Newsmaking.* Lexington, Mass., D. C. Heath, 1973.

Silj, Alessandro. *Brigate Rosse – Stato. Lo scontro spettacolo nella regia della stampa quotidiana.* Florence, Vallecchi, 1978.

Sivard, Ruth Leger. *World Military and Social Expenditures 1978.* Leesburg, Va., WMSE Publ., 1978.

Sloan, John W. 'Political Terrorism in Latin America: A Critical Analysis'. In: M. Stohl (ed.), 1979.

Smith, Anthony. *The Politics of Information. Problems of Policy in Modern Media.* London, Macmillan, 1978.

Smith, Bruce L., Harold D. Lasswell and Ralph D. Casey. *Propaganda, Communication, and Public Opinion.* Princeton, NJ., Princeton University Press, 1946.

Smith, Desmond. 'Scenario Reality. A New Brand of Terrorism'. *The Nation,* 30 March 1974.

Smythe, Dallas W. 'Communications: Blindspot of Western Marxism'. *Canadian Journal of Political and Social Theory,* Vol. 1, No. 3, Fall 1977.

Snider, Maria (ed.). *Media and Terrorism. The Psychological Impact.* Seminar, 3–4 March 1978. Newton, Kansas, Prairie View, 1978.

Sobel, Lester A. (Comp.). *Political Terrorism.* New York, Facts on File, 1975.

Sommer, Michael. 'C.B.S. News Guidelines on Terrorism Coverage Win Favor With Nation's Police Chiefs, T.V. News Directors, Survey Reveals'. Northridge, California State University, Department of Journalism Release, 31 October 1977.

Stein, Robert. 'Telling It Like It Is'. *Television Quarterly,* Winter 1973.

Stencel, Sandra. 'International Terrorism'. *Editorial Research Reports,* 2 December 1977.

Stern, J. Chester. 'News Media Relations During A Major Incident'. *The Police Journal*, No. 4, October 1976.

Stolte, Dieter. 'Das Fernsehen als Medium und Faktor in Krisenzeiten'. *Funk-Korrespondenz*, No. 2, 11 January 1979.

Stohl, Michael (ed.), *The Politics of Terrorism*. New York-Basel, Marcel Dekker, Inc., 1979.

Szeckskö, T. 'Report of the Symposium 7' (of the International Sociological Association). Uppsala, unpubl. paper, 1978.

Taylor, Peter. 'Reporting Northern Ireland'. *Index on Censorship*, Vol. 7, No. 6, November–December 1978 (also repr. in: *The British Media and Ireland, 1978*).

Tebbel, John. *The Media in America*. New York, Mentor Book, 1976.

Terrorism and the Media. *Terrorism, An International Journal*, Vol. 2, Nos. 1–2, 1979.

Terry, Herbert A. 'Television and Terrorism: Professionalism not quite the Answer'. *Indiana Law Journal*, Vol. 53, No. 4, 1978.

Thomson, Oliver. *Mass Persuasion in History. An Historical Analysis of the Development of Propaganda Techniques*. Edinburgh, Paul Harris Publ., 1977.

Trounstine, Philip J. 'We Interrupt This Program. Indiana Kidnapper Directs Live Newscasts With Shotgun'. *More*, June 1977.

Tunstall, Jeremy (ed.). *Media Sociology: A Reader*. London, Constable, 1974.

Tunstall, Jeremy. *The Media are American. Anglo-American Media in the World*. London, Constable, 1977.

Turner, Jonathan H. *The Structure of Sociological Theory*. Homewood, Ill., The Dorsey Press, 1974.

UNESCO. 'Towards a Definition of the Right to Communicate: An Expert Meeting. Draft Report'. Stockholm, 8–12 May 1978.

US Government, Department of Justice. National Advisory Committee on Criminal Justice Standards and Goals. *Disorders and Terrorism. Report of the Task Force on Disorders and Terrorism*. Washington, DC, GPO, 1976.

US Congress, House Committee on Foreign Affairs, Subcommittee on The Near East and South Asia. Hearings. International Terrorism, June 11, 18, 19, and 24, 1974. 93rd Cong., 2nd Sess. Washington, DC, GPO, 1974.

US Congress, House Committee on Internal Security. Political Kidnappings, 1968–1973. 93rd Cong., 1st Sess. Washington, DC, GPO, 1973.

US Congress, House Committee on Internal Security. Terrorism. A Staff Study. 93rd Cong., 2nd Sess. Washington, DC, GPO, 1974.

US Congress, Senate. Committee on Foreign Relations. Subcommittee on International Operations. Hearings. International Communications and Information. 95th Cong., 1st Sess., Washington, DC, GPO, 1977.

US Congress, Senate. Committee on Governmental Affairs. An Act to Combat International Terrorism. Report to accompany S.2236. 95th Cong., 2nd Sess. Report No. 95–908. Washington, DC, GPO, 1978.

US Congress, Senate. Committee on Government Operations. Subcommittee on Investigations. Hearings. Riots, Civil and Criminal Disorders. Washington, DC, GPO, 1967.

US Congress, Senate. Committee on the Judiciary Report. The Weather Underground. 94th Cong., 1st Sess., Washington, DC, GPO, 1975.

US Congress, Senate. Committee on the Judiciary. Subcommittee to Investigate the Administration of the Internal Security Act and Other Internal Security Laws. Hearings. Terroristic Activity. Parts 3, 4, 5, 7. 93rd Cong., 2nd Sess., Washington, DC, GPO, 1975.

Walker, Jerry. 'Psychologist Proposes Terrorist News Guides'. *Editor and Publisher*, 17 September 1977.

Warren Howe, Russell. 'Asset Unwitting: Covering the World for the CIA. Correspondent Tells of Employment by Secretly Funded Agency News Service'. *More*, May 1978.

Watanabe, Chujo. 'Il Caso del Giapone'. *Affari Esteri*, Anno X, No. 39, July 1978.

Watson, Francis M. *Political Terrorism: The Threat and the Response.* Washington, Robert B. Luce Co., 1976.

Weaver, Paul H. 'The New Journalism and the Old'. In: John C. Merrill and Ralph D. Barney (eds.), 1975.

Wells, Alan. *Picture-Tube Imperialism? The Impact of U.S. Television in Latin-America.* New York, Orbis, 1972.

Wilkinson, Paul. *Terrorism and the Liberal State.* London, Macmillan, 1977.

Wilkinson, Paul. 'Terrorism and the Media'. *Journalism Studies Review*, No. 3, June 1978.

Wördemann, Franz. *Terrorismus. Motive, Täter, Strategien.* München, Piper, 1977.

Wördemann, Franz. 'Mobilität, Technik und Kommunikation als Strukturelemente des Terrorismus'. In: M. Funke (ed.), 1977.

Vance, Earl L. 'Freedom of the Press for Whom?' *Virginia Quarterly Review*, 21, Summer 1945.

Yarborough, William P. 'Terrorism – The Past as an Indicator of the Future'. In: Marius H. Livingston (ed.), 1978.

ABOUT THE AUTHORS

Alex P. Schmid holds a PhD degree from the University of Zürich, Switzerland, where he received his training as a historian. He has taught European History at Creighton University (Omaha, Nebr.) and has done research in the United States and Latin America. While his dissertation dealt with the origins of the East-West conflict his orientation has since then extended to the North-South conflict and to questions of war and peace. Since 1978 he has been attached to the COMT.

Janny de Graaf received her academic training as sociologist from the University of Utrecht. She has been attached to the Polemological Institute in Groningen where she worked mainly in the field of social defence. Subsequently she has been working at the Faculty of Social Science of Leiden University where she dealt with research policy. Since 1977 she has been doing work for the Advisory Group on Research into Nonviolent Conflict Resolution and the COMT on a part-time basis.

COMT (The Centre for the Study of Social Conflicts) is part of the State University of Leiden. Its aim is to stimulate and perform empirical research on social tensions and conflicts which have their roots in (1) the aspiration for *equal* treatment and *equal* rights, and (2) the aspiration for *special* treatment and *special* rights of various groups in society.

Date Due

APR 27 '87			
FEB 18 '88			
SEP 29 '88			
NOV 17 '88			
DEC 8 '88			
MAR 16 '89			
APR 13 '89			
MAY 1 '89			
OCT 25 '90			
FEB 2 ~~1991~~			
FEB 2 1 1991			